高等学校教材

化学工程与工艺专业英语

大学英语专业阅读教材编委会组织编写

华东理工大学　胡　鸣　刘　霞　编

化学工业出版社

·北京·

内容简介

《化学工程与工艺专业英语》是根据《大学英语教学大纲》（理工科本科用）的专业阅读部分的要求编写的，供理工科大学化学工程与工艺专业或相关专业三四年级学生使用，也可供同等英语程度化学工程师或相关领域的科技人员使用。

课文及阅读材料共计四十二篇，均选自原版英文教科书、科技报告、专著及专业期刊（大部分为国外90年代以来的出版物）。其中第一部分1～4课，介绍化学过程工业；第二部分5～9课介绍基本化工工艺过程；第三部分10～17课为化学工程学科的领域；第四部分18～22课介绍过程开发的基础知识和化学工程与工艺的前沿研究领域。附录内容有：专利基本知识，化工设计的信息和数据来源，常用有机化合物名称和化学化工常用构词以及总词汇表。每篇课文均配有阅读理解练习和词汇练习。为便于学生自学，本书每课配有单词和词组表，并作必要的注释。

图书在版编目（CIP）数据

化学工程与工艺专业英语/胡鸣　刘霞编.—北京：化学工业出版社，1998.8（2025.7重印）
高等学校教材
ISBN 978-7-5025-2297-1

Ⅰ.化…　Ⅱ.①胡…　②刘…　Ⅲ.化学工业-英语-语言读物　Ⅳ.H319.4:TQ

中国版本图书馆CIP数据核字(98)第21085号

责任编辑：赵玉清　徐世峰　　　装帧设计：田彦文
责任校对：顾淑云

出版发行：化学工业出版社（北京市东城区青年湖南街13号　邮政编码100011）
印　　装：大厂回族自治县聚鑫印刷有限责任公司
787mm×1092mm　1/16　印张17　字数430千字　　2025年7月北京第1版第35次印刷

购书咨询：010-64518888　　　售后服务：010-64518899
网　　址：http: // www. cip. com. cn
凡购买本书，如有缺损质量问题，本社销售中心负责调换。

定　　价：35.00元

前　　言

组织编审出版系列的专业英语教材，是许多院校多年来共同的愿望。在高等教育面向21世纪的改革中，学生基本素质和实际工作能力的培养受到了空前重视。对非英语专业的学生而言，英语水平和能力的培养不仅是文化素质的重要部分，在很大程度上也是能力的补充和延伸。在此背景下，教育部(原国家教委)几次组织会议研究加强外语教学问题，制订有关规范，使外语教学更加受到重视。教材是教学的基本要素之一，与基础英语相比，专业英语教学的教材问题此时显得尤为突出。

国家主管部门的重视和广大院校的呼吁引起了化学工业出版社的关注，他们及时地与原化工部教育主管部门和全国化工类专业教学指导委员会请示协商后，组织全国十余个院校成立了大学英语专业阅读教材编委会。在经过必要的调研后，根据学校需求，编委会优先从各校教学(交流)讲义中确定选题，同时组织力量开展编审工作。本套教材涉及的专业主要包括化学工程与工艺、石油化工、机械工程、信息工程、生产过程自动化、应用化学及精细化工、生化工程、环境工程、制药工程、材料科学与工程、化工商贸等。

根据"全国部分高校化工类及相关专业大学英语专业阅读教材编审委员会"的要求和安排编写的《化学工程与工艺专业英语》教材，可供化工类及相关专业本科生使用，也可以作为同等程度（通过大学英语四级）的专业技术人员自学教材。

内容与结构　教材分为四部分(PART)，每个部分中含有4～8个单元(UNIT)，每单元由一篇课文和一篇阅读材料构成。阅读材料提供与课文相关的背景知识，以进一步拓宽课文内容，为学生自学（开拓视野和训练阅读技能）提供合适的材料。根据课文和阅读材料的内容，配有相应的练习题。各篇课文之间、课文与所配阅读材料之间，既有一定的内在联系，又独立成章，可根据不同学时数灵活选用。课文及阅读材料共计四十二篇，均选自原版英文教科书、科技报告、专著及专业期刊，大部分为国外90年代以来的出版物。其中：

PART 1 为化学过程工业概述，包括化学工业概况、现代化工发展过程、化工原料来源、R & D、化学工程师能胜任的工作等；

PART 2 为化学工艺学简述，主要介绍基本化工工艺过程，如硫酸、氯碱、合成氨、炼油、煤加工过程、聚合物及加工；

PART 3 为化学工程学科的主要领域，介绍传递过程、化工热力学的基本概念、典型的化工单元操作（包括设备）和化学反应工程；

PART 4 为过程开发的基础知识和化学工程前沿研究领域，如过程开发、化工设计、CAE及环境、生物和能源加工中的化学工程问题。

附录内容有：专利基本知识，化工设计的信息和数据来源，常用有机化合物名称，化学化工常用构词和总词汇表。

词汇与练习 在专业英语阅读阶段，掌握一定数量的科技词汇（包括专业词汇）是教学的主要要求之一。本教材覆盖了化学工程与工艺专业的基本内容，包含基本的化学工程与工艺的专业英语词汇和相当数量的常用科技词汇。整个教材注意前后呼应，词汇的复现率高，每个单元均有词汇练习，有利于学生比较牢固地掌握基本词汇。教材中对超出大学英语四级词汇表的单词和词组（约 1400 个）均在首次出现的课文和阅读材料后注出。附录中列出总词汇表。

大纲中对专业英语阅读阶段的学习技能有明确的要求，有针对性的练习是训练阅读技能的有效手段。本教材在设计练习时，作了一些尝试，主要的练习型式为：

①课文前设问题或要求。根据课文内容设计的问题或要求，置于课文前面，以激发学生通过阅读获取信息的欲望，有利于学生调动背景知识，变被动阅读为主动阅读。

②大部分课文配有摘要填空的练习形式，要求学生在规定时间内选用课文中的（一般不多于 3 个）词填空，培养学生通篇浏览（Surveying）、查找信息（Locating Information）及寻找关键词（Keywords）的能力，这是对阅读技能的一种强化训练，也是对学生语言能力和专业知识水平的一种有效考查方式。

③细节的理解填充题。要求对指定段落或流程所含的信息目标集中地进行分析，然后填出练习题中的步骤或化合物。由于过程中环环相扣，如不理解透彻，将无法正确回答问题。

④作读书笔记型练习。训练学生区分主要信息与次要细节的技能，通过归纳要点和对比过程，完成读书笔记。

⑤教材中没有指定英译中翻译练习，教师可从课文和阅读材料中选取。

阅读能力与阅读教学 阅读活动的基本过程是：认读——理解——吸收，这也是构成阅读能力的三个基本因素。阅读，首先要认识所读的文字符号（词汇辨识、句子结构分析），能将上下句、上下段连贯起来，明白全篇的意思，并有一定的速度。这种能力人们称之为认读能力。阅读，更需要有理解能力，所谓阅读的理解能力，是指对文章主题、所论述的原理和概念、作者的观点、以及文章的逻辑结构能够全面的了解与领会。阅读能否将读物的精华与有价值的东西储存起来并加以消化而变为自己的知识结构的有机组成部分，就要看吸收能力如何了。所谓阅读的吸收能力，是指对读物鉴别、记忆、消化的能力。如果阅读一种读物，尽管能够读下来也能理解，但读过之后就忘光了，便是无效的阅读，不能算作具备了阅读能力。

在分析阅读能力的结构时，通常没有明确提出吸收能力来，好像理解能力可以包括吸收能力，但事实上，理解代替不了吸收。认读、理解、吸收，是构成阅读能力不可缺少也不能相互替代的三个重要因素。认读是基础，理解是核心，吸收是结果，三者是一个紧密联系着的整体，人们进行阅读，先认读，后理解，再吸收，进程虽有先后之分，但三者并不是彼此孤立、互相排斥的，而是认读中有一定的理解、理解中有一定的吸收。人们边认读、边理解、边吸收的速度愈快，他们的阅读能力愈强。这本专业英语阅读教材在一定程度上展示了化学工程与工艺专业的知识结构，为全面地训练阅读能力提供了基础材料，相信能得以充分利用。

为了便于学习，我们编写了配套的《双语教学　英汉化学工程与工艺专业词典》。该词典收集了本专业常用的词汇、词组，并且运用简明的英文对概念进行解释。

叶圣陶先生在论及语文教育时指出：“阅读教学之目的，我以为首在养成读书之良好习惯。教师辅导学生认真诵习课本，其意乃在使学生渐进于善读，终于能不待教师之辅导而自臻于通篇明晓。”显然，他的话也适合英语阅读教学。应该承认，现代教学的实践性还大有加强的余地：阅读课程往往讲得过细，语言结构上下功夫过多。阅读教学应强调以学生为中心，将学生的学习积极性充分调动起来，提供较多机会让学生多读快读，反复实践，最终使学生养成良好的阅读习惯，真正提高阅读能力。希望这本专业英语阅读教材和所设计的阅读理解练习将有助于比较全面地训练和培养学生阅读能力。

致谢　本教材在成书过程中得到了化学工业出版社和华东理工大学教务处大力支持，得到了华南理工大学、大连理工大学和江苏石油化工学院等各参编单位的理解和帮助，北京化工大学吴祥芝教授审阅了全书，并提出了许多宝贵的意见，谨在此一并表示衷心感谢。本教材从结构到练习设计都是一种尝试，我们热诚希望使用本书的广大师生向我们提出宝贵意见。

编　者

1998 年 6 月

Contents

PART 1 CHEMICAL PROCESS INDUSTRY

Unit 1 Chemical Industry

Before reading the text below, try to answer following questions:

1. When did the modern chemical industry start?
2. Can you give a definition for the chemical industry?
3. What are the contributions which the chemical industry has made to meet and satisfy our needs?
4. Is the chemical industry capital- or labor-intensive? Why?

1. Origins of the Chemical Industry

Although the use of chemicals dates back to the ancient civilizations, the evolution of what we know as the modern chemical industry started much more recently. It may be considered to have begun during the Industrial Revolution, about 1800, and developed to provide chemicals for use by other industries. Examples are alkali for soapmaking, bleaching powder for cotton, and silica and sodium carbonate for glassmaking. It will be noted that these are all inorganic chemicals. The organic chemicals industry started in the 1860s with the exploitation of William Henry Perkin's [①] discovery of the first synthetic dyestuff—mauve. At the start of the twentieth century the emphasis on research on the applied aspects of chemistry in Germany had paid off handsomely, and by 1914 had resulted in the German chemical industry having 75% of the world market in chemicals. This was based on the discovery of new dyestuffs plus the development of both the contact process for sulphuric acid[②] and the Haber process for ammonia[③]. The latter required a major technological breakthrough that of being able to carry out chemical reactions under conditions of very high pressure for the first time. The experience gained with this was to stand Germany in good stead, particularly with the rapidly increased demand for nitrogen-based compounds (ammonium salts for fertilizers and nitric acid for explosives manufacture) with the outbreak of World War I in 1914. This initiated profound changes which continued during the inter-war years (1918~1939).

Since 1940 the chemical industry has grown at a remarkable rate, although this has slowed significantly in recent years. The lion's share of this growth has been in the organic chemicals sector due to the development and growth of the petrochemicals area since 1950. The explosive growth in petrochemicals in the 1960s and 1970s was largely due to the enormous increase in demand for synthetic polymers such as polyethylene, polypropylene, nylon, polyesters and epoxy resins.

The chemical industry today is a very diverse sector of manufacturing industry, within which it plays a central role. It makes thousands of different chemicals which the general public only usually encounter as end or consumer products. These products are purchased because they have the required properties which make them suitable for some particular application, e.g. a non-stick coating for pans or a weedkiller. Thus chemicals are ultimately sold for the effects that they produce.

2. Definition of the Chemical Industry

At the turn of the century there would have been little difficulty in defining what constituted the chemical industry since only a very limited range of products was manufactured and these were clearly chemicals, e.g., alkali, sulphuric acid. At present, however, many thousands of chemicals are produced, from raw materials like crude oil through (in some cases) many intermediates to products which may be used directly as consumer goods, or readily converted into them. The difficulty comes in deciding at which point in this sequence the particular operation ceases to be part of the chemical industry's sphere of activities. To consider a specific example to illustrate this dilemma, emulsion paints may contain poly (vinyl chloride)/poly (vinyl acetate). Clearly, synthesis of vinyl chloride (or acetate) and its polymerization are chemical activities. However, if formulation and mixing of the paint, including the polymer, is carried out by a branch of the multinational chemical company which manufactured the ingredients, is this still part of the chemical industry or does it now belong in the decorating industry?

It is therefore apparent that, because of its diversity of operations and close links in many areas with other industries, there is no simple definition of the chemical industry. Instead each official body which collects and publishes statistics on manufacturing industry will have its definition as to which operations are classified as "the chemical industry". It is important to bear this in mind when comparing statistical information which is derived from several sources.

3. The Need for Chemical Industry

The chemical industry is concerned with converting raw materials, such as crude oil, firstly into chemical intermediates, and then into a tremendous variety of other chemicals. These are then used to produce consumer products, which make our lives more comfortable or, in some cases such as pharmaceutical products, help to maintain our well-being or even life itself. At each stage of these operations value is added to the product and provided[④] this added value exceeds the raw material plus processing costs then a profit will be made on the operation. It is the aim of chemical industry to achieve this.

It may seem strange in textbook like this one to pose the question "do we need a chemical industry?" However, trying to answer this question will provide (i) an indication of the range of the chemical industry's activities, (ii) its influence on our lives in everyday terms, and (iii) how great is society's need for a chemical industry. Our approach in answering the question will be to consider the industry's contribution to meeting and satisfying our major needs. What are these? Clearly food (and drink) and health are paramount. Other which we shall consider in their turn are clothing and (briefly) shelter, leisure and transport.

(1) *Food.* The chemical industry makes a major contribution to food production in at least three ways. Firstly, by making available large quantities of artificial fertilizers which are used to replace the elements (mainly nitrogen, phosphorus and potassium) which are removed as nutrients by the growing crops during modern intensive farming. Secondly, by manufacturing crop protection chemicals, i.e., pesticides, which markedly reduce the proportion of the crops consumed by pests. Thirdly, by producing veterinary products which protect livestock from disease or cure their infections.

(2) *Health.* We are all aware of the major contribution which the pharmaceutical sector of the industry has made to help keep us all healthy, e.g. by curing bacterial infections with antibiotics, and even extending life itself, e.g. β-blockers to lower blood pressure.

(3) *Clothing.* The improvement in properties of modern synthetic fibers over the traditional clothing materials (e.g. cotton and wool) has been quite remarkable. Thus shirts, dresses and suits made from polyesters like Terylene [5] and polyamides like Nylon are crease-resistant, machine-washable, and drip-dry or non-iron. They are also cheaper than natural materials.

Parallel developments in the discovery of modern synthetic dyes and the technology to "bond" them to the fiber has resulted in a tremendous increase in the variety of colors available to the fashion designer. Indeed they now span almost every color and hue of the visible spectrum. Indeed if a suitable shade is not available, structural modification of an existing dye to achieve this can readily be carried out, provided there is a satisfactory market for the product.

Other major advances in this sphere have been in color-fastness, i.e., resistance to the dye being washed out when the garment is cleaned.

(4) *Shelter, leisure and transport.* In terms of shelter the contribution of modern synthetic polymers has been substantial. Plastics are tending to replace traditional building materials like wood because they are lighter, maintenance-free (i.e. they are resistant to weathering and do not need painting). Other polymers, e.g. urea-formaldehyde and polyurethanes, are important insulating materials for reducing heat losses and hence reducing energy usage.

Plastics and polymers have made a considerable impact on leisure activities with applications ranging from all-weather artificial surfaces for athletic tracks, football pitches and tennis courts to nylon strings for racquets and items like golf balls and footballs made entirely from synthetic materials.

Likewise the chemical industry's contribution to transport over the years has led to major improvements. Thus development of improved additives like anti-oxidants and viscosity index improves for engine oil has enabled routine servicing intervals to increase from 3000 to 6000 to 12000 miles. Research and development work has also resulted in improved lubricating oils and greases, and better brake fluids. Yet again the contribution of polymers and plastics has been very striking with the proportion of the total automobile derived from these materials——dashboard, steering wheel, seat padding and covering etc. — now exceeding 40%.

So it is quite apparent even from a brief look at the chemical industry's contribution to meeting our major needs that life in the world would be very different without the products of the industry. Indeed the level of a country's development may be judged by the production level and sophistication of its chemical industry.

4. Research and Development (R&D) in Chemical Industries

One of the main reasons for the rapid growth of the chemical industry in the developed world has been its great commitment to, and investment in research and development (R&D). A typical figure is 5% of sales income, with this figure being almost doubled for the most research intensive sector, pharmaceuticals. It is important to emphasize that we are quoting percentages here not of profits but of sales income, i.e. the total money received, which has to pay for raw materials, overheads, staff salaries, etc., as well. In the past this tremendous investment has paid off well, leading to[⑥]many useful and valuable products being introduced to the market. Examples include synthetic polymers like nylons and polyesters, and drugs and pesticides. Although the number of new products introduced to the market has declined significantly in recent years, and in times of recession the research department is usually one of the first to suffer cutbacks, the commitment to R&D remains at a very high level.

The chemical industry is a very high technology industry which takes full advantage of the latest advances in electronics and engineering. Computers are very widely used for all sorts of applications, from automatic control of chemical plants, to molecular modeling of structures of new compounds, to the control of analytical instruments in the laboratory.

Individual manufacturing plants have capacities ranging from just a few tonnes per year in the fine chemicals area to the real giants in the fertilizer and petrochemical sectors which range up to 500,000 tonnes. The latter requires enormous capital investment, since a single plant of this size can now cost $250 million! This, coupled with the widespread use of automatic control equipment, helps to explain why the chemical industry is capital- rather than labor-intensive.

The major chemical companies are truly multinational and operate their sales and marketing activities in most of the countries of the world, and they also have manufacturing units in a number of countries. This international outlook for operations, or globalization, is a growing trend within the chemical industry, with companies expanding their activities either by erecting manufacturing units in other countries or by taking over companies which are already operating there.

Selected from "*The Chemical Industry,* 2nd Edition, Alan Heaton, by Blackie & Son Ltd., 1997"

Words and Expressions

1. alkali ['ælkəlai] n. 碱（性，质)，强碱
2. bleaching ['bli:tʃiŋ] n. 漂白 a. 漂白的
3. silica ['silikə] n. 二氧化硅，硅石
4. sodium ['soudjəm] n. 钠，Na
5. carbonate ['kɑ:bənit] n. 碳酸盐，碳酸脂
   ['kɑ:bəneit] vt. 碳化，使化合成碳酸盐(脂)；充碳酸气于
6. inorganic [inɔ:'gænik] a. 无机的，无机物的

7. dyestuff n. 染料，颜料，着色剂
8. mauve [məuv] n. 苯胺紫(染料) a. 紫红色的，淡紫色的
9. sulphuric [sʌ l'fjurik] a. (正，含)硫的，(含)硫磺的
10. ammonia [ə'məunj ə] n. 氨(水)
11. stand … in good stead 对…很有用 （很有帮助）
12. ammonium [ə'məunjəm] n. 铵(基)
13. fertilizer ['fə:tilaizə] n. 肥料（尤指化学肥料）
14. nitric ['naitrik] a. (含)氮的，硝酸根的
15. the lion's share 较大部分，最大部分
16. petrochemical [petrəu'kemikəl] a. 石油化学的 n. 石油化学制品
17. polymer ['pɔlim ə] n. 聚合物（体），高（多）聚物
18. polyethylene [pɔli'eθili:n] n. 聚乙烯
19. polypropylene [pɔli'pr əupili:n] n. 聚丙烯
20. nylon ['nailən] n. 酰胺纤维，尼龙，耐纶
21. polyester [p ɔli'estə] n. 聚酯
22. epoxy [e'pɔksi] n. 环氧树脂
23. resin ['rezin] n. 树脂 vt. 用树脂处理
24. dilemma [di'lemə] n. 困境，进退两难；二难推论
25. emulsion [i'mʌ lʃən] n. 乳胶，乳(化，状，浊)液，乳剂
26. poly- [词头] 多，聚，重，复
27. poly n. 多，聚
28. vinyl ['vainil] n. 乙烯基，乙烯树脂
29. chloride ['kl ɔ:raid] n. 氯化物，漂白剂
30. acetate ['æsitit] n. 醋酸盐（脂），乙酸盐（酯，根）；醋酸纤维素
31. polymerization [pɔlimərai'zeiʃən] n. 聚合(反应，作用)
32. formulation [f ɔ:mju'leiʃən] n. 配方，组成；公式化，列方程式
33. ingredient [in'gri:diənt] n. （混合物的）成分，组分，配料
34. pharmaceutical [fɑ:m ə'sju:tikəl] n. 药物（品，剂） a. 医药的，制药的，药物的，
35. paramount ['pærəmaunt] a. 最高的，高过，优于（to）
36. in one's turn 值班，替代，依次
37. phosphorus ['fɔsfərəs] n. 磷 P，磷光体；启明星，金星
38. potassium [pəu'tæsi əm] n. 钾 K
39. pesticide ['pestisaid] n. 农药，杀虫剂
40. pest [pest] n. 害虫，灾害
41. veterinary ['vetərinəri] n. 兽医 a. 兽医的
42. livestock n. (总称)家畜，牲畜
43. bacterial [bæk'tiəriəl] a. 细菌的
44. antibiotic [æntibai'ɔtik] n. 抗生（菌）素，抗生素学 a. 抗菌的
45. terylene ['terili:n] n. 涤纶，聚（对苯二甲酸乙二醇）酯纤维，的确良
46. polyamide [pɔli'æmaid] n. 聚酰胺，尼龙

47. crease [kri:s] n.（衣服、纸等的）折缝，皱痕
48. drip-dry ['drip'drai] vi. 易快速晾干，晾干自挺
49. hue [hju:] n. 色彩，色调，色泽
50. spectrum ['spectrəm] n.（光，波，能，质）谱，频谱；范围，领域
51. garment ['gɑ:mənt] n. （一件）衣服；[pl.]服装
52. urea ['juəriə] n. 尿素，脲
53. formaldehyde [fɔ:'mældihaid] n. 甲醛
54. urea-formaldehyde resin 脲(甲)醛树脂
55. polyurethane n. 聚氨基甲酸(乙)酯，聚氨酯
56. athletic [æθ'letik] a. 体育的，运动的；运动员的
57. racquet = racket ['rækit] n.（网球、羽毛球等的）球拍；乒乓球拍
58. additive ['æditiv] n. 添加剂，加成剂 a. 附加的，加成的
59. antioxidant ['ænti'ɔksaidənt] n. 抗氧化剂，防老化剂
60. viscosity [vis'kɔsiti] n. 粘度
61. grease [gri:s] n. 脂肪；润滑脂（俗称牛油，黄油）
62. dashboard n. （车辆的）挡泥板，仪表板
63. overhead ['əuvəhed] n. 企业一般管理费； [化]塔顶馏出物
64. recession [ri'seʃən] n.（工商业的）衰退；（价格的）暴跌；后退
65. fine chemical 精细化学药品

Notes

① Willim Henry Perkin：1838～1907，英国合成染料发明者。1856 年 8 月 26 日，他在自家简陋的化学实验室，试图用重铬酸钾处理苯胺（含有甲苯胺）合成奎宁时，得到一种紫色的沉淀，发现能用来染丝，当时认为其具有优良的染色效果。同年申请并获得专利权，取名苯紫胺(mauve)，并在格林福格林进行工业生产，这是世界上第一个合成染料。

② contact process for sulphuric acid：接触法硫酸生产工艺。应用固体催化剂，以空气中的氧直接氧化二氧化硫，所得三氧化硫被水吸收后，得到硫酸或发烟硫酸。其生产过程通常分为二氧化硫的制备，二氧化硫的转化和三氧化硫的吸收三部分。

③ Haber process for ammonia：用氮气和氢气直接合成氨。

Fritz Haber： 1868～1939，德国物理化学家，合成氨发明者。1909 年 7 月 2 日，他在实验室内用锇催化剂将氮气和氢气在高压下直接合成，得到浓度为 6%的氨。其后，在工业化学家 Carl Busch 的协助下，成功地解决了工业生产中的技术问题。这种合成氨的方法称为 Haber-Busch Process。因发明用氮气和氢气直接合成氨的方法，Fritz Haber 获 1918 年诺贝尔化学奖。

Carl Busch：1874～1940，德国工业化学家。他的重大成就之一是使 Fritz Haber 发明的合成氨法实现工业化。因在高压化学合成技术上作出了重大贡献，获 1931 年诺贝尔化学奖。

④ 此处“provided”为连词，作“只要”解，引导一个条件从句。由于从句中 that (provided that)常省略，注意不要与动词 provide 的过去时、过去分词混淆。

⑤ Terylene: 涤纶。对苯二酸与 1，2-乙二醇缩合而产生的直链聚酯纤维的商品名，广泛用于制造织物、衣料和其他纺织品。

⑥ 分词短语作状语。此处含伴随、结果的意思。

Exercises

1. *Complete the summary of the text. Choose* ***No More Than Three Words*** *from the passage for each answer.*

The modern chemical industry came about during [1]__________________ about 1800. However, there was no [2]______________ side of the industry to speak of before 1860. By the early years of the 20th century advances into synthetic pharmaceuticals and some new dyestuffs had been made, and two important processes— [3]_________________for sulphuric acid and [4]_____________ for ammonia were developed. The major industrial developments in organic chemicals initiated in the 1930-1940 period have continued since that time. Demand for [5]___________ stimulated the explosive growth in petrochemicals in 1960s and 1970s. The chemical industry today is a very diverse sector of manufacturing industry. It makes thousands of different chemicals in the forms as raw materials, [6]__________ and products, and it's not as easy as it seems to definite "the chemical industry."

Chemical products arguably improve our lives and lifestyles, and we could not live the way we do without them. For example, agriculture relies on the chemical industry for its large quantities of [7]__________________ and [8]_____________. Modern [9]________________and synthetic dyes provide a good market for clothing. We should also draw attention to the many life saving and therapeutic drugs and medicines produced by the [10]_______________ sector of the industry. Modern synthetic polymers play an increasing role in building industry, and plastics and polymers find many applications in leisure and transport areas.

A major characteristic of the chemical industry is its great emphasis on [11]__________. The scale of operations within the industry ranges from quite small plants in the fine chemicals area to the giants of the fertilizer and [12]_______________ sectors. Heavy capital investments, extremely widespread use of [13]______________ partly explain why the industry is [14]________________.

2. *Completing the following table, by listing the chemicals as many as you can.*

Some Chemicals Used in Our Daily Life

Food		Shelter	
Health		Leisure	
Clothing		Transport	

3. *Put the following into Chinese:*

carbonate	polypropylene	epoxy	vinyl
acetate	pharmaceutical	spectrum	formaldehyde
silica	ammonium	polyester	the lion's share

4. *Put the following into English:*

钠 Na	钾 K	磷 P	氨
聚合物	聚乙烯	氯化物	粘度
烃	催化剂	炼油厂	添加剂

Reading Material 1:

Evolution of Chemical Industry

1. The Beginning of Modern Chemical Industry

The use of chemicals dates back to the ancient civilizations. For example, many chemicals were known and used by the ancient Egyptians. Evolution of an actual chemical industry is much more recent, and came about, as with many other industries, during the industrial revolution, which occurred in the U.K. around 1800 and rather later in other countries. Its initial development was stimulated by the demand of a few other industries for particular chemicals.

There was no organic chemicals side of the industry to speak of before 1856 since up to that time any organic materials were obtained from natural sources. In 1856, as has happened many times since (sometimes leading to major advances in the subject), some planned research work did not give the results expected. William Henry Perkin was trying to synthesize the antimalarial drug quinine, a naturally-occurring compound found in the bark of Cinchona trees. Using sodium dichromate he was attempting to oxidize aniline (phenylamine) sulphate to quinine, but instead obtained a black precipitate. Rather than just rejecting this reaction which had obviously failed in its purpose, he extracted the precipitate and obtained a purple compound. It showed great promise as a dye and 'mauve', as it was named became the first synthetic dyestuff. Rather ironically, thc mauve was formed because Perkin's aniline was impure—he had obtained it in the standard way by nitrating benzene and then reducing the product, but his benzene had contained significant amounts of toluene. Although only 18, and a student in London, he had the confidence to terminate his studies in order to manufacture mauve, which he did very successfully. The synthetic dyestuffs industry grew rapidly from this beginning and was dominated by Britain into the 1870s. However, chemical research in Britain by this time tended to be very academic, whereas in Germany the emphasis was much more on the applied aspects of the subject. This enabled the Germans to forge ahead in the discovery of new dyes.

The very sound base which their success in dyestuffs provided for the large German companies—BASF①, Bayer②, Hoechst③—particularly in terms of large financial resources and scientific research expertise and skills, enabled them to diversify into and develop new areas of the chemical industry. By the early years of the 20th century advances into synthetic pharmaceuticals had been made. The synthetic dyestuffs technology can fairly be termed a strategic technology, for it led to a wide range of changes in the fine chemicals industry, including pharmaceuticals, and it brought about the establishment of the first permanent industrial research laboratories. These were instituted in German dyestuffs firms about 120 years ago. The industrial research laboratory is now a common feature of large firms, whether in chemical or in other industries.

BASF concentrated on inorganic chemistry and achieved notable successes in developing the contact process for sulphuric acid and the Haber process for ammonia production. The latter particularly was a major technological breakthrough, since it required novel, very specialized plant to handle gases at high temperatures and pressures. Thus by 1914 Germany dominated the world scene and was well ahead in both applied chemistry and technological achievement.

However, the outbreak of World War I changed this situation dramatically. Firstly, in both Britain and Germany stimulus was given to those parts of the industry producing chemicals required for explosives manufacture, e.g. nitric acid. Secondly, Germany was particularly isolated from its raw material supplies and could not of course export its products, such as dyestuffs, which led to shortages in Britain and the U.S.A. The result was a rapid expansion in the manufacture of dyestuffs in these countries. In contrast Germany had to rapidly develop production of nitrogen-based compounds particularly nitric acid for explosives manufacture and ammonium-salts for use in fertilizers. Commercialization of the Haber process (catalytic oxidation of ammonia leading to nitric acid) had come at just the right time to make this possible.

2. Inter-war years, 1918～1939

The war had alerted governments to the importance of the chemical industry, and the immediate post-war years were boom years for the British and American industries. During the war and immediately afterwards most countries had, largely out of necessity, expanded their chemical industry. With its large and expanding home market and lack of competition from imports the American chemical industry grew rapidly during the 1920s. This was in complete contrast to the situation in most other countries at this time. Germany continued to dominate the international scene.

As indicated previously, during this time the American industry was growing steadily, although largely in isolation. Up until 1940 it was also the only country to have petrochemical plants. The availability for some years of their own supplies of crude oil, and refineries, led to interest in the use of petroleum fractions for the synthesis of organic compounds and started in the 1920s with the manufacture of iso-propanol from the refinery offgas propylene.

Apart from the start of the trend towards very large companies, and bigger manufacturing units, the inter-war period will be remembered as marking the beginning of two areas which have had profound effects on the industry's subsequent development, growth, and profitability. The first, petrochemicals, has already been referred to above. The second, the synthetic polymer sector, has over the last few decades owed much to the development of petrochemicals. This has grown into the most important sector of the whole chemical industry.

3. Second World War period, 1939～1945

In general terms the impact on the chemical industry was similar to that of the First World War. Thus Germany especially was cut off from its raw-material supplies and therefore relied entirely on synthetic materials, e.g. poly (styrene-butadiene) rubber, and gasoline produced from coal. Britain and America were not affected to quite the same extent but demand for polymers like nylon and polyethylene for parachutes and electrical insulation was high. By the end of the war facilities for synthetic polymer production had expanded considerably in all three countries.

4. Post-1945 period

The major changes in the world-wide chemical industry since 1945 have been concerned with organic chemicals, in particular the raw materials used to produce key intermediates such as ethylene (ethene), propylene (propene), benzene and toluene. The situation was starting to change due to events in the oil industry. Worldwide demand for petroleum products was increasing, this being most apparent for transport. Increasing ownership of automobiles and rapid development of air transport raised demand for gasoline. Processes were developed in the refineries to convert low demand fractions, e.g. gas oil, into high-demand lower-boiling fractions, e.g. gasoline. Alkenes such as ethylene and propylene were produced as by-products. Thus they were available for chemical synthesis and at a very cheap price largely because of the vast scale of operation. Note that until this time ethylene had been obtained by dehydration of ethanol which in turn had been made by fermentation of carbohydrates. By 1959 oil was on a par with coal as the major source of chemicals in Europe, mirroring the position of the American industry some two decades previously. Although the processing costs of the oil tended to increase this was counterbalanced by the ever-increasing size of the operations (hence the benefits of the economy-of-scale effect) and the improved efficiency of the processes. Thus the economic advantages were swinging very much in oil's direction, and by 1969, oil dominated the scene, and this has continued to do ever since. Petrochemicals had truly come of age.

Let us consider further the reasons for the explosive growth of the petrochemicals industry. As indicated, oil-refinery processes such as cracking supplied key chemical intermediates—ethylene and propylene at low prices compared with traditional methods for their preparation. However this factor alone cannot account completely for the vast increase in the tonnage of organic chemicals produced from petroleum sources. Much of the credit may be placed with research chemists, process-development chemists and chemical engineers. Once it was realized that abundant quantities of ethylene and propylene were available, research chemists had the incentive to develop processes for the production of many other compounds. Success in the laboratory led to process development and eventually construction of manufacturing units. Consideration of the chemical reagents and reactants used in many of these processes shows the importance and influence on the development of the petrochemical industry of one particular area of chemistry, namely catalysis. This influence has been a two-way process: research into catalysis has been stimulated by the needs of the industry and, in turn, better, more efficient catalysts have been discovered which have improved process efficiency and economics, and may even have rendered an existing process obsolete by permitting introduction of an entirely new, more economic route. Introduction of these catalysts has made possible not only entirely new routes and interconversions of compounds, but also immensely shorter reaction times (sometimes now just a few seconds) compared with the corresponding non-catalytic route. Another major advantage has been that catalysts have introduced better control of the reaction, particularly improved selectivity towards the desired product. This is a vital aim in chemicals production, since very few processes yield only the desired product and by-product formation represents material and efficiency loss. Furthermore separation of product from by-products can be a major cost item in the overall process economics. A notable example is the introduction of catalytic cracking units in place of purely thermal cracking units for ethylene production. Evolution of manufacturing processes utilizing these new catalysts has often necessitated technological developments. Examples are design and construction of equipment to handle very high-pressure gas reactions, facilities for rapid quenching of products (as in cracking to cheat the kinetics and obtain predominantly alkenes rather than alkynes when the process has to be operated under conditions favoring the latter) and development of fluidized-bed reactors.

A major advance in polymer chemistry was provided by the work of Karl Ziegler[④] and Giulio Natta, which led in 1955 to the introduction of some revolutionary catalysts which bear their name. During the late 1970s production of linear low-density polyethylene (LLDPE) was commercialized.

A very important trend during the post-Second World War period has been the increasing size of plants, and nowhere is this more apparent than in the petrochemicals sector[⑤], where capacities of 100,000 tonnes per annum are commonplace. Large integrated chemical complexes have evolved, due to this increase in scale, and the need to locate petrochemical plants adjacent to refineries, so many of the downstream processes, which utilize petrochemical intermediates, are located on the same site, and this arrangement can lead to reduced utility costs. For example, a large complex of units can justify its own power station to produce electricity and steam.

This trend to larger-sized individual chemical plants and large complexes of chemical plants has been matched by movement to bigger chemical companies by mergers, or takeovers, or both, as we have already seen happening in the 1920s with the formation of ICI[⑥]. Nowadays the multinational giants dominate the international chemical scene.

The chemical industry has been to the fore during the last decade or two in utilizing the tremendous advances in electronics. Thus complete automation (even full computer control) of large continuous plants is commonplace. An additional advantage is the automatic data collection of throughput, temperatures, pressures, etc. This can be invaluable when subsequent analysis of the data may suggest small adjustments to the plant to improve its efficiency and hence reduce product costs and improve profitability. The rapid developments in microelectronics which have led to reduced selling prices for microprocessors is making their introduction for fairly small plants an economical and practical proposition.

Control of pollution, i.e, effluent control and treatment, is another important factor which has markedly influenced the industry over the past decade. Indeed there are legal requirements to be met in control of the emission or discharge of effluent. Although, as indicated previously, utilization of by-products is a feature of the industry, nevertheless some effluents are generated, and due to the very large scale of operation the quantity can be substantial. Its treatment and disposal can be a considerable cost item of the process. Equipment for the prevention of loss of untreated wastes can also add significantly to the capital and running costs of a plant.

Since the rapid rise in the price of oil in 1973, energy costs have been a major concern of chemical producers. The chemical industry is a major energy consumer and therefore even small percentage savings in energy costs can mean tens or hundreds of thousands of dollars or pounds, and the difference between profit and loss. It is no surprise to find therefore that immense efforts are now being made to assess and analyse the energy usage of plants to see where savings can be made.

The most exciting area of development at the start of the 1980s, arising from the immense amount of research and development work which the chemical and related industries carry out each year, is biotechnology. In biotechnology genes are manipulated to ensure that the micro-organism will synthesize the desired specific chemical. Although the risks and practical problems are considerable, the rewards for their solution are immense. The technology is still in its infancy and its effect on the chemical industry as a whole is difficult to predict. Clearly it will make a major contribution to pharmaceuticals—as the successful development of insulin—and production of interferon and antibiotics are on the near horizon. In contrast it is difficult to see biotechnology being a competitive route to bulk chemical intermediates like ethylene and benzene, because of its slowness and the high product separation costs. However, it is an area whose development chemists are watching with interest and fascination.

Selected from "*An Introduction to Industrial Chemistry,* 2nd Edition, C.A. Heaton, Blackie & Son Ltd., 1997"

Words and Expressions

1. antimalarial a. 抗疟疾的
2. quinine [kwi'ni:n] n. 奎宁，金鸡纳碱（霜）
3. Cinchona [siŋ'kəunə] n. 金鸡纳树属，金鸡纳皮，奎宁
4. sodium dichromate n. 重铬酸钾
5. oxidize ['ɔksidaiz] vt. 使氧化
6. aniline ['æniliːn] n. 苯胺
7. phenylamine n. 苯胺
8. sulphate ['sʌlfeit] n. 硫酸盐（酯）
9. precipitate [pri'sipitit] n. 沉淀物
   [pri'sipiteit] v. 沉淀，析出
10. ironically [ai'rɔnikli] ad. 令人啼笑皆非地，讽刺地
11. nitrate ['naitreit] n. 硝酸盐（根，酯）
12. benzene ['benzi:n] n. 苯
13. reduce [ri'dju:s] v.（使）还原；减少
14. toluene ['tɔljui:n] n. 甲苯
15. forge ahead 向前迈进，迎头赶上
16. institute ['institju:t] vt. 设立，创立
17. stimulus ['stimjuləs] n. 刺激，促进因素
18. catalytic [kætə'litik] a. 催化的
19. oxidation [ɔksai'deiʃən] n. 氧化（反应，作用）

20. alert [ə'lɑ:t] vt. 使警觉，使留心
21 refinery [ri'fainəri] n. 炼油厂，提炼厂
22. fraction ['frækʃən] n. 馏分，分馏物；分数，部分
23. amalgamation [əmælgə'meiʃən] n. 合并，混合；汞合，汞齐作用
24. iso- [词头]（相）等，（相）同的，（同分）异构
25. propanol ['prəupənɔl] n. 丙醇
26. offgas n. 废气，气态废物
27. propylene ['prəupili:n] n. 丙烯
28. styrene ['staiəri:n] n. 苯乙烯
29. butadiene [bju:tə'daii:n] n. 丁二烯
30. poly (styrene-butadiene) rubber 丁苯橡胶
31. ethylene ['eθili:n] n. 乙烯
32. ethene ['eθi:n] n. 乙烯
33. propene n. 丙烯
34. alkene ['ælki:n] n. 烯烃
35. dehydration [di:haidreit] v.; n. 去（脱，除）水（物），（使）干燥
36. ethanol ['eθənɔl] n. 乙醇，酒精
37. fermentation [fə:men'teiʃən] n. 发酵
38. carbohydrate ['kɑ:bou'haidreit] n. 碳水化合物，糖
39. on a par with 和...同等，等于...
40. cracking n. 裂化，裂解
41. incentive [in'sentiv] a. 刺激的，鼓励的 n. 刺激，诱因
42. reagent [ri: 'eidʒənt] n. 试剂，反应物
43. reactant [ri: 'æktənt] n. 反应物
44. catalysis [kə'tælisis] n. 催化（作用，反应）
45. obsolete ['ɔbsəli:t] a. 已废弃的，过时的
46. catalyst ['kætəlist] n. 催化剂
47. render ['rendə] v. 使得，使变为；提炼，提取
48. thermal ['θə:məl] a. 热（量，力）的，温的
49. quench [kwentʃ] v.; n. 急冷，淬冷
50. kinetics [kai'netiks] n. 动力学
51. alkyne ['ælkain] n. 炔（属烃）
52. integrate ['intigreit] vt. 使一体化，使结合；[数]求…的积分
53. merger [mə:dʒə] n. （企业等的）合并，吞并；合并者
54. fore [fɔ:] ad. 在前面 n. 前部
55. to the fore 在前面，在显著的位置；在近处
56. throughput n. 生产量，生产率，生产能力
57. microelectronics n. 微电子学，微电子技术
58. microprocessor n. 微信息处理机
59. effluent ['efluənt] a.; n 流出（的，物），废水及废气

60. biotechnology　n. 生物工艺学
61. gene　[dʒiːn]　n. 基因
62. manipulate　[mə'nipjuleit]　v. 操作，控制，运算
63. micro-organism　n. 微生物
64. infancy　['infənsi]　n. 初期，摇篮时代；婴儿期，幼年期
65. insulin　['insjulin]　n. 胰岛素
66. interferon　[intəː'fiərɔn]　n. 干扰素
67. fascination　[fæsi'neiʃən]　n. 感染力，吸引力

Notes

① BASF: Basf Aktiengesellschaft，巴斯夫公司，德国的大型化工公司，创建于 1865 年，其前身是巴登苯胺纯碱公司。1913 年在路德维希港建成世界第一套合成氨工业装置，是一个经营范围很广的大型跨国公司。

② Bayer: Bayer Aktiengesellschaf，拜耳股份公司，德国的大型化工企业，创建于 1863 年，1889 年发明驰名世界的药物：阿司匹林，是一个大型的跨国公司。

③ Hoechst: Hoechst Aktiengesellschaft，赫司特公司，德国的大型化学公司，总部设在法兰克福，创建于 1863 年。该公司是世界上最大的医药制造厂商之一。

④ Karl Ziegler: 齐格勒, K.1898～1973，德国有机化学家。1953 年，他发现用烷基铝和四氯化钛为催化剂，乙烯可在常压下高收率地聚合。

Giulio Natta: 纳塔, K.1903～1979，意大利化学家。1954 年，他在 Karl Ziegler 乙烯低压聚合制成聚乙烯的基础上，发现用三氯化钛和烷基铝作催化剂，丙烯可在低压下高收率地聚合，生成立体定向聚合物聚丙烯。

Karl Ziegler 和 Giulio Natta 开创的配位催化聚合和立体定向聚合，开拓了高分子科学和工艺的崭新领域，被称为 Ziegler-Natta 催化剂及 Ziegler-Natta 聚合。两人因此而共获 1963 年诺贝尔化学奖。

⑤ 倒装句。以否定词开头的句子，主谓语一般颠倒。

⑥ ICI: Imperial Chemical Industries Limited，卜内门化学工业公司，又译帝国化学工业公司，英国最大的化工企业，也是世界最大的化学公司之一，组建于 1926 年，总部设在伦敦。

Unit 2 Research and Development

Before reading the text below, try to answer these questions:

1. Can you make a distinction between the terms of "research" and "development"?
2. What is the main reason for carrying out R&D in industry?
3. How many types of R&D are of most concern to the chemical industry?
4. Which area is the most research intensive in chemical industry?

Research and development, or R&D as it is commonly referred to, is an activity which is carried out by all sectors of manufacturing industry but its extent varies considerably, as we will see shortly. Let us first understand, or at least get a feel for, what the terms mean. Although the distinction between research and development is not always clear-cut, and there is often considerable overlap, we will attempt to separate them. In simple terms research can be thought of as the activity which produces new ideas and knowledge whereas development is putting those ideas into practice as new processes and products. To illustrate this with an example, predicting the structure of a new molecule which would have a specific biological activity and synthesizing it could be seen as research, whereas testing it and developing it to the point where it could be marketed as a new drug could be described as the development part.

1. Fundamental Research and Applied Research

In industry the primary reason for carrying out R&D is economic and is to strengthen and improve the company's position and profitability. The purpose of R&D is to generate and provide information and knowledge to reduce uncertainty, solve problems and to provide better data on which management can base decisions. Specific projects cover a wide range of activities and time scales, from a few months to 20 years.

We can pick out a number of areas of R&D activity in the following paragraphs but if we were to start with those which were to spring to the mind of the academic, rather than the industrial, chemist then these would be basic, fundamental (background) or exploratory research and the synthesis of new compounds. This is also labeled "blue skies" research.

Fundamental research is typically associated with university research. It may be carried out for its own intrinsic interest and it will add to the total knowledge base but no immediate applications of it in the "real world" will be apparent[①]. Note that it will provide a valuable training in defining and solving problems, i.e. research methodology for the research student who carries it out, under supervision. However, later "spin offs" from such work can lead to useful applications. Thus physicists claim that but for the study and development of quantum theory we might not have had computers and nuclear power[②]. However, to take a specifically chemical example, general studies on a broad area such as hydrocarbon oxidation might provide information which would be useful in more specific areas such as cyclohexane oxidation for the production of nylon intermediates.

Aspects of synthesis could involve either developing new, more specific reagents for controlling particular functional group interconversions, i.e. developing synthetic methodology or complete synthesis of an entirely new molecule which is biologically active. Although the former is clearly fundamental the latter encompasses both this and applied aspects. This term ‘applied’ has traditionally been more associated with research carried out in industrial laboratories, since this is more focused or targeted. It is a consequence of the work being business driven.

Note, however, that there has been a major change in recent years as academic institutions have increasingly turned to industry for research funding, with the result that much more of their research effort is now devoted to more applied research. Even so, in academia the emphasis generally is very much on the research rather than the development.

2. Types of Industrial Research and Development

The applied or more targeted type of research and development commonly carried out in industry can be of several types and we will briefly consider each. They are: (i) product development, (ii) process development, (iii) process improvement and (iv) applications development. Even under these headings there are a multitude of aspects so only a typical example can be quoted in each case. The emphasis on each of these will vary considerably within the different sectors of the chemical industry.

(1) **Product development.** Product development includes not only the discovery and development of a new drug but also, for example, providing a new longer-acting anti-oxidant additive to an automobile engine oil. Developments such as this have enabled servicing intervals to increase during the last decade from 3000 to 6000 to 9000 and now to 12000 miles. Note that most purchasers of chemicals acquire them for the effects that they produce, i.e. a specific use. Teflon^{TM}, or polytetrafluoroethylene (PTFE), may be purchased because it imparts a non-stick surface to cooking pots and pans, thereby making them easier to clean.

(2) **Process development**. Process development covers not only developing a manufacturing process for an entirely new product but also a new process or route for an existing product. The push for the latter may originate for one or more of the following reasons: availability of new technology, change in the availability and/or cost of raw materials. Manufacture of vinyl chloride monomer is an example of this. Its manufacturing route has changed several times owing to changing economics, technology and raw materials. Another stimulus is a marked increase in demand and hence sales volume which can have a major effect on the economics of the process. The early days of penicillin manufacture afford a good example of this.

The ability of penicillin to prevent the onset of septicemia in battle wounds during the Second World War (1939～1945) resulted in an enormous demand for it to be produced in quantity. Up until then it had only been produced in small amounts on the surface of the fermentation broth in milk bottles! An enormous R&D effort jointly in the U.S. and the U.K. resulted in two major improvements to the process. Firstly a different strain[③] of the mould *(penicillium chrysogenum)* gave much better yields than the original *penicillium notatum*. Secondly the major process development was the introduction of the deep submerged fermentation process[④]. Here the fermentation takes place throughout the broth, provided sterile air is constantly, and vigorously, blown through it. This has enabled the process to be scaled up enormously to modern stainless steel fermenters having a capacity in excess of 50000 liters. It is salutary to note that in the first world war (1914～1919) more soldiers died from septicemia of their wounds than were actually killed outright on the battlefield!

Process development for a new product depends on things such as the scale on which it is to be manufactured, the by-products formed and their removal/recovery, and required purity. Data will be acquired during this development stage using semi-technical plant (up to 100 liters capacity) which will be invaluable in the design of the actual manufacturing plant. If the plant is to be a very large capacity, continuously operating one, e.g. petrochemical or ammonia, then a pilot plant will first be built and operated to test out the process and acquire more data, these semi-technical or pilot plants will be required for testing, e.g., a pesticide, or customer evaluation, e.g., a new polymer.

Note that by-products can have a major influence on the economics of a chemical process. Phenol manufacture provides a striking example of this. The original route, the benzenesulphonic acid route, has become obsolete because demand for its by-product sodium sulfite (2.2 tons/1 ton phenol) has dried up. Its recovery and disposal will therefore be an additional charge on the process, thus increasing the cost of the phenol. In contrast the cumene route owes its economic advantage over all the other routes to the strong demand for the by-product acetone (0.6 tons/1 ton phenol). The sale of this therefore reduces the net cost of the phenol.

A major part of the process development activity for a new plant is to minimize, or ideally prevent by designing out, waste production and hence possible pollution. The economic and environmental advantages of this are obvious.

Finally it should be noted that process development requires a big team effort between chemists, chemical engineers, and electrical and mechanical engineers to be successful.

(3) **Process improvement**. Process improvement relates to processes which are already operating. It may be a problem that has arisen and stopped production. In this situation there is a lot of pressure to find a solution as soon as possible so that production can restart, since 'down time' costs money.

More commonly, however, process improvement will be directed at improving the profitability of the process. This might be achieved in a number of ways. For example, improving the yield by optimizing the process, increasing the capacity by introducing a new catalyst, or lowering the energy requirements of the process. An example of the latter was the introduction of turbo compressors in the production of ammonia by the Haber process. This reduced utility costs (mainly electricity) from $6.66 to $0.56 per ton of ammonia produced. Improving the quality of the product, by process modification, may lead to new markets for the product.

In recent years, however, the most important process improvement activity has been to reduce the environmental impact of the process, i.e., to prevent the process causing any pollution. Clearly there have been two interlinked driving forces for this. Firstly, the public's concern about the safety of chemicals and their effect on the environment, and the legislation which has followed as a result of this. Secondly the cost to the manufacturer of having to treat waste (i.e., material which cannot be recovered and used or sold) so that it can be safely disposed of, say by pumping into a river. This obviously represents a charge on the process which will increase the cost of the chemical being made. The potential for improvement by reducing the amount of waste is self-evident.

Note, however, with a plant which has already been built and is operating there are usually only very limited physical changes which can be made to the plant to achieve the above aims. Hence the importance, already mentioned, of eliminating waste production at the design stage of a new plant. Conserving energy and thus reducing energy cost has been another major preoccupation in recent years.

(4) **Applications development.** Clearly the discovery of new applications or uses for a product can increase or prolong its profitability. Not only does this generate more income but the resulting increased scale of production can lead to lower unit costs and increased profit. An example is PVC whose early uses included records and plastic raincoats. Applications which came later included plastic bags and particularly engineering uses in pipes and guttering.

Emphasis has already been placed on the fact that chemicals are usually purchased for the effect, or particular use, or application which they have. This often means that there will be close liaison between the chemical companies' technical sales representatives and the customer, and the level of technical support for the customer can be a major factor in winning sales. Research and development chemists provide the support for these applications developments. An example is CF_3CH_3F. This is the first of the CFC replacements and has been developed as a refrigerant gas. However, it has recently been found that it has special properties as a solvent for extracting natural products from plant materials. In no way was this envisaged when the compound was first being made for use as a refrigerant gas, but it clearly is an example of applications development.

3. Variations in R & D Activities across the Chemical Industry

Both the nature and amount of R&D carried out varies significantly across the various sectors of the chemical industry. In sectors which involve large scale production of basic chemicals and where the chemistry, products and technology change only slowly because the processes are mature, R&D expenditure is at the lower end of the range for the chemical industry. Most of this will be devoted to process improvement and effluent treatment. Examples include ammonia, fertilizers and chloralkali production from the inorganic side, and basic petrochemical intermediates such as ethylene from the organic side.

At the other end of the scale lie pharmaceuticals and pesticides (or plant protection products). Here there are immense and continuous efforts to synthesize new molecules which exert the desired, specific biological effect. A single company may generate 10,000 new compounds for screening each year. Little wonder that some individual pharmaceutical company's annual R&D expenditure is now approaching $1000 million! Expressing this in a different way they spend in excess of 14% of sales income (note not profits) on R&D.

Selected from "*An Introduction to Industrial Chemistry,* 2nd Edition, C.A. Heaton, by Blackie & Son Ltd., 1997"

Words and Expressions

1. clear-cut a. 明确的，鲜明的；轮廓清楚的
2. overlap ['əuvəlæp] n. 重迭（部分）
3. blue sky a. 纯理论的；（股票等）价值极微的
4. intrinsic [in'trinsik] a. 内在的，固有的；本质的
5. supervision [sju:pə'vi ʒən] n. 监督，管理
6. spin off n. 伴随（附带）的结果，有用的副产品
7. quantum ['kwɔntəm] n. 量子
8. hydrocarbon ['haidrəu'kɑ:bən] n. 烃，碳氢化合物
9. encompass [in'kʌmpəs] vt. 包含，包括；完成；围绕
10. multitude ['mʌltitju:d] n. 大批，大群，大量，众多
11. teflon ['teflɔn] n. （商品名）特氟隆，聚四氟乙烯
12. TM ＝ trademark n. 商标
13. polytetrafluoroethylene n. 聚四氟乙烯
14. impart [im'pɑ:t] vt. 给予，把…分给；告诉
15. cyclohexane [saikləu'heksein] n. 环己烷
16. monomer ['mɔnəmə] n. 单体，单聚物
17. penicillin [peni'silin] n. 青霉素，盘尼西林
18. septicemia [septi'si:miə] n. 败血症
19. functional group 官能团
20. broth [brɔ:θ] n.肉汤（指细菌培养液），液体培养基
21. strain [strein] n. 菌株（种），品系，种
22. mould [məuld] n. 霉菌；（模）型，模（具）
23. penicillium chrysogenum 黄青霉
24. penicillium notatum 青霉菌
25. sterile ['sterail] a. 无菌的，消过毒的
26. scale-up n. （按比例）放大，增加，升高
27. stainless ['steinlis] a. 不锈的；纯洁的
28. fermenter ['fə:mentə] n. 发酵罐
29. purity ['pjuəriti] n. 纯度，品位；纯净，洁净；纯化
30. salutary ['sæljutəri] a. 有益的，有益于健康的
31. semi-technical n. 半工业化的
32. pilot-plant n. 中间（试验性）工厂，试验生产装置
33. phenol ['fi:nɔl] n. (苯)酚，石碳酸
34. benzenesulphonic acid 苯磺酸

35. sulphite ['sʌlfait] n. 亚硫酸盐（酯）
36. cumene ['kju:mi:n] n. 枯烯，异丙基苯
37. acetone ['æsitəun] n. 丙酮
38. down time 停车时间，故障期
39. optimize ['ɔptimaiz] v. （使）最优（佳）化，优选
40. turbo ['tə:bəu] n. 涡轮（透平）（机）
41. legislation [ledʒi s'lei ʃən] n. 法规，立法
42. self-evident ['self'evid ənt] a. 不言而喻的，自明的，不需证明的
43. conserve [kən'sə:v] vt. 节省；保存；守恒
44. preoccupation [pri:ɔkju'pei ʃən] n. 急务，使人全神贯注的事物
45. prolong [prə'lɔŋ] vt. 延伸，引伸；延长，拖延
46. PVC = poly vinyl chloride n. 聚氯乙烯
47. gutter ['gʌ tə] n. 排水沟，水槽
48. liaison [li(:)'eizən] n.; v. 联络，联系（人），协作
49. CFC = chlorofluorocarbon n. 含氯氟烃
50. refrigerant [ri'fridʒərənt] n. 致冷剂，冷冻剂
51. solvent ['sɔlvənt] n. 溶剂，溶媒
52. extract [iks'trækt] vt. 萃取，提炼
53. envisage [in'vizidʒ] vt. 设想，预计，重视
54. expenditure [iks'penditʃə] n. （时间、金钱等的）支出，花费，使用
55. chlor(o)- [词头] 氯（化）
56. chloralkali n. 氯碱

Notes

① 用 no 否定名词，构成完全否定；用 not 否定名词，构成部分否定。
② “but for ＋名词”表示“要不是”、“没有”之意，一般用于虚构的假设句中。
③ strain: 菌种，用于发酵过程作为活细胞催化剂的微生物。
④ deep submerged fermentation process: 深层发酵过程 发酵过程按培养基的性质分为固体培养和液体培养，液体培养又可分为表面培养和深层培养，前者产品仅存在于发酵液的表面，后者产品则遍布于整个发酵液中。目前，大多数发酵产品采用分批深层培养法制备。

Exercises

1. *Complete the summary of the text above. Choose* ***No More Than Three Words*** *from the passage for each answer.*

All sectors of manufacturing industry carry out research and development, or [1]________ . Research refers to the activities which create new [2]______________, and then they are put into practice as new [3]_________________ by development. Furthermore, research can be classified as [4]_________ research, carried out mainly by academic institutions, and [5]__________ research, carried out mainly by industrial laboratories.

This article explores four types of research and development in chemical industry: (1)

[6]______________, discovering and developing a chemical with specific use; (2) process development, resulting a process for a new product or a new route for [7]_____________; the latter may be caused by using new technology, changing raw materials or increasing in demand. If a very large plant is to be built for a new product, a semi-technical or [8]___________ will first be built and operated. Usually the process development needs a big team effort between scientists and engineers. (3) process improvement, finding a solution for an emerging case or improving the [9]__________ of the process. Recently attentions are devoted to reducing the [10]__________ of the process and to reducing [11]__________. (4) applications development, discovery of new applications or uses for a product and providing [12]____________ for the customer.

The character and amount of R&D vary greatly across the sectors of the chemical industry. In the basic chemical sector, R&D expenditure is lower than that of other sectors and now most of it is devoted to [13]__________ and [14]___________. By contrast, [15]___________ and pesticide sectors spend a lot of money on R&D.

2. *Complete the following table by consulting the reading material* ***"The Anatomy of a Chemical Manufacturing Process".***

Stage	*Purpose*
Raw material storage	To smooth out fluctuations and interruptions in supply
Feed preparation	To make feed [16]___________, or in the right form
[17]__________	To convert raw materials to the desired product
Product separation	To separate the product from any [18]__________ and [19]__________
Purification	To meet [20]__________________
[21]__________	To match production with sales

3. *Put the following into Chinese:*

quantum	strain	mould	phenol
sulphate	carbide	foul	scrub
semi-technical	fermenter	CFC	refrigerant

4. *Put the following into English:*

试剂	单体	丙酮	脉动
乙炔	硫	盐酸	停车时间
杂质	反应器	（使）优化	纯度

Reading Material 2:

The Anatomy of a Chemical Manufacturing Process

The basic components of a typical chemical process are shown in Fig. 1-1, in which each block represents a stage in the overall process for producing a product from the raw materials. Fig. 1-1 represents a generalized process; not all the stages will be needed for any particular process, and the complexity of each stage will depend on the nature of the process. Chemical engineering design is concerned with the selection and arrangement of the stages, and the selection, specification and design of the equipment required to perform the stage functions.

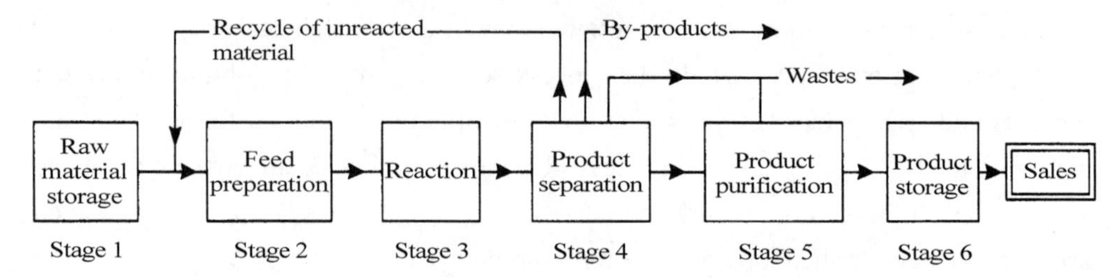

Fig. 1-1 Anatomy of a chemical process

Stage 1. Raw material storage

Unless the raw materials (also called essential materials, or feed stocks) are supplied as intermediate products (intermediates) from a neighboring plant, some provision will have to be made to hold several days, or weeks storage to smooth out fluctuations and interruptions in supply. Even when the materials come from an adjacent plant some provision is usually made to hold a few hours, or even days, supply to decouple the processes. The storage required will depend on the nature of the raw materials, the method of delivery, and what assurance can be placed on the continuity of supply. If materials are delivered by ship (tanker or bulk carrier) several weeks stocks may be necessary; whereas if they are received by road or rail, in smaller lots, less storage will be needed.

Stage 2. Feed preparation

Some purification, and preparation, of the raw materials will usually be necessary before they are sufficiently pure, or in the right form, to be fed to the reaction stage. For example, acetylene generated by the carbide process contains arsenical and sulphur compounds, and other impurities, which must be removed by scrubbing with concentrated sulphuric acid (or other processes) before it is sufficiently pure for reaction with hydrochloric acid to produce dichloroethane. Liquid feeds will need to be vaporized before being fed to gas-phase reactors, and solids may need crushing, grinding and screening.

Stage 3. Reactor

The reaction stage is the heart of a chemical manufacturing process. In the reactor the raw materials are brought together under conditions that promote the production of the desired product; invariably, by-products and unwanted compounds (impurities) will also be formed.

Stage 4. Product separation

In this first stage after the reactor the products and by-products are separated from any unreacted material. If in sufficient quantity, the unreacted material will be recycled to the reactor. They may be returned directly to the reactor or to the feed purification and preparation stage. The by-products may also be separated from the products at this stage.

Stage 5. Purification

Before sale, the main product will usually need purification to meet the product specification. If produced in economic quantities, the by-products may also be purified for sale.

Stage 6. Product storage

Some inventory of finished product must be held to match production with sales. Provision for product packaging and transport will also be needed, depending on the nature of the product. Liquids will normally be dispatched in drums and in bulk tankers (road, rail and sea), solids in sacks, cartons or bales.

The stock held will depend on the nature of the product and the market.

1. Ancillary processes

In addition to the main process stages shown in Figure 1-1, provision will have to be made for the supply of the services (utilities) needed, such as process water, cooling water, compressed air, steam. Facilities will also be needed for maintenance, firefighting, offices and other accommodation, and laboratories.

2.Continuous and batch processes

Continuous processes are designed to operate 24 hours a day, 7 days a week, throughout the year. Some down time will be allowed for maintenance and, for some processes, catalyst regeneration. The plant attainment, that is, the percentage of the available hours in a year that the plant operates, will usually be 90 to 95%.

$$\text{Attainment}\ \% = \frac{\text{hours operated}}{8760} \times 100$$

Batch processes are designed to operate intermittently. Some, or all, the process units being frequently shut down and started up.

Continuous processes will usually be more economical for large scale production. Batch processes are used where some flexibility is wanted in production rate or product specification.

The choice between batch or continuous operation will not be clear cut, but the following rules can be used as a guide.

Continuous	*Batch*
1. Production rate greater than 5×100 kg/h	1. Production rate less than 5×100 kg/h
2. Single product	2. A range of products or product specifications
3. No severe fouling	3. Severe fouling
4. Good catalyst life	4. Short catalyst life
5. Proven processes design	5. New product
6. Established market	6. Uncertain design

Selected from "*Chemical Engineering, Vol 6*, 2nd Edition, R.K. Sinnott, Pergamon Press, 1996"

Words and Expressions

1. anatomy [ə'nætəmi] n. 解剖，分解；构造，组织
2. specification [spesifi'keiʃən] n. 说明书；（pl.）（尺寸）规格，技术要求；明细表

3. fluctuation [flʌktju'eiʃən] n. 波动，脉动；振幅
4. decouple [di'kʌpl] v. 消除...间的影响，分隔；去耦
5. bulk [bʌlk] a. 散装的；大块的
6. bulk carrier 散装大船
7. lot [lɔt] n. （商品的）一批；批量；份额
8. acetylene [ə'setili:n] n. 乙炔
9. carbide ['kɑ:baid] n. 碳化物；碳化钙
10. arsenical [ɑ:'sennikəl] a. (含)砷的 n. 含砷制剂
11. sulphur ['sʌlfə] n. 硫 S, 硫磺
12. impurity [im'pjuəriti] n. 杂质，夹杂物；不纯，污染
13. scrub [skrʌb] v. 气体洗涤，涤气，洗涤，清洗
14. hydrochloric acid 盐酸
15. dichloroethane n. 二氯乙烷
16. vaporize ['veipəraiz] vt. （使）汽化，（使）蒸发
17. screen [skri:n] v. 筛分，筛选；屏蔽，隐藏
18. reactor [ri'æktə] n. 反应器，反应堆
19. inventory ['invəntri] n. 库存量；（商品、物资等）清单
20. dispatch [dis'pætʃ] vt. （迅速地）发送，派遣；迅速办理，了结
21. carton ['kɑ:tən] n. 纸板箱（或盒）
22. bale [beil] n. 大包，大捆
23. regeneration [ridʒenə'reiʃən] n. 再生，更新，新生
24. attainment [ə'teinmənt] n. 开工率
25. batch [bætʃ] a. 间歇的，分批的
26. intermittently [intə'mitəntli] ad. 间歇地；断断续续地；周期性地
27. foul [faul] n. 污物（垢） v. 结垢，弄脏

Unit 3 Typical Activities of Chemical Engineers

After completing this unit, you should be able to:

1. Identify the differences between the work of chemists and that of chemical engineers.
2. Describe some of the typical activities of the chemical engineer.
3. Define the functions of the "pilot-plant".
4. List the main products of the design stage.

The classical role of the chemical engineer is to take the discoveries made by the chemist in the laboratory and develop them into money-making, commercial-scale chemical processes. The chemist works in test tubes and Parr bombs with very small quantities of reactants and products (e.g., 100 ml), usually running "batch", constant-temperature experiments. Reactants are placed in a small container in a constant temperature bath. A catalyst is added and the reactions proceed with time. Samples are taken at appropriate intervals to follow the consumption of the reactants and the production of products as time progresses.

By contrast, the chemical engineer typically works with much larger quantities of material and with very large (and expensive) equipment. Reactors can hold 1,000 gallons to 10,000 gallons or more. Distillation columns can be over 100 feet high and 10 to 30 feet in diameter. The capital investment for one process unit in a chemical plant may exceed $100 million!

The chemical engineer is often involved in "scaling up" a chemist-developed small-scale reactor and separation system to a very large commercial plant. The chemical engineer must work closely with the chemist in order to understand thoroughly the chemistry involved in the process and to make sure that the chemist gets the reaction kinetic data and the physical property data needed to design, operate, and optimize the process. This is why the chemical engineering curriculum contains so many chemistry courses.

The chemical engineer must also work closely with mechanical, electrical, civil, and metallurgical engineers in order to design and operate the physical equipment in a plant—the reactors, tanks, distillation columns, heat exchangers, pumps, compressors, control and instrumentation devices, and so on. One big item that is always on such an equipment list is piping. One of the most impressive features of a typical chemical plant is the tremendous number of pipes running all over the site, literally hundreds of miles in many plants. These pipes transfer process materials (gases and liquids) into and out of the plant. They also carry utilities (steam, cooling water, air, nitrogen, and refrigerant) to the process units.

To commercialize the laboratory chemistry, the chemical engineer is involved in development, design, construction, operation, sales, and research. The terminology used to label these functions is by no means uniform from company to company, but a rose by any other name is still a rose. Let us describe each of these functions briefly. It should be emphasized that the jobs we shall discuss are "typical" and "classical," but are by no means the only things that chemical engineers do. The chemical engineer has a broad background in mathematics, chemistry, and physics. Therefore, he or she can, and does, fill a rich variety of jobs in industry, government, and academia.

1. Development

Development is the intermediate step required in passing from a laboratory-size process to a commercial-size process. The "pilot-plant" process involved in development might involve reactors that are five gallons in capacity and distillation columns that are three inches in diameter. Development is usually part of the commercialization of a chemical process because the scale-up problem is a very difficult one. Jumping directly from test tubes to 10,000-gallon reactors can be a tricky and sometimes dangerous endeavor. Some of the subtle problems involved which are not at all obvious to the uninitiated include mixing imperfections, increasing radial temperature gradients, and decreasing ratios of heat transfer areas to heat generation rates.

The chemical engineer works with the chemist and a team of other engineers to design, construct, and operate the pilot plant. The design aspect involves specifying equipment sizes, configuration, and materials of construction. Usually pilot plants are designed to be quite flexible, so that a wide variety of conditions and configurations can be evaluated.

Once the pilot plant is operational, performance and optimization data can be obtained in order to evaluate the process from an economic point of view. The profitability is assessed at each stage of the development of the process. If it appears that not enough money will be made to justify the capital investment, the project will be stopped.

The pilot plant offers the opportunity to evaluate materials of construction, measurement techniques, and process control strategies. The experimental findings in the pilot plant can be used to improve the design of the full-scale plant.

2. Design

Based on the experience and data obtained in the laboratory and the pilot plant, a team of engineers is assembled to design the commercial plant. The chemical engineer's job is to specify all process flow rates and conditions, equipment types and sizes, materials of construction, process configurations control systems, safety systems, environmental protection systems, and other relevant specifications. It is an enormous responsibility.

The design stage is really where the big bucks are spent. One typical chemical process might require a capital investment of $50 to $100 million. That's a lot of bread! And the chemical engineer is the one who has to make many of the decisions. When you find yourself in that position, you will be glad that you studied as hard as you did (we hope) so that you can bring the best possible tools and minds to bear on the problems.

The product of the design stage is a lot of paper:

(1) *Flow Sheets* are diagrams showing all the equipment schematically, with all streams labeled and their conditions specified (flow rate, temperature, pressure, composition, viscosity,

density, etc.).

(2) *P and I (Piping and Instrumentation) Drawings* are drawings showing all pieces of equipment (including sizes, nozzle locations, and materials), all piping (including sizes, materials, and valves), all instrumentation (including locations and types of sensors, control valves, and controllers), and all safety systems (including safety valve and rupture disk locations and sizes, flare lines, and safe operating conditions).

(3) *Equipment Specification Sheets* are sheets of detailed information on all the equipment precise dimensions, performance criteria, materials of construction, corrosion allowances, operating temperatures, and pressures, maximum and minimum flow rates, and the like. These "spec sheets" are sent to the equipment manufacturers for price bids and then for building the equipment.

3. Construction

After the equipment manufacturers (vendors) have built the individual pieces of equipment, the pieces are shipped to the plant site (sometimes a challenging job of logistics, particularly for large vessels like distillation columns). The construction phase is the assembling of all the components into a complete plant. It starts with digging holes in the ground and pouring concrete for foundations for large equipment and buildings (e.g., the control room, process analytical laboratory, and maintenance shops).

After these initial activities, the major pieces of equipment and the steel superstructure are erected. Heat exchangers, pumps, compressors, piping, instrument sensors, and automatic control valves are installed. Control system wiring and tubing are run between the control room and the plant. Electrical wiring, switches, and transformers are installed for motors to drive pumps and compressors. As the process equipment is being installed, it is the chemical engineer's job to check that it is all hooked together properly and that each piece works correctly.

This is usually a very exciting and rewarding time for most engineers. You are seeing your ideas being translated from paper into reality. Steel and concrete replace sketches and diagrams. Construction is the culmination of years of work by many people. You are finally on the launch pad, and the plant is going to fly or fizzle! The moment of truth is at hand.

Once the check-out phase is complete, "startup" begins. Startup is the initial commissioning of the plant. It is a time of great excitement and round-the-clock activity. It is one of the best learning grounds for the chemical engineer. Now you find out how good your ideas and calculations really are. The engineers who have worked on the pilot plant and on the design are usually part of the startup team.

The startup period can require a few days or a few months, depending on the newness of the technology, the complexity of the process, and the quality of the engineering that has gone into the design. Problems are frequently encountered that require equipment modifications. This is time consuming and expensive: just the lost production from a plant can amount to thousands of dollars per day. Indeed, there have been some plants that have never operated, because of unexpected problems with control, corrosion, or impurities, or because of economic problems.

The engineers are usually on shift work during the startup period. There is a lot to learn in a short time period. Once the plant has been successfully operated at its rated performance, it is turned over to the operating or manufacturing department for routine production of products.

4. Manufacturing

Chemical engineers occupy a central position in manufacturing (or "operations" or "production," as it is called in some companies). Plant technical service groups are responsible for the technical aspects of running an efficient and safe plant. They run capacity and performance tests on the plant to determine where the bottlenecks are in the equipment, and then design modifications and additions to remove these bottlenecks.

Chemical engineers study ways to reduce operating costs by saving energy, cutting raw material consumption, and reducing production of off-specification products that require reprocessing. They study ways to improve product quality and reduce environmental pollution of both air and water.

In addition to serving in plant technical service, many engineers have jobs as operating supervisors. These supervisors are responsible for all aspects of the day-to-day operation of the plant, including supervising the plant operators who run the plant round the clock on a three-shift basis, meeting quality specifications, delivering products at agreed-upon times and in agreed-upon quantities, developing and maintaining inventories of equipment spare parts, keeping the plant well maintained, making sure safe practices are followed, avoiding excessive emissions into the local environment, and serving as spokespersons for the plant to the local community.

5. Technical Sales

Many chemical engineers find stimulating and profitable careers in technical sales. As with other sales positions, the work involves calling on customers, making recommendations on particular products to fill customer's needs, and being sure that orders are handled smoothly. The sales engineer is the company's representative and must know the company's product line well. The sales engineer's ability to sell can greatly affect the progress and profitability of the company.

The marketing of many chemicals requires a considerable amount of interaction between engineers in the company producing the chemical and engineers in the company using the chemical. This interaction can take the form of advising on how to use a chemical or developing a new chemical in order to solve a specific problem of a customer.

When the sales engineer discovers problems that cannot be handled with confidence, he or she must be able to call on the expertise of specialists. The sales engineer may sometimes have to manage a joint effort among researchers from several companies who are working together to solve a problem.

6. Research

Chemical engineers are engaged in many types of research. They work with the chemist in developing new or improved products. They develop new and improved engineering methods (e.g., better computer programs to simulate chemical processes, better laboratory analysis methods for characterizing chemicals, and new types of reactors and separation systems). They work on improved sensors for on-line physical property measurements. They study alternative process configurations and equipment.

Research engineers are likely to be found in laboratories or at desks working on problems. They usually work as members of a team of scientists and engineers. Knowledge of the process and common types of process equipment helps the chemical engineer make special contributions to the research effort. The chemical engineer's daily activities may sometimes closely resemble those of the chemist or physicist working on the same team.

Selected from "*Chemical Process Analysis*, by L.L. William, Prentice Hall, 1988"

Words and Expressions

1. Parr bomb　派氏氧弹
2. gallon　['gælən]　n. 加仑
(the imperial ~英制加仑 ＝4.546 升　the wine ~美制加仑 ＝3.785 升)
3. distillation　[disti'leiʃən]　n. 蒸馏（作用），馏分
4. curriculum　[kə'rikjuləm]　n. （一门，全部）课程
5. metallurgical　[metə'lə:dʒikəl]　a. 冶金（学、术）的
6. heat exchanger　热交换器
7. literally　['litərəli]　ad. [口]不加夸张地，确实地
8. terminology　[tə:mi'nɔlədʒi]　n. 术语，专门用语
9. tricky　['triki]　a. （工作等）复杂的，棘手的；靠不住的
10. endeavor　[in'devə]　n. 努力，尽力
11. subtle　['sʌtl]　a. 微细的，巧妙的；稀薄的
12. gradient　['greidiənt]　n. 梯度，变化率，坡度
13. configuration　[kənfigju'reiʃən]　n. 结构，构造
14. buck　[bʌk]　n.（美俚）元
15. flow sheet　工艺流程图，程序方框图
16. schematicallyad. 用示意图，用图解法，示意地，大略地
17. composition　[kɔmpə'ziʃən]　n. 组成，成分，结构
18. nozzle　['nɔzl]　n. 喷嘴（管，头），接管嘴
19. valve　[vælv]　n. 阀，活门
20. sensor　['sensə]　n. 传感器，探测器
21. rupture　['rʌptʃə]　n.;v. 破裂，断裂，破损
22. rupture disk　安全（隔）膜
23. flare line　火舌管，（石油）废气燃烧管路
24. criterion　[krai'tiəriən]　n. (pl.) criteria 判据，准则，判断标准
25. corrosion　[kə'rəuʒən]　n. 腐蚀，锈蚀
26. spec = specification
27. bid　[bid]　v.; n. 出（报，喊）价，投标

28. vendor ['vendə:] n. 卖主，小贩，自动售货机
29. logistics [lə'dʒistiks] n. 后勤(学)，后勤保障
30. concrete ['kɔnkri:t] n. 混凝土 a. 混凝土的
31. superstructure ['sju:pəstrʌktʃə] n. 上层（上部）结构，上层建筑
32. sketch [sketʃ] n. 示意图，简图，设计图
33. culmination [kʌlmi'neiʃən] n. 顶点，极点，最高潮
34. fizzle ['fizl] vi.（在开始时大有成功希望的计划等）终于失败
35. startup n. 开动，运转
36. commission [kə'miʃən] n. 交工试运转，投产
37. round-the-clock 连续一整天（或一昼夜）
38. shift [ʃift] n. (换，轮）班，工作班
39. agreed-upon a. 约定的，(各方)同意的
40. spare part n. 备件
41. simulate ['simjuleit] vt. 模拟，仿真，模型化，模型试验
42. on-line 联机，在线，机内

Exercises

1. *Complete the notes below with words taken from the text above. Use* ***No More Than Three Words*** *for each answer.*

(1) The chemical engineer must work closely with the chemist, as well as [1]_________, [2]________, [3]_______, and metallurgical engineers, in order to [4]____________ a laboratory-size process to a [5]________________ process.

(2) Usually a chemical plant may compose of many process units, such as [6]__________, tanks, [7]___________, heat exchangers, [8]________, compressors, [9]______________________devices, and so on.

(3) With a broad background in [10]___________, chemistry, and physics, a chemical engineer can take a position in [11]__________, government, and [12]__________.

(4) Pipes transfer process materials into and out of the plant, and carry utilities, such as [13]______, [14]________________ , air, nitrogen and refrigerant, to the process units.

2. *Complete the table below. Choose* ***No More Than Three Words*** *from the text for each answer.*

Stage	*Activities or products*	*Cooperators*
Development	● *Design, construct*, and operate the pilot plant. ● Evaluate the process from [15]_____________ point of view ● Get information [16]____________ the design of the full-scale plant	The chemist Other engineers
Design	● Flow sheets ● [17]_______________ ● [18]________________________	Other engineers
[19]___________	● Check if everything is OK. ● Start up the plant	● The startup team

续表

Stage	*Activities or products*	*Cooperators*
Manufacturing	● Test the plant [20]____________ ● Modify design and move [21]____________ ● Improve the process ● Supervise the routine operation	Technical service group
[22]____________	● Call on customers ● Give suggestion on particular products ● Arrange orders	Engineers in the company Specialists Engineers from several companies
Research	● Develop [23]____________ products ● Develop new or improved [24]____________ ● Improve sensors ● Study more desirable process [25]____________ and equipment	Scientist and engineers

3. *Put the following into Chinese:*

reactant	distillation	compressor	pilot-plant
specification	flow sheet	nozzle	corrosion
sensor	atrophy	on-line	commission

4. *Put the following into English:*

间歇的	反应器	放大	热交换器
创新	术语	阀	流程图
梯度	组成	杂质	模拟

Reading Material 3:

Excel in Your Engineering

When I reflect on my 20-plus years of experience as a chemical engineer, I realize how wonderful my profession is. As engineers, we provide the essential link between technology and humanity. Our job is to make the world better for its human inhabitants while protecting the environment. And we fulfill our mission amongst the demands and guidelines of the business world.

But sometimes we get so bogged down in the everyday aspects of our jobs that we lose sight of the big picture. We forget to appreciate engineering—though it is challenging, creative, interesting, significant, and even fun.

For example, there's nothing like getting engrossed in a tough technical problem and coming up with a neat solution. Do you find yourself hurrying to the office because you look forward to working? Do you ever wake up in the middle of the night thinking about a problem and lie there working out the details of a brilliant solution? Do you get up to write notes so you won't forget your breakthrough in the morning?

Engineering can be that wonderful. And being involved in your work doesn't mean you're a nut or a workaholic. We should like what we do: Enjoying something and doing it well is a "chicken-and-egg" situation. We tend to like activities we perform well, and to be good at things we enjoy. So here's some advice for both enjoying and improving your engineering work.

1. Enhance technical skills

Engineering provides many opportunities to develop existing skills and to learn new ones. In fact, we have to keep learning or we atrophy—that's the nature of any profession. The ability to grow is one reward of a good job. As your interests and involvements change, and as technology changes, you need to keep learning

You can foster your skills by keeping informed of new advances in technology. Read the industry literature and see what's new at conferences. Vendors often offer seminars that can help you in your work. Professional societies can also be good sources of up-to-data information.

2. Hone interpersonal skills

Not all the development opportunities relate to technical matters. Successful engineering practice is strongly dependent on interpersonal and communications skills. It's important to learn about people, motivation, organizational behavior, written and oral communication and visual aids. With these skills, as with any others, practice makes perfect (or at least very proficient).

In addition, remember that we are also "business people" and, as such, should keep up on trends in the business world, particularly in our industry. These communications skills can help develop relations both within and outside the company.

Activities outside of the workplace can be good opportunities for enhancing nontechnical skills. They can help you improve interpersonal, leadership and communication capabilities.

For example, it's very easy to get into leadership positions in volunteer organizations. All you have to do is attend some meetings and show that you're willing to help out, and soon you'll move right into whatever you want to do.

3. Do the whole job

You're probably familiar with the concept of "completed staff work" (CSW). According to this concept, a subordinate presents his or her boss with solutions, or at least options, rather than problems. The reasoning is that the person closest to the problem is better prepared than anyone—even the boss—to make a decision and to implement it. Decisions are best made at the lowest practical level.

Before passing your work on to the boss, try to make the work as complete as you can. That means not only writing the report, but also the cover letter and any transmittal notes it will need to flow smoothly through channels. Think through any political ramifications and make appropriate contacts to preclude problems. Anticipate questions and prepare for them. If your boss looks good, you look good.

By maximizing the quality and quantity of your work, you maximize your value to your employer. Learn to do many things well. Be the engineer who can write a project proposal, plan and perform experiments, design equipment, analyze data, develop a mathematical model, write and present results, and bring in the next job. If you do it yourself—or lead others in doing it—you will be indispensable.

4. See the big picture

Many engineers with little experience view their job too narrowly. They're content to just do what they're asked. They may be creative in carrying out designated tasks, and they may see some minor extensions of it, but they don't explore widely enough.

But the "big picture" is not just the concern of higher-level people. Everything that happens in the company affects all of its employees. In turn, each employee can contribute to the well being of the company.

You can get involved in long-range planning, business development, and diversification into new products or services. The people who are already involved in these matters will welcome your help. Although you might start out with a small role, you will soon be contributing more and more. Such efforts often begin by demanding a little more of your personal time, but are later sanctioned by your supervisors as you prove your capability.

5. Be a leader

There's always a need for leadership of technical activities, and many engineers are suited to this. Leaders aren't born: leadership skills are developed.

Leadership is different from management. For example, consider a large group of people in a jungle; their task is to cut a path through the underbrush. Managers recruit the workers, teach them how to use a machete, provide them with appropriate clothing, arrange their transportation to the job site and ensure that they are fed.

But the leader is the one at the front of the group, showing them where to cut the path. Or perhaps the leader tells the group that this is the wrong jungle and they need to go elsewhere.

Managers take charge of administrative, executive and business matters. They supervise employees' work to make sure that operations are flowing smoothly. Leaders, on the other hand, are those who break ground, bring in new technologies, and point the way toward innovation.

You don't have to have any assigned management responsibility to be a leader. People respond to leaders—with or without prestigious titles.

As a matter of fact, you may be able to develop true leadership skills better if you don't have administrative responsibilities. When you don't have jurisdictional authority over people, you find other ways to influence them. Instead of ordering people to do things, you make them want to do them—and that's the best way.

6. Be a mentor

As we gain experience, we can help younger engineers develop their potential. People pick up a lot of their attitudes toward work, approaches to problems, and working methods from their senior colleagues. If you are a senior engineer, your impact on new employees is particularly strong and important.

New engineers should be able to take a sufficiently broad view of their jobs and not limit themselves. It's rewarding to accomplish work through others, to see them develop into stronger engineers and move into positions of more responsibility.

Sometimes part of your success as an engineer may be hiring or training someone who goes on to do things you can do yourself. You can help a promising engineer with capabilities beyond your own. And if you have a hand in developing someone who goes on to a really high position in your company, be proud of your accomplishment.

7. Beware of diversions

A multifaceted profession, engineering involves other disciplines. But think about your chosen path before becoming involved in a peripheral area.

For example, many engineers become enamored with computers. Today's personal computers can certainly enhance our productivity. Remember, however, that a computer is a tool just like a telephone or a calculator. Don't let yourself value the means over the end. If you're working on computer tasks that support personnel can do more efficiently, you're probably not employing your time well.

Some engineers are so fascinated by computers that they have in reality shifted from being engineers to being computer scientists. There's certainly merit in doing what you enjoy, but issue a caution. Remember that you had good reasons for going into engineering in the first place, and if you drift into another area, you may later find it difficult to return to your engineering duties.

Management is another popular diversion. For some engineers, going into management is a positive move. Management is challenging and rewarding, and many engineers are well suited to it. In addition, having an engineer-turned-manager is helpful to the other engineers. Moving in and out of management positions, especially in the lower levels of management, can actually be good for an engineer's career.

However, the longer you stay in management, the more you run the risk of no longer being able to return to engineering. Most engineers who move into lower-level management positions are wise to regard them as a temporary diversion from their true profession.

8. Keep fit

Good health is essential to doing a good job. When you're fit, you have more energy and feel better generally. Thus you can put more into your work, as well as into other aspects of your life. Because most engineers have predominantly sedentary jobs, it is important to eat carefully and get enough exercise.

9. Enjoy your profession

As professional engineers, we need to keep developing and broadening our skills. We need to expand the scope of our work and reach the full potential we have, to the benefit of both ourselves and our employer. For most engineers, the best job security is being able to do high-quality engineering work, which is always in great demand. Finally, we should relish the varied challenges and excitement that constitute engineering at its best.

By Douglas Hissong, Exxon Production Research Co. *Chemical Engineering,* April 1993, 157

Words and Expressions

1. bog down （使）陷入泥沼（困境），（使）停顿，阻碍
2. engross [in'grəus] vt. （使）全神贯注，吸引（注意）
3. nut [nʌt] n. 螺带（帽）；
   (美俚)傻瓜，（行为或信仰方面的）怪人，狂热者
4. workaholic [wə:kə'hɔlik] n. 为免遭辞退而工作过分卖力的人
5. chicken-and-egg a. 鸡与蛋孰先难定的，因果（或先后次序）难定的
6. atrophy ['ætrəfi] vi. 退化，衰退，萎缩
7. foster ['fɔstə] vt. 培养，促进，鼓励；养育
8. seminar ['seminɑ:] n. 研究班，（专家）研讨班，讨论会
9. hone [həun] vt. 把...放在磨石上磨
10. motivation [məuti'veiʃən] n. 动机的形成，促进因素，动力
11. enhance [in'hɑ:ns] vt. 提高，增强
12. subordinate [sə'bɔ:dinit] a. 下级的，次要的，从属的
13. implement ['impliment] vt. 实现，完成，履行
14. ramification [ræmifi'keiʃən] n. 细节，门类；结果；衍生物
15. preclude [pri'klu:d] vt. 预防，排除
16. sanction ['sæŋkʃən] n.;v. （习俗上对行为等）赞许，支持，鼓励；承认
17. jungle ['dʒʌŋgl] n. 丛林， 密林
18. underbrush ['ʌndəbrʌʃ] n. 下木，下层林木（长在树林下的矮树丛）
19. recruit [ri'kru:t] vt. 征募，吸收（新成员）
20. machete [mə'tʃeiti] n. (中美 、南美人割甘蔗或当武器用的）大砍刀
21. innovation [inəu'veiʃən] n. 创新，改革；新方法，新事物
22. prestigious [pres'ti:dʒəs] a. 有威信的，受尊敬的
23. jurisdiction [dʒuəris'dikʃən] n. 权限，管辖权
24. mentor ['mentɔ:] n. 顾问，指导者，教练，师傅
25. multifaceted [mʌlti'fæsitid] n. （多面体的）面，（题目、思想等的）面
    vt. 在…上刻面
26. peripheral [pə'rifərəl] a. 周边的，周围的，边缘的
27. enamore [i'næmə] vt. 使倾心，使迷恋
28. the means 手段
29. the end 目标
30. fascinate ['fæsineit] v. 使着迷，强烈吸引住
31. relish ['reliʃ] vt. 乐于，爱好，欣赏，玩味

Unit 4 Sources of Chemicals

After completing this unit, you should be able to:

1. Compare the sources of inorganic chemicals with that of organic chemicals.
2. Give an example of the extraction process for processing inorganic chemicals.
3. Distinguish between non-renewable resource and renewable resource. And show the relative values of oil in the different forms.
4. Evaluate the advantages and disadvantages of the fermentation process.

The number and diversity of chemical compounds is remarkable: over ten million are now known. Even this vast number pales into insignificance when compared to the number of carbon compounds which is theoretically possible. This is a consequence of catenation, i.e., formation of very long chains of carbon atoms due to the relatively strong carbon-carbon covalent bonds, and isomerism. Most of these compounds are merely laboratory curiosities or are only of academic interest. However, of the remainder there are probably several thousands which are of commercial and practical interest. It might therefore be expected that there would be a large number of sources of these chemicals. Although this is true for inorganic chemicals, surprisingly most organic chemicals can originate from a single source such as crude oil (petroleum).

1. Inorganic Chemicals

Table 1-1 Major sources of inorganic chemicals

Source	*Examples of uses*
Phosphate rock	Fertilizers, detergents
Salt	Chlorine, alkali production
Limestone	Soda ash, lime, calcium carbide
Sulphur	Sulphuric acid production
Potassium compounds	Caustic potash, fertilizers
Bauxite①	Aluminum salts
Sodium carbonate	Caustic soda, cleaning formulations
Titanium compounds	Titanium dioxide pigments, lightweight alloys
Magnesite	Magnesium salts
Borates	Borax, boric acid, glazes
Fluorite②	Aluminum fluoride, organofluorine compounds

Since the term "inorganic chemical" covers compounds of all the elements other than carbon, the diversity of origins is not surprising (see Table 1-1). Some of the more important sources are metallic ores (for important metals like iron and aluminum), and salt or brine (for chlorine, sodium, sodium hydroxide and sodium carbonate). In all these cases at least two different elements are combine together chemically in the form of a stable compound. If therefore the individual element or elements, say the metal, are required then the extraction process must involve chemical treatment in addition to any separation methods of a purely physical nature. Metal ores, or minerals, rarely occur on their own in a pure form and therefore a first step in their processing is usually the separation from unwanted solids, such as clay or sand. Crushing and grinding of the solids followed by sieving may achieve some physical separation because of differing particle size. The next stage depends on the nature and properties of the required ore. For example, iron-bearing ores can often be separated by utilizing their magnetic properties in a magnetic separator. Froth flotation is another widely used technique in which the desired ore, in a fine particulate form, is separated from other solids by a difference in their ability to be wetted by an aqueous solution. Surface active (anti-wetting) agents are added to the solution, and these are typically molecules having a non-polar part, e.g., a long hydrocarbon chain, with a polar part such as an amino group at one end. This polar grouping attracts the ore, forming a loose bond. The hydrocarbon grouping now repels the water, thus preventing the ore being wetted, and it therefore floats. Other solids, in contrast, are readily wetted and therefore sink in the aqueous solution. Stirring or bubbling the liquid to give a froth considerably aids the "floating" of the agent-coated ore which then overflows from this tank into a collecting vessel, where it can be recovered. The key to success is clearly in the choice of a highly specific surface-active agent for the ore in question.

2. Organic Compounds

In contrast to inorganic chemicals which, as we have already seen, are derived from many different sources, the multitude of commercially important organic compounds are essentially derived from a single source. Nowadays in excess of 99% (by tonnage) of all organic chemicals is obtained from crude oil (petroleum) and natural gas via petrochemical processes. This is a very interesting situation—one which has changed over the years and will change again in the future—because technically these same chemicals could be obtained from other raw materials or sources. Thus aliphatic compounds, in particular, may be produced via ethanol, which is obtained by fermentation of carbohydrates. Aromatic compounds on the other hand are isolated from coal-tar, which is a by-product in the carbonization of coal. Animal and vegetable oils and fats are a more specialized source of a limited number of aliphatic compounds, including long-chain fatty acids such as stearic (octadecanoic) acid, $CH_3(CH_2)_{16}CO_2H$, and long-chain alcohols such as lauryl alcohol (dodecanol), $CH_3(CH_2)_{11}OH$.

The formation of fossil fuels[③], i.e. oil, gas and coal reserves, takes millions of years and once used they cannot be replaced. They are therefore referred to as *non-renewable resources*. This contrasts with carbohydrates which, being derived from plants, can be replaced relatively quickly. A popular source is sugar-cane—once a crop has been harvested and the ground cleared, new material may be planted and harvested, certainly in less than one year. Carbohydrates are therefore described as *renewable resources*. The total annual production of dry plant material has been estimated as 2×10^{11} tonnes.

Fossil fuels—natural gas, crude oil and coal—are used primarily as energy sources and not as sources of organic chemicals. For instance various petroleum fractions are used as gas for domestic cooking and heating, petrol or gasoline for automobiles, and heavy fuel oil for heating buildings or generating steam for industrial processes. Typically only around 8% of a barrel of crude oil is used in chemicals manufacture. The following figures demonstrate why the chemical industry can compete with the fuel- or energy-using industries for the crude oil

Form of oil	*Relative value of oil*
Crude oil	1
Fuel	2
Typical petrochemical	10
Typical consumer product	50

Clearly alternative energy sources to fossil fuels are now available if we have the will to use them, and we can confidently expect other alternatives to become available in the not too distant future. It is therefore essential that we retain our precious oil supplies for chemicals production. The statement that "the last thing you should do with oil is burn it" becomes more valid every year. It is interesting, and salutory, to note that as early as 1894 Mendeleyev (the Russian chemist who developed the Periodic Table) reported to his government that "oil was too valuable a resource to be burned and should be preserved as a source of chemicals".

Organic chemicals from carbohydrates (biomass). The main constituents of plants are carbohydrates which comprise the structural parts of the plant. They are polysaccharides such as cellulose and starch. Starch occurs in the plant kingdom in large quantities in foods such as cereals, rice and potatoes, cellulose is the primary substance from which the walls of plant cells are constructed and therefore occurs very widely and may be obtained from wood, cotton, etc. Thus, not only is the potential for chemicals considerable, but the feedstock is renewable.

The major route from biomass to chemicals is via fermentation processes. However these processes cannot utilize polysaccharides like cellulose and starch, and so the latter must first be subjected to acidic or enzymic hydrolysis to form the simpler sugars (the mono- or disaccharides, e.g. sucrose) which are suitable starting materials.

Fermentation processes utilize single-cell micro-organisms typically yeasts, fungi, bacteria or moulds to produce particular chemicals. Some of these processes have been used in the domestic situation for many thousands of years, the best-known example being fermentation of grains to produce alcoholic beverages. Indeed up until about 1950 this was the most popular route to aliphatic organic chemicals, since the ethanol produced could be dehydrated to give ethylene, which is the key intermediate for the synthesis of a whole range of aliphatic compounds. Although chemicals production in this way has been declining there is a lot of interest in producing automobile fuel in this way.

Disadvantages reflected in this can be divided into two parts (i) raw materials (ii) the fermentation process. Raw-material costs are higher than that of crude oil, because biomass is an agricultural material and therefore in comparison its production and harvesting is very labor-intensive. Also, being a solid material transportation is more difficult and expensive. Major disadvantages of fermentation compared with petrochemical processes are, firstly, the time scale, which is usually of the order of days compared to literally seconds for some catalytic petrochemical reactions, and secondly, the fact that the product is usually obtained as a dilute aqueous solution (< 10% concentration). The separation and purification costs are therefore very high indeed. Since the micro-organism is a living system, little variation in process conditions is permitted. Even a relatively small increase in temperature to increase the reaction rate may result in death of the micro-organism and termination of the process.

On the other hand particular advantages of fermentation methods are that they are very selective and that some chemicals which are structurally very complex, and therefore extremely difficult to synthesize, and/or require a multi-stage synthesis, are easily made. Notable examples are various antibiotics, e.g., penicillins, cephalosporins and streptomycins.

Provided that the immense practical problems associated with the rapidly developing field of genetic engineering, where micro-organisms such as bacteria are 'tailor-made' to produce the required chemical, can be overcome, then the interest in fermentation methods will be very considerable. However it seems unlikely that bulk chemicals, i.e. those required in very large quantities such as ethylene and benzene, will be produced in this way in the foreseeable future because of the slow reaction rate and the very high product separation costs.

Organic chemicals from animal and vegetable oils and fats. Animal and vegetable oils and fats——commonly known as lipids——are composed of mixtures of glycerides, which are esters of the trihydric alcohol, glycerol (propane-l, 2, 3-triol). There are many different sources of these oils. Some popular sources are soya, corn, palm-kernel, rapeseed and olive, animal fats and even sperm whales. The oils are isolated by solvent extraction and considerable quantities are used in the food industries as cooking oils and fats, and for production of butter, margarine and various other foodstuffs such as ice-cream. There is still controversy about the effect of the R-groups[④] in these foodstuffs on human health, particularly on high cholesterol levels in blood which may lead to high blood pressure and heart disease. Opinion now seems to favor a high proportion of unsaturated groups as being beneficial in lowering cholesterol levels and reducing the risk of heart attacks. This has led to a trend away from cooking fats and ordinary butter or margarine (which are all rich in saturated R-groups) to cooking oils and the use of margarines rich in polyunsaturates.

Being esters, the use of lipids for chemicals production starts with hydrolysis. Although this can be either acid- or alkali-catalyzed, the latter is preferred since it is an irreversible reaction, and under these conditions the process is known as saponification.

It is important to note that saponification, hydrolysis (fat splitting) and hydrogenolysis reactions do not each use a single glyceride (or methyl ester). In practice, the vegetable oil which is used is a mixture of various glycerides and the product is therefore a mixture which requires separating.

Selected from "*The Chemical Industry,* 2nd Edition, Alan Heaton, Blackie & Son Ltd. 1997"

Words and Expressions

1. pale [peil] vi. 变苍白，变暗淡

2. catenation [kæti'nei ʃən] n. 耦合，连接
3. covalent [kəu'veilənt] a. 共价的
4. bond [bɔnd] n.;v. （化学）键，键合
5. isomerism [ai'sɔmərizm] n. 同分异构(现象)
6. phosphate ['fɔsfeit] n. 磷酸盐（酯），磷肥
7. detergent [di'tə:dʒənt] n. 洗涤剂，去污剂
8. chlorine ['klɔ:ri:n] n. 氯（气） Cl
9. calcium ['kælsiəm] n. 钙 Ca
10. bauxite ['bɔ:ksait] n. 铝土矿，矾土
11. aluminum [ə'lju:minəm] n. = aluminium 铝 Al
12. caustic ['kɔ:stik] a. 苛性的 n. 苛性物，氢氧化物
13. soda ['səudə] n. 苏打，纯碱，碳酸钠；碳酸氢钠，小苏打
14. potash ['pɔtæʃ] n. 钾碱
15. titanium [tai'teinjəm] n. 钛 Ti
16. dioxide [dai'ɔksaid] n. 二氧化物
17. pigment ['pigm ənt] n. 颜料，色料；色素
18. magnesite ['mægnisait] n. 镁矿
19. magnesium [mæg'ni:zjəm] n. 镁 Mg
20. borate ['bɔ:reit] n. 硼酸盐（酯）
21. borax ['bɔ:ræks] n. 硼砂
22. boric acid 硼酸
23. glaze [gleiz] n. 釉面，上釉 vt. 上釉于，给陶（瓷）器上釉
24. fluorite ['flu ərait] n. 萤石，氟石
25. fluoride [flu əraid] n. 氟化物
26. organofluorine compound n. 有机氟化合物
27. brine [brain] n. 盐水，卤水，海水
28. hydroxide [hai'drɔksaid] n. 氢氧化物
29. extraction [iks'træk ʃən] n. 萃取，提炼；抽出物，提取的
30. sieve [siv] vt. 筛分，过筛，过滤
31. froth flotation 泡沫浮选
32. particulate [pə'tikjulit] a. 颗粒的，微粒的 n. 颗粒，微粒，粒子
33. aqueous ['eikwiəs] a.（含，多，似）水的，水成（化，样，多）的
34. surface-active agent 表面活性剂
35. amino ['æminəu] a. 氨基的
36. repel [ri'pel] v. 排斥，推开，击退，弹回
37. overflow [əuvə'fləu] v. 溢出，溢流
38. via prep.［拉丁语］经（过），（经）由，通过；借助于
39. aliphatic [æli'fætikl] a. 脂肪族的，无环的
40. aromatic [ærəu'mætik] a. 芳香（族）的，芳（香）烃的
41. coal-tar 煤焦油

42. carbonization [kɑ:bənai'zei ʃən] n. 碳化处理，渗炭，焦化
43. fatty acid 脂肪酸
44. stearic [sti'ərik] a. 硬脂的
45. stearic acid 硬脂酸，十八（碳）（烷）酸
46. octadecanoic acid 十八（碳）（烷）酸
47. alcohol ['ælkəhɔl] n. （乙）醇，酒精
48. lauryl ['lɔrəl] n. 月桂基，十二烷基
49. dodecanol n. 十二（烷）醇
50. fossil fuel 化石燃料，石油
51. sugar-cane n. 甘蔗
52. biomass ['baiəumæs] n. 植物茎杆或动物废弃物；生物量
53. polysaccharide [pɔli'sæk əraid] n. 多糖
54. cellulose ['seljul əus] n. 纤维素，细胞膜质 a. 细胞的
55. starch [st ɑ:t ʃ] n. 淀粉，浆（糊）
56. cereal ['siəriəl] n.;a. 谷类（的），谷子，谷物（的）
57. enzymic [en'zaimik] a. 酶的，酵素的
58. hydrolysis [hai'dr ɔlisis] n. 水解（作用），加水分解
59. mono- [词头]单一，单一的
60. di- [词头]二，重，双
61. saccharide ['sæk əraid] n. 糖类，糖化物
62. sucrose ['sju:krəus] n. 蔗糖，砂糖
63. yeast [ji:st] n. 酵母，发酵粉
64. fungi ['f ʌŋgai] n. (fungus 的复数) 真菌
65. bacteria [bæk'tiəriə] n. (bacterium 的复数) 细菌
66. beverage ['bevəridʒ] n. 饮料
67. dehydrate [di:'haidreit] v.; n. 脱水，干燥
68. decline [di'klain] v.;n. 下降，减少，倾斜，衰落
69. dilute [dai'lju:t] a. 稀（薄，释）的，淡的 v. 稀释，冲淡
70. cephalosporin [sefələu'sp ɔ:rin] n. 头孢菌素
71. streptomycin [streipt əu'maisin] n. 链霉素
72. foreseeable a. 可预见到的
73. lipid = lipiod n. 类脂（化合物），类脂体
74. glyceride ['glisəraid] n. 甘油脂
75. ester ['estə] n. 酯
76. tri- [词头]三（重，倍，回）
77. trihydric a. 三价的，三元的，含有三个 OH 基的，三价酸式的
78. glycerol ['glisərɔl] n. 甘油，丙三醇
79. propane ['proupein] n. 丙烷
80. –triol [词尾]三醇
81. soya ['sɔiə] n. 或 soybean 大豆, 黄豆

82. palm [pɑ:m] n. 棕榈（树，叶，枝）
83. kernel ['k ə:nl] n.（果实的）核，仁；原子核，核心
84. rapeseed n. 油菜籽
85. olive ['ɔliv] n. 橄榄 a. 橄榄（色）的
86. sperm [sp ə:m] n. 巨头（抹香）鲸，鲸油
87. whale [hweil] n. 鲸（鱼）
88. margarine [m ɑ:d ʒə'ri:n] n. 人造黄油，代黄油
89. controversy ['k ɔntrə və:si] n. 争论，论战
90. cholesterol [k ɔ'lestə rɔl] n. 胆固醇
91. unsaturated [ʌ n'sæt ʃəreitid] a. 不饱和的
92. saponification [sæpə nifi'kei ʃə n] n. 皂化（作用）
93. splitting ['splitiŋ] n. 分解，分裂，蜕变
94. hydrogenolysis n. 氢解（作用），用氢还原
95. methyl ['meθil] n. 甲基

Notes

① bauxite: 铝土矿，工业价值最大的含铝矿物，主要成分是氧化铝，还含有二氧化硅、氧化铁和水等。

② fluorite: 萤石，是最主要的含氟矿物，主要成分是氟化钙。萤石主要用作冶金工业的助熔剂，是无机盐工业的重要原料。

③ fossil fuels: 化石燃料，指埋藏地层中的不同地质年代的植物和动物遗体，经漫长地质条件的变化，在温度、压力和微生物的作用下而形成的一类可燃性矿物，包括煤、石油、天然气、油页岩及油砂等。

④ R-group: 指烷基基团。

Exercises

1. *Complete the summary of the text above. Choose **No More Than Three Words** from the passage for each answer.*

There are enormous kinds of chemical compounds and the origins of [1]______________ are diverse, whereas most organic chemicals can [2]___________ a single source. Now over 99% of organic chemicals are obtained from crude oil and natural gas via [3]_____________________. [4]____________ and salt or brine are the important inorganic chemical sources. Some physical separation methods and the chemical treatment compose the [5]_________________.

Organic chemicals can be made from [6]_________________, such as crude oil, natural gas and coal or [7]______________, such as carbohydrates. Although relative value of oil is much higher if it is used in chemical industry, most of it is still used as [8]_______________.

Carbohydrates may be a potential source of organic chemicals, viz. a major route of the [9]_________. Although this process is very [10]__________ and it can make some very complex chemicals, it fails to compete with petrochemical for its high [11]___________ cost, very slow reaction rate and very high [12]_______________________ costs. Another source of organic chemicals is animal and vegetable oils and fats, which are mainly used in [13]__________ and soap making.

2. *Refer to the paragraph of "**Inorganic Chemicals**", complete the following notes and diagram.*

Froth Flotation Process

Scientific basis: a difference in the ability [14]______________

[15]____________: the choice of a highly specific surface-active agent

Steps:

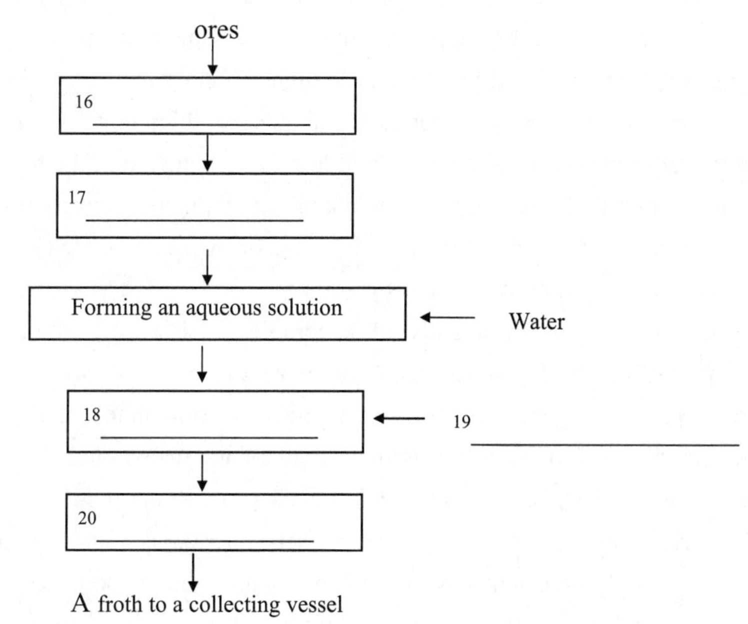

3. *Put the following into Chinese:*

covalent	isomerism	froth flotation	borate
fluoride	amino	hydrolysis	eater
naphthene	naphtha	enzymic	xylene

4. *Put the following into English:*

氢氧化物	脂肪族的	芳香族的	甲烷
酯	不饱和的	烯烃	烷烃

Reading Material 4:

Organic Chemicals from Oil, Natural Gas and Coal

Sources of organic chemicals are surprisingly few in number and it is technically possible for each to act as the raw material for the synthesis of the majority of all the organic chemicals of commercial importance. The choice between them is therefore largely a matter of economics, which has been greatly influenced by the scale of operation. The dominant position of oil and natural gas as the source of more than 90% of all organic chemicals is due in considerable measure to the very large scale on which the petrochemical industry operates. This feature is shared with the oil-refining industry from which it developed and which provides its feedstocks.

1. Organic chemicals from oil and natural gas

The petroleum or crude-oil processing industry dates from the 1920s, and in these early days its operations were confined to separation of the oil into fractions by distillation. These various fractions were then used as energy sources, but the increasing sales of automobiles pushed up demand for the gasoline or petrol fraction. Development of processes such as cracking and reforming was stimulated and by this means higher-boiling petroleum fractions, for which demand was low, were converted into materials suitable for blending as gasoline. Additionally these processes produced olefins or alkenes, and at this particular time there was no outlet for these as petroleum products. Subsequent research and development showed that they were very useful chemical intermediates from which a wide range of organic chemicals could be synthesized. This was the start of the petrochemical industry.

Crude oil. consists principally of a complex mixture of saturated hydrocarbons—mainly alkanes (paraffins) and cycloalkanes (naphthenes) with smaller amounts of alkenes and aromatics—plus small amounts (< 5% in total) of compounds containing nitrogen, oxygen or sulphur. The presence of the latter is undesirable since many sulphur-containing compounds, e.g. mercaptans, have rather unpleasant odors and also, more importantly, are catalyst poisons and can therefore have disastrous effects on some refinery operations and downstream chemical processes. In addition, their combustion may cause formation of the air pollutant sulphur dioxide. They are therefore removed at an early stage in the refining of the crude oil (or else they tend to concentrate in the heavy fuel oil fraction). The complex mixture of hydrocarbons constituting crude oil must first be separated into a series of less complex mixtures or fractions. Since the components are chemically similar, being largely alkanes or cycloalkanes, and ranging from very volatile to fairly involatile materials, they are readily separated into these fractions by continuous distillation. The separation is based on the boiling point and therefore accords largely with the number of carbon atoms in the molecule. Table 1-2 shows the typical fractions which are obtained, together with an indication of their boiling range, composition and proportion of the starting crude oil.

In terms of producing chemicals it is the lower-boiling fractions which are of importance particularly the gases and the naphtha① fractions. However consideration of the nature of the components of these fractions (they are largely alkanes and cycloalkanes) suggests that they will not be suitable for chemical synthesis as they stand. Alkanes are well known for their lack of chemical reactivity—indeed their old name, paraffins, is derived from two Latin words, *parum* and *affinis*, meaning, “little affinity”. They need to be converted into more reactive molecules and this is achieved by chemical reactions which produce unsaturated hydrocarbons such as alkenes and aromatics. As expected, because of the alkanes’ lack of reactivity, the reaction conditions are very vigorous, and high temperatures are required. Alkenes are produced by a process known as cracking, which may be represented in very simple terms as

$$2C_6H_{14} \xrightarrow[\text{catalyst}]{800\sim1000^\circ C} CH_4+3C_2H_4+C_2H_6+C_3H_6$$

Table 1-2 Distillation of crude oil

Fraction	Boiling range (℃) (at atmospheric pressure)	Number of Carbon atoms in molecule	Approximate % by volume
CRUDE OIL → GASES	<20	1~4	1~2
→ LIGHT GASOLINES OR LIGHT NAPHTHA	20~70	5~6 }	20~40
→ NAPHTHA (MID-RANGE)	70~170	6~10 }	
→ KEROSENE	170~250	10~14	10~15
→ GAS OIL	250~340	14~19 }	15~20
→ DISTILLATE FEEDSTOCKS for LUBRICATING OIL and WAXES,or HEAVY FUEL OILS	340~500	19~35 }	40~50
→ BITUMEN	>500 i.e. Residue	>35 }	

In practice the feedstock, being a crude-oil fraction such as gases or naphtha, is a mixture and therefore the product consists of a number of unsaturated and saturated compounds. Cracking is used to break down the longer-chain alkanes, which are found in (say) the gas-oil fraction, producing a product akin to a naphtha (gasoline) fraction.

Aromatics are made from alkanes and cycloalkanes by a process aptly named reforming[2]. As in cracking, the feedstock is a mixture of compounds. A substantial conversion (c. 50%) to aromatic compounds is achievable. The principal components, benzene, toluene and the xylenes, are separated for further processing.

Separation and purification of products is a major cost item in industrial chemical processes. It is important not only to isolate the desired products but also to recover the by-products. The economic success of many processes involves finding uses for co-produced materials. Greater selectivity in the reaction will minimize by-product formation and hence reduce the purification requirements. It is often economically desirable to run a reaction at a lower conversion level in order to increase selectivity even though this increases the amount of recycling of reactants.

Natural gas. is found in the same sort of geological areas as crude oil, and may occur with it or separately. It consists mainly of methane plus some ethane, propane and small amounts of higher alkanes.

Steam reforming[3] of natural gas is a very large scale and important reaction for producing synthesis gas (syngas[4]), which is a mixture of carbon monoxide and hydrogen, viz.

$$\underset{\text{Natural gas}}{CH_4+H_2O} \xrightarrow[850℃]{\text{Ni catalyst}} \underset{\text{syngas}}{CO + 3H_2}$$

The importance of syngas as an intermediate for the production of a variety of organic chemicals is demonstrated later. Large quantities of hydrogen, produced as indicated above, are used in ammonia synthesis using the high-temperature and high-pressure Haber process, viz.

$$N_2+ 3H_2 \rightleftharpoons 2\ NH_3$$

2. Organic chemicals from coal

Coal., like crude oil (petroleum), is a fossil fuel which forms over a period of millions of years from the fossilized remains of plants. It is therefore also a non-renewable resource. However, reserves of coal are several times greater than those of petroleum. Extraction and handling of the coal is more difficult, and expensive, than for oil. Although the precise nature of coal varies somewhat with its source (like crude oil), analysis of a representative sample shows it to be very different from oil.

Carbonization of coal. Traditionally, and even today to some extent, chemicals have been obtained from coal via its carbonization. This is brought about by heating the coal in the absence of air at a temperature of between 800 and 1200℃, viz.

$$\text{coal} \xrightarrow{800 \text{ and } 1200\ ^{\circ}\text{C}} \text{coke + town gas +crude benzole+ coal-tar}$$

The major product by far is the coke, followed by the town gas (a mixture of largely carbon monoxide and hydrogen) with only small amounts of crude benzole and coal-tar (~ 50 kg per 1000 kg of coal carbonized) being formed, but it is from these that chemicals are obtained. It is therefore clear that for the carbonization process to be viable there must be a market for the coke produced. The steel industry is the main outlet for this, and therefore demand for coal carbonization is closely linked to the fortunes of this industry. The demand for coal carbonization has fallen considerably over the past few decades and it is not economically feasible to carry out this operation merely to obtain the crude benzole, coal-tar, and chemicals derived from them.

Coal-tar is a complex mixture of compounds (over 350 have been identified) which are largely aromatic hydrocarbons plus smaller amounts of phenols. The initial step in the isolation of individual chemicals from coal-tar is continuous fractional distillation (cf.[⑤] oil) which yields the fractions shown in Table 1-3.

Each of these fractions still consists of a mixture of compounds, albeit a much simpler and less complex mixture than the coal-tar itself. Some are used directly, e.g. absorbing oil is used for absorbing benzene produced during carbonization of coal and it is also used—under the name creosote—for preserving timber. More usually they are subjected to further processing to produce individual compounds. Thus the light-oil fraction is washed with mineral acid (to remove organic bases such as pyridine, plus thiophene), then with alkali (to remove tar acids, i.e. phenols). The remaining neutral fraction is subjected to fractional distillation which separates benzene, toluene and the xylenes.

Table 1-3 Distillation of coal-tar

Fraction	Boiling range (℃) (at atmospheric pressure)	Approximate % by volume	Main components
COAL TAR → AMMONIACAL LIQUOR			
→ LIGHT OIL	up to 180		benzene,toluene, xylenes(dimethyl benzenes),pyridine, picolines (methyl-pyridines)
→ TAR ACIDS (carbolic oil)	180～230	8	phenols,cresols (methylphenols), naphthalene
→ ABSORBING OIL (creosote oil)	230～270	17	methylnaphthalenes quinolines, lutidines (dimethylpyridines)
→ ANTHRACENE OIL	270～350	12	anthracene, phenanthrene, acenaphthene
→ RESIDUE (pitch)		60	

In view of the difficulties of obtaining chemicals from coal via carbonization and coal-tar (discussed above), it is not surprising that alternative routes starting from this source have been under very active investigation for some years now. These routes have all reached at least the pilot-plant stage of development and indeed some have achieved full commercialization. They may be grouped under two headings: (i) gasification and (ii) liquefaction.

There is no doubt about the switch from oil to coal as a source of organic chemicals; the only uncertainty concerns the time-scale and rate at which it happens.

Selected from "*Industrial Organic Chemicals in Perspective*, by Harold A. Witcoff and Bryan G.Reuben, Wiley-Intersecience, 1980"

Words and Expressions

1. reforming [ri'fɔ:miŋ] n. 重整，转化
2. saturate ['sætʃəreit] v. 使饱和；浸透 a. 饱和的
3. olefin ['əuləfin] n.（链）烯（烃），烯族烃
4. alkane ['ælkein] n. 烷(属)烃，(链)烷
5. paraffin ['pærəfin] n. 链烷（属）烃，石蜡
6. cycloalkane n. 环烷烃
7. naphthene ['næfθi:n] n. 环烷烃

8. mercaptan [mə'kæpt ən] n. 硫醇
9. disastrous [di'zɑ:strəs] a. 灾难性的，造成惨重损失的
10. combustion [kəm'bʌ stʃən] n. 燃烧
11. volatile ['vɔlətail] a. 易挥发的，挥发性的
12. naphtha ['næfθə] n. 石脑油，粗汽油，(粗)挥发油
13. kerosene ['kerəsi:n] n. 煤油，火油
14. distillate ['distileit] n. 馏出物，馏出液；精华
15. lubricate ['lju:brikeit] vt. 使润滑
16. bitumen ['bitjumin] n. 地沥青
17. reactivity [riæk'tiviti] n. 反应性，反应活性；反应
18. affinity [ə'finiti] n. 亲和力，亲和势，化合力
19. reactive [ri'æktiv] a. 反应性的，活性的；反应的
20. be akin to 类似（于），近似
21. aptlyad. 适当地，合适地
22. xylene ['zaili:n] n. 二甲苯
23. geological [dʒiɔ'lɔdʒikəl] a. 地质(学，上)的
24. methane ['mi:θein] n. 甲烷，沼气
25. ethane ['eθein] n. 乙烷
26. syngas 合成气
27. monoxide [mɔ'nɔksaid] n. 一氧化物
28. viz = videlicet [拉丁语]即，就是
29. benzole ['benzɔl] n. (粗)苯，安息油
30. coke [kəuk] n. 焦炭，焦 vt. 炼焦，焦化
31. viable ['vaiəbl] a. 可行的
32. ammoniacal [æməu'naiəkəl] a. (含)氨的，氨性的
33. dimethyl benzene 二甲苯
34. pyridine ['piridin] n. 吡啶，氮（杂）苯
35. picoline ['pikəli:n] n. 皮考啉，甲基吡啶
36. methyl-pyridine 甲基吡啶
37. tar acid 焦油酸
38. carbolic acid = phenol 苯酚，石炭酸
39. cresol [kri:sɔl] n. 甲酚，甲氧甲酚，甲氧基
40. methylphenol 甲酚
41. naphthalene ['næfθəli:n] n. 萘
42. creosote ['kri əs əut] n. 木馏油，木材防腐油
43. methylnaphthalene 甲基萘
44. quinoline ['kwinəli:n] n .喹啉，氮(杂)茂
45. lutidine =dimethyl pyridine n. 二甲基吡啶，卢剔啶
46. anthracene ['ænθrəsin] n. 蒽，并三苯
47. phenanthrene [fi'nænθri:n] n. 菲

48. acenaphthene [æs'næpθi:n] n. 苊
49. albeit [ɔ:l'bi:it] conj. 虽然，即使
50. timber ['timbə] n. 木材，树木
51. mineral acid 无机酸
52. base [beis] n. 碱
53. thiophene ['θaiə fi:n] n. 噻吩，硫（杂）茂
54. gasification [gæsifi'keiʃən] n. 气化法，气化作用
55. liquefaction [likwi'fækʃən] n. 液化（作用）= liquification

Notes

① naphtha: 石脑油，一种轻质油，指易挥发的石油产品，由原油蒸馏或油田伴生气经冷凝液化而得，其沸点范围一般为 30～220℃（相当于粗汽油）。

② reforming：重整或转化。在石油炼制过程中，在氢气和催化剂存在的条件下加热，使原油蒸馏所得的轻汽油馏分（或石脑油）转变成富含芳烃的高辛烷值汽油（重整汽油），并副产液化石油气和氢气的过程，称为（催化）重整（catalytic reforming）。在合成气生产过程中，以天然气或轻质油为原料，在高温下与水蒸气发生反应制取合成气的过程，称为（蒸汽）转化（steam reforming）。

③ steam reforming for producing syngas: 合成气蒸汽转化法，此法以天然气或石脑油为原料，与水蒸气反应制取合成气。

④ syngas: 合成气，以氢气和一氧化碳为主要成分用于化学合成的一种原料气。由煤、石油或天然气等转化而来。按其来源、组成和用途不同，可称其为煤气、合成氨原料气或甲醇合成气等。

⑤ cf. = confer; compare 比较；对照；参看。

PART 2 CHEMICAL TECHNOLOGIES

Unit 5 Basic Chemicals

Before reading the text below, try to answer these questions:

1. Can you list some kinds of basic chemicals which are produced in the highest volume?
2. What is the main task of the basic chemical industry?
3. Have you got any idea about the scale and price of a basic chemical?
4. What are the challenges that the basic chemical industry is now facing?

We can divide the various sectors of the chemical industry into these two types: the higher –volume sector and low-volume sector. In the *high-volume sector,* individual chemicals are typically produced on the tens to hundreds of thousands of tonnes per annum scale. As a result, the plants used are dedicated to the single product, operate in a continuous manner and are highly automated, including computer control. Sectors categorized as high-volume are sulphuric acid, phosphorus-containing compounds, nitrogen-containing compounds, chlor-alkali[①] and related compounds, plus petrochemicals and commodity polymers such as polythene. With the exception of the latter, they are key intermediates, or *base chemicals,* which are feedstocks for the production of a wide range of other chemicals, many of which are also required in large quantities.

In contrast, *low-volume sectors* are largely involved in fine-chemicals manufacture, and individual products are produced only on the tens of tonnes to possibly a few thousand tonnes scale. However, they have a very high value per unit weight, in contrast to high-volume products. Fine chemicals are usually produced in plants operating in a batch manner and the plants may be multiproduct ones. Thus, low-volume sectors are agrochemicals, dyestuffs, pharmaceuticals, and speciality polymers such as PEEK.

Basic chemicals are the orphans of the chemical industry. They are not glamorous, like drugs, and are sometimes not very profitable (and at the very least the profits come in unpredictable cycles of boom and bust). They are not seen or used directly by the general public and so their importance is not often understood. Even within the industry their importance is often insufficiently appreciated. Without them, however, the rest of the industry could not exist.

Basic chemicals occupy the middle ground between raw materials (that is, things that are mined, quarried or pumped from the ground) and end-products. One distinguishing feature of basic chemicals is the scale on which they are manufactured; everything from really big to absolutely enormous. Fig. 2-1 shows the top 25 chemicals in the USA market by volume in 1993, just to give a feel for the sort of chemicals and volumes concerned. Basic chemicals are typically manufactured in plants that produce hundreds of thousands of tonnes of product per year. A plant that produces

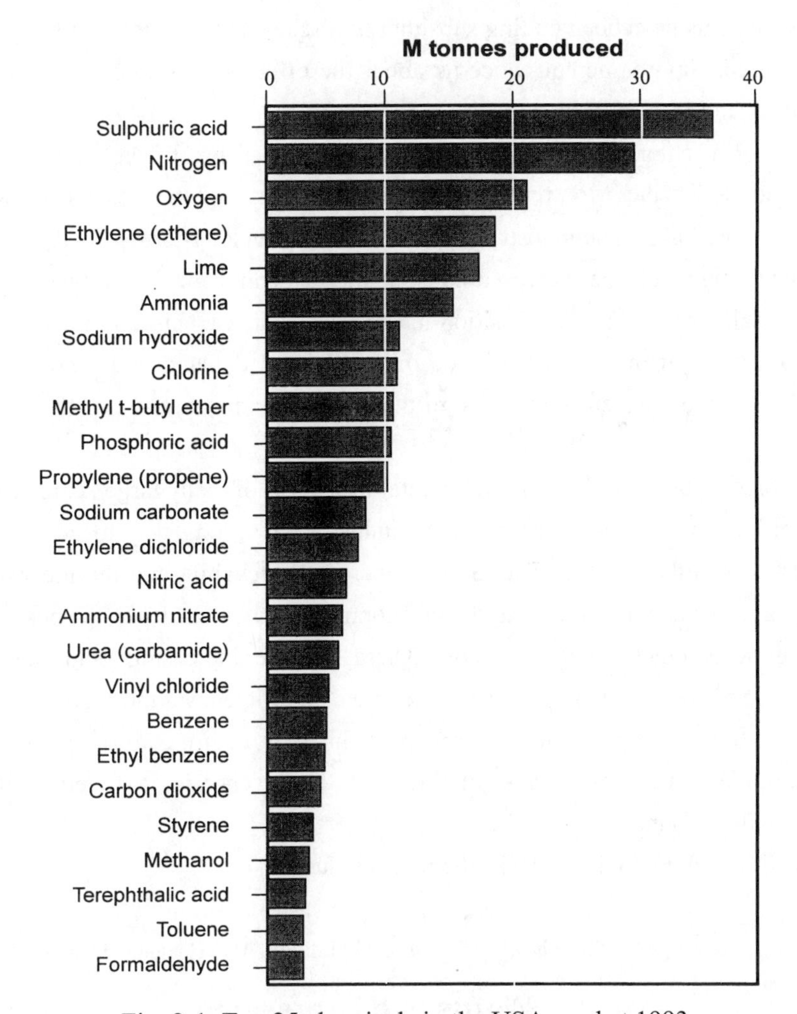

Fig. 2-1 Top 25 chemicals in the USA market,1993

100,000 tonnes per year will produce about 12.5 tonnes every hour. Another distinguishing and important feature of basic chemicals is their price: most of them are fairly cheap.

The job of the basic chemical industry is to find economical ways of turning raw materials into useful intermediates. There is little leeway for any company to charge premium prices for its products, so the company that makes the products at the cheapest cost will probably be the most profitable. This situation means that companies must always be on their toes looking for new and more economical ways of making and transforming their raw materials.

Many basic chemicals are the products of oil refining, while parts of the industry—the sulphur, nitrogen, phosphorus and chloro-alkali industries—put elements other than carbon and hydrogen into chemicals. In combination, these products and the basic products of the petrochemical industry can be combined to produce the myriad of important chemicals that feed the rest of the chemical industry.

The basic chemicals industry is now facing one of the biggest challenges in its history. The main consumer of the industry's key products—the agriculture industry—has stopped growing and is severely cutting back its demand for fertilizers. Western farmers have been producing too much food and governments have been cutting subsidies, with the result that less land is being farmed and less fertilizer used. Environmental concerns about the effects of excessive fertilizer run-off have also reduced demand for fertilizers.

Products such as chlorinated compounds have come under threat from environmentalists. Some will be banned under the Montreal Protocol②, but others are not harmful and may survive environmentalist pressures. The industry can no longer rely on long-term growth in demand.

The industry may well see increased consolidation as companies swap plants to achieve better economies of scale or better market position in specific products. This could leave an industry with far fewer players but with a better balance of supply and demand and better profitability. The industry will move more to serving the rest of the chemical industry and less to serving the farming industry.

Another threat is the perceived environmental messiness of many large-scale processes. Despite the relative efficiency of many big plants, the industry has a long way to go to achieve the best environmental standards possible. The drive to increased recycling and the ideal of emission-free plants will be a major factor influencing the development of the industry in the next decade.

Technical developments will not stop. There will be increasing emphasis on plants and processes that do not pollute. Companies will compete on efficiency—those able to produce the best quality products at the cheapest price will prosper. This will require companies to keep investing in technical improvements. New ways of bringing basic chemicals together to form useful intermediates will be found.

There is still much to do in the basic chemicals industry.

Selected from "*The Chemical Industry,* 2nd Edition, Alan Heaton, by Blackie & Son Ltd., 1997"

Words and Expressions

1. dedicate ['dedikeit] vt. 把（时间、力量等）用在…(to)；奉献
2. commodity [kə'mɔditi] n. 日用品，商品
3. polythene ['pɔliθi:n] n. 聚乙烯 （=polyethylene）
4. butyl- ['bju:til] n. 丁基
5. ether ['i:θə] n. 醚，乙醚；以太
6. phosphoric [fɔs'fɔrik] a. 磷的，含磷的，含五价磷的
7. carbamide ['kɑ:bəmaid] n. 尿素，碳酰二胺
8. ethyl ['eθil] n. 乙基，乙烷基
9. methanol ['meθænɔl] n. 甲醇
10. terephthalic acid 对苯二甲酸
11. agrochemical [ægrəu'kemikəl] n. 农用化学品；农业化肥；农产品中提炼出的化学品
12. speciality [speʃi'æliti] n. 特制品，特殊产品；专门化，专业（化）
13. PEEK ＝ polyetheretherketone 聚醚醚酮
14. orphan ['ɔ:fən] n. 孤儿，无人支持之事物
15. glamorous ['glæmərəs] a. 吸引人的，动人的

16. boom [bu:m] n. （商业等的）景气，繁荣；激增，暴涨
17. bust [bʌ st] n. 商业上的大不利；失败
18. quarry ['kwɔri] v. 挖掘，（露天）开采
19. end-product 最后产物，最终结果
20. leeway ['li:wei] n. 余地，可允许的误差；落后
21. premium ['pri:mjəm] n. 额外费用；奖励，奖金
22. on one's toes 准备行动的
23. myriad ['miriəd] n. （一）万，无数
24. subsidy ['sʌ bsidi] n. 补助费，津贴
25. run-off ['rʌ nɔ:f] n. 流出，流泻，径流；流量
26. chlorinate ['klɔ:rineit] vt. 使氯化，使与氯化合，用氯气处理
27. ban [bæn] vt. 禁止，取缔
28. protocol ['prəutəkɔl] n. (条约等的)草案，会谈备忘录，(外交)协定书
29. consolidation [kən'sɔli'deiʃən] n. 巩固，加强；合并，联合
30. swap [swɔp] vt. 用…作交易，交换
31. perceive [pə'si:v] vt. 觉察，发觉；看见，看出；领悟，理解
32. messiness n. 混乱，弄脏，肮脏；困境
33. emission-free a. 无排放的，零排放的

Notes

① chlor-alkali industry: 以饱和食盐水溶液为原料，用电解法生产烧碱（氢氧化钠）、氯气和氢气，并由此生产纯碱（碳酸钠）及一系列含氯产品，如盐酸、高氯酸钾、次氯酸钙、光气、二氧化氯等。工业生产方法有：隔膜（diaphragm）电解法，水银（mercury）电解法，离子膜（membrane）电解法。

② the Montreal Protocol: 《关于消耗臭氧层物质的蒙特利尔议定书》, 1992 年 11 月在哥本哈根签署，规定冻结或削减消耗臭氧层物质的生产。

Exercises

1. *Summarize the information on the two sectors of chemical industry by completing the table below.*

	High-volume sector	*Low-volume sector*
Production scale		
Products / a plant		
Operation manner		
Price or profit		
Usage		
Challenges		
Products in the sector		

2. *Complete the following block flow diagram. Use the words from the reading passage (referring to the last three paragraphs of **"Major Sectors of Chemical Industry"**).*

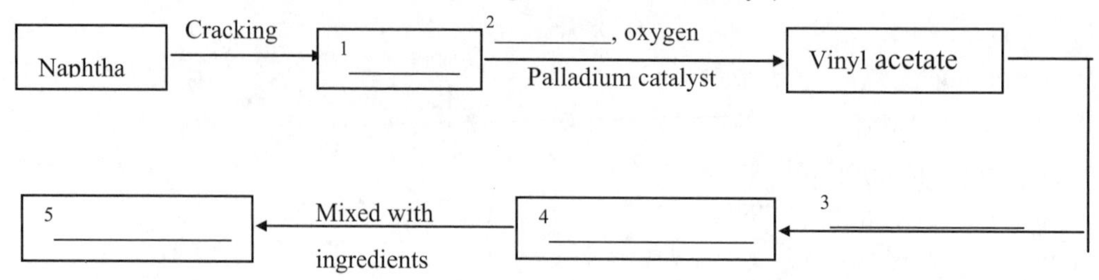

3. *Put the following into Chinese:*

commodity	ether	speciality	end-product
on one's toes	elastomer	hydrate	plasticizer
sulphonate	formulate	metallurgy	phosphoric acid

4. *Put the following into English:*

烷基	芳基	乙基	丁基
离子	乙醇	甲醇	醋酸
均相的	系数	摩擦	无排放的

Reading Material 5:

Major Sectors of the Chemical Industry

The chemical industry takes a relatively small number of natural raw materials such as oil and natural gas, limestone and salt and converts them (by chemical processing or chemical reactions) into several thousand chemical intermediates. As we have already seen, these are then converted into end or consumer products. It is important to note that value is added at every stage in this process and the final product may have a value many times that of the raw materials which were used at the beginning. Clearly the increase in value added at each stage must exceed the processing costs if the company is to realize a profit on its activities.

The major sectors of the chemical industry are:

- Petrochemicals
- Polymers
- Dyestuffs
- Agrochemicals
- Pharmaceuticals
- Chlor- alkali products
- Sulphuric acid (sulphur industry)
- Ammonia and fertilizers(nitrogen industry)
- Phosphoric acid and phosphates (phosphorus industry)

The petrochemicals sector provides the key intermediates or building blocks (derived from oil and natural gas) such as ethylene, propylene, benzene and toluene. These are the starting points for the synthesis of an enormous range of industrial organic chemicals, which are produced in the downstream processing of the key intermediates in some of the other sectors listed.

The polymers sector is the major user of petrochemical intermediates and consumes almost half the total output of organic chemicals which are produced. It covers plastics, synthetic fibers, rubbers, elastomers and adhesives, and it was the tremendous demand for these new materials with their special, and often novel, properties which brought about the explosive growth of the organic chemicals industry between 1950 and 1970.

Although the dyestuffs sector is much smaller than the previous two, it has strong links with them. This arose because the traditional dyestuffs, which were fine for natural fibers like cotton and wool, were totally unsuitable for the new synthetic fibers like nylons and polyesters. A great deal of research and technological effort within the sector has resulted in the amazingly wide range of colors in which modern clothing is available. Along with drugs and plant-protection agents (pesticides), dyestuffs are examples of fine chemicals, i.e. chemicals produced in relatively small tonnages which are of high purity and high value per unit weight.

Agrochemicals (pesticides) in recent years, along with the pharmaceuticals sector, have constituted a bluechip sector of the chemical industry, i.e. a very profitable one for those companies which can continue to operate in it.

Pharmaceuticals have been the glamorous sector of the industry for some years now because of their high levels of profitability—although this often seems to attract criticism that profits on some drugs are too high. The latter comments have to be set against the very high risks and costs (in excess of $160 million per marketable compound) of discovering and developing new products.This sector is unique in both its relationship with its customers and the fact that demand for its products is little affected by economic recessions, in great contrast to all the other sectors.

The chlor-alkali products sector produces principally the very high-tonnage chemicals chlorine and sodium hydroxide. It is an area which demonstrates very nicely the influence of new technology and energy costs on chemicals production.

Sulphuric acid (sulphur industry) is the most important chemical of all in tonnage terms. Its production can be regarded as having reached maturity some years ago, but even now work is being done to remove the last traces of unreacted SO_2 (for environmental reasons).

Ammonia and fertilizers is a sector in which it has been difficult to achieve a balance between capacity and demand, and this has often led to major cost cutting and losses for many companies. In tonnage terms it is one of the most important sectors and it is based on the Haber process for ammonia. This is very energy demanding (moderately high temperatures and very high pressures) and a fortune is awaiting anyone who can find a viable alternative route. It will not be easy since no one has yet succeeded despite 70 years of intensive research effort!

Various phosphates are produced from phosphoric acid which is made either by adding sulphuric acid to phosphate rock (wet process)[①] or by burning phosphorus in air to give phosphorus pentoxide, which is then hydrated. Major uses of phosphoric acid are the production of phosphate and compound fertilizers, formation of sodium tripolyphosphate (which is used as a builder in detergents where it forms stable water-soluble complexes with calcium and magnesium ions) and the production of organic derivatives like triphenyl and tricresyl phosphate. These are used as plasticizers for synthetic polymers and plastics.

Soaps and detergents represent an interesting and rather different sector. Interesting in that early production of soap, with its demand for alkali, can be viewed as the beginnings of the modern chemical industry. Different from the other sectors in that its products are sold directly to the public and market share probably has more to do with packaging and marketing than the technical properties of the product. Many of its products can be derived from both petrochemical intermediates and from animal and vegetable oils and fats, e.g., alkyl and aryl sulphonates.

Although some chemicals, such as organic solvents, are used directly, most require further processing and formulating before they can be put to their end uses. In some cases, where novel materials have been discovered, major technological advances were required before they could be processed and their unique properties utilized. Such a material is polytetrafluoroethylene, which is better known as PTFE or under its trade names Fluon (ICI) and Teflon (Dupont). When this was first made its special properties of great chemical stability, excellent electrical insulation, very low coefficient of friction (hence its non-stick applications) and very wide working temperature range were quickly recognized. However, its use was delayed for several years because it could not be processed by conventional techniques and it had to await the development of powder metallurgy techniques.

In order to appreciate the downstream processing and technology, let us take as an example polyvinyl acetate② and one of its applications as a binder in such that a homogeneous film is produced on evaporation of the water base. What processing steps are involved in making the polyvinyl acetate and in finally formulating the paint?

The story starts with crude oil or natural gas fractions, e.g. naphtha, which are cracked to give principally ethylene. The ethylene is then reacted with acetic acid and oxygen over a supported palladium catalyst to produce the vinyl acetate. Finally this is polymerized to polyvinyl acetate which is then mixed with the other ingredients to produce the emulsion paint.

The above examples teach us an important lesson, although it is the chemists who make and discover the new chemicals which may have special properties, a considerable input from engineers and technologists may be required before the chemical can be processed and converted into a suitable form in which it can be used. This emphasizes an important aspect of research and technology in the chemical industry, namely the importance of inter-disciplinary teamwork.

Selected from "*An Introduction to Industrial Chemistry,* 2nd Edition, C.A. Heaton, Blackie & Son Ltd., 1997"

Words and Expressions

1. elastomer [i'læstəmə] n. 合成橡胶，人造橡胶；弹性体，高弹体
2. adhesive [əd'hi:siv] n. 胶粘剂，粘结剂
3. blue-chip a. （在行业中）最赚钱, 第一流的；（股票等）热门的，靠得住的
4. maturity [mə'tjuərity] n. 成熟；老化，陈化
5. pentoxide n. 五氧化物
6. hydrate ['haidreit] v. （使）水合，（使）成水合物

7. tripolyphosphate　n. 三聚磷酸盐（酯）
8. builder　['bildə]　n. 组分，增加洗涤剂清洁作用的物质
9. ion　['aiən]　n. 离子
10. derivative　[di'rivətiv]　n. 衍生物；导数
11. triphenyl　[trai'fi:nil]　n. 三苯基
12. tricresyl phosphate　磷酸三甲苯酯
13. plasticizer　['plæstisaizə]　n. 增塑剂
14. alkyl　['ælkil]　n. 烷基，烃基
15. aryl　['æril]　n. 芳基
16. sulphonate　['sʌlfəneit]　n. 磺酸盐，磺化　vt. 使磺化
17. formulate　['fɔ:mjuleit]　vt. 配方（制），按配方制造
18. insulation　[insju'leiʃən]　n. 绝缘，绝热；孤立，隔离
19. coefficient　[kəui'fiʃənt]　n. 系数
20. friction　['frikʃən]　n. 摩擦，摩擦力
21. metallurgy　[me'tælədʒi]　n. 冶金学，冶金术
22. binder　['baində]　n. 粘合剂；铺路沥青
23. homogeneous　[hɔmə'dʒi:njəs]　a. 均相的，均匀的，同质的
24. evaporation　[ivæpə'reiʃən]　n. 蒸发，挥发，汽化
25. acetic　[ə'si:tik]　a. 醋（酸）的，酸的
26. acetic acid　醋酸
27. palladium　[pə'leidiəm]　n. 钯　Pd
28. teamwork　n. 协力，协作，配合，协同作战

Notes

① wet process for phosphoric acid: 湿法磷酸，用硫酸（或盐酸、硝酸，主要为硫酸）分解磷矿，然后将生成的磷酸和硫酸钙分离。而热法磷酸是黄磷在空气中燃烧生成五氧化二磷，再经水吸收制成。

② polyvinyl acetate: 聚醋酸乙烯酯 PVA。由醋酸乙烯聚合而成，主要用于黏合剂和涂料的组分。

Unit 6 Chlor-Alkali and Related Processes

After completing this unit, you should be able to:

1.List some major products in the chlor-alkali processes.

2.Describe briefly the Solvay ammonia soda process.

3.Outline the main steps in making sulfuric acid.

4.Point out the major uses of some main products described in the text.

Historically the bulk chemical industry was built on chlor-alkali and related processes. The segment is normally taken to include the production of chlorine gas, caustic soda (sodium hydroxide), soda-ash (derivatives of sodium carbonate in various forms) and, for convenience, lime-based products.

Soda-ash and sodium hydroxide have competed with each other as the major source of alkali ever since viable processes were discovered for both. The peculiar economics of electrolytic processes mean that you have to make chlorine and caustic soda together in a fixed ratio whatever the relative demand for the two totally different types of product, and this causes swings in the price of caustic soda which can render soda-ash more or less favorable as an alkali.

Both chlorine/caustic soda and soda-ash production are dependent on cheap readily available supplies of raw materials. Chlorine/caustic soda requires a ready supply of cheap brine and electricity, soda-ash requires brine, limestone and lots of energy. Soda-ash plants are only profitable if their raw materials do not have to be transported far. The availability of such supplies is a major factor in the location of many of the chemical industry's great complexes.

1. Lime-Based Products

One of the key raw materials is lime. Limestone consists mostly of calcium carbonate ($CaCO_3$) laid down over geological time by various marine organisms. High-quality limestones are often good enough to be used directly as calcium carbonate in further reactions. Limestone is usually mined in vast open-cast quarries, many of which will also carry out some processing of the materials.

The two key products derived from limestone are quicklime (CaO) and slaked lime ($Ca(OH)_2$). Quicklime is manufactured by the thermal decomposition (1200~1500 ℃) of limestone according to the equation:

$$CaCO_3 \longrightarrow CaO + CO_2$$

Typically limestone is crushed and fed into the higher end of a sloping rotating kiln① where the decomposition takes place and quicklime is recovered from the end. Most frequently, however, the quicklime is not isolated for further reactions, rather, other compounds are fed in with the lime to give final products at the low end of the kiln. For example, alumina, iron ore and sand can be fed in to give Portland cement[2]. Soda-ash manufacture often adds coke to the limestone which burns to give extra carbon dioxide needed for soda-ash manufacture. Slaked lime which is more convenient to handle than quicklime—is manufactured by reacting quicklime with water.

About 40% of the output of the lime industry goes into steel-making, where it is used to react with the refractory silica present in iron ore to give a fluid slag which floats to the surface and is easily separated from the liquid metal. Smaller, but still significant, amounts are used in chemical manufacture, pollution control and water treatment. The most important chemical derived from lime is soda-ash.

2. Soda-Ash

The Solvay process[3][4]. The process, which was perfected by Ernest Solvay in 1865, is based on the precipitation of $NaHCO_3$ when an ammoniated solution of salt is carbonated with CO_2 from a coke-fired lime kiln. The $NaHCO_3$ is filtered, dried, and calcined to Na_2CO_3. The filtered ammonium chloride process liquor is made alkaline with slaked lime and the ammonia is distilled out for recycle to the front end of the process. The resultant calcium chloride is a waste or by-product stream.

For a simple basic product the Solvay process appears exceedingly complicated. The basic principle of the reaction is to take salt (NaCl) and calcium carbonate ($CaCO_3$) as inputs and to produce calcium chloride and sodium carbonate as outputs. However, the reactions occurring between input and output are not remotely obvious and involve the use of ammonia and calcium hydroxide as intermediate compounds.

The essential principle is that, by carefully controlling the concentration of the components (especially ammonia and salt), sodium bicarbonate can be precipitated from solutions containing salt, carbon dioxide and ammonia. The key to making the process work is controlling the strength of the solutions and the rates of crystallization.

The essential steps of the process are as follows. Ammonia is absorbed in an ammonia absorber into brine which has previously been purified to reduce the amount of calcium and magnesium ions (which tend to precipitate during the process in all the wrong places, blocking pipe-work). The solution (nominally containing sodium chloride and ammonium hydroxide) is then passed down a tower where it absorbs carbon dioxide (passing up the tower) to form ammonium carbonate at first and later ammonium bicarbonate. By the next stage of the plant sodium chloride and ammonium bicarbonate have metathesised to sodium bicarbonate (which precipitates) and ammonium chloride. Filtration separates the solid bicarbonate from the remaining solution. The bicarbonate is passed to a rotary dryer where it loses water and carbon dioxide to give a fluffy crystalline mass known as light soda-ash which is mostly sodium carbonate. The fluffy mass is light because the original crystal shape is retained on the loss of carbon dioxide, leaving many voids. It is usually more convenient to make a more dense material and this is achieved by adding water (which causes recrystallization in a denser form) and further drying.

It is debatable whether the actual chemistry given above is a good description of the process, but it certainly aids understanding. For a detailed understanding, a great deal needs to be known about solubility products of multicomponent systems. The important thing to know is that the system is complex and requires careful control at all parts of the process in order for it to operate effectively.

One disadvantage of the process is the amount of calcium chloride produced. Far more is produced than can be used, so much of the production is simply dumped (it is not a particularly noxious or nasty product). It would be advantageous to use all the input material in this process, for example producing hydrogen chloride from the chloride.

Uses of soda-ash. Of all soda-ash, 50% is sold to the glassmaking industry as it is a primary raw material for glass manufacture. The fortunes of the industry are therefore strongly tied to glass demand. Soda-ash also competes directly with sodium hydroxide as an alkali in many chemical processes. Sodium silicates are another important class of chemicals derived from soda-ash by reaction with silica at 1200~1400℃. Silica-gel is a fine sodium silicate with a large surface area and is used in catalysts, chromatography and as a partial phosphate replacement in detergents and soaps.

3. Electrolytic Processes for Chlorine/Caustic Soda

Introduction. Both chlorine and caustic soda have, at various times in the history of the chemical industry, been greatly in demand, but unfortunately for operators of electrochemical plants, not always at the same time. Chlorine has been valued as a bleach, or a raw material for the production of bleaching powder, as a disinfectant in water supplies and as a raw material for plastics and solvents manufacture. Caustic soda has been used in the production of soda-ash, soap, textiles, and as a very important raw material in an incredible variety of chemical processes.

All the electrolytic processes have in common the electrolysis of salt to give chlorine and sodium hydroxide. The vast majority of production electrolyses a solution of salt, but there are some significant plants that electrolyze molten salt to give liquid sodium and chlorine. These are used by industries that need the liquid sodium, mainly in the production of tetra-alkyl lead petroleum additives, though the petroleum additive companies are diversifying and other uses may appear. There are essentially three different types of cell used for aqueous electrolysis: mercury cells, diaphragm cells and membrane cells. Membrane cells are really the only technology that is viable for new capacity in modern plants, but a large amount of old capacity still exists and many companies have not found it economical to replace even their mercury cells, despite the environmental implications.

All electrolytic reactions are based on the idea of using electrons as a reagent in chemical reactions. The basic reactions of brine electrolysis can be written as follows:

$$\text{Anode } 2Cl^- - 2e^- \longrightarrow Cl_2$$

$$\text{Cathode } 2H_2O + 2e^- \longrightarrow H_2 + 2OH^-$$

The overall reaction is:

$$2Na^+ + 2Cl^- + 2H_2O \longrightarrow NaOH + Cl_2 + H_2$$

This reaction has a positive free energy ($\Delta G = 421.7$ kJ/mol at 25℃) and needs to be driven uphill by electricity.

Like many basic chemical processes, though the reaction appears to be gloriously simple, there are some significant complications. For a start, the reaction products need to be kept apart: hydrogen and chlorine will react explosively if they are allowed to mix. Chlorine reacts with hydroxide to give hypochlorous acid (HOCI) and chloride (both wasting product and creating by-products). The hypochlorous acid and hypochlorite (ClO^-) in turn react to give chlorate (ClO_3^-), protons and more chloride. Hydroxide reacts at the anode to form oxygen, which can contaminate the chlorine. All the reactions reduce efficiency and/or create difficult separation or contamination problems that need to be sorted out before any products can be sold. The key to understanding the various types of process used for the electrolysis is the way they separate the reaction products. There are basically three types of electrolytic cell for brine electrolysis, though there are many variations of detail among the cells from different manufacturers.

4. The Uses of Chlorine and Sodium Hydroxide

Sodium hydroxide has so many chemical uses that it is difficult to classify them conveniently. One of the largest uses is for paper-making, where the treatment of wood requires a strong alkali. In some countries this consumes 20% of production. Another 20% is consumed in the manufacture of inorganic chemicals such as sodium hypochlorite (the bleach and disinfectant). Various organic syntheses consume about another fifth of the production. The production of alumina and soap uses smaller amounts.

Chlorine is widely used in a variety of other products. About a quarter of all production world-wide goes into vinyl chloride, the monomer for making PVC. Between a quarter and a half goes into a variety of other products. Depending on the country, up to 10% goes into water purification. Up to 20% goes into the production of solvents (methylchloroform, trichloroethene, etc.) though many of these are being phased out because of the Montreal Protocol. About 10% world-wide goes into the production of inorganic chlorine-containing compounds. A very significant use in some countries is for the bleaching of wood pulp, though this is another use coming under environmental pressure.

Selected from "*An Introduction to Industrial Chemistry,* 2nd Edition, C.A. Heaton, Blackie & Son Ltd., 1997"

Words and Expressions

1. segment ['segmənt] n. 部分；切片
2. soda-ash n. 纯碱，无水碳酸钠，苏打灰
3. peculiar [pi'kju:ljə] a. 特有的，独特的，特殊的；奇怪的
4. electrolytic [i'lektrəu'litik] a. 电解的，电解质的
5. open-cast a.;ad. 露天开采的（地）
6. quicklime ['qwiklaim] n. 生石灰，氧化钙
7. slakedlime n. 熟石灰，消石灰
8. kiln [kiln, kil] n. 窑,炉 v. 窑烧
9. decomposition [di:kəmpə'ziʃən] n. 分解,离解
10. alumina [ə'lju:minə] n. 矾土，氧化铝
11. Protland cement 硅酸盐水泥，波特兰水泥，普通水泥
12. refractory [ri'fræktəri] a. 难熔的，耐火的 n. 耐火材料
13. slag [slæg] n. (炉,熔,矿）渣

14. the Solvay process　索尔维法
15. ammoniated　[ə'məunieitid]　a. 充氨的，含氨的
16. calcine　['kælsin]　v.; n. 煅烧,烧成（灰）
17. alkaline　['ælkəlain]　n. 碱性　a. 强碱的
18. distil(l)　[dis'til]　vt. 蒸馏，用蒸馏法提取；提取…的精华
19. bicarbonate　[bai'kɑ:bənit]　n. 碳酸氢盐，酸式碳酸盐
20. crystallization　[kristəlai'zeiʃən]　n. 结晶（作用，过程）
21. metathesis　[me'tæθəsis]　n. 复分解(作用), 置换(作用)
22. filtration　[fil'treiʃən]　n. 过滤
23. rotary dryer　旋转干燥器
24. fluffy　['flʌfi]　a. 蓬松的,松软的
25. crystalline　['kristəlain]　a. 结晶的，结晶状的；水晶的
26. void　[vɔid]　n. 空隙，空隙率；空间，空位
27. solubility　[sɔlju'biliti]　n. 溶解度，溶解性
28. solubility product　溶度积
29. noxious　['nɔkʃəs]　a. 有毒的，有害的，不卫生的
30. nasty　['nɑ:sti]　a. 难处理的，极脏的，（气味）令人作呕的
31. silicate　['silikit]　n. 硅酸盐(酯)
32. silica-gel　(氧化)硅胶
33. chromatography　['krəumətəgrɑ:f]　n. 色谱(法,学), 色层法
34. electrochemical　[i'lektrə'kemikəl]　a. 电化学的
35. disinfectant　[disin'fektənt]　n. 消毒剂，杀菌剂
36. incredible　[in'kredəbl]　a. 难以置信的，不可思议的，惊人的
37. electrolysis　[ilek'trɔlisis]　n. 电解法，电解作用，电分析
38. electrolyse　[i'lektrəlaiz]　vt. 电解　（= electrolyze）
39. tetra-alkyl lead　四烷基铅
40. mercury　['mə:kjuri]　n. 汞, 水银 Hg
41. diaphragm　['daiəfræm]　n. 隔膜，隔板
42. membrane　['membrein]　n. 膜，膜片，隔板
43. anode　['ænəud]　n. 阳极，正极
44. cathode　['kæθəud]　n. 阴极，负极
45. hypochlorous acid　次氯酸
46. hypochlorite　[haipə'klɔ:rait]　n. 次氯酸盐
47. chlorate　['klɔ:rit]　n. 氯酸盐
48. proton　['prəutɔn]　n. 质子
49. contaminate　[kən'tæmineit]　vt. 污染，弄脏，毒害
50. methylchloroform　n. 三氯乙烷，甲基氯仿
51. trichloroethene　n. 三氯乙烯
52. pulp　[pʌlp]　n. 浆状物，纸浆；矿浆

Notes

① kiln:窑，指高温下（一般大于 800℃）通过焙烧（roasting）过程烧制产品的热工设备。roasting:

焙烧，固体物料在高温不发生熔融的条件下进行的化学反应，可以有氧化、热解、还原、卤化等。其中不加添加剂的焙烧，也称为煅烧，如石灰石化学加工制成氧化钙，同时制得二氧化碳气体。

② Portland cement: 硅酸盐水泥，一类以高碱性硅酸盐为主要化合物的水硬性水泥的总称，因其凝结硬固后的外观、颜色与早期英国用于建筑的优质波特兰石头相似，故西方国家通称为波特兰水泥。

③ the Solvay process: 索尔维法，又称氨碱法，由比利时人 Ernest Solvay 提出，是纯碱生产的最主要方法。先将原盐溶化成饱和盐水，除去杂质，然后吸收氨制成氨盐水，再进行碳化得碳酸氢钠，过滤后煅烧而得纯碱。

④ Ernest Solvay: 1838~1922，比利时工业化学家，1861 年，他在煤气厂从事稀氨水的浓缩工作时，在用盐水吸收氨和二氧化碳的试验中得到碳酸氢钠，同年，他获得了用食盐、氨和二氧化碳制取碳酸钠的工业生产方法的专利，称为索尔维法，又称氨碱法。

Exercises

1. *Summarize the information on the main products in chlor-alkali and sulfuric acid sectors, by completing the following table.*

Product	*Raw material*	*Major steps or Principal reactions*	*Uses*
Soda-ash			
Chlorine			
Caustic soda			
Sulfuric acid			

2. *Referring to the paragraph of* ***"Soda-Ash"****, completing the following simplified diagrammatic flow sheet for* ***the Solvay ammonia soda process.***

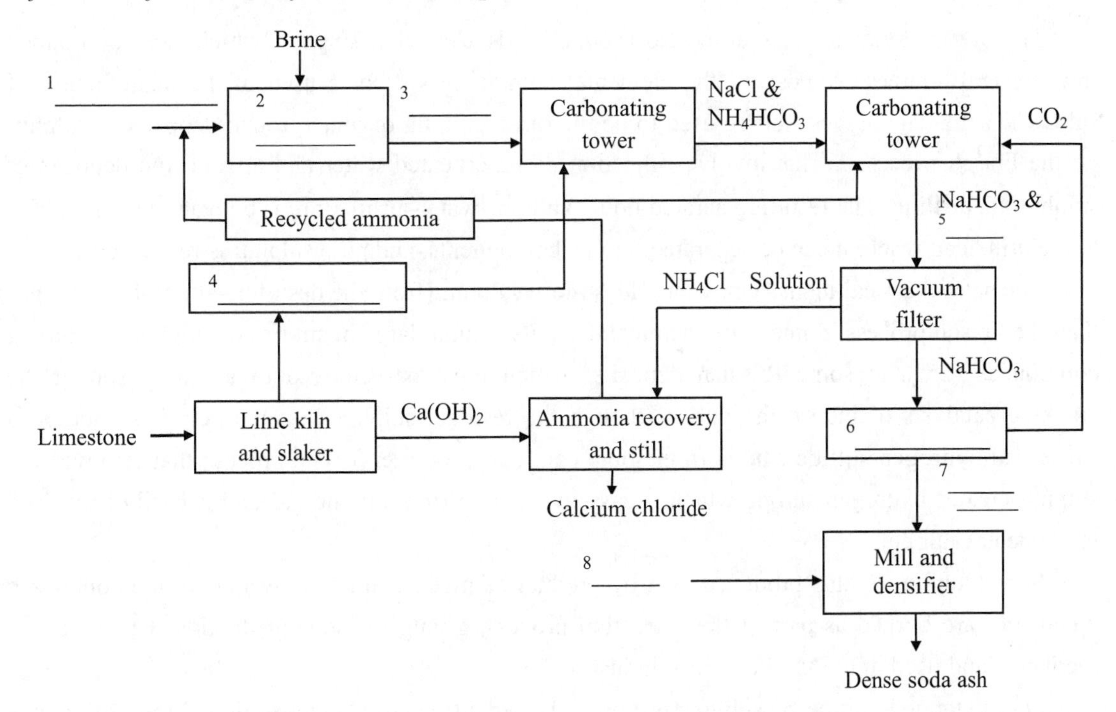

3. *Put the following into Chinese:*

oleum	mercury	soda ash	metathesis
PVC	alkaline	desulphurisation	membrane
carbonate	caustic sodium	proton	polytetrafluoroethylene

4. *Put the following into English:*

电解	分解	氯化物	还原
催化剂	氧化反应	动力学	沉淀
钙	镁	树脂	表面活性剂

Reading Material 6:

Sulphuric Acid

1. Introduction

Sulphuric acid is the chemical that is produced in the largest tonnage. Such is its importance as a raw material for other processes that its production was, until recently, considered a reliable indicator of a country's industrial output and the level of its industrial development. It is still used in an incredible variety of different processes and remains one of the most important chemicals produced.

2. Raw materials

The raw material for sulphuric acid production is elemental sulphur, which can be obtained from several sources. Almost all the elemental sulphur produced is used in the manufacture of sulphuric acid. The biggest source used to be the direct mining of underground deposits of sulphur by the Frasch process①. This involves injection of superheated water and air into the deposits of sulphur via drilling. The resulting aerated liquid sulphur-water-air mixture is buoyant enough to rise to the drill head where it can be separated into its components, and pure sulphur is recovered.

The petrochemical industry now provides more sulphur (from the desulfurisation of oil and gas) than the Frasch process. Some petrochemical deposits contain large quantities of sulphur-containing compounds (25% in some Russian deposits) which must be removed to avoid poisoning the cracking catalysts or indeed the public (though the residual sulphur in some petrol is enough to cause bad hydrogen sulfide smells from some catalytic converters). The process that removes the sulphur creates hydrogen sulfide which is easy to separate from oil and gas and is easily converted to elemental sulphur.

Some sulphur is also produced as a by-product of metal extraction. Many sulfide-containing metal ores are burned as part of the extraction process, giving off sulphur dioxide, which can be recovered and used in the sulphuric acid industry.

One untapped source of sulphur is the coal used in electricity generation. More sulphur is emitted from power stations than is used by the chemical industry. Most of this ends up in the atmosphere where it causes acid rain, though power stations are increasingly having to scrub their flue gases. Unfortunately, there is at present no convenient way to recover this sulphur in a useable form.

3. The Manufacturing Process

The production of sulphuric acid has three stages:

(1) The burning of sulphur in air to give sulphur dioxide

$$S + O_2 \longrightarrow SO_2$$

(2) The reaction of sulphur dioxide and oxygen to give sulphur trioxide

$$2SO_2 + O_2 \longrightarrow 2SO_3$$

(3) The absorption of sulphur trioxide in water to give sulphuric acid.

The first stage is simple, with few of the all too common complications that beset many industrially important "simple" reactions. Molten sulphur is sprayed into a furnace in a current of dry air at about 1000 ℃ to produce a gas stream containing about 10% sulphur dioxide. The stream is cooled in a boiler where the energy of the exothermic reaction can be extracted and the temperature brought down to 420℃.

The second stage is the key to the process. The direct reaction between sulphur dioxide and oxygen to give sulphur trioxide is slow and requires a catalyst. In the old lead chamber process② nitrogen dioxide (NO_2) was used for the oxidation though in practice mixtures of nitrogen oxides were used. This process has now been completely superseded by the contact process, which speeds the direct reaction via a solid-state catalyst of vanadium pentoxide (V_2O_5). The catalyst is normally absorbed on an inert silicate support and lasts for about 20 years.

The reaction between oxygen and sulphur dioxide is exothermic so the equilibrium favors the product at lower temperatures. So much heat is produced by the reaction that it is difficult to achieve good yields in a single-bed reactor: the reactor warms up so much that the reaction goes into reverse. Most plants therefore used several reactor stages (with coolers between the reactors) so that the heat produced does not drive the reaction backwards. The first reactor chamber converts the mixture of oxygen and sulphur dioxide into a stream about 60%~65% converted to products at about 600℃. It is then cooled to about 400℃ and passed into the next layer of catalyst, and so on. After three layers 95%~96% of the starting materials have been converted to products (this is near the maximum possible conversion unless sulphur trioxide is removed).

The gas mixture can then be passed into the initial absorption tower where some sulphur trioxide is removed. The remaining gas mixture is then reheated and passed back into a fourth converter which enables overall conversion of up to 99.7% to be achieved.

The final stage involves passing the gas mixture into the final absorption tower where the sulphur trioxide is hydrated with water to give, at the end of the tower, a 98%~99% acid solution. If excess sulphur trioxide is used the mixture consists of, effectively, sulphur trioxide dissolved in pure sulphuric acid this is known as oleum.

4. Uses of Sulphuric Acid

A large amount (66% of total production in the peak year) of sulphuric acid is used in the manufacture of phosphoric acid for fertilizer (phosphate rock plus acid gives impure phosphoric acid), though this use is now declining as demand for fertilizers declines. Some more goes into production of ammonium sulphate, a low-grade fertilizer.

More interesting are some of the more speciality uses of the compound, which are less significant in volume but are possibly more important for the rest of the industry. There are many important large-scale industrial syntheses that use sulphuric acid, for example the manufacture of ethanol from ethene, one of the routes to titanium dioxide (a white pigment important to the paint industry), the production of hydrofluoric acid from calcium fluoride (the ultimate source of about 70% of all the fluorine in fluorinated compounds), the production of aluminum sulphate (an important water-treatment chemical), the production of sulphonated surfactants (detergents and many other applications). Many uses are based on the fact that sulphuric acid represents a cheap source of protons. For example, the manufacture of hydrofluoric acid from fluoride-containing minerals involves mixing them with concentrated sulphuric acid in a rotating kiln the fluoride is protonated to hydrogen fluoride by the acid and the hydrogen fluoride is given off as a gas.

Selected from "*An Introduction to Industrial Chemistry,* 2nd Edition, C.A. Heaton, Blackie & Son Ltd., 1997"

Words and Expressions

1. Frash process 地下熔融法
2. aerate ['ɛəreit] vt. 充气,鼓气,通风,鼓风
3. buoyant ['bɔiənt] a. 有浮力的，能浮的，易浮的
4. desulphurisation [di:sʌlfərai'zeiʃən] n. 脱硫，除硫
5. sulfide ['sʌlfaid] n. 硫化物
6. untapped a. 未利用的，未开发的
7. flue [flu:] n. 烟道，风道
8. beset [bi'seit] vt. 包围,缠绕,为…所苦
9. exothermic [eksəu'θə:mik] a. 放热的
10. lead chamber process 铅室法
11. supersede [sju:pə'si:d] vt. 代替，取代，废弃
12. vanadium [və'neidjəm] n. 钒 V
13. inert [i'nə:t] a. 惰性的，不活泼的；惯性的
14. equilibrium [i:kwi'libriəm] n. 平衡
15. absorption [əb'sɔ:pʃən] n. 吸收（作用）
16. oleum n. 发烟硫酸
17. hydrofluoric [haidrəuflu'ɔrik] a. 氟化氢的，氢氟酸的
18. fluorine ['fluəri:n] n. 氟 F
19. fluorinated ['fluərineitid] a. 氟化的

20. surfactant [sə:'fæktənt] n. 表面活性剂
21. protonate v. 使质子化

Notes

① Frasch process: 地下熔融法，又称弗拉施法，由美国人 Herman Frasch(1851~1914)于 1894 年发明。先在矿区地表钻孔至含硫层，然后插入直径各为 20cm、10cm、2.5cm 的三层同心套管，向外管中压入 160~165℃的过热水，使地下硫磺熔化，再向直径 2.5cm 的管内通入热的压缩空气，使液硫从 10cm 的管上升压出，液硫经脱气后固化，或以液态储运，产品纯度可达 99.7%~99.8%。

② lead chamber process: 铅室法，利用高级氮氧化物（主要是三氧化二氮）使二氧化硫氧化并生成硫酸，因以铅制的方形空室为主要设备而得名，是硫酸工业发展史上最古老的工业生产方法。

Unit 7 Ammonia, Nitric Acid and Urea

Before reading the text below, try to answer following questions:

1.Do you know the amount of energy consumed in ammonia process every year?

2.When was the Haber process for ammonia synthesis developed?

3.Can you list the major uses of ammonia?

4.How many stages are involved in the conversion of ammonia to nitric acid?

5.What are the main raw materials for urea?

Dinitrogen makes up more than three-quarters of the air we breathe, but it is not readily available for further chemical use. Biological transformation of nitrogen into useful chemicals is embarrassing for the chemical industry, since all the effort of all the industry's technologists has been unable to find an easy alternative to this. Leguminous plants can take nitrogen from the air and convert it into ammonia and ammonium-containing products at atmospheric pressure and ambient temperature; despite a hundred years of effort, the chemical industry still needs high temperatures and pressures of hundreds of atmospheres to do the same job. Indeed, until the invention of the Haber process, all nitrogen-containing chemicals came from mineral sources ultimately derived from biological activity.

Essentially all the nitrogen in manufactured chemicals comes from ammonia derived from the Haber-based process. So much ammonia is made (more molecules than any other compound, though because it is a light molecule greater *weights* of other products are produced), and so energy-intensive is the process, that ammonia production alone was estimated to use 3% of the World's energy supply in the mid-1980s.

1. The Haber Process For Ammonia Synthesis

Introduction. All methods for making ammonia are basically fine-tuned versions of the process developed by Haber, Nernst and Bosch in Germany just before the First World War.

$$N_2 + 3H_2 \rightleftharpoons 2NH_3$$

In principle the reaction between hydrogen and nitrogen is easy; it is exothermic and the equilibrium lies to the right at low temperatures. Unfortunately, nature has bestowed dinitrogen with an inconveniently strong triple bond, enabling the molecule to thumb its nose at thermodynamics. In scientific terms the molecule is kinetically inert, and rather severe reaction conditions are necessary to get reactions to proceed at a respectable rate. A major source of "fixed" (meaning, paradoxically, "usefully reactive") nitrogen in nature is lightning, where the intense heat is sufficient to create nitrogen oxides from nitrogen and oxygen.

To get a respectable yield of ammonia in a chemical plant we need to use a catalyst. What

Haber discovered—and it won him a Nobel prize—was that some iron compounds were acceptable catalysts. Even with such catalysts extreme pressures (up to 600 atmospheres in early processes) and temperatures (perhaps 400℃) are necessary.

Pressure drives the equilibrium forward, as four molecules of gas are being transformed into two. Higher temperatures, however, drive the equilibrium the wrong way, though they do make the reaction faster, chosen conditions must be a compromise that gives an acceptable conversion at a reasonable speed. The precise choice will depend on other economic factors and the details of the catalyst. Modern plants have tended to operate at lower pressures and higher temperatures (recycling unconverted material) than the nearer-ideal early plants, since the capital and energy costs have become more significant.

Biological fixation also uses a catalyst which contains molybdenum (or vanadium) and iron embedded in a very large protein, the detailed structure of which eluded chemists until late 1992. How it works is still not understood in detail.

Raw materials. The process requires several inputs: energy, nitrogen and hydrogen. Nitrogen is easy to extract from air, but hydrogen is another problem. Originally it was derived from coal via coke which can be used as a raw material (basically a source of carbon) in steam reforming, where steam is reacted with carbon to give hydrogen, carbon monoxide and carbon dioxide. Now natural gas (mainly methane) is used instead, though other hydrocarbons from oil can also be used. Ammonia plants always include hydrogen-producing plants linked directly to the production of ammonia.

Prior to reforming reactions, sulphur-containing compounds must be removed from the hydrocarbon feedstock as they poison both the reforming catalysts and the Haber catalysts. The first desulphurisation stage involves a cobalt-molybdenum catalyst, which hydrogenates all sulphur-containing compounds to hydrogen sulfide. This can then be removed by reaction with zinc oxide (to give zinc sulfide and water).

The major reforming reactions are typified by the following reactions of methane (which occur over nickel-based catalysts at about 750℃):

$$CH_4 + H_2O \longrightarrow \underset{\text{Synthesis gas}}{CO + 3\,H_2}$$

$$CH_4 + 2H_2O \longrightarrow CO_2 + 4\,H_2$$

Other hydrocarbons undergo similar reactions.

In the secondary reformers, air is injected into the gas stream at about 1100℃. In addition to the other reactions occurring, the oxygen in the air reacts with hydrogen to give water, leaving a mixture with close to the ideal 3: 1 ratio of hydrogen to nitrogen with no contaminating oxygen. Further reactions, however, are necessary to convert more of the carbon monoxide into hydrogen and carbon dioxide via the shift reaction:

$$CO + H_2O \longrightarrow CO_2 + H_2$$

This reaction is carried out at lower temperatures and in two stages (400℃ with an iron catalyst and 220℃ with a copper catalyst) to ensure that conversion is as complete as possible.

In the next stage, carbon dioxide must be removed from the gas mixture, and this is accomplished by reacting the acidic gas with an alkaline solution such as potassium hydroxide and/or mono- or di-ethanolamine.

By this stage there is still too much contamination of the hydrogen-nitrogen mixture by carbon monoxide (which poisons the Haber catalysts), and another step is needed to get the amount of CO down to ppm levels. This step is called methanation and involves the reaction of CO and hydrogen to give methane (i.e. the reverse of some of the reforming steps). The reaction operates at about 325℃ and uses a nickel catalyst.

Now the synthesis gas mixture is ready to go into a Haber reaction.

Ammonia production. The common features of all the different varieties of ammonia plant are that the synthesis gas mixture is heated, compressed and passed into a reactor containing a catalyst. The essential equation for the reaction is simple:

$$N_2 + 3H_2 \rightleftharpoons 2NH_3$$

What industry needs to achieve in the process is an acceptable combination of reaction speed and reaction yield. Different compromises have been sought at different times and in different economic circumstances. Early plants plumped for very high pressure (to get the yield up in a one-pass reactor), but many of the most modern plants have accepted much lower one-pass yields at lower pressures and have also opted for lower temperatures to conserve energy. In order to ensure the maximum yield in the reactor the synthesis gas is usually cooled as it reaches equilibrium. This can be done by the use of heat exchangers or by the injection of cool gas into the reactors at an appropriate point. The effect of this is to freeze the reaction as near to equilibrium as possible. Since the reaction is exothermic (and the equilibrium is less favorable for ammonia synthesis at higher temperatures) the heat must be carefully controlled in this way to achieve good yields.

The output from the Haber stage will consist of a mixture of ammonia and synthesis gas so the next stage needs to be the separation of the two so that the synthesis gas can be recycled. This is normally accomplished by condensing the ammonia (which is a good deal less volatile than the other components, ammonia boils at about –40℃).

Uses of ammonia. The major use of ammonia is not for the production of nitrogen-containing chemicals for further industry use, but for fertilizers such as urea or ammonium nitrates and phosphates. Fertilizers consume 80% of all the ammonia produced. In the USA in 1991, for example, the following ammonia-derived products were consumed, mostly for fertilizers (amounts in millions of tonnes); urea (4.2); ammonium sulphate (2.2), ammonium nitrate (2.6); diammonium hydrogen phosphate (13.5).

Chemical uses of ammonia are varied. The Solvay process for the manufacture of soda ash uses ammonia, though it does not appear in the final product since it is recycled. A wide variety of processes take in ammonia directly, including the production of cyanides and aromatic nitrogen-containing compounds such as pyridine. The nitrogen in many polymers (such as nylon or acrylics) can be traced back to ammonia, often via nitriles or hydrogen cyanide. Most other processes use nitric acid or salts derived from it as their source of nitrogen. Ammonium nitrate, used as a nitrogen-rich fertilizer, also finds a major use as a bulk explosive.

2. Nitric Acid

Production. Much of the nitrogen used by the chemical industry to make other raw materials is not used directly as ammonia, rather, the ammonia is first converted into nitric acid. Nitric acid production consumes about 20% of all the ammonia produced.

The conversion of ammonia to nitric acid is a three-stage process:

(i) $4NH_3 + 5O_2 \longrightarrow 4NO + 6H_2O$

(ii) $2NO + O_2 \longrightarrow 2NO_2$

(iii) $3NO_2 + H_2O \longrightarrow 2HNO_3 + NO$

The first reaction is catalyzed by platinum (in practice platinum-rhodium gauze), as can be observed on the bench with a piece of platinum wire and some concentrated ammonia solution. It might, at first sight, seem that the overall reaction to the acid would be easy; unfortunately, there are complications as nature is a good deal less tidy than chemists and engineers would prefer.

Industrially the first reaction is carried out at about 900 ℃ in reactors containing platinum-rhodium gauze, the temperature being maintained by the heat produced by the reaction. At these temperatures some important side reactions are also fast. Firstly, the ammonia and air mixture can be oxidized to dinitrogen and water (this reaction tends to happen on the wall of the reaction vessel if it is hot, so it needs to be deliberately cooled). Secondly, the decomposition of the first reaction product, nitric oxide, to dinitrogen and oxygen is promoted by the catalyst. It is therefore important to get the product out of the reactor as fast as possible, though this must be balanced against the need to keep the raw materials in contact with the catalyst long enough for them to react. Thirdly, the product, nitric oxide, reacts with ammonia to give dinitrogen and water, so it is important not to let too much ammonia through the catalyst beds or the result will be wasted raw material that cannot be recovered. Control of these conflicting needs is achieved by careful reactor design and by fine control of temperature and flow-rates through the reactors. The actual contact time is usually about 3×10^{-4}s.

The second and third stages have fewer complications, but both are slow and there are no known—cost-effective—catalysts. Typically, a mixture of air and nitric oxide is passed through a series of cooling condensers where partial oxidation occurs, the reaction is favored by low temperatures. The nitrogen dioxide is absorbed from the mixture as it is passed down through a large bubble-cap absorption tower; 55%~60% nitric acid emerges from the bottom.

This nitric acid cannot be concentrated much by distillation as it forms an azeotrope with water at 68% nitric acid. Nitric acid plants typically employ a tower containing 98% sulphuric acid to give 90% nitric acid from the top of the tower. Near 100% acid can be obtained if necessary by further dehydration with magnesium nitrate.

Uses of nitric acid. About 65% of all the nitric acid produced is reacted with ammonia to make ammonium nitrate; 80% of this is used as fertilizer, the rest as an explosive. The other major use of nitric acid is in organic nitrations. Almost all explosives are ultimately derived from nitric acid (most are nitrate esters—e.g. nitrogiycerine or nitrated aromatics—e.g., trinitrotoluene). Nitration using mixtures of sulphuric and nitric acid is the first step in the synthesis of important nitro- and amino-aromatic intermediates such as aniline (the first step is nitration of an aromatic, then reduction of the nitro group to an amino). Many important dyestuffs and pharmaceuticals are ultimately derived from such reactions, though the quantities involved are small. Polyurethane plastics are built around aromatic isocyanates ultimately derived from nitrated toluene and benzene; this use consumes about 5%~ 10% of nitric acid production.

3. Urea

Production. One other product of some significance is made directly from ammonia in large quantities: urea (H_2NCONH_2). About 20% of all ammonia is made into urea. It is synthesized by high pressure reaction (typically 200~400 atm and 180~210℃) of carbon dioxide with ammonia in a two-stage reaction:

(i) $CO_2 + 2NH_3 \longrightarrow NH_2CO_2^- NH_4^+$ (ammonium carbamate)

(ii) $NH_2CO_2^- NH_4^+ \longrightarrow NH_2CONH_2 + H_2O$

The high pressure reaction achieves about 60% conversion of carbon dioxide to the carbamate (stage 1) and the resulting mixture is then passed into low-pressure decomposers to allow for the conversion to urea. Unreacted material is passed back to the start of the high-pressure stage of the process as this greatly improves overall plant efficiency. The solution remaining after the second stage can either be used directly as a liquid nitrogenous fertilizer or concentrated to give solid urea of 99.7% purity.

Uses. The high nitrogen content of urea makes it another useful nitrogenous fertilizer, and this accounts for the vast majority of the market for the compound. Other uses are significant but use only about 10% of all the urea produced. The biggest other use is for resins (melamine-formaldehyde and urea-formaldehyde) which are used, for example, in plywood adhesives and Formica surfaces.

Selected from "*An Introduction to Industrial Chemistry,* 2nd Edition, C.A. Heaton, Blackie & Son Ltd., 1997"

Words and Expressions

1. dinitrogen n. 分子氮，二氮
2. leguminous [le'gju:minəs] a. 豆科的，似豆科植物的
3. ambient ['æmbiənt] a. 周围的，包围着的
4. bestow [be'stəu] vt. 把…赠与（给）
5. thumb one's noise (at) (对…)作蔑视的手势
6. thermodynamics ['θ:məudai'næmiks] n. 热力学
7. paradoxically [pærə'dɔksikəli] ad. 似非而可能是，自相矛盾地，荒谬地
8. molybdenum [mɔ'libdinəm] n. 钼 Mo
9. embed [im'bed] vt. 把…嵌入；栽种
10. protein ['prouti:n] n. 蛋白质，朊
11. elude [i'lju:d] vt. 使困惑，难倒
12. cobalt ['kəubɔ:lt] n. 钴 Co

13. hydrogenate [hai'drɔdʒineit] vt. 使与氢化合，使氢化
14. zinc [zink] n. 锌 Zn
15. nickel ['nikl] n. 镍 Ni
16. secondary reformer 二段（次）转化炉（器）
17. shift reaction 变换反应，转移反应
18. ethanolamine n. 乙醇胺
19. methanation n. 甲烷化作用
20. plump [plʌmp] vi. 投票赞成，坚决拥护（for）
21. one-pass 单程，非循环过程
22. opt [ɔpt] vi. 选择，挑选 (for, between)
23. diammonium hydrogen phosphate 磷酸氢二铵
24. cyanide ['saiənaid] n. 氰化物
25. acrylic a. 聚丙烯的，丙烯酸（衍生物）的
26. nitrile ['naitrail] n. 腈
27. platinum ['plætinəm] n. 铂 Pt，白金
28. rhodium ['rəudiəm] n. 铑 Rh
29. gauze [gɔ:z] （金属丝，纱，线）网
30. bench [bentʃ] n. 实验台，装置
31. deliberately [di'libəritli] ad. 故意地，蓄意地；审慎地，深思熟虑地
32. bubble-cap tower 泡罩塔
33. azeotrope [ə'zi:ətrəup] n. 恒沸物，共沸混合物
34. nitroglycerine [naitrəu'glisəri:n] n. 硝化甘油(炸药)，硝酸甘油
35. trinitrotoluene [trai'naitrəu'tɔljui:n] n. 三硝基甲苯，TNT 炸药
36. nitration [nai'treiʃən] n. 硝化（作用），渗氮（法）
37. nitro- [词头] 硝基
38. polyurethane 聚氨酯，聚氨基甲酸乙酯
39. isocyanate 异氰酸盐(酯)
40. carbamate ['kɑ:bəmeit] n. 氨基甲酸酯
41. ammonium carbamate 氨基甲酸铵
42. nitrogenous [nai'trɔdʒinəs] a. 含氮的
43. melamine ['meləmi:n] n. 密胺，三聚氰(酰)胺
44. plywood ['plaiwud] n. 胶合板
45. Formica [fɔ:'maik] n. 佛米卡（一种家具表面抗热塑料贴面）

Exercises

1. *Completing the following paragraph about the ammonia synthesis process, by using* ***No More Than Three Words*** *in the passage of* ***"The Haber Process for Ammonia Synthesis"****.*

Ammonia is one of the most important chemicals being manufactured in large tonnage today. Its production is linked to the population explosion. Although nitrogen is generally [1]____________, Fritz Haber showed that thermodynamically the reaction of nitrogen with hydrogen was feasible. In 1911 he discovered that [2]________________ (catalysts) would facilitate production and process development started.

Ammonia synthesis from elements nitrogen and hydrogen is a reversible, [3]_____ reaction and proceeds with a decrease in the number of moles. In theory, the [4]_________ will be greater if conditions of high-pressure and low temperature are used. However, in industry, [5]_______ is important, and a relatively low percentage conversion is accepted. Modern plants have tended to operate at [6]____________ and [7]_____________ than the early plants, since the [8]_____ and [9]_________ costs have become more significant. The unconverted materials are recycled.

From where do the reactants of nitrogen and hydrogen originate? The answer is generally "from coal, oil, natural gas, water and air". With natural gas as the raw material, the plants depend on [10]______________ to produce hydrogen and [11]________________. Air is blended into a [12]________________ to supply nitrogen. Through [13]_________________ the carbon monoxide is then reacted with steam to produce hydrogen and carbon dioxide; the latter is removed and the last traces of carbon monoxide and carbon dioxide converted to [14]_______.The purified hydrogen and nitrogen with the ratio of [15]__________ are compressed and fed to the ammonia synthesis loop.

2. *Competing the following table, by referring to the reading material of* ***"Haber-Bosch Process"***.

1787	C. Berthollet	discovers the composition of ammonia
1903	Fritz Haber	
1909	Fritz Haber	
1909~1914	C. Bosch, A. Mittasch	
1913	in BASF	
1919	Fritz Haber	
1920s	in Britain and America	
1931	C. Bosch	

3. *Put the following into Chinese*:

soda ash	refractory	silicate	chromatography
mercury	alkaline	desulphurisation	membrane
anode	cathode	contaminate	inert

4. *Put the following into English:*

电解	分解	复分解	还原
沉淀	结晶	过滤	吸收
溶解度	溶度积	平衡	放热的

Reading Material 7:

Haber-Bosch Process

In his *Essay on Population* (1798), Malthus argued that, since food supplies could never keep pace with population growth, poverty, famine, death and misery were ineluctable consequences of life. Although famous for its use by Darwin to evoke the mechanism of natural selection for evolution, the Malthusian spectre haunted the nineteenth century. Indeed, had yields per acre not been increased in the 1840s by nitrogen and phosphorus fertilizers, or American wheat been introduced to Europe in the 1870s, there might well have been famine in England, as there was in Ireland in the 1840s.①

Even so, at the end of the century, the chemist, William Crookes②, could argue that supplies of nitrogen fertilizer were finite and that, if food supplies were to be further increased to ward off the Malthusian threat, some means would be found to tap the vast reservoir of nitrogen in the air.

It is the chemist who must come to the rescue of the threatened communities. It is through the laboratory that starvation may ultimately be turned to plenty.

Following the eighteenth-century nomenclature of Stephen Hales, chemists referred to this as the problem of fixation of nitrogen. The rise of the Nobel explosives industry based upon nitroglycerine and dynamite was also to increase demand for nitric acid and therefore of a convenient method of synthesis from nitrogen.

One obvious way of fixing nitrogen was to use the method long ago discovered by Cavendish③ whereby nitrogen and oxygen were sparked together to form oxides of nitrogen from which nitric acid could be prepared. The snag was that, industrially, such a process demanded extremely high temperatures (2000~3000℃) and therefore uneconomic amounts of electricity. Since such a process was only available with cheap hydroelectricity, it was only worked for some years in Norway after 1903 when a process was perfected by Olaf Birkeland (a physicist) and Sam Eyde (an engineer). Despite its limitations, the Birkeland-Eyde attracted the attention of academic chemists such as Fritz Haber (1868~1934) and Walther Nernst (1864~1941), who were interested in the thermodynamics of reactions. In 1903 Haber showed that ammonia could be synthesized at the not unreasonable temperature of 1000℃ if an iron catalyst was used:

$$3H_2 + N_2 \longrightarrow 2NH_3$$

However, the yield was infinitesimal and of no commercial significance.

To Haber's embarrassment, this was publicly challenged by Nernst, who pointed out that Haber had paid insufficient attention to pressure as a factor in driving the equilibrium to the right. Haber therefore reinvestigated the matter thoroughly from first principles and derived optimum thermodynamic conditions for the reactions. Using an osmium, uranium carbide or iron catalyst, a pressure of 200 atmospheres (402kPa) and a temperature of 500℃, Haber persuaded the firm of BASF that the synthesis did have commercial possibilities. That was in 1909. It took the engineer, Carl Bosch (1874~1940), and the firm's chief chemist, Alwin Mittasch (1869~1953)④, a further five years to scale up the process. One of the chief problems was the design of a pressure converter of some 65 tons, which involved Krupps in the development of new steel forging techniques. Bosch also had to develop a cheaper method for preparing hydrogen, since electrolysis of water was far too expensive. (Nitrogen was available from industrial plants via liquefaction of air by this date.) Bosch achieved this by passing steam over coke.

The first pilot plant for ammonia synthesis was built by BASF in 1913. With the outbreak of war this pilot plant was quickly enlarged to a production capacity of 60 000 tons of ammonia per annum, thus making Germany potentially, if not actually, self-sufficient in nitric acid for explosives production.

Although the conquest of ammonia synthesis was widely publicized (Haber was to be awarded the Nobel prize for chemistry in 1919 even though he had directed research on gases for chemical warfare, and Bosch received the Nobel prize in 1931), BASF revealed nothing concerning the economics of production. When war broke out in 1914, and British supplies of nitrate for fertilizer and explosives were blockaded by U-boats, Britain and her allies were forced to look closely at the economics of the synthesis. Drawing the erroneous conclusion that the process was prohibitively expensive, the British government developed instead the cyanamide process, which German chemists had used as a route to cheap fertilizers since the 1890s. In this, calcium carbide absorbed nitrogen directly to form the fertilizer, calcium cyanamide. The cyanamide could also be decomposed with steam to form ammonia, which, complemented by ammonia recovered from gasworks, could be converted to nitric acid for the explosives industry.

The British invested heavily in cyanamide factories only to discover in 1919, when BASF's books were inspected, that estimates of the costs of ammonia synthesis had been way out. Consequently, in the 1920s, and very rapidly, the Haber-Bosch process was introduced in Britain and America and soon superseded all rivals. Moreover, its introduction acted as a stimulus and model for all subsequent twentieth-century industry, almost all of which began to involve high-pressure synthesis. As Haber's son has put it:

The construction of huge plants, designed to handle continuously large volumes of high temperatures and pressures, imposed novel operating practices on works engineers, and contributed to the rapid development of chemical engineering, and also to improved types of steel, and new designs of valves and gas compressing machinery.

He adds that "the impact of the ammonia synthesis may be compared in significance with the adoption of petroleum and natural gas for chemical manufacture in Europe in the 1950s and 1960s".

The Haber-Bosch process was of considerable social, economic and scientific importance. Scientifically it was an elegant study of the thermodynamics of gaseous reactions and a demonstration of its commercial significance, socially and economically, it resolved the specter of Malthus and of starving millions; environmentally, with its absence of waste products and polluting odors, it was a model for a cleaner and more socially responsible industry.

Apart from cleaner and more efficient processes suggested by electrochemical processes in the alkali industry and by ammonia synthesis, twentieth-century industry has also been concerned with the economics of scale and scope, including the transfer from wasteful and inefficient batch manufacture to continuous flow. This has been made possible by the exploitation of the remarkable powers of catalysts and through process control by instrumental monitoring. The key factor has been the development of the petrochemicals industry since the 1920s, when chemical engineers at MIT first devised quantitative tools for analyzing fractional distillations, and when John Griebe was hired by the Dow Company to develop automatic control technology. Later, in the 1940s, industrial analysis was further refined by the development of infrared spectroscopy —to the enhancement of post-war research in organic chemistry.

But it has been the chemical industry's ability to substitute a cheaper synthetic product for a natural one, followed by the exploitation of such materials in novel applications, that has been the real hallmark of twentieth-century industry in the public mind.

Selected from "*The Fontana History of Chemistry*, William H. Brock, Fontana Press, 1992"

Words and Expressions

1. famine ['fæmin] n. 饥荒；严重的缺乏
2. ineluctable [ini'lʌktəbl] a. 不可避免的，必然发生的
3. evoke [i'vəuk] vt. 引起,召唤，制定出
4. mechanism ['mekənizm] n. 机理；机制；历程；机械
5. spectre ['spektə] n. 鬼怪，幽灵
6. haunt [hɔ:nt] vt. （鬼魂等）常出没于，作祟；常去，缠住
7. ward [wɔ:d] vt. 挡住，避开，防止（off）
8. tap [tæp] vt. 开发，发掘
9. nomenclature [nəu'menklətʃə] n. 术语，命名（法），名称，（某一学科的）术语表
10. dynamite ['dainəmait] n. 黄色炸药，硝化甘油炸药
11. snag [snæg] n. 暗礁，隐患，意外困难
12. hydroelectricity n. 水电
13. infinitesimal [infini'tesiməl] a. 无穷小的；细微末节的
14. optimum ['ɔptiməm] a.;n. 最佳（的，点，值），最优（的，值）
15. osmium ['ɔzmiəm] n. 锇 Os
16. uranium [juə'reinjəm] n. 铀 U
17. warfare ['wɔ:fεə] n. 战争（状态），竞争，斗争
18. U-boat ['ju:bəut] n. 潜水艇
19. blockade [blɔ'keid] n.;vt. 封锁，禁运
20. erroneous [i'rəunjəs] a. 错误的，不正确的
21. prohibitively [prə'hibitivli] ad. （价格）过高地
22. cyanamide [saiə'næmaid] n. 氰胺，氨基氰
23. elegant ['eligənt] a. 优雅的，精美的
24. quantitative ['kwɔntitətiv] a. 定量的；数量的
25. fractional distillation 分馏（作用）
26. infrared ['infrə'red] a. 红外线的，红外区的
27. spectroscopy [spek'trɔskəpi] n. 光谱学
28. hallmark ['hɔ:lmɑ:k] n. 标志，品质证明

Notes

① 假设条件从句中谓语有 were, had, should 时，可省去 if，把这些词提到句首。这是假设条件句的一种句型。

② William Crookes: 1832~1919,英国化学家和物理学家，铊的发现者，曾任英国皇家学会会长。

③ Cavendish: Henry Cavendish, 1731~1810, 英国化学家。1871 年他的家族捐赠一笔资金，在剑桥大学里建立卡文迪什实验室来纪念他。

④ Alwin Mittasch: 1869~1953, 德国化学家，为寻找合适的合成氨催化剂，在他的建议下，德国巴登苯胺纯碱公司于 1912 年用 2000 种不同的催化剂进行了 6500 次试验，终于研制成功价廉易得的铁催化剂，该公司于 1912 年建成了世界上第一座日产 39 吨合成氨的装置。

Unit 8 Petroleum Processing

After completing this unit, you should be able to:

1.Identify the major constitutes of petroleum.

2.List some important precursors of petrochemicals from petroleum refining.

3.List the unit operation and conversion processes in petroleum refining.

4.Describe briefly cracking and reforming processes.

Petroleum, the product of natural changes in organic materials over millennia, has accumulated beneath the earth's surface in almost unbelievable quantities and has been discovered by humans and used to meet our varied fuel wants. Because it is a mixture of thousands of organic substances, it has proved adaptable to our changing needs. It has been adapted, through changing patterns of processing or refining, to the manufacture of a variety of fuels and through chemical changes to the manufacture of a host of pure chemical substances, the petrochemicals.

Modern units operate continuously. First a tubular heater supplies hot oil to an efficient distillation column which separates the material by boiling points into products similar to those obtained with the batch still, but more cleanly separated; then later units convert the less salable parts of the crude (the so-called bottom half of the barrel) into desired salable products. The processes used include various cracking units (which make small molecules from large ones), polymerization, reforming, hydrocracking, hydrotreating, isomerization, severe processing known as coking, and literally dozens of other processes designed to alter boiling point and molecular geometry.

1. Constituents of Petroleum

Crude petroleum is made up of thousands of different chemical substances including gases, liquids, and solids and ranging from methane to asphalt. Most constituents are hydrocarbons, but there are significant amounts of compounds containing nitrogen (0 to 0.5%), sulfur (0 to 6%), and oxygen (0 to 3.5%). No one constituent exists in large quantity in any crude.

Aliphatics, or open chain hydrocarbons

***n-Paraffin Series or n-alkanes, C_nH_{2n+2}*.** This series comprises a larger fraction of most crudes than any other. Most straight-run (i.e., distilled directly from the crude) gasolines are predominantly n-paraffins. These materials have poor antiknock properties.

***Iso-Paraffin Series or Iso-alkanes, C_nH_{2n+2}*.** These branched chain materials perform better in internal-combustion engines than n-paraffins and hence are considered more desirable. They may be formed by catalytic reforming, alkylation, polymerization, or isomerization. Only small amounts exist in crudes.

Olefin, or Alkene Series, C_nH_{2n} . This series is generally absent in crudes, but refining processes such as cracking (making smaller molecules from large ones) produce them. These relatively unstable molecules improve the antiknock quality of gasoline, although not as effectively as iso-paraffins. On storage they polymerize and oxidized, which is undesirable. This very tendency to react, however, makes them useful for forming other compounds, petrochemicals, by additional chemical reactions. Ethylene, propylene, and butylene (also called ethene, propene, and butene) are examples. Cracked gasolines contain many higher members of the series.

Ring Compounds

Naphthene Series or Cycloalkanes, C_nH_{2n} . This series, not to be confused with naphthalene, has the same chemical formula as the olefins, but lacks their instability and reactivity because the molecular configuration permits them to be saturated and unreactive like the alkanes, these compounds are the second most abundant series of compounds in most crudes. The lower members of their group are good fuels; higher molecular weight ones are predominant in gas oil and lubricating oils separated from all types of crudes.

Aromatic, or Benzenoid Series, C_nH_{2n-6} . Only small amounts of this series occur in most common crudes, but they are very desirable in gasoline since they have high antiknock value, good storage stability, and many uses besides fuels. Many aromatics are formed by refining processes. Examples are: benzene, toluene, ehylbenzene, and xylene.

Lesser Components. Sulfur has always been an undesirable constituent of petroleum. The strong, objectionable odor of its compounds originally brought about efforts to eliminate them from gasoline and kerosene fraction. Chemical reactions were at first directed at destroying the odor. Later it was found that sulfur compounds had other undesirable effects (corrosion, reducing the effect of tetraethyl lead as an antiknock agent, air pollution). At present, wherever possible, the sulfur compounds are being removed and frequently the sulfur thus removed is recovered as elemental sulfur. Nitrogen compounds cause fewer problems than sulfur compounds, are less objectionable, and are generally ignored.

With the general adoption of catalytic cracking and finishing processes, it was discovered that the occurrence of metals present only in traces (Fe, Mo, Na, Ni, V, etc.) was troublesome as they are strong catalyst poisons. Now methods to remove these substances are being perfected. Salt has been a major problem for many years. It is practically always present in raw crude, usually as an emulsion, and must be removed to prevent corrosion. It breaks down heating in the presence of hydrocarbons to produce hydrochloric acid. Mechanical or electrical desalting is preliminary to most crude-processing steps.

Petroleum crudes vary widely, each kind requiring different refining procedures. The terms paraffin base, asphalt (naphthene), and mixed base are often applied to differentiate crudes on the basis of the residues produced after simple distillation.

Pure chemical compounds are not regularly separated by refining processes. Some of the simpler, low molecular weight ones are isolated for processing into petrochemicals. Most petroleum products are mixtures separated on the basis of boiling point ranges and identified by the ultimate uses to which they are well adapted.

Common refinery fractions are:

Natural (or casing-head) gasoline and natural gas
LPG
Light distillates
Motor gasolines
Solvent naphthas
Jet fuel
Kerosene
Light heating oils

Intermediate distillates
Heavy fuel oils
Diesel oils
Gas oils
Heavy distillates
Heavy mineral oils (medicinal)
Heavy flotation oils
Lubricating oils

Waxes (candles, sealing, paper treating, insulating)
Residues
Lubricating oil
Fuel oils
Petrolatum
Road oils
Asphalts
Coke

2. Products of Refining

Precursors of Petrochemicals. As markets change, there is constant alteration in the materials used for the manufacture of petrochemicals. Almost any synthesis desired can be brought about; the problem is to do it at low cost with the equipment available. In earlier times, acetylene was used extensively for making petrochemicals, but it is difficult to make and store, so ethylene has now become the principal raw material for further synthesis. Precursors are reactive materials usually made by breaking down larger molecules, called feedstocks. Ethylene is currently being made from LPG, naphtha, gas oil, diesel fuel, ethane, propane, and butane, with coal a possibility soon to be explored, and some testing of liquefied coal already completed. The principal precursors are:

Acetylene　Propylene　Benzene　Xylenes
Ethylene　Butene　Toluene　Naphthalene

Ethylene, manufacturing from distillates, natural gas, or gas liquids, is the largest volume organic material. The conditions for its manufacture lie somewhere between those usually thought of as refining and those encountered in chemical production. Extremely large plants are built and being built. Some plants have a production capacity as large as 7×10^{8} kg/year.

Propylene is rarely produced except as a coproduct with ethylene. Steam cracking of ethylene produces most of it, and virtually all of it is used for polymer production. The remainder, used mostly for chemical production, comes from oil refinery fluid catalytic crackers. Refinery propylene is used mainly for alkylation.

Aromatics are usually thought of as coal-derived, but the amount from that source in 1980 was almost vanishingly small, 4 percent of the benzene, 0.9 percent of the toluene, and only 0.1 percent of the xylenes. Benzene can be made by dehydrogenation of cyclohexane or substituted cyclohexanes, by aromatization of methycyclopentane, and by demethylation of toluene or xylenes. The demand for aromatics is large and attention is being given to find catalysts to produce more BTX (benzene-toluene-xylene) for chemical and high-grade fuel use.

Naphthalene is used in smaller quantities than the lighter aromatics, but its consumption is far from trivial. Dealkylation of a selected reformate stream using chromate-aluminum carbide catalyst gives a product which is purified to be purer than that formed form coal tar.

Light distillates. Aviation gasoline, (automobile) motor gasoline, naphthas, petroleum solvents, jet-fuel, and kerosene are the fractions generally regarded as light distillates. Any given refinery rarely makes all of them. Gasoline is the most important product, and around 45 percent of the crude processed now ends up as gasoline.

Intermediate distillates. These include gas oil, light and heavy domestic furnace oils, diesel fuels, and distillates used for cracking to produce more gasoline. These distillates are used mainly for transportation fuels in heavy trucks, railroads, small commercial boats, standby and peak-shaving power plants, farm equipment, and wherever diesels are used to produce power. Home heating furnaces use these distillates.

Heavy distillates. These are converted into lubricating oils, heavy oils for a variety of fuel uses, waxes, and cracking stock.

Residues. Some constituents are simply not volatile enough to be distilled, even under vacuum. These include asphalt, residual fuel oil, coke, and petrolatum. These difficulty salable materials are by-products of the refining process, and while many are extremely useful, most are difficult to dispose of and are relatively unprofitable.

Petroleum-derived chemicals, commonly known as petrochemicals, are made from petroleum and natural gas. Production of some of these products is very large, and over 1000 organic chemicals are derived from petroleum. Examples are carbon black, butadiene, styrene, ethylene glycol, polyethylene, etc.

3. Processing or Refining

Refining involves two major branches, separation processes and conversion processes. Particularly in the field of conversion, there are literally hundreds of processes in use, many of them patented. Even in a given refinery running a single crude, daily changes to accommodate changing markets and changing parameters of the conversion apparatus take place. No refinery on any day will operate exactly as shown, but all refineries will operate along the basic lines indicated.

Separation processes. The unit operations used in petroleum refining are the simple, usual ones, but the interconnections and interactions may be complex. Most major units are commonly referred to as stills. A crude still consists of heat exchangers, a furnace, a fractionating tower, steam strippers, condensers, coolers, and auxiliaries. There are usually working tanks for temporary storage at the unit; frequently there are treating tanks, used for improving the color and removing objectionable components, particularly sulfur; blending and mixing tanks; receiving and storage tanks for crude feed; a vapor recovery system; spill and fire control systems; and other auxiliaries. For the refinery as a whole, a boiler house and usually an electrical generating system are added. A control room with instruments to measure, record, and control, thus keeping track of material which permits heat and material balances, forms the heart of the system. One of the major functions of the instruments is to permit accurate accounting of the materials and utilities used.

Conversion Processes. About 70 percent of the crude processed is subjected to conversion processing both carbonium ion and free radical mechanisms occur. The presence of catalysts, the temperature, and pressure determine which type predominates. The following are examples of the more important basic reactions which occur: cracking or pyrolysis, polymerization, alkylation, hydrogenation, hydrocracking, isomerization, and reforming or aromatization.

Select from "*Shreve's Chemical Process Industries*, 6th edition, N. Shreve, McGraw-Hill, 1993"

Words and Expressions

1. millennium [mi'leniəm] n. 一千年
2. tubular ['tju:bjulə] a. 管的，管式的，由管构成的
3. still [stil] n. 蒸馏釜，蒸馏
4. salable ['seiləbl] a. 畅销地，销路好的
5. hydrocracking n. 加氢裂化, 氢化裂解
6. isomerization n. 异构化(作用)
7. constituent [kəns'titjuənt] n. 组成，组分，成分
8. asphalt ['æsfælt] n. （地）沥青，柏油
9. straight run gasoline 直馏汽油
10. antiknock ['ænti'nɔk] a. 抗爆的，防爆的，抗震的
11. alkylation [ælki'leiʃən] n. 烷基化，烷基取代
12. butene ['bju:ti:n] n. 丁烯
13. benzenoid a. 苯（环）型的
14. ethylbenzene n. 乙（基）苯
15. tetraethyl lead 四乙基铅
16. finishing ['finiʃiŋ] n. 精加工，最终加工
17. desalt ['di:'sɔ:lt] vt. 脱盐
18. paraffin base crude 石蜡基石油
19. asphalt base crude 沥青基石油
20. naphthene base crude 环烷基石油
21. mixed base crude 混合基石油
22. differentiate [difə'renʃieit] v. 区分，区别；求微分，求导数
23. residue ['reizidju:] n. 残余物，残渣，剩余物
24. casing-head gas 油井气，油田气
25. LPG = liquefied petroleum gas 液化石油气
26. light distillate 轻馏分
27. motor gasoline 动力汽油, 车用汽油
28. solvent naphtha 溶剂石脑油
29. jet fuel 喷气式发动机燃料
30. light heating oil 轻质燃料油
31. intermediate distillate 中间馏分
32. diesel ['di:zəl] n. 内燃机，柴油机
33. diesel oil 柴油
34. gas oil 粗柴油, 瓦斯油, 汽油
35. heavy distillate 重馏分

36. heavy mineral oil　重质矿物油
37. medicinal　[me'disinl]　a. 药的，药用的　n. 药物，药品
38. heavy flotation oil　重质浮选油
39. lubricating oil　润滑油
40. petrolatum　[petrə'leitəm]　石蜡油, 软石蜡, 矿酯
41. road oil　铺路沥青
42. precursor　[pri'kə:sə]　产物母体, 前身, 先驱
43. butane　['bju:tein]　n. 丁烷
44. dehydrogenation　[di: 'haidrədʒ'neiʃən]　n. 脱氢（作用）
45. aromatization　n. 芳构化
46. demethylation　n. 脱甲烷（作用）
47. methylcyclopentane　n. 甲基环戊烷
48. trivial　['triviəl]　a. 普通的，不重要的，无价值的
49. chromate　['krəumeit]　n. 铬酸盐
50. aviation　[eivi'eiʃən]　n. 航空，飞行
51. standby　['stændbai]　a. 备用的，后备的　n. 备用设备
52. carbon black　炭黑
53. glycol　['glaikɔl]　n. 乙二醇
54. patent　['peitənt]　n. 专利，专利权　vt. 取得…的专利权
55. parameter　[pə'ræmitə]　n. 参数，系数
56. fractionate　['færkʃəneit]　vt. 使分馏，把…分成几部分
57. stripper　['stripə]　n. 汽提塔, 解吸塔
58. carbonium　n. 阳碳, 正碳
59. carbonium ion mechanism　正碳离子机理
60. radical　['rædikəl]　n. 基，原子团；根部；根式
61. free radical mechanism　自由基机理
62. predominate　[pri'dɔmineit]　vi. 占优势，居支配地位
63. pyrolysis　[pai'rɔlisis]　n. 热解（作用），高温分解
64. hydrogenation　[haidrɔdʒ'neiʃən]　n. 加氢（作用）

Exercises

1. *Complete the summary of Reading Material 8. Choose* ***No More Than Three Words*** *from the passage for each answer.*

Coal forms the world's largest reserve of concentrated raw material from which chemicals can be extracted and produced, and it also is a cheap source of heat and power used for processing. Coal, taking the place of oil, will be a source of [1]___________ in the near future, and much research and development is being conducted for the coal-conversion processes. In order to use existing plant and processes, the [2]_____________ in coal-derived liquid feedstocks must be improved in favor of more hydrogen and sulphur is to be removed.

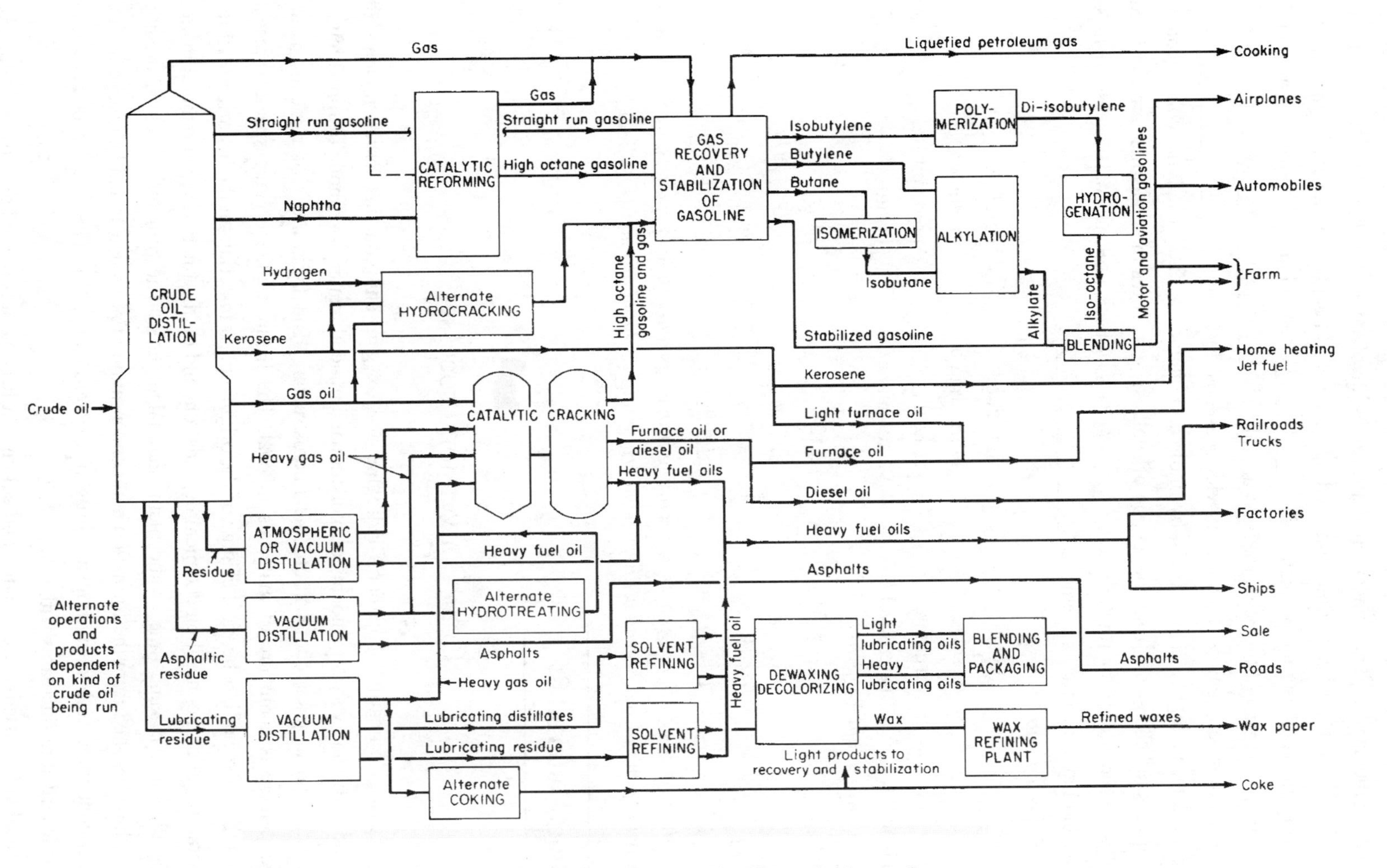

Fig. 2-2 Generalized overall refinery from crude oil to salable products

In [3]________________ process, the main products are fuel gas,[4]________________, light oils and ammonia gas. The fundamental processes involved in the liquefaction of coal are [5]____________, solvent extraction and hydrogenation. Although the advances in chemical engineering and catalysts, the problems—[6]______________ and high [7]____________—remain in this process. And many of the new processes are only at [8]__________________.

Gasification of coal is used to provide gaseous fuels by [9]_________________ coal gasification technologies, liquid fuels by indirect liquefaction, i.e., catalytic conversion of synthesis gas and chemicals from conversion of synthesis gas. Three main gasifiers are fixed bed, [10]________ and trained or rotating bed. [11]__________has been used in coal process to make gaseous and liquid fuels and to remove [12]________________.

2. *Put the following into Chinese:*

antiknock	alkylation	finishing	desalt
differentiate	diesel oil	lubricating oil	precursor
stripper	carbonium	radical	predominate
degradation	heterocyclic	stationary	in situ

3. *Put the following into English*:

管式的	加氢裂解	异构化	组成
热解	腐蚀	残余物	液化石油气
脱氢	芳构化	专利	参数
降解	定量地	定性地	选择性

4. *Identify the overall relationship between refining processes and refined products, by referring to the following generalized overall refinery from crude oil to salable products*(Fig. 2-2).

Reading Material 8:

Coal-Conversion Processes

Coal consists primarily of carbon, hydrogen, and oxygen, and contains lesser amounts of nitrogen and sulfur and varying amounts of moisture and mineral matter. The mode of formation of coal, the variation in plant composition, the microstructure, and the variety of mineral matter indicate that there is a mixture of materials in coal. The nature of the organic species present depends on the degree of biochemical change of the original plant material, on the historic pressures and temperatures after the initial biochemical degradation, and on the finely divided mineral matter deposited either at the same time as the plant material or later. The principal types of organic compounds have resulted from the formation and condensation of polynuclear and heterocyclic ring compounds containing carbon, hydrogen, nitrogen, oxygen, and sulfur. The fraction of carbon in aromatic ring structures increases with rank.

Nearly all coal is used in combustion and coking. At least 80% is burned directly in boilers for generation of electricity or steam for industrial purposes. Small amounts are used for transportation, space heating, firing of ceramic products, etc. The rest is essentially pyrolyzed[①] to produce coke, coal gas, ammonia, coal tar, and light oil products from which many chemicals are produced. Combustible gases and chemical intermediates are also produced by the gasification of coal, and different carbon products are produced by various heat treatments. A small amount of coal is used in miscellaneous applications such as fillers, pigments, foundry material, and water filtration.

There is no doubt about the switch from oil to coal as a source of organic chemicals; the only uncertainty concerns the time-scale and rate at which it happens.

Coal-conversion processes under development are directed towards producing either gaseous or liquid feedstocks which approximate in composition to petroleum-derived feedstocks. They can then be utilized directly in existing petrochemical plant and processes. To achieve this, however, two problems must be overcome, which are a consequence of the differing natures of coal and oil. Firstly, the H:C ratios are different for coal and for petroleum-derived liquid feedstocks. Secondly, significant amounts of heteroatoms are present in coal, particularly sulphur which may reach levels as high as 3%. The sulphur has to be removed for two reasons: (i) on combustion it will form the atmospheric pollutant SO_2, and (ii) it is a potent catalyst poison, and most of the downstream petrochemical processes are catalytic. However, its removal from coal is difficult and it is therefore removed from the conversion products in stead.

Coal Processing to Synthetic Fuels and Other Products

The primary approaches to coal processing or coal conversion are thermal decomposition, including pyrolysis or carbonization[②], gasification, and liquefaction by hydrogenation. The hydrogenation of coal is not currently practiced commercially.

High Temperature Carbonization. High temperatures and long processing times are used in carbonizing coking coals in coke ovens or gas retorts. Besides metallurgical or gas coke the products include fuel gas, crude tar, light oils[③] (benzene, toluene and xylene, referred to as BTX, and solvent naphtha), and ammonia gas.

Most coal chemicals are obtained from high temperature tar with an average yield over 5% of the coal which is carbonized. The yields in coking are about 70% of the weight of feed coal. Tars obtained from vertical gas retorts have a much more uniform chemical composition than those from coke ovens. Two or more coals are usually blended. The conditions of carbonization vary depending on the coals used and affect the tar composition. Coal-tar chemicals include phenols, cresols, xylenes, benzene, toluene, naphthalene, and anthracene.

The largest consumer of coke is the iron and steel industry. Coke is also used to make calcium carbide, from which acetylene is made. Synthesis gas for methanol and ammonia production is also made from gasification of coke.

Low Temperature Carbonization. Lower temperature carbonization of lump coal at ca 700℃ primarily used for production of solid smokeless fuel, gives a quantitatively and qualitatively different yield of solid, liquid, and gaseous products than does the high temperature processes.

Although a number of low temperature processes have been studied, only a few have been used commercially. These have been limited in the types of coal that are acceptable, and the by-products are less valuable than those obtained from high temperature processing.

Liquefaction. Liquefaction of coal, via hydrogenation, is quite an old process which was operated commercially in Germany during World War II when external fuel supplies were cut off. Tens of millions of tonnes of gasoline were produced in this way during this period. Interestingly, Germany is today playing a leading part in the development of more efficient processes. For the resulting liquids to be suitable chemical feedstocks the H:C ratio must be improved in favor of more hydrogen. Clearly this can be achieved in two ways—either by adding hydrogen or by removing carbon. Although many of the new processes are only at the pilot-plant stage of development, their superiority over the old methods is due to increased sophistication of the chemical engineering employed plus improvements in the catalysts available. The basic problems, however, remain the same—poor selectivity in producing the desired fractions and a relatively high rate of consumption of hydrogen.

The fundamental processes involved are pyrolysis, solvent extraction and hydrogenation. Differences between the techniques being developed lie in how these fundamental processes are combined. Note that in the above processes the main product is a highly carbonaceous solid material known as char. This is either burnt to provide process heat or reacted with water and oxygen to produce hydrogen.

The liquids produced by coal liquefaction are similar to fractions obtained by distillation of crude oil (although they are much richer in aromatics), and therefore require further treatment, e.g. cracking, before being used for synthesis.

Gasification. A number of gasifiers are either available commercially or in various stages of development. These are described as fixed bed, fluidized bed, and entrained or rotating bed. The fixed bed involves an upward flow of reaction gas through a relatively stationary bed of hot coal. The gas velocity is slow enough to avoid blowing the coal out of the bed. The fluidized bed operates at higher gas velocities than the fixed bed and utilizes somewhat smaller particles. The entrained bed operates with parallel flows of reaction gas and finely pulverized coal particles to minimize reaction time and maximize throughput of product. The rotating bed is similar to a kiln, which operates with the coal entering at the upper part of the inclined kiln. Rotation avoids clinking and exposes fresh surfaces to enhance completion of the reaction.

Surface Gasification technology. Gasification of coal for fuel gas and chemical intermediate production has been developed commercially and improvements in technology are being studied in a number of facilities. In the United States, the purpose of a number of programs has shifted from production of a substitute natural gas (methane) to electric power generation through the integrated gasification-combined-cycle (IGCC) plants. The interest in this use of coal results from the low emission levels that can be achieved and the potential for higher power generation efficiency.

Future large gasification plants, intended to produce ca $7\times10^{6}\,m^3$ standard of methane per day, are expected to be sited near a coal field having an adequate water supply. It is cheaper to transport energy in the form of gas through a pipeline than coal by either rail or pipeline. The process chosen is expected to utilize available coal in the most economical manner.

Underground Coal Gasification (UCG). Underground coal gasification is intended to gasify a coal seam *in situ*, converting the coal into gas and leaving the ash underground. This approach avoids the need for mining and reactors gasification. UCG is presently considered most interesting for deep coal or steeply sloping seams. This approach involves drilling holes to provide air or oxygen for gasification and removal of product gases and liquids.

A low calorific value gas, which includes nitrogen from air, could be produced for boiler or turbine use in electric power production, or an intermediate calorific value gas containing no nitrogen for an industrial fuel gas, or syntheses gas for chemical and methane production could be provided. This approach is still noncommercial in part because it is not economically competitive.

Although many environmental and safety problems can be avoided using UCG, there is some concern about groundwater contamination as a result of the process.

The chemistry of underground gasification has much in common with surface gasification, however, many of the parameters cannot be controlled because the reaction occurs in a remote site. Heat energy to drive the gasification comes primarily from carbon combustion to produce CO and then CO_2. Because many coal seams are also aquifers there is a considerable amount of water intrusion, which leads to steam generation at the expense of the reaction energy. As a result the rate of air or oxygen passage through the injection wells and seam is adjusted to maintain a low level of moisture in the product gas. The steam is beneficial for char gasification and some is consumed in the water gas shift reaction to produce H_2 and CO_2 from H_2O and CO. Some H_2 reacts with C to produce CH_4, which enhances the calorific value of the gas.

Liquid Fuels and Chemicals from Gasification of Coal. Gasification of coal using steam and oxygen in different gasifiers provides varying proportions of carbon monoxide and hydrogen. Operations at increasing pressures increase the formation of methane. Because mixtures of CO and H_2 are used as the start of chemical synthesis and methane is not wanted or needed for chemical processes, the conditions favoring its formation are avoided. The product gases may then be passed over catalysts to obtain specific products. Iron-based catalysts are used to produce hydrocarbons in the Fischer-Tropsch process[4], or zinc or copper catalysts are used to make methyl alcohol.

The Fischer-Tropsch process has not been economical in competitive markets. The South African Sasol plant has operated successfully using the modification of the Fischer-Tropsch process. The original plant was designed to produce 227,000 t/yr of gasoline, diesel oil, solvents, and chemicals from 907,000 metric tons of noncaking high ash subbituminous coal. The success of the Sasol project is attributed to the availability of cheap coal and the reliability of the selected components.

A variety of pilot plants using fluid-bed gasifiers have been built in the United States, Germany, and elsewhere. The Winkler process[5] is the only one that has been used on a large scale. It was developed in Germany in the 1920s to make synthesis gas at atmospheric pressure. Plans were being made to develop a pressurized version.

Bioprocessing and Biotreatment of Coal. The use of biotechnology to process coal to make gaseous and liquid fuels is an emerging field. Bacteria and enzymes have been studied to establish the technical feasibility of conversion.

The earliest work was done on microbial decomposition of German hard coals. Reactors have been designed to use a variety of bacteria and fungi to break down the large molecular structure into smaller units that may be useful as intermediates (solubilization) or as liquid and gaseous fuels (conversion). Efforts have focused on lower rank coals, lignite or brown coal and subbituminous coal, because of greater reactivity. The conversion processes frequently introduce chemically combined oxygen through hydrolysis or related reactions to make the solid soluble in the reaction mixture as an initial step. Further reaction involves biological degradation of the resulting material to form gases or liquids.

The large-scale processing of coal is expected to involve plants similar to sewage treatment facilities in the handling of liquid and solid materials. The reaction rates are substantially lower than those achieved in high temperature gasifiers and liquefaction reactors requiring much larger systems to achieve comparable coal throughput.

Biological processes are also being studied to investigate ability to remove sulfur species in order to remove potential contributors to acid rain. These species include benzothiophene-type materials, which are the most difficult to remove chemically, as well as pyritic material. The pyrite may be treated to enhance the ability of flotation processes to separate the mineral from the combustible parts of the coal. Genetic engineering techniques are being applied to develop more effective species.

Selected from "*Encyclopedia of Chemical Technology*, Vol. 6, R. E. Kirk and D.F. Othmer, Interscience, 3rd edition 1996"

Words and Expressions

1. biochemical ['baiəu'kemikəl] a. 生物化学的
2. degradation [degrə'deiʃən] n. 降解；退化；（能量的）衰变；降级
3. heterocyclic [hetərə'saiklik] a. 杂环的
4. ceramic [si'ræmik] a. 陶器的，陶瓷的，制陶的
5. pyrolyze ['paiərəlaiz] vt. 热(分)解
6. filler ['filə] n. 填充物，填料
7. miscellanneous [misi'leiniəs] a. 杂的, 各种的, 多方面的
8. foundry ['faundri] n. 铸造, 翻砂
9. heteroatom n. 杂原子, 异质原子
10. coal carbonization 煤干馏
11. gas retort 干馏甑，干馏炉
12. retort [ri'tɔ:t] n. 干馏釜, 甑
13. ca = circa ['sə:kə] [拉丁语] prep.; ad. 大约
14. quantitatively ad. 定量地
15. qualitatively ad. 定性地
16. superiority [sju: 'piəriəriti] n. 优越（性），优势
17. selectivity [silek'tiviti] n. 选择性，选择
18. carbonaceous [kɑ:bə'neiʃəs] a. 碳的，碳质的，含碳的

19. char [tʃɑ:] n. 炭，木炭
20. gasifier n. 气化炉
21. fixed bed 固定床
22. fluidized bed 流化床
23. entrained bed 气流床
24. rotating bed 转动床, 旋转床
25. stationary ['steiʃənəri] a. 静止的，固定的，不变的
26. pulverize ['pʌlvəraiz] vt. 使成粉末，研磨，粉碎
27. clink [kliŋk] v.;n. 响裂（钢锭缺陷），（铸件）裂纹，（发出）碰撞声
28. surface gasification 地面煤气化
29. underground coal gasification 地下煤气化
30. seam [si:m] n. (煤，矿)层
31. *in situ* 就地，原地，在现场
32. calorific value 热值，发热量
33. boiler ['bɔilə] n. 锅炉
34. turbine ['tə:bin] n. 透平（机），叶轮机，汽轮机，涡轮（机）
35. aquifer n. 蓄水层，含水层
36. intrusion [in'tru:ʒən] n. 侵入
37. subbituminous coal (黑色，褐色)次烟煤
38. microbial [mai'krəubiəl] a. 微生物的, (因)细菌(而引起)的
39. hard coal 硬煤，无烟煤
40. solubilization [sɔljubilai'zeiʃən] n. 溶液化，增溶（化）
41. lignite ['lignait] n. 褐煤
42. sewage ['sju:idʒ] n. 污水，下水道（系统）
43. benzothiophene n. 苯并噻吩
44. pyritic [pai'ritik] a. 黄铁矿的
45. pyrite [paiərait] n. 黄铁矿

Notes

① pyrolyze: 热解，指物质受热发生分解的反应过程。热解过程不涉及催化剂以及其他能量（如紫外线辐射）所引起的反应。

② coal carbonization: 煤干馏，指煤在隔绝空气条件下加热分解，生成焦炭（或半焦）、煤焦油、粗苯（主要成分为单环芳烃）、煤气等产物的过程。按加热终温的不同，可分为三种：高温干馏，中温干馏，低温干馏。

③ light oil: 轻质油或轻油。在煤化工行业，把煤焦油以及煤直接液化产物中的沸点低于210℃的轻馏分称作轻质油或轻油。

④ Fischer-Tropsch process: 费-托合成法，以合成气为原料在催化剂和适当反应条件下，合成以石蜡烃为主的液体燃料的工艺过程。工艺流程主要包括：煤气化、气体净化、变换和重整、合成和产品精制改质等。Franz Fischer: 1877~1947, 德国燃料化学家，1925 年与 H. Tropsch 合作发明了用水煤气在常压下催化合成石油，以制取汽油、柴油和石蜡油等（费-

托合成法），从而开创了自煤间接液化制取液体燃料的途径。

⑤ Winkler process: 以德国人 F. Winkler 命名的一种煤气化工艺。以氧和水蒸气为气化剂，使煤在沸腾气化炉中进行气化。1926 年在德国工业化。目前多用于制氢气、合成氨原料气和燃料煤气。

Unit 9 Polymers

> *Before reading the text below, try to answer these questions:*
>
> 1. Can you give a definition for polymer?
> 2. Do you have any idea about the prices of commodity polymers, engineering polymers and advanced polymeric materials?
> 3. What do the terms of LDPE, HDPE, LLDPE, PP, PVC and PS stand for?
> 4. What are the most important parameters in making polymers?

Polymers are all around us. They are the main components of food (starch, protein), clothes (silk, cotton, polyester, nylon), dwellings (wood-cellulose, paints) and also our bodies (nucleic acids, polysaccharides, proteins). No distinction is made between biopolymers and synthetic polymers. Indeed many of the early synthetic polymers were based upon naturally occurring polymers, e.g. celluloid (cellulose nitrate), vulcanization of rubber, rayon (cellulose acetate).

Polymers are constructed from monomer units, connected by covalent bonds. The definition of a polymer is:

"a substance, —R—R—R—R— or, in general —$[R]_n$—, where R is a bifunctional entity (or bivalent radical) which is not capable of a separate existence"

where n is the *degree of polymerization*, DP_n .This definition excludes simple organic and inorganic compounds, e.g. CH_4, NaCl, and also excludes materials like diamond, silica and metals which appear to have the properties of polymers, but are capable of being vaporized into monomer units.

The molecular weight (MW) (strictly relative molecular mass) can be obtained from the MW of the monomer (or repeat unit) multiplied by n. Thus the MW of CH_4 or NaCl is 18 or 58.5 respectively, whereas the MW of a polymer can be > 100. When the value of n is small, say 2~20, the substances are called *oligomers*[①], often these oligomers are capable of further polymerizations and are then referred to as macromers.

By definition, 1 mole of a polymer contains 6×10^{27} polymer molecules and therefore 1g mole = MW of the polymer in grams, which, in theory, can be > 10^6 g. However, by convention, 1 g mole usually refers to the MW of the repeat unit; thus 1 g mole of polyethylene—$(CH_2)_n$— is taken as 14 g (the end groups, being negligible, are ignored).

A polymer with a MW of 10^7, if fully extended, should have a length of ~ 1mm and a diameter of ~ 0.5 nm. This is equivalent in size to uncooked spaghetti ~ 2 km in length. However, in reality, in bulk polymers the chain is never fully extended—a random coil configuration is adopted sweeping out a space of diameter ~ 200 nm. It therefore has the appearance of cooked spaghetti or worms (or more correctly, worms of different length). The movements of these polymer chains are determined by several factors, such as:

(i) Temperature

(ii) Chemical make-up of the backbone —C—C—C— chain; whether the chain is flexible (aliphatic structure) or rigid (aromatic)

(iii) The presence or absence of side-chains on the backbone

(iv) The *inter*-polymer chain attraction (weak—dipole/dipole, H-bonding—or strong covalent bonds, cross-linking)

(v) The MW and molecular weight distribution (MWD) of the polymer.

Nearly all of the properties of polymers can be predicted if the above factors are known, e.g. whether the polymer is amorphous or partially crystalline; the melting temperature of the crystalline phase (T_m) (actually it is more of a softening temperature over several degrees); is the polymer brittle or tough; its rigidity or stiffness (called modulus), whether the polymer dissolves in solvents, etc.

Polymers are really effect chemicals in that they are used as materials, e.g. plastics, fibers, films, elastomers, adhesives, paints, etc., with each application requiring different polymer properties. Many of the initial uses of plastics were inappropriate, which led to the belief that plastics were "cheap and nasty". However, recent legislation on product liability and a better understanding of the advantages and disadvantages of plastics have changed this position.

Economics, that is the cost of making and fabricating the polymer is of prime importance. This has led to a rough grouping of polymers into commodity polymers, engineering polymers, and advanced polymeric materials.

1. Commodity Polymers

Examples of these are:

Polyethylene:
- low density polyethylene (LDPE)
- high density polyethylene (HDPE)
- linear low density polyethylene (LLDPE)

Polypropylene (PP)

Poly vinyl chloride (PVC)

Polystyrene (PS)

Each of these is prepared on the 10 million tonnes/year scale. The price is <$1500/tonne.

2. Engineering Polymers

The materials have enjoyed the highest percentages growth of any polymers in the last ten years and are principally used as replacements for metals for moderate temperature (< 150 ℃) and environmental conditions or they may have outstanding chemical inertness and/or special properties, e.g. low friction polytetrafluoroethylene (PTFE). These engineering polymers include

Acetal (or polyoxymethylene, POM)

Nylons (polyamides)

Polyethylene or polybutylene terephthalate (PET or PBT)
Polycarbonate (of bisphenol A) (PC)
Polyphenylene oxide (PPO) (usually blended with styrene).
The prices are (\$3000~\$15000)/tonne.

3. Advanced Polymeric Materials

These have very good temperature stability (many hours/days at 250~300℃) and when reinforced with fibers (e.g., glass, carbon or Aramid fibres)②, i.e. composites, they are stronger than most metals on a weight/weight basis. They are usually only used sparingly, often in critical parts of a structure. Their price can be as high as \$150,000/tonne.

4. Making of Polymers

Approximately 100 million tonnes of polymers are made annually, in plants ranging from 240,000 tonnes/year continuous single-stream polypropylene plants to a single batch preparation of a few kilograms of advanced performance composites. The highest tonnage polymers are LDPE, HDPE, LLDPE, PP, PVC and PS.

The most important parameters in making polymers are quality control and reproducibility. They are different from simple organic compounds such as acetone, where often a simple distillation gives the desired purity. There are many different grades of the "same" polymer, depending on the final application, e.g., different MW, MWD, extent of branching, cross-linking, etc., and these variations are multiplied when copolymers (random, alternating and block) are considered. Many of the properties are fixed during polymerization and cannot be altered by post-treatment. Blending is sometimes carried out to obtain desired properties or just to up-grade production polymer that may be lightly off-specification.

A polymerization process consists of three stages:

(1) *Monomer preparation.* This is not discussed here, other than to emphasize that the purity of the monomer is paramount. Thus monofunctional impurities in step-growth, and radical scavengers, chain-transfer impurities and catalyst poisons (e.g. water in ionic propagation) in chain polymerizations are all significant.

(2) *Polymerization.* As stated above, uniformity of polymer properties is absolutely necessary, this not only includes MW, etc., but other factors such as color, shape of polymer particle (if the polymer is not palletized or granulated), catalyst residues, odor (especially when used for food application), etc.

The polymerization operation has to cope with the following parameters.

(i) Homogeneous or heterogeneous reactions.

(ii) In homogeneous systems, large increases in viscosity, affecting kinetics of polymerization, heat transfer and efficiency of mixing.

(iii) Most chain-growth polymerizations are exothermic, giving out several hundred kilowatts per ton of polymer produced; this heat has to be removed, since most polymerization are performed at constant temperature (isothermal). Heat removal is achieved by heat transfer through reactor walls, reactor design (long tubular reactors with high surface area/volume ratio), added cold reagents (monomer and/or solvent) or by using the latent heat of evaporation of monomer or solvents.

(iv) Control of MW and MWD, branching and cross-linking in the polymer. The polymerization process affects these whether batch, semi-batch (polymerizing reaction mixture is fed through to further reactors) or continuous. The residence time③ of polymerization, whether narrow or broad, also determines MW and MWD.

As a general rule, once a process has been perfected it is not altered, unless economics dictate a change—for example, gas-phase polymerization performed in the absence of a solvent, thus eliminating solvent purification, recovery, fire hazard, etc.

(3) *Polymer recovery.* Unless the polymerization takes place in bulk, separation from the solvent has to be carried out. The conventional methods for recovering chemicals e.g., crystallization, distillation, adsorption, etc. are not normally to be used because polymers possess properties such as high viscosity and low solubility in solvents, and are sticky and non-volatile. Nevertheless, precipitation by using a non-solvent followed by centrifuging, or by coagulation of an emulsion or latex and removal of the solvent by steam-stripping (to keep the temperature down and prevent decomposition) can be used. Devolatilisation of the solvent or unused monomer from the polymer can be performed during pellitization in an extruder.

Selected from "*An Introduction to Industrial Chemistry,* 2nd Edition, C.A. Heaton, Blackie & Son Ltd., 1997"

Words and Expressions

1. nucleic acid 核酸
2. biopolymer n. 生物聚合物
3. celluloid ['seljulɔid] n. 赛璐珞, 硝酸纤维素
4. vulcanization [vʌlkənai'zeiʃən] n. 硫化，硬化
5. rayon ['reiɔn] n. 人造丝，人造纤维
6. bifunctional a. 双官能团的
7. entity ['entiti] n. 存在，实体，统一体
8. degree of polymerization 聚合度
9. diamond ['daiəmənd] n. 金刚石，钻石
10. oligomer n. 低聚物，齐(分子量)聚(合)物
11. macromer n. 高聚物
12. spaghetti [spə'geti] n. 通心粉
13. backbone ['bækbəun] n. 构架, 骨干, 主要成分
14. dipole ['daipoul] n. 偶极(子)
15. H-bond n. 氢键
16. cross-link ['krɔ:sliŋk] v. (聚合物)交联, 横向耦合
17. amorphous [ə'mɔ:fəs] a. 无定形的, 非晶体的

18. brittle ['britl] a. 脆的，易碎的
19. stiffness ['stifnis] n. 刚性(度)，韧性
20. modulus ['mɔdjuləs] n. 模数，系数，指数
21. liability [laiə'biliti] n. 责任，义务
22. fabricate ['fæbrikeit] vt. 制造，生产，制备；装配，安装，组合
23. linear ['liniə] a. （直）线的，直线型的；线性的，线性化的
24. poly vinyl chloride 聚氯乙烯
25. polystyrene [pɔli'staiəri:n] 聚苯乙烯
26. acetal ['æsitæl] n. 乙缩醛，乙醛缩二乙醇
27. polyoxymethylene n. 聚甲醛，聚氧化亚甲基
28. polybutylene terephthalate 聚丁烯对苯二酸酯
29. polycarbonate n. 聚碳酸酯
30. bisphenol A n. 双酚 A
31. polyphenylene oxide 聚苯氧化物
32. composite ['kɔmpəzit] n. 复合材料，合成[复合，组合]物
33. reproducibility n. 再生性，还原性，重复性
34. copolymer [kəu'pɔlimə] n. 共聚物
35. random ['rændəm] a. 随机的，无规则的，偶然的
36. scavenger ['skævindʒə] n. 清除剂，净化剂
37. propagation [prɔpə'geiʃən] n. 增长，繁殖，传播，波及
38. pelletize ['pelitaiz] v. 造粒，做成丸(球，片)状
39. granulate ['grænjuleit] vt. 使成颗粒，使成粒状
40. heterogeneous ['hetərəu'dʒi:njəs] a. 多相的，非均匀的
41. kilowatt ['kiləwɔt] n. 千瓦（特）
42. isothermal [aisəu'θə:məl] a.;n. 等温（的），等温线（的）
43. latent heat 潜热
44. residence time 停留时间
45. adsorption [æd'sɔpʃən] n. 吸附（作用）
46. centrifuge ['sentrifjudʒ] n.;v. 离心；离心机，离心器
47. coagulation [kəuægju'leiʃən] n. 凝结(聚，固)；胶凝，絮凝
48. latex ['leiteks] n. 橡胶，乳状液，(天然橡胶，人造橡胶)乳液
49. devolatilization n. 脱(去)挥发份(作用)
50. extruder [eks'tru:də] n. 挤压机，(螺旋)压出机

Notes

① oligomer: 齐聚物。单体聚合生产分子量较低的低聚物，称为齐聚反应 oligomerization，产物称为齐聚物。

② Aramid fibres: 芳香族聚酰胺类纤维。由含有重复出现的酰胺基团 (—CO—NH—) 直接连接到两个芳香环的线性聚合物所纺制的纤维 (Aramid 是由 aromatic amide 缩写而成)。这种纤维具有特别高的强度，常用于复合材料。

③ residence time (in reactor): 停留时间，指物料在反应器中停留的时间。在连续操作设备中，由于物料的逆向混合（返混，backmixing），在同一时刻进入设备的物料可能分别取不同的流动路径，在设备内的停留时间也不相同，从而形成一定的分布，称为停留时间分布(residence time distribution)。

Exercises

1. *Complete the table below by referring back to the information in the passage.*

Abbreviation	*Name of polymer*	*Name in Chinese*
LDPE		
HDPE		
LLDPE		
PET or PBT		
PVC		
PS		
POM		
PP		
PC		
PPO		
PTFE	Polytetrafluoroethylene	聚四氟乙烯
PF	Phenol-formaldehyde resins	酚醛树脂
PMMA	Poly (methyl methacrylate)	聚甲基丙烯酸甲酯
UF	Urea-formaldehyde resins	脲醛树脂

2. *Put the following into Chinese:*

oligomer　macromer　copolymer　propagation
uvlcanization　stiffness　fabricate　linear
reproducibility　residence time　coagulation　foresight
coordination　stereochemical　plug flow　injection-moulding

3. *Put the following into English*:

官能团　单体　构架　模数
复合材料　非均相的　潜热　显热
热固性的　热塑性的　无定形的　交联
随机的　等温的　吸附　离心

4. *Go through the reading material of* ***"Polymerization Techniques"*** *and complete the chart below. Not every space can be filled in from the information given; if this is the case, just leave a blank.*

Name of polymer	*Company or Inventor*	*Year introduced*
Phenol-formaldehyde resin	Baekland	1909
Urea-formaldehyde resin		1929
Alkyd resin		
Poly(styrene-butadiene)		

续表

Name of polymer	*Company or Inventor*	*Year introduced*
Poly (acrylonitrile-butadiene)		
Poly (vinyl chloride)		
Polystyrene		
Polyethylene		
Nylon		
Polyacrylonitrile		
Terylene		
Epoxy resins		
Polypropylene		
LLDPE		

Reading Material 9:

Polymerization Techniques

1. The History Perspectives of Polymerization Techniques

The chemical industry's interest in polymers dates back to the 19th century. In those days it was a case of synthetically modifying natural polymers with chemical reagents to either improve their properties or produce new materials with desirable characteristics. Notable examples were nitration of cellulose giving the explosive nitrocellulose.

The first fully synthetic polymer to be introduced (1909) was a phenol-formaldehyde resin known as bakelite. Although the reaction had been discovered some twenty years previously, it was only after a careful and systematic study of it that it was properly controlled to give a useful thermosetting resin[①]. In the late 1920s two other types of thermosetting resins followed, namely urea-formaldehyde, and alkyd resins. Assisted by advances in high-pressure technology, a more scientific approach to the study of synthetic polymers (macromolecules) led to the discovery and production of several important polymers in the 1930s and early 1940s. These plastics, elastomers and synthetic fibers have had a profound effect not only on the chemical industry but also on the quality of all our lives.

Germany had the foresight to realize the importance of this area, and they dominated the early research and development work. Their commercial successes ranged from rubber-like materials—the co-polymers poly (styrene-butadiene) and poly (acrylonitrile- butadiene) to thermoplastics[②] like poly (vinyl chloride) and polystyrene.

In the U.K., Gibson of ICI was studying high-pressure reactions of alkenes in autoclaves. His reaction with ethylene appeared to have failed since he obtained a small amount of a waxy white solid. Fortunately his curiosity led him to investigate this. It proved to be polyethylene, first produced commercially by ICI in 1938.

America's interest was led by the Dupont Company and its major success was the commercial introduction of the first nylon in 1941. This certainly was a reward for perseverance and effort since their first researches on the subject to commercial production took 12 years and reportedly cost $12 million.

The major industrial developments in organic chemicals initiated in the 1930~1940 period have continued since that time. Most important of all is the introduction of purely synthetic polymers. Although much of this growth was due to the increased demand for the polymers introduced in the 1930s and 1940s—urea-formaldehyde resins, nylon, polyethylene (low-density), poly (vinyl chloride), and butadiene co-polymers—new polymers have also made a significant contribution. The most familiar examples (together with their year of commercial introduction and the company responsible) are polyacrylonitrile (1948, Du Pont); Terylene (1949, ICI), epoxy resins (1955, Du Pont) ; and polypropylene (1956, Montecatini). Their special properties and economic advantage have enabled them to displace traditional materials. Thus plastics such as poly (vinyl chloride) have replaced wood in window frames and metal drainpipes, since they are unaffected by weathering, lighter in weight, and maintenance-free. Synthetic fibers like nylon and terylene have enabled non-drip, machine-washable, and crease-resistant clothing to be introduced, and we are made aware many times each day of the widespread usage of synthetic plastics in all facets of the packaging industry. Indeed, so profound is the influence of plastics and polymers on our lives (something we tend to take for granted) that it is difficult to imagine our existence without them. Not only are all these polymers well established now, but also are the processes for making them. It must also be mentioned in passing that the actual use of these polymers required major technological advances in developing processes to get the material in the correct form for its particular applications. Techniques such as injection-moulding[③] and blow-moulding are the result. Existing dyestuffs would not adhere to these synthetic materials and so new ones were in turn discovered and developed. Polymer science and technology has grown into a large field of study.

A major advance in polymer chemistry was provided by the work of Karl Ziegler and Giulio Natta, which led in 1955 to the introduction of some revolutionary catalysts which bear their name. The great significance of this event was highlighted by them being awarded a Nobel Prize in 1963 for their work. Ziegler-Natta catalysts are mixtures of a trialkyl aluminium plus a titanium salt and they bring about the polymerization by a coordination mechanism in which the monomer is inserted between the catalyst and the growing polymer chain. Industrial interest in this centered on the fact that it gave more control over the polymerization process. Significantly, it allowed the polymerization to occur under milder conditions and produced a very stereoregular polymer. Taking polypropylene as an example, the Ziegler-Natta catalyst gives the isotactic product whereas a free-radical process leads to the atactic stereochemical form. These stereochemical forms show differences in their properties, for example, the isotactic polymer chains can pack together better and this form has a higher degree of crystallinity and hence a higher softening point than the atactic variety. Ziegler-Natta polymerization of ethylene gives high-density polyethylene (HDPE) which is different in some properties from the low-density form (LDPE) produced by free-radical polymerization.

During the late 1970s production of linear low-density polyethylene (LLDPE) was commercialized. Here the polymer chain is much more linear containing only short branching chains, in contrast to conventional LDPE. The polymer has greater strength and toughness, particularly in film applications, than ordinary low-density polyethylene.

Over recent years in addition to continuing production of the bulk polymers described above many companies have developed certain speciality polymers. These can be thought of as polymers whose structure has been tailor-made to yield certain specific properties, and therefore have limited, very specialized applications. For example, polymers which are exceedingly thermally and oxidatively stable are required for space capsules which will re-enter the earth's atmosphere. To develop these requires particular knowledge and skills. There is therefore little competition in producing these polymers; the market for them, although small, is assured and the product therefore commands a high price by comparison with "standard" polymers.

2. Polymerization Techniques

Most polymerizations are performed in the liquid phase using either a batch or a continuous process. The continuous method is preferred because it lends itself to smoother operation leading to a more uniform product, because of modern on-line analysis techniques. It also has lower operating costs. However, continuous processes have difficulties. The residence time of the polymer in the reactor will be variable, unless plug-flow is adopted using tube reactors. This may result in:

(i) Catalyst residues in the polymer, e.g., peroxides, which may degrade the polymer during granulation or processing.

(ii) The polymer may have a broad MWD with some decomposition, e.g., cross-linking (for long residence times).

(iii) The polymer may adhere to the reactor walls, requiring shutdown for cleaning.

(iv) Repeated changes in polymer grade may be required, during change-over the polymer will be a mixture making the polymer unsuitable for use.

There are five general methods of polymerization:

(i) Bulk (or mass)

(ii) Solution

(iii) Slurry (or precipitation)

(iv) Suspension (or dispersion)

(v) Emulsion

Further lesser-used methods include:

(vi) Interfacial

(vii) Reaction injection moulding (RIM)[④],

(viii) Reactive processing of molten polymers.

Selected from "*The Fontana History of Chemistry*, William H. Brock, Fontana Press, 1992"

Words and Expressions

1. phenol-formaldehyde resin　酚醛树脂
2. bakelite　['beikəlait]　n. 胶木，酚醛树脂，电木
3. thermoset　['θə:məset]　n. 热固性　a. 热固性的
4. urea-formaldehyde resin　脲醛树脂
5. alkyd resin　醇酸树脂，聚酯树脂
6. autoclave　['ɔ:təkleiv]　n. 压煮器，高压釜
7. perseverance　a. 能坚持的
8. thermoplastic　['θə:məu'plæstik]　n. 热塑性塑料　a.热塑性的
9. injection-moulding　塑料注塑成型，注模
10. blow-moulding　吹模法
11. coordination　[kəuɔ:di'neiʃən]　n. 配位，配合
12. stereoregular　a. 有规立构的，立体定向的
13. atactic　a. 无规立构的
14. isotactic　a. 全同立构的，等规立构的
15. plug flow　活塞流，平推流
16. peroxide　[pə'rɔksaid]　n. 过氧化物
17. bulk polymerization　本体聚合
18. solution polymerization　溶液聚合
19. slurry polymerization　淤浆聚合
20. suspension polymerization　悬浮聚合
21. emulsion polymerization　乳液聚合
22. interficial polymerization　界面聚合
23. reaction injection moulding　反应注射成型
24. reactive proccssing of molten polymers　熔融聚合物的反应加工

Notes

① thermosetting resin: 热固性树脂。指在加热、加压下或在固化剂、紫外光作用下，进行化学反应，交联固化成为不溶物质的一大类合成树脂。该反应是不可逆的，一经固化，再加热加压也不可能再度软化或流动。

② thermoplastics: 热塑性树脂，可反复加热软化、冷却固化的一大类合成树脂（也包括常见的天然树脂）。

③ injection-moulding: 注射成型，简称注塑。塑料在注塑机加热料筒中塑化后，由柱塞或往复螺杆注射到闭合模具的模腔中形成制品的塑料加工方法。

④ reaction injection moulding: 反应注射成型，简称 RIM，成型过程中有化学反应的一种注射成型方法。这种方法所用原料不是聚合物，而是将两种或两种以上的液体单体或预聚物，以一定比例分别加到混合头中，在加压下混合均匀，立即注射到闭合模具中，在模具内聚合固化，定型成制品。

PART3 CHEMICAL ENGINEERING

Unit 10 What Is Chemical Engineering?

Before reading the text, try to answer the following questions:

1.Can you tell the difference between the chemical engineering and the mechanical engineering?

2.When did the concept of "unit operation" first appear?

3.Can you list some core courses of chemical engineering?

4.What are the future trends in chemical engineering?

In a wider sense, *engineering* may be defined as a scientific presentation of the techniques and facilities used in a particular industry. For example, mechanical engineering refers to the techniques and facilities employed to make machines. It is predominantly based on mechanical forces which are used to change the appearance and/or physical properties of the materials being worked, while their chemical properties are left unchanged. Chemical engineering encompasses the chemical processing of raw materials, based on chemical and physico-chemical phenomena of high complexity.

Thus, chemical engineering is that branch of engineering which is concerned with the study of the design, manufacture, and operation of plant and machinery in industrial chemical processes.

Chemical engineering is above all based on the chemical sciences, such as physical chemistry, chemical thermodynamics, and chemical kinetics. In doing so, however, it does not simply copy their findings, but adapts them to bulk chemical processing. The principal objectives that set chemical engineering apart from chemistry as a pure science, is "to find the most economical route of operation and to design commercial equipment and accessories that suit it best of all". Therefore, chemical engineering is inconceivable without close ties with economics, physics, mathematics, cybernetics, applied mechanics, and other technical sciences.

In its early days, chemical engineering was largely a descriptive science. Many of the early textbooks and manuals on chemical engineering were encyclopedias of the commercial production processes known at the time. Progress in science and industry has brought with it an impressive increase in the number of chemical manufactures. Today, petroleum for example serves as the source material for the production of about 80 thousand chemicals. The expansion of the chemical process industries on the one hand and advances in the chemical and technical sciences on the other have made it possible to lay theoretical foundations for chemical processing.

As the chemical process industries forged ahead, new data, new relationships and new generalizations were added to the subject-matter of chemical engineering. Many branches in their own right have separated from the main stream of chemical engineering, such as process and plant design, automation, chemical process simulation and modeling, etc.[1]

1. A Brief Historical Outline

Historically, chemical engineering is inseparable from the chemical process industries. In its early days chemical engineering which came into being with the advent of early chemical trades was a purely descriptive division of applied chemistry.

The manufacture of basic chemical products in Europe appears to have begun in the 15th century when small, specialized businesses were first set up to turn out acids, alkalis, salts, pharmaceutical preparations, and some organic compounds.

For all the rhetoric of nineteenth-century academic chemists in Britain urging the priority of the study of pure chemistry over applied, their students who became works chemists were little more than qualitative and quantitative analysts. Before the 1880s this was equally true of German chemical firms, who remained content to retain academic consultants who pursued research within the university and who would occasionally provide the material for manufacturing innovation. By the 1880s, however, industrialists were beginning to recognize that the scaling up of consultants' laboratory preparations and syntheses was a distinctly different activity from laboratory investigation. They began to refer to this scaling problem and its solution as "chemical engineering" —— possibly because the mechanical engineers who had already been introduced into works to maintain the steam engines and pumps in an industry of growing complexity were the very men who seemed best able to understand the processes involved. The academic dichotomy of head and hand died slowly.

Unit Operations. In Britain when in 1881 there was an attempt to name the new Society of Chemical industry as the "Society of Chemical Engineers", the suggestion was turned down. On the other hand, as a result of growing pressure from the industrial sector, the curricula of technical institutions began to reflect, at last, the need for chemical engineers rather than competent analysts. No longer was mere description of existing industrial processes to suffice. Instead, the expectation was that the processes generic to various specific industries would be analyzed, thus making room for the introduction of thermodynamic perspectives, as well as those being opened up by the new physical chemistry of kinetics, solutions and phases.

A key figure in this transformation was the chemical consultant, George Davis (1850~1907)①, the first Secretary of the Society of Chemical Industry. In 1887 Davis, then a lecturer at the Manchester Technical School, gave a series of lectures on chemical engineering, which he defined as the study of "the application of machinery and plant to the utilization of chemical action on the large scale". The course, which revolved around the type of plant involved in large-scale industrial operations such as drying, crashing, distillation, fermentation, evaporation and crystallization, slowly became recognized as a model for courses elsewhere, not only in Britain, but overseas. The first fully fledged course in chemical engineering in Britain was not introduced until 1909; though in America, Lewis Norton (1855~1893) of MIT pioneered a Davis-type course as early as 1888.

In 1915, Arthur D. Little②, in a report on MIT's programme, referred to it as the study of "unit operations" and this neatly encapsulated the distinctive feature of chemical engineering in the twentieth century. The reasons for the success of the Davis movement are clear: it avoided revealing the secrets of specific chemical processes protected by patents or by an owner's reticence——factors that had always seriously inhibited manufacturers from supporting academic programmes of training in the past. Davis overcame this difficulty by converting chemical industries "into separate phenomena which could be studied independently" and, indeed, experimented with in pilot plants within a university or technical college workshop.

In effect he applied the ethics of industrial consultancy by which experience was transmitted "from plant to plant and from process to process in such a way which did not compromise the private or specific knowledge which contributed to a given plant's profitability". The concept of unit operations held that any chemical manufacturing process could be resolved into a coordinated series of operations such as pulverizing, drying, roasting, electrolyzing, and so on. Thus, for example, the academic study of the specific aspects of turpentine manufacture could be replaced by the generic study of distillation, a process common to many other industries. A quantitative form of the unit operations concept emerged around 1920, just in time for the nation's first gasoline crisis. The ability of chemical engineers to quantitatively characterize unit operations such as distillation allowed for the rational design of the first modern oil refineries. The first boom of employment of chemical engineers in the oil industry was on.

During this period of intensive development of unit operations, other classical tools of chemical engineering analysis were introduced or were extensively developed. These included studies of the material and energy balance of processes and fundamental thermodynamic studies of multicomponent systems.

Chemical engineers played a key role in helping the United States and its allies win World War II. They developed routes to synthetic rubber to replace the sources of natural rubber that were lost to the Japanese early in the war. They provided the uranium-235 needed to build the atomic bomb, scaling up the manufacturing process in one step from the laboratory to the largest industrial plant that had ever been built. And they were instrumental in perfecting the manufacture of penicillin, which saved the lives of potentially hundreds of thousands of wounded soldiers.[2]

The Engineering Science Movement. Dissatisfied with empirical descriptions of process equip-ment performance, chemical engineers began to reexamine unit operations from a more fundamental point of view. The phenomena that take place in unit operations were resolved into sets of molecular events. Quantitative mechanistic models for these events were developed and used to analyze existing equipment. Mathematical models of processes and reactors were developed and applied to capital-intensive U.S. industries such as commodity petrochemicals.

Parallel to the growth of the engineering science movement was the evolution of the core chemical engineering curriculum in its present form. Perhaps more than any other development, the core curriculum is responsible for the confidence with which chemical engineers integrate knowledge from many disciplines in the solution of complex problems.

The core curriculum provides a background in some of the basic sciences, including mathematics, physics, and chemistry. This background is needed to undertake a rigorous study of the topics central to chemical engineering, including:

- multicomponent thermodynamics and kinetics,
- transport phenomena,
- unit operations,
- reaction engineering,
- process design and control, and
- plant design and systems engineering.

This training has enabled chemical engineers to became leading contributors to a number of interdisciplinary areas, including catalysis, colloid science and technology, combustion, electro-chemical engineering, and polymer science and technology.

2. Basic Trends In Chemical Engineering

Over the next few years, a confluence of intellectual advances, technologic challenges, and economic driving forces will shape a new model of what chemical engineering is and what chemical engineering do.

The focus of chemical engineering has always been industrial processes that change the physical state or chemical composition of materials. Chemical engineers engage in the synthesis, design, testing scale-up, operation, control and optimization of these processes. The traditional level of size and complexity at which they have worked on these problems might be termed the *mesoscale*. Examples of this scale include reactors and equipment for single processes (unit operations) and combinations of unit operations in manufacturing plants. Future research at the mesoscale will be increasingly supplemented by dimensions—the *microscale* and the dimensions of extremely complex systems—the *macroscale*.

Chemical engineers of the future will be integrating a wider range of scales than any other branch of engineering. For example, some may work to relate the macroscale of the environment to the mesoscale of combustion systems and the microscale of molecular reactions and transport. Other may work to relate the macroscale performance of a composite aircraft to the mesoscale chemical reactor in which the wing was formed, the design of the reactor perhaps having been influenced by studies of the microscale dynamics of complex liquids.

Thus, future chemical engineers will conceive and rigorously solve problems on a continuum of scales ranging from microscale to macroscale. They will bring new tools and insights to research and practice from other disciplines: molecular biology, chemistry, solid-state physics, materials science, and electrical engineering. And they will make increasing use of computers, artificial intelligence, and expert system in problem solving, in product and process design, and in manufacturing.

Two important developments will be part of this unfolding picture of the discipline.

- Chemical engineers will become more heavily involved in product design as a complement to process design. As the properties of a product in performance become increasingly linked to the way in which it is processed, the traditional distinction between product and process design will become blurred. There will be a special design challenge in established and emerging industries that produce proprietary, differentiated products tailored to exacting performance specifications. These products are characterized by the need for rapid innovatory as they are quickly superseded in the marketplace by newer products.

- Chemical engineers will be frequent participants in **multidisciplinary** research efforts. Chemical engineering has a long history of fruitful interdisciplinary research with the chemical sciences, particularly industry. The position of chemical engineering as the engineering discipline with the strongest tie to the molecular sciences is an asset, since such sciences as chemistry, molecular biology, biomedicine, and solid-state physics are providing the seeds for tomorrow's technologies. Chemical engineering has a bright future as the "interfacial discipline", that will bridge science and engineering in the multidisciplinary environments where these new technologies will be brought into being.[3]

[1] *Basic Chemical Engineering*, A.M Kutepov, Mir Publishers, 1988

[2] *The Fontana History of Chemistry*, William H. Brock, Fontana Press, 1992

[3] *Frontiers in Chemical Engineering: Research Needs and Opportunities*, National Academy Press, 1988

Words and Expressions

1. accessory [æk'sesəri] n. (pl.) 辅助设备（装置），附件 a. 附属的，辅助的
2. inconceivable [inkən'si:vəbl] a. 不可想象的，不可思议的，难以置信的
3. cybernetics [saibə'netiks] n. 控制论
4. encyclopedia [ensaikləu'pi:djə] n. 百科全书；某科全书
5. generalization [dʒenərəlai'zeiən] n. 归纳，概述，通则；普遍化，法则化
6. subject-matter 主题，题材，要点，内容
7. advent ['ædvənt] n. 到来，出现，来临
8. with the advent of 随着…的到来（出现）
9. rhetoric ['retərik] n. 言语，修辞学
10. priority [prai'ɔriti] n. （在）先，（在）前；优先（权，次序），重点
11. qualitative ['kwɔlitətiv] a. 定性的；质的，质量的；性质上的
12. consultant [kən'sʌltənt] n. 顾问，咨询者
13. dichotomy [di'kɔtəmi] n. 两分法
14. curricula [kə'rikjulə] n. curriculum 的复数
15. suffice [sə'fais] vi. 足够，有能力 vt. 满足（…的需要）
16. generic [dʒi'nerik] a. （同，定）属的，类（属性）的；一般的，普通的
17. revolve [ri'vɔlv] v. （使）绕（旋）转；循环；思索，反复思考
18. revolve around M 围绕着 M 盘算，绕 M 旋转
19. fledged a. 羽毛已长成的
20. encapsulate [in'kæpsjuleit] v. 压缩，节略；封装，用胶囊包起来
21. reticence ['retisəns] n. 缄默，保留
22. inhibit [in'hibit] vi. 有禁止力，起抑制作用 vt. 禁止；抑制，约束

23. ethics ['eθiks] n. 职业规矩，道德标准，伦理观
24. coordinate [kəu'ɔdinit] n. 坐标；一致；配位 a. 坐标的，协调的，配位的
    [kəu'ɔdineit] v. 使协调，配合，配位
25. turpentine ['tə:pəntain] n. 松节油，松香水
26. ally ['ælai] n. 同盟国（者）；伙伴，助手 v. 结盟
27. instrumental [instru'mentl] a. 有帮助的，起作用的；仪器的
28. capital-intensive a. 资本密集的，资本集约的
29. rigorous ['rigərəs] a. 严格的，严密的，精确的；严厉的，苛刻的
30. colloid ['kɔlɔid] n. 胶体，胶粒 a. 胶状的，胶体的
31. confluence ['kɔnfluəns] n. 合流（点），汇合（处）；集合，聚集
32. meso- [词头]中（间，等，央），中等的；内消旋；介，新
33. mesoscale n. 中间尺度（刻度，标度）
34. micro- [词头]微（量，型，观）；显微；百万分之一
35. microscale n. 微（观）尺度（刻度，标度）
36. macro- [词头]宏（观），大（量），常量
37. macroscale n. 宏观尺度（刻度，标度）
38. dynamics [dai'næmiks] n. （动）力学，动态（特性）
39. conceive [kən'si:v] v. 设想，想象；想到(出)(of)
40. continuum [kən'tinjuəm] n. 连续介质；连续（统一体）；连续光谱
41. insight ['insait] n. 见识，洞察（力），理解，领会
42. artificial intelligence 人工智能
43. expert system 专家系统
44. unfold [ʌn'fəuld] v. 展开，显露，呈现；发展，伸展
45. complement ['kɔmplimənt] n. 补充，互补，补充物；配套
46. blur [blə:] v. （使）变模糊；弄污
47. proprietary [prə'praiətəri] a. 专利的，专有的，有专利权的 n. 所有权，业主
48. asset ['æset] n. 宝贵的人（或物）；财产
49. biomedicine n. 生物医学
50. interfacial [intə'feiʃəl] a. 界面的，面际的，层间的

Notes

① George Davis: 1850~1907，英国化学工程开拓者，1881 年，他协助创立英国化学工业协会，1901 年，他把在曼彻斯特工学院讲学的内容，整理成为《化学工程手册》，这是第一部化学工程专著。

② Arthur D. Little：1863~1935，美国化学工程的先驱，1886 年他在美国首创了商业性咨询研究所，曾任美国化学学会会长及美国化学工程师协会会长。

Exercises

1. *In the future, chemical engineering will evolve to address challenges that span a wide range of intellectual disciplines and physical scales (from the molecular scale to planetary scale).*

Completing the following table by matching the scales (Microscale, Mesoscale and Macroscale) with the activities listed.

- Atomic and molecular studies of catalysts
- Chemical processing in the manufacture of integrated circuits
- Studies of the dynamics of suspensions and microstructured fluids
- Improving the rate and capacity of separations equipment
- Design of injection molding equipment to produce car bumpers made from polymers
- Designing feedback control systems for bioreactors
- Operability analysis and control system synthesis for an entire chemical plant
- Mathematical modeling of transport and chemical reactions of combustion-generated air pollutants
- Manipulating a petroleum reservoir during enhanced oil recovery through remote sensing of process data, development and use of dynamic models of underground interactions, and selective injection of chemicals to improve efficiency of recovery

2. *Completing following table, by referring to the reading material of* ***"Curriculum of Chemical Engineering".***

Course	*Course contents*
Science and Math.	
Chemical Engineering	
Other Engineering	
Humanities and Social Science	

3. *Put the following into Chinese:*

cybernetics	encyclopedia	ethics	accessory
shortcut	coordinate	expert system	artificial intelligence
generalization	proprietary	interfacial	off-the-shelf

4. *Put the following into English:*

热力学	动力学	力学	水力学
积分	微分	化学计量	动量
有帮助的	胶体	连续介质	定性的

Reading Material 10:

Curriculum of Chemical Engineering

As chemical engineering knowledge developed, it was inserted into university courses and curricula. Before World War I, chemical engineering programs were distinguishable from chemistry programs in that they contained courses in engineering drawing, engineering thermodynamics, mechanics, and hydraulics taken from engineering departments. Shortly after World War I the first text in unit operations was published (W. H. Walker, W. K. Lewis[①], and W. H. McAdams, *Principles of Chemical Engineering,* New York McGraw-Hill, 1923). Courses in this area became the core of chemical engineering teaching.

By the mid-1930s, chemical engineering programs included courses in (i) stoichiometry (using material and energy conservation ideas to analyze chemical process steps), (ii) chemical processes or "unit operations," (iii) chemical engineering laboratories "in which equipment was operated and tested", and (iv) chemical plant design (in which cost factors were combined with technical elements to arrive at preliminary plant designs). The student was still asked to take the core chemistry courses, including general, analytical, organic, and physical chemistry. However, in addition, he or she took courses in mechanical drawing, engineering mechanics, electric circuits, metallurgy, and thermo-dynamics with other engineers.

Since World War II chemical engineering has developed rapidly. As new disciplines have proven useful, they have been added to the curriculum. Chemical engineering thermodynamics became generally formulated and taught by about 1945. By 1950, courses in applied chemical kinetics and chemical reactor design appeared. Process control appeared as an undergraduate course in about 1955, and digital computer use began to develop about 1960.

The idea that the various unit operations depended on common mechanisms of heat, mass, and momentum transfer developed about 1960. Consequently, courses in transport phenomena assumed an important position as an underlying, unifying basis for chemical engineering education. New general disciplines that have emerged in the last two decades include environmental and safety engineering, biotechnology, and electronics manufacturing processing. There has been an enormous amount of development in all fields, much of it arising out of more powerful computing and applied mathematics capabilities.

1. Science and Mathematics Courses

Chemistry.

Chemical engineers continue to need background in organic, inorganic and physical chemistry, but also should be introduced to the principles of instrumental analysis and biochemistry.

- Valuable conceptual material should be strongly emphasized in organic chemistry including that associated with biochemical processes.
- Much of thermodynamic is more efficiently taught in chemical engineering, and physical chemistry should include the foundations of thermodynamics.

Physics.

Biology.

- Biology has emerged from the classification stage, and modern molecular biology holds great promise for application. Future graduates will become involved with applying this knowledge at some time in their careers.
- A special course is required on the functions and characteristics of living cells with some emphasis on genetic engineering as practiced with microorganisms.

Materials Science.

● Course work should include the effects of microstructure on physical, chemical, optical, magnetic and electronic properties of solids.

● Fields of study should encompass ceramics, polymers, semiconductors, metals, and composites.

Mathematics.

Computer Instruction.

● Although students should develop reasonable proficiency in programming, the main thrust should be that use of standard software including the merging of various programs to accomplish a given task. Major emphasis should be on how to analyze and solve problems with existing software including that for simulation to evaluate and check such software with thoroughness and precision.

● Students should learn how to critically evaluate programs written by others.

● All courses involving calculations should make extensive use of the computer and the latest software. Such activity should be more frequent as students progress in the curriculum. Adequate computer hardware and software must be freely available to the student through superior centralized facilities and/or individual PC's. Development of professionally written software for chemical engineering should be encouraged.

2. Chemical Engineering Courses

Thermodynamics.

● The important concepts of the courses should be emphasized; software should be developed to implement the concepts in treating a wide variety of complex, yet interesting, problems in a reasonable time. The value of analysis of units and dimensions in checking problems should continue to be emphasized.

● Examples in thermodynamics should involve problems from a variety of industries so that the subject comes alive and its power in decision making is clearly emphasized.

Kinetics, Catalysis, and Reactor Design and Analysis.

● This course also needs a broad variety of real problems, not only design but also diagnostic and economic problems. Real problems involve real compounds and the chemistry related to them.

● Existing software for algebraic and differential equation solving make simulation and design calculation on many reactor systems quite straightforward.

● Shortcut estimating methods should be emphasized in addition to computer calculations.

● The increased production of specialties makes batch and semibatch reactor more important, and scale-up of laboratory studies is an important technique in the fast-moving specialties business.

Unit Operations

The unit operations were conceived as an organized means for discussing the many kinds of equipment-oriented physical processes required in the process industries. This approach continues to be valid. Over the years some portions have been given separate status such as transport phenomena and separations while some equipment and related principles have not been included in the required courses, as is the case with polymer processing, an area in which all chemical engineers should have some knowledge.

● Transport phenomena principles can be made more compelling by using problems from a wide range of industries that can be analyzed and solved using the principles taught.

● Some efficiency may be gained by teaching several principles and procedures for developing specifications and selection the large number of equipment items normally purchased off-the-shelf or as standard designs.

● A great deal of time can be saved in addressing designed equipment such as fractionators and absorbers be emphasizing rigorous computer calculations and the simplest shortcut procedures. Most intermediate calculation procedures and graphical methods should be eliminated unless they have real conceptual value.

Process Control.

● This course should emphasize control strategy and precise measurement in addition to theory.

● Some hands-on experience using current practices of computer control with industrial-type consoles should be encouraged.

● Computer simulation of processes for demonstration of control principles and techniques can be most valuable, but contact with actual control devices should not be ignored.

Chemical engineering laboratories.

● Creative problem solving should be emphasized.

● Reports should be written as briefly as possible; they should contain an executive summary with clearly drawn conclusions and brief observations and explanations with graphical rather than tabular representation of data. A great deal of such graphing can be done in the laboratory on computers with modern graphics capabilities. Detailed calculations should be included in an appendix.

● Some part of the laboratory should be structured to relate to product development.

Design/Economics.

● In the design course in engineering, students learn the techniques of complex problem solving and decision making within a framework of economic analysis. The very nature of processes requires a system approach; the ability to analyze a total system is one of the special attributes of chemical engineers that will continue to prove most sought after in a complex technological world.

● Because of the greater diversity of interests and job opportunities, some consideration should be given to providing a variety of short design problem of greatest personal interest.

● The design approach can be most valuable in diagnosing plant problems, and some practice in this interesting area should be provided.

● Rigorous economic analysis and predictive efforts should be required in all decision processes.

● Safety and environmental considerations should also be emphasized.

● Modern simulation tools should be made available to the students.

Other Engineering Courses.

The electrical engineering courses should emphasize application of microprocessors, lasers, sensing devices, and control systems as well as the traditional areas of circuits and motors. The course should provide insight into the principles on which each subject is based.

Remaining courses in engineering mechanics and engineering drawing should be considered for their relevance to current and future chemical engineering practice.

3. Other courses

Economics and Business Courses.

It is difficult to find a single course in economics or business departments that covers the various needs of engineers. The qualitative ability of engineers makes it possible to teach following topics in a single-semester course—in many cases in the Chemical Engineering Department: business economics, project economic analysis, economic theory, marketing and market studies, and national and global economics.

Humanities and Social Science Courses.

It is important to understand the origins of one's own culture as well as that of others.

Communication Course.

Since improved communication skills require continuous attention, the following requirements may be useful:

- Oral presentations in at least one course each year.
- Several literature surveys in the junior and senior years.
- Introduce computer-based communication systems.

Area of Specialization.

The elective areas should be generous in hours to maximize freedom of choice. Each department will have to consider its own and its total university resources and strengths as well as the quality and preparation of its students. The suggested areas are:

- Life sciences and applications
- Materials sciences and applications
- Catalysis and electrochemical science and applications
- Separations technology
- Computer applications technology
- Techniques of product development and marketing
- Polymer technology

Each of these areas should be strongly career-oriented. The interest in a given area will depend on opportunities perceived by the students.

Selected from "*Chemical Process Analysis*, by L.L. William, Prentice-Hall, 1988" & "CEP, V81, No10, 9-14"

Words and Expressions

1. mechanics [mi'kæniks] n. 力学，机械学

2. hydraulics [hai'drɔ:liks] n. 水力学；液压系统
3. stoichiometry [stɔiki'ɔmitri] n. 化学计算，化学计量，理想配比法
4. momentum [məu'mentəm] n. 动量，冲量
5. underlie [ʌndə'lai] v. 构成（作为）…的基础；位于…的下面
6. unify ['ju:nifai] vt. 统一，使一致，使成一体
7. proficiency [prə'fiʃənsi] n. 熟练，精通
8. software ['sɔftwεə] n. 软件，程序，程序计算方法；设计计算方法
9. thoroughness ['θʌrənis] n. 彻底性，充分性，完全性
10. hardware ['hɑ:dwεə] n. 硬件，硬设备，计算机
11. centralize ['sentrəlaiz] v. 集中，形成中心，由中心统一管理
12. diagnostic [daiəg'nɔstik] a. 诊断的，（有）特征的 n. 诊断，症状，特征
13. algebraic [ældʒi'breiik] a. 代数（学）的
14. differential [difə'renʃəl] a.; n. 微分（的），差分（的）；（有）差别（的）
15. straightforward [streit'fɔ:wəd] a. 直接了当的，简单明了的，易懂的
16. shortcut ['ʃɔ:tkʌt] n. 近路，捷径 v. 简化
17. orient ['ɔ:riənt] v. 定向，取向，定位；（使）适应
18. off-the-shelf a. 成品的，现成的
19. console ['kɔnsəul] n. 控制台，操纵台；托架，支柱
20. appendix [ə'pendiks] n. 附录，附言；附属（物），附加（物）
21. diagnose ['daiəgnəuz] v. 判断，诊断；确定，分析，识别，断定（…的原因）
22. sensing device 传感装置(器)，遥感装置
23. relevance ['relivəns] n. 关联，关系；适当，贴切，中肯
24. humanity [hju: 'mæniti] n. 人性，人类； the humanities 人文学科
25. maximize ['mæksimaiz] v. 使达到最大，使极大，极限化

Notes

① W. K. Lewis：Warren Kendall Lewis，1882~1975，美国化学工程界先驱者，被誉为化学工程之父, 1910 年后, 终身任教于麻省理工学院。

Unit 11 Chemical and Process Thermodynamics

After completing this unit, you should be able to:

1. Identify the application of thermodynamics.
2. Discuss the nature of thermodynamics.
3. State and describe briefly each of the three thermodynamic laws.
4. Explain the mechanisms of heat flow: conduction, convection and radiation.

Before committing a great deal of time and effort to the study of a subject, it is reasonable to ask the following two questions: what is it? What is it good for? Regarding thermodynamics, the second question is more easily answered, but an answer to the first is essential to an understanding of the subject. Although it is doubtful that many experts or scholars would agree on a simple and precise definition of thermodynamics, necessity demands that a definition be attempted. However, this is best accomplished after the applications of thermodynamics have been discussed.

1. Applications of Thermodynamics

There are two major applications of thermodynamics, both of which are important to chemical engineers:

(i) The calculation of heat and work effects associated with processes as well as the calculation of the maximum work obtainable from a process or the minimum work required to drive a process.

(ii) The establishment of relationships among the variables describing systems at equilibrium.

The first application is suggested by the name *thermodynamics*, which implies heat in motion. Most of these calculations can be made by the direct implementation of the first and second laws. Examples are calculating the work of compressing a gas, performing an energy balance on an entire process or a process unit, determining the minimum work of separating a mixture of ethanol and water, or evaluating the efficiency of an ammonia synthesis plant.

The application of thermodynamics to a particular system results in the definition of useful properties and the establishment of a network of relationships among the properties and other variables such as pressure, temperature, volume, and mol fraction. Actually, application 1 would not be possible unless a means existed for evaluating the necessary thermodynamic property changes required in implementing the first and second laws. The property changes are calculated from experimentally determined data via the established network of relationships. Additionally, the network of relationships among the variables of a system allows the calculation of values of variables which are either unknown or difficult to determine experimentally from variables which are either available or easier to measure. For example, the heat of vaporizing a liquid can be calculated from measurements of the vapor pressure at several temperatures and the densities of the liquid and vapor phases at several temperatures, and the maximum conversion obtainable in a chemical reaction at any temperature can be calculated from calorimetric measurements performed on the individual substances participating in the reaction.

2. The Nature of Thermodynamics.

The laws of thermodynamics have an empirical or experimental basis, and in the delineation of its applications the reliance upon experimental measurement stands out. Thus, thermodynamics might be broadly defined as a means of extending our experimentally gained knowledge of a system or as a framework for viewing and correlating the behavior of the system. To understand thermodynamic, it is essential to keep an experimental perspective, for if we do not have a physical appreciation for the system or phenomenon studied, the methods of thermodynamics will have little meaning. We should always ask the following questions: How is this particular variable measured? How, and form what type of data, is a particular property calculated?

Because of its experimental foundation, thermodynamics deals with macroscopic properties, or properties of matter in bulk, as opposed to microscopic properties which are assigned to the atoms and molecules constituting matter. Macroscopic properties are either directly measurable or calculable from directly measurable properties without recourse to a specific theory. Conversely, while microscopic properties are ultimately determined from experimental measurements, their authenticity depends on the validity of the particular theory applied to their calculation. Herein lies the power and authority of thermodynamics: Its results are independent of theories of matter and are thus respected and confidently accepted.

In addition to the certitude accorded its results, thermodynamics enjoys a broad range of applicability. Thus, it forms an integral part of the education of engineers and scientists in many disciplines. Nevertheless, this panoramic scope is often unappreciated because each discipline focuses only on the few applications specific to it. Actually, any system which can exist in observable and reproducible equilibrium states is amenable to the methods of thermodynamics. In addition to fluids, chemically reacting systems, and systems in phase equilibrium, which are of major interest to chemical engineers, thermodynamics has also been successfully applied to systems with surface effects, stressed solids, and substances subjected to gravitational, centrifugal, magnetic, and electric fields.

Through thermodynamics the potentials which define and determine equilibrium are identified and quantified. These potentials also determine the direction in which a system will move as well as the final state it will reach but offer no information concerning the time required to attain the final state. Thus, time is not a thermodynamic variable, and the study of rates is outside the bounds or thermodynamics except in the limit as the system nears equilibrium. Here rate expressions should be thermo-dynamically consistent.

The experiments and observations on which the laws of thermodynamics are based are neither grand nor sophisticated. Also, the laws themselves are stated in rather pedestrian language. Yet, from this apparently unimpressive beginning a grand structure has evolved which is a tribute to the inductive powers of the human mind. This never fails to inspire awe in the thoughtful and serious student and has led Lewis[①] and Randall to refer to thermodynamics as a cathedral of science. The metaphor is well chosen for in addition to technical accomplishment and structural integrity one also sees beauty and grandeur. It is no small wonder that the study of thermodynamics can be technically rewarding, intellectually stimulating, and, for some, a pleasurable experience.

3. The Thermodynamic Laws

The First Law. The first law of thermodynamics is simply a statement of the conservation of energy. As shown in Fig. 3-1, the sum of all the energy leaving a process must equal the sum of all the energy entering, in the steady state. The laws of conservation of mass and energy are followed implicitly by engineers designing and operating processes of all kinds. Unfortunately, taken by itself, the first law has led to much confusion when attempting to evaluate process efficiency. People talk of energy conservation being an important effort, but in fact, no effort is required to conserve energy—it is naturally conserved.

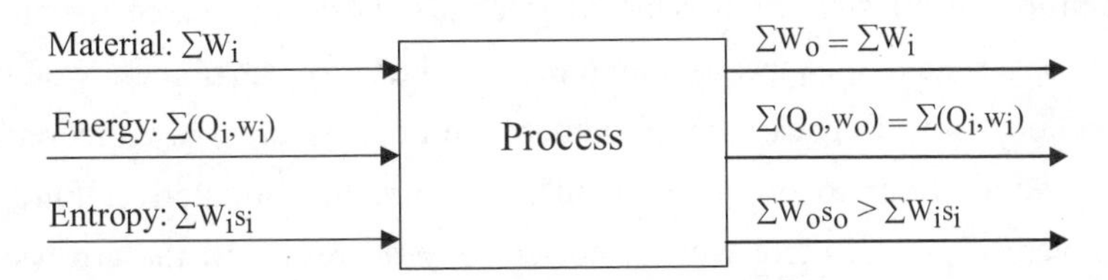

Fig.3-1 Mass and energy are naturally conserved but entropy is created in every process.

The conclusions which can be drawn from the first law are limited because it does not distinguish among the various energy forms. Shaft work introduced by a reflux pump will leave a column as heat to the condenser just as readily as will heat introduced at the reboiler. Some engineers have fallen into the trap of lumping all forms of energy together in attempting to determine process efficiency. This is obviously not justified—the various energy forms have different costs.

The Second Law. There are many different statements of the second law as applied to cycles in which heat is converted into work. At this point, a more general statement is desirable: The conversion of energy from one form to another always results in an overall loss in quality. Another is: All systems tend to approach equilibrium (disorder). These statements point out the difficulty in expressing the second law. It cannot really be done satisfactorily without defining another term describing quality or disorder.

That term is *entropy*. This property of state quantifies the level of disorder in a fluid, body, or system. Absolute zero entropy is defined as the state of a pure, crystalline solid at absolute zero temperature. Each molecule is surrounded by identical molecules in a perfectly ordered structure at rest. Motion, randomness, contamination, uncertainty, all add disorder and therefore contribute to entropy. Conversely, order is valuable, whether in the clarity of a gem stone, the purity of a chemical product, the cleanliness of a living space, or the freshness of air and water. Order commands a high price and can be created only by applying work. Most of our work is expended in creating or restoring order in the home, the workplace, and the environment. High entropy in the environment is one of the externalized costs of manufacturing.

The purpose of every productive process is to reduce entropy by separating mixtures into pure products, reducing uncertainty in our knowledge, or creating works of art from raw materials. In general, there is a progression of decreasing entropy from feedstocks to products. However, this is an uphill struggle inasmuch as the natural tendency is for entropy to increase as systems approach equilibrium.

The driving force for the decrease in entropy required of production is a concomitant increase in entropy by a greater amount in the rest of the universe. Generally speaking, this increase is sustained within the same plant and is therefore responsible for the decrease in product entropy. Whereas the entropy decrease resides in the conversion of feedstocks unto products, the greater increase is indicated by the conversion of fuels, electricity, air, and water, into combustion products, wastewater, and waste heat.

The bottom line of Fig. 3-1 describes the second law, just as the middle line describes the first law. The total entropy of all streams leaving a process must always exceed that of all streams entering. If the entropy were to balance, as do the mass and energy, the process would be *reversible*, i.e., it could function as well backward. Reversible processes are only theoretically possible, requiring dynamic equilibrium to exist continually-they are not productive. Furthermore, if the inequality were reversed, i.e., if there were a not entropy decrease, all the arrows would also be reversed and the process would be forced to run backward. In essence, it is the entropy rise that drives the process: It is the same driving force that makes water flow downhill, heat flow from hot to cold, vessels leak, glass break, metals corrode. In short, all things approach equilibrium with their surroundings.

The first law requires the conservation of energy and gives equal weight to all types of energy changes. While no process is immune to its authority, this law does not recognize the quality of energy nor does it explain why spontaneously occurring processes are never observed to spontaneously reverse themselves. The repeatedly confirmed observation that work may be completely converted into heat but that the reverse transformation never occurs quantitatively leads to the recognition that heat is a lower quality of energy. The second law with its origins deeply rooted in the study of the efficiency of heat engines recognizes the quality of energy. Through this law the existence of a heretofore unrecognized property, the entropy, is revealed, and it is shown that this property determines the direction of spontaneous change. The second law in no way diminishes the authority of the first law; rather it extends and reinforces the jurisdiction of thermodynamics.

The Third law. The third law of thermodynamics provides an absolute scale of values for entropy by stating that for changes involving only perfect crystalline solids at absolute zero, the changes of the total entropy is zero. This law enables absolute values to be stated for entropies.

Selected from "*Chemical and Process Thermodynamics*, B.G. Kyle, Prentice-Hall, Inc., 1984"

Words and Expressions

1. (be) good for 对…适用，有效，有利，有好处
2. delineation [dilini'eiʃən] n. 描述，叙述
3. macroscopic [mækrəu'skɔpic] a. 宏观的；肉眼可见的
4. microscopic [maikrəs'kɔpic] a. 微观的，微小的；显微镜的
5. authenticity [ɔ:θen'tisiti] n. 可靠性,真实性
6. validity [və'liditi] n. 有效，合法性；正确，确实
7. certitude ['sə:titju:d] n. 确实，必然性
8. panoramic [pænə'ræmik] a. 全景的，全貌的
9. amenable [ə'mi:nəbl] a. 服从的，适合于…的（to）
10. centrifugal [sen'trifjugəl] a. 离心力的，利用离心力的
11. potential [pə'tenʃəl] n. 势（能），位（能），电势（位，压）
12. pedestrian [pi'destriən] a. 普通的，平凡的 n. 非专业人员
13. unimpressive ['ʌnim'presiv] a. 给人印象不深的，平淡的，不令人信服的
14. inductive [in'dʌktiv] a. 引入的，导论的，诱导的，归纳的
15. awe [ɔ:] n.;v. （使）敬畏（畏惧）
16. cathedral [kə'θi:drəl] n.（一个教区内的）总教堂，大教堂
a.（像）大教堂的，权威的
17. metaphor ['metəfə] n. 隐喻，比喻
18. integrity [in'tegriti] n. 完整，完全，完善
19. grandeur ['grændʒə] n. 宏伟，壮观；伟大，崇高；富丽堂皇，豪华
20. implicitly ad. 含蓄地；无疑地，无保留地，绝对地
21. shaft [ʃɑ:ft] n. （传动，旋转）轴
22. reflux ['ri:flʌks] n. 回流，倒流
23. condenser [kən'densə] n. 冷凝器
24. reboiler n. 再沸器
25. entropy ['entrəpi] n. 熵
26. gem [dʒem] n. 宝石，玉，珍宝
27. externalize [eks'tə:nəlaiz] vt. 使客观化，使具体化，给…以外形
28. inasmuch as 因为，由于
29. concomitant [kən'kɔmitənt] a. 相伴的，伴随的
30. unto ['ʌntu] prep. [古][诗] 到，对；直到，到…为止
31. reversible [ri'və:səbl] a. 可逆的，双向的
32. immune [i'mju:n] a. 免除的，可避免的；不受影响的
33. spontaneous [spɔn'teinjəs] a. 自发的，自然的
34. heretofore ['hiətu'fɔ:] ad. 至今，到现在为止；在此以前
35. diminish [di'miniʃ] v. 减少，递减，削弱，由大变小

Notes

① Lewis：Gilbert Newton Lewis，1875~1946，美国物理化学家，提出了活度、逸度、离子强度等概念及共价键理论、广义酸碱理论等，1923 年与 M.Randall 合著《化学物质的热力学和自由能》一书。

Exercises

1. *Some words which are a part of our everyday vocabulary have a special or more restricted meaning in a thermodynamic context. Study following terminologies of thermodynamics.*

System	Any part of the universe we choose to study or analyze. It may be enclosed within real boundaries, or the boundaries may be imaginary.
State	The term refers to the condition in which the system exists. In thermodynamics this always means a state in which equilibrium obtains.
Surroundings	The remainder of the universe, when the system and its boundaries have been chosen.
Closed system	A system does not exchange mass with the surroundings. It may exchange heat and work with the surroundings and thereby undergo changes in energy and volume or experience other property changes, but its mass remains constant.
Open system	A system does exchange mass with its surroundings.
Isothermal	Any process occurring in a system takes place at constant temperature
Adiabatic system	When a process occurs in either an open or closed system without the exchange of heat with the surroundings, both the process and the system are termed.
Isolated system	A system which exchange neither mass, heat , nor work with the surroundings
State variables	The term refers to a variable whose value depends on the state in which the system exists. Between two states the change in a state variable is always the same regardless of which path the system travels. Temperature, pressure and volume are examples of state variables.
Path variables	Changes in path variables depend on the path traveled by the system. These variables have meaning only when applied to a process in which the path between two states is specified. Work and heat are path variables.
Extensive properties	One which depends on the size of the system. Extensive properties are also additive. Volume is an example of an extensive property.
Intensive properties	Properties which do not depend on the size of the system. Examples are temperature, pressure, and specific volume (or density).

2. *Put the following into Chinese:*

(be)good for	authenticity	centrifugal	potential
shaft	condenser	reboiler	diminish
buoyancy	agitator	simultaneously	magnitude

Btu	conductivity	heretofore	validity

3. *Put the following into English:*

焓	熵	宏观的	微观的
通量	湍流的	自发的	可逆的
传导	对流	扩散	绝热地
横截面	旋涡	无因次的	回流

Reading Material 11:

Heat Transfer

Practically all the operations that are carried out by the chemical engineer involve the production or absorption of energy in the form of heat. The laws governing the transfer of heat and the types of apparatus that have for their main object the control of heat flow are therefore of great importance.

1. Nature of Heat Flow

When two objects at different temperatures are brought into thermal contact, heat flows from the object at the higher temperature to that at the lower temperature. The net flow is always in the direction of the temperature decrease. The mechanisms by which the heat may flow are three: conduction, convection, and radiation.

Conduction. If a temperature gradient exists in a continuous substance, heat can flow unaccompanied by any observable motion of matter. Heat flow of this kind is called *conduction*. In metallic solids, thermal conduction results from the motion of unbound electrons, and there is close correspondence between thermal conductivity and electrical conductivity. In solids which are poor conductors of electricity, and in most liquids, thermal conduction results from the transport of momentum of individual molecules along the temperature gradient. In gases conduction occurs by the random motion of molecules, so that heat is "diffused" from hotter regions to colder ones. The most common example of conduction is heat flow in opaque solids, as in the brick wall of a furnace or the metal wall of a tube.

Convection. When a current of macroscopic particle of fluid crosses a specific surface, such as the boundary of a control volume, it carries with it a definite quantity of enthalpy. Such a flow of enthalpy is called a *convective flow of heat* or simply *convection*. Since convection is a macroscopic phenomenon, it can occur only when forces act on the particle or stream of fluid and maintain its motion against the forces of friction. Convection is closely associated with fluid mechanics. In fact, thermodynamically, convection is not considered as heat flow but as flux of enthalpy. The identification of convection with heat flow is a matter of convenience, because in practice it is difficult to separate convection from true conduction when both are lumped together under the name convection. Examples of convection are the transfer of enthalpy by the eddies of turbulent flow and by the current of warm air flowing across and away from an ordinary radiator.

Natural and forced convection. The forces used to create convection currents in fluids are of two types. If the currents are the result of buoyancy forces generated by differences in density and the differences in density are in turn caused by temperature gradients in the fluid mass, the action is called *natural convection*. The flow of air across a heated radiator is an example of natural convection. If the currents are set in motion by the action of a mechanical device such as a pump or agitator, the flow is independent of density gradients and is called *forced convection*. Heat flow to a fluid pumped through a heated pipe is an example of forced convection. The two kinds of force may be active simultaneously in the same fluid, and natural and forced convection then occur together.

Radiation. Radiation is a term given to the transfer of energy through space by electromagnetic waves. If radiation is passing through empty space, it is not transformed into heat or any other form of energy nor is it diverted from its path. If, however, matter appears in its path, the radiation will be transmitted, reflected, or absorbed. It is only the absorbed energy that appears as heat, and this transformation is quantitative. For example, fused quartz transmits practically all the radiation that strikes it: a polished opaque surface will absorb most of the radiation received by it and will transform such absorbed energy quantitatively into heat.

Monatomic and diatomic gases are transparent to thermal radiation, and it is quite common to find that heat is flowing through masses of such gases both by radiation and by conduction-convection. Examples are the loss of heat from a radiator or unlagged steam pipe to the ambient air of the room and heat transfer in furnaces and other high-temperature gas-heating equipment. The two mechanisms are mutually independent and occur in parallel, so that one type of heat flow can be controlled or varied independently of the other. Conduction-convection and radiation can be studied separately and their separate effects added together in cases where both are important. In very general terms radiation becomes important at high temperatures and is independent of the circumstances of the flow of the fluid. Conduction-convection is sensitive to flow conditions and is relatively unaffected by temperature level.

2. Rate of Heat Transfer

Heat flux. Heat-transfer calculations are based on the area of the heating surface and are expressed in Btu per hour per square foot (or watts per square meter) of surface through which the heat flows. The rate of heat transfer per unit area is called the *heat flux*. In many types of heat-transfer equipment the transfer surfaces are constructed from tubes or pipe. Heat fluxes may then be based either on the inside area or the outside area of the tubes. Although the choice is arbitrary, it must be clearly stated, because the numerical magnitude of the heat fluxes will not be the same for both.

Average temperature of fluid stream. When a fluid is being heated or cooled, the temperature will vary throughout the cross section of the stream. If the fluid is being heated, the temperature of the fluid is a maximum at the wall of the heating surface and decreases toward the center of the stream. If the fluid is being cooled, the temperature is a minimum at the wall and increases toward the center. Because of these temperature gradients throughout the cross section of the stream, it is necessary, for definiteness, to state what is meant by the temperature of the stream. It is agreed that it is the temperature that would be attained if the entire fluid stream flowing across the section in question were withdrawn and mixed adiabatically to a uniform temperature, The temperature so defined is called the *average* or *mixing-up stream temperature*.

3. Overall Heat-Transfer Coefficient

It is reasonable to expect the heat flux to be proportional to a driving force. In heat flow, the driving force is taken as $T_k - T_c$, where T_k is the average temperature of the hot fluid and T_c is that of the cold fluid. The quantity $T_k - T_c$ is the *overall local temperature difference* ΔT. It is clear that ΔT can vary considerably from point to point along the tube, and, therefore, since the heat flux is proportional to ΔT, the flux also varies with tube length. It is necessary to start with a differential equation, by focusing attention on a differential area *dA* through which a differential heat flow *dq* occurs under the driving force of a local value of ΔT. The local flux is then *dq/dA* and is related to the local value of ΔT by the equation

$$\frac{\mathrm{d}q}{\mathrm{d}A} = U\Delta T = U(T_k - T_c)$$

The quantity *U*, defined by equation above as a proportionality factor between d*q*/d*A* and ΔT, is called the *local overall heat-transfer coefficient*.

Dimensionless groups. The values of heat-transfer coefficients for the various types of films that are encountered in convective-heat transfer are obtained from experimental data. The limited amount of data that has been obtained can be extended by means of several dimensionless groups which relate various thermal and physical properties of fluids as well as flow rates or velocities. The various dimensionless groups are combined in equations, and the experimental data are analyzed to obtain the exponents for each group and the coefficients of proportionality.

The name of a person who is being honored or who proposed the particular relationship of physical properties is usually applied to the group. Bi, Nu, Pe, Re and St are several of the more common dimensionless group used for analyzing heat transfer and for obtaining heat-transfer coefficients.

Selected from "*Unit Operations of Chemical Engineering*, 4th edition, Warren L. McCabe, McGraw-Hill,Inc.,1985"

Words and Expressions

1. conduction [kən'dʌkʃən] n. 传导(性，率，系数)，导热(电)(性，率，系数)
2. unbound electron 自由电子
3. conductivity [kəndʌk'tiviti] n. 传导率，导热系数
4. diffuse [di'fju:z] v. 扩散，散布
5. opaque [əu'peik] a. 不透明的；不传导的；无光泽的
6. convection [kən'vekʃən] n. (热，电)对流，迁移
7. enthalpy [en'θælpi] n. 焓，热函，（单位质量的）热含量

8. flux [flʌks] n. 通量
9. eddy ['edi] n. (水，风，气等的)涡，旋涡
10. turbulent ['tə:bjulənt] a. 湍流的，紊流的；扰动的
11. radiator ['reidieitə] n. 辐射体，散热器，暖气装置
12. buoyancy ['bɔiənsi] n. 浮力，浮性
13. agitator ['ædʒiteitə] n. 搅拌器，搅拌装置
14. simultaneously ad. 同时地；同时发生地
15. divert [di'və:t] vt. 使转向，使变换方向，转移
16. fuse [fju:z] v. 熔融，熔化
17. quartz [kwɔ:z] n. 石英，水晶
18. transparent [træns'pɛərənt] a. 透明的，半透明的，某种辐射线可以透过的
19. unlagged a. 未保温的，未隔热的；未绝缘的，
20. Btu = British thermal unit 英热量单位 (＝252 卡)
21. numerical [nju: 'merikəl] a. 数（量，字，值）的，用数字表示的
22. magnitude ['mægnitju:d] n. （数）量级；大小
23. cross section （横）截面，剖面，断面
24. definiteness ['definitnis] n. 明确，确定，肯定
25. adiabatically [ædiə'bætikəli] ad. 绝热地
26. dimensionless [di'men ʃənlis] a. 无因次的，无量纲的
27. exponent [eks'pəunənt] n. 指数，幂(数)，阶

Unit 12 What Do We Mean by Transport Phenomena?

> *Before reading the text, try to answer the following questions:*
> 1. What are the three research areas of transport phenomena?
> 2. Why should engineers study transport phenomena?
> 3. Do you think that all problems can be solved by the methods of transport phenomena?
> 4. Can you describe briefly the famous Reynolds experiment?

Transport phenomena is the collective name given to the systematic and integrated study of three classical areas of engineering science: (i) energy or heat transport, (ii) mass transport or diffusion, and (iii) momentum transport or fluid dynamics. Of course, heat and mass transport occur frequently in fluids, and for this reason some engineering educators prefer to includes these processes in their treatment of fluid mechanios. Since transport phenomena also includes heat conduction and diffusion in solids, however, the subject is actually of wider scope than fluid mechanics. It is also distinguished from fluid mechanics in that the study of transport phenomena makes use of the similarities between the equations used to describe the processes of heat, mass, and momentum transport. These analogies, as they are usually called, can often be related to similarities in the physical mechanisms whereby the transport takes place. As a consequence, an understanding of one transport process can readily lead to an understanding of other processes. Moreover, if the differential equations and boundary conditions are the same, a solution need be obtained for only one of the processes since by changing the nomenclature that solution can be used to obtain the solution for any other transport process.

It must be emphasized, however, that while there are similarities between the transport processes, there are also important differences, especially between the transport of momentum (a vector) and that of heat or mass (scalars). Nevertheless, a systematic study of the similarities between the transport processes makes it easier to identify and understand the differences between them.

1. How We Approach the Subject

In order to demonstrate the analogies between the transport processes, we will study each of the process in parallel—instead of studying momentum transport first, then energy transport, and finally mass transport. Beside promoting understanding, there is another pedagogical reason for not using the serial approach that is used in other textbooks: of the three processes, the concepts and equations involved in the study of momentum transport are the most difficult for the beginner to understand and to use. Because it is impossible to cover heat and mass transport thoroughly without prior knowledge of momentum transport, one is forced under the serial approach to take up the most difficult subject (momentum transport) first. On the other hand, if the subjects are studied in parallel, momentum transport becomes more understandable by reference to the familiar subject of heat transport. Furthermore, the parallel treatment makes it possible to study the simpler concepts first and proceed later to more difficult and more abstract ideas. Initially we can emphasize the physical processes that are occurring rather than the mathematical procedures and representations. For example, we will study one-dimensional transport phenomena first because it can be treated without requiring vector notation and we can often use ordinary differential equations instead of partial differential equations, which are harder to solve. This procedure is also justified by the fact that many of the practical problems of transport phenomena can be solved by one-dimensional models.

2. Why Should Engineers Study Transport Phenomena?

Since the discipline of transport phenomena deals with certain laws of nature, some people classify it as a branch of engineering. For this reason the engineer, who is concerned with the economical design and operation of plants and equipment, quite properly should ask how transport phenomena will be of value in practice. There are two general types of answers to those questions. The first requires one to recognize that heat, mass, and momentum transport occur in many kinds of engineering equipment, e.g., heat exchangers, compressors, nuclear and chemical reactors, humidifiers, air coolers, driers, fractionaters, and absorbers. These transport processes are also involved in the human body as well as in the complex processes whereby pollutants react and diffuse in the atmosphere. It is important that engineers have an understanding of the physical laws governing these transport processes if they are to understand what is taking place in engineering equipment and to make wise decisions with regard to its economical operation.

The second answer is that engineers need to be able to use their understanding of natural laws to design process equipment in which these processes are occurring. To do so they must be able to predict rates of heat, mass, or momentum transport. For example, consider a simple heat exchanger, i.e., a pipe used to heat a fluid by maintaining its wall at a higher temperature than that of the fluid flowing through it. The rate at which heat passes from the wall of the pipe to the fluid depends upon a parameter called the heat-transfer coefficient, which in turn depends on pipe size, fluid flow rate, fluid properties, etc. Traditionally heat-transfter coefficients are obtained after expensive and time-consuming laboratory or pilot-plant measurements and are correlated through the use of dimensionless empirical equations. Empirical equations are equations that fit the data over a certain range; they are not based upon theory and cannot be used accurately outside the range for which the data have been taken.

The less expensive and usually more reliable approach used in transport phenomena is to predict the heat-transfer coefficient from equations based on the laws of nature. The predicted result would be obtained by a research engineer by solving some equations (often on a computer). A design engineer would then use the equation for the heat-transfer coefficient obtained by the research engineer.

Keep in mind that the job of designing the heat exchanger would be essentially the same no matter how the heat-transfer coefficients were originally obtained. For this reason, some courses in transport phenomena emphasize only the determination of the heat-transfer coefficient and leave the actual design procedure to a course in unit operations. It is of course a " practical" matter to be able to obtain the parameters, i.e., the heat-transfer coefficients that are used in design, and for that reason a transport phenomena course can be considered an engineering course as well as one in science.

In fact, there are some cases in which the design engineer might use the methods and equations of transport phenomena directly in the design of equipment. An example would be a tubular reactor, which might be illustrated as a pipe, e.g., the heat exchanger described earlier, with a homogeneous chemical reaction occurring in the fluid within. The fluid enters with a certain concentration of reactant and leaves the tube with a decreased concentration of reactant and an increased concentration of product.

If the reaction is exothermic, the reactor wall will usually be maintained at a low temperature in order to remove the heat generated by the chemical reaction. Therefore the temperature will decrease with radial position, i.e., with the distance from the centerline of the pipe. Then, since the reaction rate increases with temperature, it will be higher at the center, where the temperature is high, than at the wall, where the temperature is low. Accordingly, the products of the reaction will tend to accumulate at the centerline while the reactants accumulate near the wall of the reactor. Hence, concentration as well as temperature will vary both with radial position and with length. To design the reactor we would need to know, at any given length, the mean concentration of product. Since this mean concentration is obtained from the point values averaged over the cross section, we actually need to obtain the concentration at every point in the reactor, i.e., at every radial position and at every length. But to calculate the concentration at every point we need to know the reaction rate at every point, and to calculate the rate at every point we need to know both the temperature and the concentration at every point! Furthermore, to calculate the temperature we also need to know the rate and the velocity of the fluid at every point. We will not go into the equations involved, but obviously we have a complicated set of partial differential equations that must be solved by sophisticated procedures, usually on a computer. It should be apparent that we could not handle such a problem by the empirical design procedures used in unit operations courses for a heat exchanger. Instead the theory and mathematical procedures of transport phenomena are essential, unless one wishes to go to the expense and take the time to build pilot plants of increasing size and measure the conversion in each. Even then the final scale-up is precarious and uncertain.

Of course, not all problems today can be solved by the methods of transport phenomena. However, with the development of the computer, more and more problems are being solved by these methods. If engineering students are to have an education that is not become obsolete, they must be prepared, through an understanding of the methods of transport phenomena, to make use of the computations that will be made in the future. Because of its great potential as well as its current usefulness, a course in transport phenomena may ultimately prove to be the most practical and useful course on a student's undergraduate career.

Selected from "*Fundamentals of Transport Phenomena*, Ray W. Fahien, McGraw-Hill, 1983"

Words and Expressions

1. similarity [simi'læriti] n. 相似性，类似，相像
2. analogy [ə'nælədʒi] n. 类似，相似（性），类推
3. vector ['vektə] n. 矢量，向量
4. scalar ['skeilə] n. 标量，纯量
5. pedagogical [pedə'gɔdʒikəl] a. 教学法的，教师的
6. dimensional [di'menʃənl] a. …维的；因次的；维数的；尺寸的
7. humidifier n. 增湿器，湿润器
8. radial ['reidiəl] a. 径向的，（沿）半径的
9. precarious [pri'kεəriəs] a. 靠不住的，不安全的；不稳定的，不确定的

Exercises

1. *Completing the table below, by using your knowledge about the relationship of transport phenomena and unit operations.*

	Unit operations
Momentum transfer	
Heat transfer	
Mass transfer	

2. *Filling in the spaces in each sentence, by referring to the reading material of* ***"Fluid Flow Phenomena"*.**

(1) Studies have shown that the transition from laminar to turbulent flow in tubes is not only a function of velocity but also of [1]____________ and [2] ____________ of the fluid and the [3] ____________ .These variables are combined into the [4]_________ number, which is dimensionless.

(2) The type of flow occurring in a fluid in a channel is important in fluid dynamics problems. The first type of flow at low velocities where the layers of fluid seem to slide by one another without [5]______ or swirls be present is called [6]___________ and Newton's law of viscosity holds. The second type of flow at higher velocities where eddies are present giving the fluid a fluctuating nature is called [7]___________________.

(3) Since turbulent flow is important in many areas of engineering, the nature of turbulence has been extensively investigated. Measurements of the [8]_____________ of the eddies in turbulent flow have helped explain turbulence.

(4) In the boundary-layer region near solid, the fluid motion is greatly affected by this [9]___________. In the bulk of the fluid away from the boundary layer the flow can often be adequately described by the theory of [10]_________ with zero viscosity. However, in the thin boundary layer, [11]___________ is important. Since the region is thin, simplified solutions can be obtained for the boundary-layer region. [12]________ originally suggested this division of

the problem into two parts, which has been used extensively in [13] ______________ .

3. *Put the following into Chinese:*

dimensional	humidifier	nozzle	onset
conduit	adhere	finite	lateral
transition	shed light on	flask	viscous

4. *Put the following into English:*

矢量	标量	相似性	类似
剪应力	界面张力	脉动	临界速度
层流	湍流	势流	错流

Reading Material 12:

Fluid-Flow Phenomena

The behavior of a flowing fluid depends strongly on whether or not the fluid is under the influence of solid boundaries. In the region where the influence of the wall is small, the shear stress may be negligible and the fluid behavior may approach that of an ideal fluid, one which is incompressible and has zero viscosity. The flow of such an ideal fluid is called *potential flow* and is completely described by the principles of Newtonian mechanics and conservation of mass. Potential flow has two important characteristics: (i) neither circulations nor eddies can form within the stream, so that potential flow is also called irrotational flow, and (ii) friction cannot develop, so that there is no dissipation of mechanical energy into heat.

Potential flow can exist at distances not far from a solid boundary. A fundamental principle of fluid mechanics, originally stated by Prandtl in 1904, is that, except for fluids moving at low velocities or possessing high viscosities, the effect of the solid boundary on the flow is confined to a layer of the fluid immediately adjacent to the solid wall. This layer is called the *boundary layer*, and shear forces are confined to this part of the fluid. Outside the boundary layer, potential flow survives. Most technical flow processes are best studied by considering the fluid stream as two parts, the boundary layer and the remaining fluid. In some situations such as flow in a converging nozzle, the boundary layer may be neglected, and in others such as flow through pipes, the boundary layer fills the entire channel, and there is no potential flow.

Within the current of an incompressible fluid under the influence of solid boundaries, four important effects appear: (i) the coupling of velocity-gradient and shear-stress fields, (ii) the onset of turbulence, (iii) the formation and growth of boundary layers, and (iv) the separation of boundary layers from contact with the solid boundary.

The velocity field. When a stream of fluid is flowing in bulk past a solid wall, the fluid adheres to the solid at the actual interface between solid and fluid. The adhesion is a result of the force fields at the boundary, which are also responsible for the interfacial tension between solid and fluid. If, therefore, the wall is at rest in the reference frame chosen for the solid-fluid system, *the* *velocity of the fluid at the interface is zero*. Since at distances away from the solid the velocity is finite, there must be variations in velocity from point to point in the flowing stream. Therefore, the velocity at any point is a function of the space coordinates of that point, and a velocity field exists in the space occupied by the fluid. The velocity at a given location may also vary with time. When the velocity at each location is constant, the field is invariant with time and the flow is said to be steady.

One-dimensional flow. Velocity is a vector, and in general the velocity at a point has three components, one for each space coordinate. In many simple situations all velocity vectors in the field are parallel or practically so, and only one velocity component, which may be taken as a scalar, is required. This situation, which obviously is much simpler than the general vector field, is called *one-dimensional flow*; an example is flow through straight pipe.

Laminar flow. At low velocities fluids tend to flow without lateral mixing, and adjacent layers slide past one another like playing cards. There are neither cross-currents nor eddies. This regime is called laminar flow. At higher velocities turbulence appears and eddies form, which, as discussed later, lead to lateral mixing.

Tubulence It has long been known that a fluid can flow through a pipe or conduit in two different ways. At low flow rates the pressure drop in the fluid increases directly with the fluid velocity; at high rates it increases much more rapidly, roughly as the square of the velocity. The distinction between the two types of flow was first demonstrated in a classic experiment by Osborne Reynolds, reported in 1883. A horizontal glass tube was immersed in a glass-walled tank filled with water. A controlled flow of water could be drawn through the tube by opening a valve. The entrance to the tube was flared, and provision was made to introduce a fine filament of colored water from the overhead flask into the stream at the tube entrance. Reynolds found that, at low flow rates, the jet of colored water flowed intact along with the mainstream and no cross mixing occurred. The behavior of the color band showed clearly that the water was flowing in parallel straight lines and that the flow was laminar. When the flow rate was increased, a velocity, called the *critical velocity*, was reached at which the thread of color became wavy and gradually disappeared, as the dye spread uniformly throughout the entire cross section of the stream of water. This behavior of the colored water showed that the water no longer flowed in laminar motion but moved erratically in the form of crosscurrents and eddies. This type of motion is *turbulent flow*.

Reynolds number and transition from laminar to turbulent flow. Reynolds studied the conditions under which one type of flow changes into the other and found that the critical velocity, at which laminar flow changes into turbulent flow, depends on four quantities: the diameter of the tube, and the viscosity, density, and average linear velocity of the liquid. Furthermore, he found that these four factors can be combined into one group and that the change in kind of flow occurs at a definite value of the group. The grouping of variables so found was

$$Re^{❶} = \frac{D\overline{V}\rho}{\mu} = \frac{D\overline{V}}{\nu} \tag{1}$$

❶Re 原文写为 N_{Re}。

where D = diameter of tube

$\overline{V}$ = average velocity of liquid

μ = viscosity of liquid

ρ = density of liquid

ν = kinetic viscosity of liquid

The dimensionless group of variables defined by Eq. (1) is called the *Reynolds number Re*. It is one of the named dimensionless groups. Its magnitude is independent of the units used, provided the units are consistent.

Additional observations have shown that the transition from laminar to turbulent flow actually may occur over a wide range of Reynolds numbers. Laminar flow is always encountered at Reynolds numbers below 2,100 but it can persist up to Reynolds numbers of several thousand under special conditions of well-rounded tube entrance and very quiet liquid in the tank. Under ordinary conditions of flow, the flow is turbulent at Reynolds numbers above about 4,000. Between 2,100 and 4,000 a *transition region* is found, where the type of flow may be either laminar or turbulent, quite so and statistical analysis of the frequency distributions has proved to be useful in characterizing the turbulence.

Nature of turbulence. Because of its importance in many branches of engineering, turbulent flow has been extensively investigated in recent years, and a large literature has accumulated on this subject. Refined methods of measurement have been used to follow in detail the actual velocity fluctuations of the eddies during turbulent flow, and the results of such measurements have shed much qualitative and quantitative light on the nature of turbulence.

Turbulent flow consists of a mass of eddies of various sizes coexisting in the flowing stream. Large eddies are continually formed. They break down into smaller eddies, which in turn evolve still smaller ones. Finally, the smallest eddies disappear. At a given time, and in a given volume, a wide spectrum of eddy sizes exists. The size of the largest eddy is comparable with the smallest dimension of the turbulent stream; the diameter of the smallest eddies is about 1 mm. Smaller eddies than this are rapidly destroyed by viscous shear. Flow within an eddy is laminar. Since even the smallest eddies contain about 10^{16} molecules, all eddies are of macroscopic size, and turbulent flow is not a molecular phenomenon.

Any given eddy possesses a definite amount of mechanical energy, much like that of a small spinning top. The energy of the largest eddies is supplied by the potential energy of the bulk flow of the fluid. From an energy standpoint turbulence is a transfer process in which large eddies, formed from the bulk flow, pass energy of rotation along a continuous series of smaller eddies. Mechanical energy is not appreciably dissipated into heat during the breakup of large eddies into smaller and smaller ones, but such energy is not available for maintaining pressure or overcoming resistance to flow and is worthless for practical purposes. This mechanical energy is finally converted to heat when the smallest eddies are obliterated by viscous action.

Selected from "*Unit Operations of Chemical Engineering*, 4th edition, Warren L. McCabe, McGraw-Hill, Inc.,1985"

Words and Expressions

1. shear stress 剪应力
2. negligible ['neglidʒəbl] a. 可忽略的，不计的，很小的
3. potential flow 势流
4. irrotational [irəu'teiʃənl] a. 无旋的，不旋转的
5. dissipation [disi'peiʃən] n. 耗散，损耗，消散
6. boundary layer 边界层
7. converge [kən'və:dʒ] v. 会聚，汇合，[数]收敛
8. onset ['ɔnset] n. （有力的）开始，发动，
9. adhere [əd'hiə] v. 粘附（于），附着（于）；坚持；追随
10. finite ['fainait] a. 有限的，受限制的
11. tension ['tenʃən] n. 张力，弹力
12. laminar ['læminə] a. 层流的，层状的
13. lateral ['lætərəl] a. 横向的，水平的
14. cross-current n. 错流，正交流
15. conduit ['kɔndit] n. 导管，输送管，(大)管道
16. immerse [i'mə:s] vt. 浸（入，没），沉入；专心，埋头于，投入
17. flare [flεə] v. 端部张开，（向外）扩张（成喇叭形）
18. flask [flɑ:sk] n. 烧瓶，长颈瓶
19. filament ['filəmənt] n. （细）丝，（细）线；灯丝，游丝
20. mainstream ['meinstri:m] n. 干流，主流；主要倾向
21. critical velocity 临界速度
22. erratically ad. 不规律的，不稳定的
23. transition [træn'siʃən] n. 过渡（段），转变，变化
24. fluctuation [flʌktju'eiʃən] n. 脉动，波动，起伏，增减
25. shed light on 阐明，把…弄明白
26. viscous ['viskəs] a. 粘（性，滞，稠）的，
27. dissipate ['disipeit] v. 使耗散，消除，消耗
28. obliterate [ə'blitəreit] vt. 除去，删去，消除

Unit 13 Unit Operations in Chemical Engineering

Before reading this unit, try to answer the following questions:

1.Is chemical reaction involved in unit operations?

2.Who first presented the concept of unit operations clearly?

3.How many kinds of unit operations can you list?

4.Can you identify two major physical models: ideal contact and rate of transfer?

Chemical processes may consist of widely varying sequences of steps, the principles of which are independent of the material being operated upon and of other characteristics of the particular system. In the design of a process, each step to be used can be studied individually if the steps are recognized. Some of the steps are chemical reactions, whereas others are physical changes. The versatility of chemical engineering originates in training to the practice of breaking up a complex process into individual physical steps, called unit operations, and into the chemical reactions. The unit-operations concept in chemical engineering is based on the philosophy that the widely varying sequences of steps can be reduced to simple operations or reactions, which are identical in fundamentals regardless of the material being processed. This principle, which became obvious to the pioneers during the development of the American chemical industry, was first clearly presented by A. D. Little in 1915:

Any chemical process, on whatever scale conducted, may be resolved into a coordinated series of what may be termed "unit actions," as pulverizing, mixing, heating, roasting, absorbing, condensing, lixiviating, precipitating, crystallizing, filtering, dissolving, electrolyzing and so on. The number of these basic unit operations is not very large and relatively few of them are involved in any particular process. The complexity of chemical engineering results from the variety of conditions as to temperature, pressure, etc., under which the unit actions must be carried out in different processes and from the limitations as to materials of construction and design of apparatus imposed by the physical and chemical character of the reacting substances.

The original listing of the unit operations quoted above names twelve actions, not all of which are considered unit operations. Additional ones have been designated since then, at a modest rate over the years but recently at an accelerating rate. Fluid flow, heat transfer, distillation, humidification, gas absorption, sedimentation, classification, agitation, and centrifugation have long been recognized. In recent years increasing understanding of new techniques—and adaptation of old but seldom used separative techniques—has led to a continually increasing number of separations, processing operations, or steps in a manufacture that could be used without significant alteration in a variety of processes. This is the basis of a terminology of "unit operations," which now offers us a list of techniques.

1. Classification of Unit Operations

(1) *Fluid flow.* This concerns the principles that determine the flow or transportation of any fluid from one point to another.

(2) *Heat transfer.* This unit operation deals with the principles that govern accumulation and transfer of heat and energy from one place to another.

(3) *Evaporation.* This is a special case of heat transfer, which deals with the evaporation of a volatile solvent such as water from a nonvolatile solute such as salt or any other material in solution.

(4) *Drying.* In this operation volatile liquids, usually water, are removed from solid materials.

(5) *Distillation.* This is an operation whereby components of a liquid mixture are separated by boiling because of their differences in vapor pressure.

(6) *Absorption.* In this process a component is removed from a gas stream by treatment with a liquid.

(7) *Membrane separation.* This process involves the diffusion of a solute from a liquid or gas through a semipermeable membrane barrier to another fluid.

(8) *Liquid-liquid extraction.* In this case a solute in a liquid solution is removed by contacting with another liquid solvent which is relatively immiscible with the solution.

(9) *Liquid-solid leaching.* This involves treating a finely divided solid with a liquid that dissolves out and removes a solute contained in the solid.

(10) *Crystallization.* This concerns the removal of a solute such as a salt from a solution by precipitating the solute from the solution.

(11) *Mechanical physical separations.* These involve separation of solids, liquids, or gases by mechanical means, such as filtration, settling, and size reduction, which are often classified as separate unit operations.

Many of these unit operations have certain fundamental and basic principles or mechanisms in common. For example, the mechanism of diffusion or mass transfer occurs in drying, absorption, distillation, and crystallization. Heat transfer occurs in drying, distillation, evaporation, and so on.

2. Fundamental Concepts

Because the unit operations are a branch of engineering, they are based on both science and experience. Theory and practice must combine to yield designs for equipment that can be fabricated, assembled, operated, and maintained. The following four concepts are basic and form the foundation for the calculation of all operations.

The Material Balance

If matter may be neither created nor destroyed, the total mass for all materials entering an operation equals the total mass for all materials leaving that operation, except for any material that may be retained or accumulated in the operation. By the application of this principle, the yields of a chemical reaction or engineering operation are computed.

In continuous operations, material is usually not accumulated in the operation, and a material balance consists simply in charging (or debiting) the operation with all material entering and crediting the operation with all material leaving, in the same manner as used by any accountant. The result must be a balance.

As long as the reaction is chemical and does not destroy or create atoms, it is proper and frequently very convenient to employ atoms as the basis for the material balance. The material balance may be made for the entire plant or for any part of it as a unit, depending upon the problem at hand.

The Energy Balance

Similarly, an energy balance may be made around any plant or unit operation to determine the energy required to carry on the operation or to maintain the desired operating conditions. The principle is just as important as that of the material balance, and it is used in the same way. The important point to keep in mind is that all energy of all kinds must be included, although it may be converted to a single equivalent form.

The Ideal Contact (the equilibrium stage model)

Whenever the materials being processed are in contact for any length of time under specified conditions, such as conditions of temperature, pressure, chemical composition, or electrical potential they tend to approach a definite condition of equilibrium which is determined by the specified conditions. In many cases the rate of approach to these equilibrium conditions is so rapid or the length of time is sufficient that the equilibrium conditions are practically attained at each contact. Such a contact is known as an equilibrium or ideal contact. The calculation of the number of ideal contacts is an important step required in understanding those unit operations involving transfer of material from one phase to another, such as leaching, extraction, absorption, and dissolution.

Rates of an Operation (the rate of transfer model)

In most operations equilibrium is not attained either because of insufficient time or because it is not desired. As soon as equilibrium is attained no further change can take place and the process stops, but the engineer must keep the process going. For this reason rate operations, such as rate of energy transfer, rate of mass transfer, and rate of chemical reaction, are of the greatest importance and interest. In all such cases the rate and direction depend upon a difference in potential or driving force. The rate usually may be expressed as proportional to a potential drop divided by a resistance. An application of this principle to electrical energy is the familiar Ohm's law for steady or direct current.

In solving rate problems as in heat transfer or mass transfer with this simple concept, the major difficulty is the evaluation of the resistance term are generally computed from an empirical correlation of many determinations of transfer rates under different conditions.

The basic concept that rate depends directly upon a potential drop and inversely upon a resistance may be applied to any rate operation, although the rate may be expressed in different ways with particular coefficients for particular cases.

Selected from "*Transport Processes and Unit Operations*, 2nd Edition, Christie J. Geankoples, Allyn and Bacon, Inc. , 1983"

Words and Expressions

1. lixiviate [lik'sivieit] vt. 浸提(析，出)，溶滤
2. dissolve [di'zɔlv] v.;n. 使溶解，溶化
3. humidification [hju:midifi'keiʃən] n. 增湿作用，湿润
4. sedimentation [sedimen'teiʃən] n. 沉积，沉淀，沉降，淀积
5. semipermeable ['semi'pə:mjəbl] a. 半渗透性的
6. immiscible [i'misibl] a. 不混溶的，不互溶的
7. leaching ['li:tʃiŋ] n. 浸取,浸提
8. solute ['sɔlju:t] n. 溶质，溶解物
9. settling ['setliŋ] n. 沉降，沉淀
10. debit ['debit] vt.;n. （记入）借方
11. equilibrium stage 平衡级
12. dissolution [disə'lju:ʃən] n. 溶解，溶化
13. correlation [kɔri'leiʃən] n. 相关（性），（相互，对比）关系

Exercises

1. *Complete the summary of the text. Choose* ***No More Than Three Words*** *from the passage for each answer.*

In the chemical and other processing industries, many similarities exist in their physical processing. We can take these seemingly different [1]________ processes and break them down into a series of separate and distinct steps called [2]______________ and the fundamentals in a unit operation should be [3]_______. When [4]___________ first presented the concept, he listed twelve actions. Now some new techniques are emerging as unit operations in variety of processes.

In this passage, some major unit operations are classified according to their function and the phase or phases treated as: [5]____________ , heat transfer, evaporation, drying, distillation, absorption, [6]_________________, liquid-liquid extraction, leaching, [7]_____________, and mechanical physical separations which often include [8]___________, settling and size reduction.

A number of scientific principles and techniques are basic to the treatment of the unit operations. Some are elementary concepts such as the [9]_____________, energy balance, the ideal contact or [10]____________________, and rates of an operation or the rate-of-transfer model.

2. *Filling in the spaces in the figure of "solid-liquid separations" below, by referring to the reading materials* ***"Filtration"*** *and* ***"Centrifugal Separation"***.

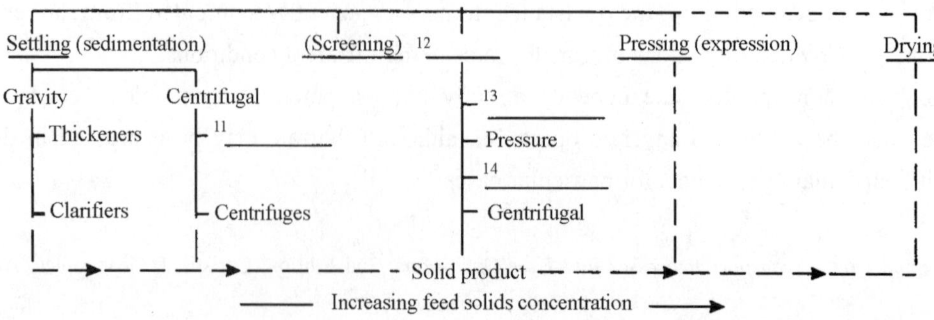

3. *Put the following into Chinese:*

lixiviation	filter aid	flammability	isotope
sedimentation	settling	correlation	funnel
baffle	agglomeration	configuration	tangentially
droplet	vortex	drag	holdup

4. *Put the following into English:*

溶解	溶液	溶质	溶剂
平衡级	不互溶的	浸取	过滤
提纯	板框压滤机	旋风分离器	逆流
板式塔	填料塔	孔板	液泛

Reading Material 13:

1. Filtration

The separation of solids from a suspension in a liquid by means of a porous medium or screen which retains the solids and allows the liquid to pass is termed filtration.

In general, the pores of the medium will be larger than the particles which are to be removed, and the filter will work efficiently only after an initial deposit has been trapped in the medium. In the chemical laboratory, filtration is often carried out in a form of Buchner funnel, and the liquid is sucked through the thin layer of particles using a source of vacuum: in even simpler cases the suspension is poured into a conical funnel fitted with a filter paper. In the industrial equivalent of such an operation, difficulties are involved in the mechanical handling of much larger quantities of suspension and solids. A thicker layer of solids has to form and, in order to achieve a high rate of passage of liquid through the solids, higher pressures will be needed, and it will be necessary to provide a far greater area.

The volumes of the suspensions to be handled will vary from the extremely large quantities involved in water purification and ore handling in the mining industry to relatively small quantities in the fine chemical industry where the variety of solids will be considerable. In most instances in the chemical industry it is the solids that are required and their physical size and properties are of paramount importance.

The most commonly used filter medium is woven cloth, but a great variety of other media is also used. Filter aids are often used to increase the rate of filtration of difficult slurries. They are either applied as a precoat to the filter cloth or added to the slurry, and deposited with the solids, assisting in the formation of a porous cake.

Industrial filters use vacuum, pressure, or centrifugal force to drive the liquid (filtrate) through the deposited cake of solids. Filtration is essentially a discontinuous process. With batch filters, such as plate and frame presses, the equipment has to be shut down to discharge the cake; and even with those filters designed for continuous operation, such as rotating-drum filters, periodic stoppages are necessary to change the filter cloths. Batch filters can be coupled to continuous plant by using several units in parallel, or by providing buffer storage capacity for the feed and product.

The principal factors to be considered when selecting filtration equipment are:

(i) The nature of the slurry and the cake formed.

(ii) The solids concentration in the feed.

(iii) The throughput required.

(iv) The nature and physical properties of the liquid: viscosity, flammability, toxicity, corrosiveness

(v) Whether cake washing is required.

(vi) The cake dryness required.

(vii) Whether contamination of the solid by a filter aid is acceptable.

(viii) Whether the valuable product is the solid or the liquid, or both.

The overriding factor will be the filtration characteristics of the slurry, whether it is fast filtering (low specific cake resistance) or slow filtering (high specific cake resistance). The filtration characteristics can be determined by laboratory or pilot plant tests.

The principle types of industrial scale filter used are: Nutsch (gravity and vacuum operation), plate and frame press (pressure operation), leaf filters (pressure and vacuum operation), rotary drum filters (usually vacuum operation), disc filters (pressure and vacuum operation), belt filters (vacuum operation), horizontal pan filters (vacuum operation), centrifugal filters.

2. Gas-Solids Separations (Gas Cleaning)

The primary need for gas-solid separation processes is for gas cleaning: the removal of dispersed finely divided solids (dust) and liquid mists from gas streams. Process gas streams must often be cleaned up to prevent contamination of catalysts or products, and to avoid damage to equipment, such as compressors. Also, effluent gas streams must be cleaned to comply with air-pollution regulations and for reasons of hygiene, to remove toxic and other hazardous materials.

There is also often a need for clean, filtered, air for process using air as a raw material, and where clean working atmospheres are needed: for instance, in the pharmaceutical and electronics industries.

Gas-cleaning equipment can be classified according to the mechanism employed to separate the particles: gravity settling, impingement, centrifugal force, filtering, washing and electrostatic precipitation.

Gravity settlers (settling chambers) Settling chambers are the simplest form of industrial gas-cleaning equipment, but have only a limited use; they are suitable for coarse dusts, particles larger than 50 μm. They are essentially long, horizontal, rectangular chambers; through which the gas flows. The solids settle under gravity and are removed from the bottom of the chamber.

Impingement separators Impingement separators employ baffles to achieve the separation. The gas stream flows easily round the baffles, whereas the solid particles, due to their higher momentum, tend to continue in their line of flight, strike the baffles and are collected. Impingement separators cause a higher pressure drop than settling chambers, but are capable of separating smaller particle sizes, 10~20 μm.

Centrifugal separators (cyclones) Cyclones are the principal type of gas-solids separator employing centrifugal force, and are widely used. They are basically simple constructions; can be made from a wide range of materials; and can be designed for high temperature and pressure operation. Cyclones are suitable for separating particles above about 5 μm diameter; smaller particles, down to about 0.5 μm, can be separated where agglomeration occurs.

The most commonly used design is the reverse-flow cyclone; other configurations are used for special purposes. In a reverse-flow cyclone the gas enters the top chamber tangentially and spirals down to the apex of the conical section; it then moves upward in a second, smaller diameter, spiral, and exits at the top through a central vertical pipe. The solids move radically to the walls, slide down the walls, and are collected at the bottom.

Filters. The filters used for gas cleaning separate the solid particles by a combination of impingement and filtration; the pore sizes in the filter media used are too large simply to filter out the particles. A typical example of this type of separator is the bag filter, which consists of a number of bags supported on a frame and housed in a large rectangular chamber. The deposited solids are removed by mechanically vibrating the bag, or by periodically reversing the gas flow.

Wet scrubbers (washing) In wet scrubbing the duct is removed by counter-current washing with a liquid, usually water, and the solids are removed as a slurry. Spray towers, and plate and packed columns are used, as well as a variety of proprietary designs. Venturi and orifice scrubbers are simple forms of wet scrubbers. The turbulence created by the venturi or orifice is used to atomize water sprays and promote contact between the liquid droplets and dust particles. The agglomerated particles of dust and liquid are then collected in a centrifugal separator, usually a cyclone.

Electrostatic precipitators Electrostatic precipitators are capable of collecting very fine particles, < 2 μm, at high efficiencies. However, their capital and operating costs are high, and electrostatic precipitation should only be considered in place of alternative processes, such as filtration, where the gases are hot or corrosive. Electrostatic precipitators are used extensively in the metallurgical, cement and electrical power industries. Their main application is probably in the removal of the fine fly ash formed in the combustion of pulverized coal in powerstation boilers. The basic principle of operation is simple. The gas is ionized in passing between a high-voltage electrode and an earthed (grounded) electrode; the dust particles become charged and are attracted to the earthed electrode. The precipitated dust is removed from the electrodes mechanically, usually by vibration, or by washing. Wires are normally used for the high-voltage electrode, and plates or tubes for the earthed electrode.

3. Centrifugal Separations

There is now a wide range of situations where centrifugal force is used in place of the gravitational force in order to effect separations. The resulting accelerations may be several thousand times that attributable to gravity. Some of the benefits include far greater rates of separation; the possibility of achieving separations which are either not practically feasible, or actually impossible, in the gravitational field; and a substantial reduction of the size of the equipment.

Centrifugal fields can be generated in two distinctly different ways:

(i) By introducing a fluid with a high tangential velocity into a cylindrical or conical vessel as in the *hydrocyclone* and in the *cyclone separator*. In this case, the flow pattern in the body of the separator approximates to a *free vortex* in which the tangential velocity varies *inversely* with the radius. Generally, the larger and heavier particles will collect and be removed near the walls of the separator, and the smaller and lighter particles will be taken off through an outlet near the axis of the vessel.

(ii) By the use of the *centrifuge*. In this case the fluid is introduced into some form of rotating bowl and is rapidly accelerated. Because the frictional drag within the fluid ensures that there is very little *rotational slip* or relative motion between fluid layers within the bowl, all the fluid tends to rotate at a constant angular velocity ω and a *forced vortex* is established. Under these conditions, the tangential velocity will be directly proportional to the radius at which the fluid is rotating.

Here, attention is focused on the operation of the centrifuge. Some of the areas where it is extensively used are as follows:

(i) For separating particles on the basis of their size or density. This is effectively using a centrifugal field to achieve a higher rate of sedimentation than could be achieved under gravity.

(ii) For separating immiscible liquids of different densities, which may be in the form of dispersions or even emulsions in the feed stream. This is the equivalent of a gravitational decantation process.

(iii) For filtration of a suspension. In this case centrifugal force replaces the force of gravity or the force attributable to an applied pressure difference across the filter.

(iv) For the drying of solids and, in particular, crystals. Liquid may be adhering to the surface of solid particles and may be trapped between groups of particles. Drainage may be slow in the gravitational field, especially if the liquid has a high viscosity. Furthermore, liquid is held in place by surface tension forces which must be exceeded before liquid can be freed. This is particularly important with fine particles. Thus, processes which are not possible in the gravitational field can be carried out in the centrifuge.

(v) For breaking down of emulsions and colloidal suspensions. A colloid or emulsion may be quite stable in the gravitational field where the dispersive forces, such as those due to Brownian motion, are large compared with the gravitational forces acting on the fine particles or droplets. In a centrifugal field which may be several thousand times more powerful, however, the dispersive forces are no longer sufficient to maintain the particles in suspension and separation is effected.

(vi) For the separation of gases. In the nuclear industry isotopes are separated in the gas centrifuge in which the accelerating forces are sufficiently great to overcome the dispersive effects of molecular motion. Because of the very small difference in density between isotopes and between compounds of different isotopes, fields of very high intensity are needed.

(vii) For mass transfer processes. Because far greater efficiencies and higher throughputs can be obtained before flooding occurs, centrifugal packed bed contactors are finding favor and are replacing ordinary packed columns in situation where compactness is important, or where it is desirable to reduce the holdup of materials undergoing processing because of their hazardous properties.

Selected from "*Chemical Engineering, Vol 2*, 4th Edition, R.K. Sinnott, Pergamon Press, 1992"

Words and Expressions

1. porous ['pɔ:rəs] a. 多孔的，疏松的；能渗透的
2. pore [pɔ:] n. 细(毛，微，气)孔，孔隙
3. filter ['filtə] n. （过）滤器(机，层，纸) v. 过滤
4. funnel ['fʌnl] n. 漏斗 a. 漏斗状的
5. conical ['kɔnikəl] a. （圆）锥形的
6. purification [pjuərifi'keiʃən] n. 净化，提纯
7. filter aid 助滤剂
8. slurry ['slə:ri] n. 稀浆，淤浆；悬浮液(体)
9. filtrate ['filtreit] v. 过滤，滤除
   ['filtrit] n. 滤液，滤过的水
10. plate and frame press 板框式压滤机
11. rotating-drum filter 转鼓式过滤机
12. flammability n. 易燃性，可燃性，燃烧性
13. toxicity [tɔk'sisiti] n. 毒性，毒力
14. overriding [əuvə'raidiŋ] a. 基本的，最主要的，占优势的
15. Nutsch ['nʌtʃ] n. （真空）吸滤机
16. leaf filter 叶滤机
17. disc filter 盘滤机
18. belt filter 带式过滤机
19. horizontal pan filter 卧式盘滤机
20. hygiene ['haidʒi:n] n. 卫生（学），保健学
21. comply [kəm'plai] vi. 同意，遵照，履行，根据（with）
22. toxic ['tɔksik] a. （有）毒的，毒性的 n. 毒药(物，剂)
23. gravity settling 重力沉降
24. impingement separator 撞击式分离器
25. impingement n. （气体等的）撞击；水捶
26. electrostatic [i'lektrəu'stætik] a. 静电的
27. coarse [kɔ:s] a. 粗的，大的
28. rectangular [rek'tæŋgjulə] a. 矩形的，长方形的
29. baffle ['bæfl] n. 挡板；折流板；缓冲板
30. cyclone ['saikləun] n. 旋风分离器，旋流器
31. agglomeration [əglɔmə'reiʃən] n. 附聚，凝聚，成团

32. reverse-flow cyclone　回流型旋风分离器
33. tangentially　ad. 成切线
34. spiral　['spaiərəl]　a. 螺旋（形）的，螺线的
35. apex　['eipeks]　n. 顶点，最高点，脊
36. bag filter　袋滤器
37. wet scrubber　湿洗器
38. counter current　逆流
39. spray tower　喷淋塔
40. plate tower　板式塔
41. packed tower　填充塔，填料塔
42. venturi scrubber　文丘里涤气器
43. venturi　[ven'tu:ri]　n. 文氏管
44. orifice scrubber　孔板涤气器
45. orifice　['ɔrifis]　n. 孔板；锐孔
46. droplet　['drɔplit]　n. 液滴，微滴，小滴
47. atomize　['ætəmaiz]　vt. 使雾化，喷雾
48. ionize　['aiənaiz]　vt. 使电离，离子化，游离（化）
49. electrode　[i'lektrəud]　n. 电极
50. earth　[ə:θ]　vt. 接地，通地
51. hydrocyclone　n. 水力旋流器
52. vortex　['vɔ:teks]　n. 旋涡；涡流（面），涡旋（体）
53. drag　[dræg]　n. 阻力，曳力
54. angular　['æŋgjulə]　a. 角的，角度的，有角的
55. decantation　[di:kæn'teiʃən]　n. 倾析（法），倾滤，滗析
56. Brownian motion　布朗运动
57. isotope　['aisəutəup]　n. 同位素
58. flooding　['flʌdiŋ]　液泛，溢流
59. compactness　n　致密（性），密集（性），紧凑
60. holdup　n. 滞留量，滞液量

Unit 14 Distillation

Before reading this unit, try to answer the following questions:

1.What does the distillation process primarily depend on?

2.How is the equilibrium stage concept used in the distillation design?

3.Can you list several kinds of plates and packings? What are their features?

4.When should we utilize batch distillation in stead of continuous one?

Separation operations achieve their objective by the creation of two or more coexisting zones which differ in temperature, pressure, composition, and/or phase state. Each molecular species in the mixture to be separated reacts in a unique way to differing environments offered by these zones. Consequently, as the system moves toward equilibrium, each establishes a different concentration in each zone, and this results in a separation between the species.

The separation operation called *distillation* utilizes vapor and liquid phases at essentially the same temperature and pressure for the coexisting zones. Various kinds of device such as *dumped* or *ordered packings* and *plates* or *trays* are used to bring the two phases into intimate contact. Trays are stacked one above the other and enclosed in a cylindrical shell to form a *column*. Packings are also generally contained in a cylindrical shell between hold-down and support plates.

1. Continuous Distillation

The *feed* material, which is to be separated into fractions, is introduced at one or more points along the column shell. Because of the difference in gravity between vapor and liquid phases, liquid runs down the column, cascading from tray to tray, while vapor flows up the column, contacting liquid at each tray.

Liquid reaching the bottom of the column is partially vaporized in a heated *reboiler* to provide *boil-up*, which is sent back up the column. The remainder of the bottom liquid is withdrawn as *bottoms*, or bottom product. Vapor reaching the top of the column is cooled and condensed to liquid in the *overhead condenser*. Part of this liquid is returned to the column as *reflux* to provide liquid overflow. The remainder of the overhead stream is withdrawn as *distillate*, or overhead product.

This overall flow pattern in a distillation column provides countercurrent contacting of vapor and liquid streams on all the trays through the column. Vapor and liquid phases on a given tray approach thermal, pressure, and composition equilibriums to an extent dependent upon the efficiency of the contacting tray.

The *lighter* (lower-boiling) components tend to concentrate in the vapor phase, while the *heavier* (higher-boiling) components tend toward the liquid phase. The result is a vapor phase that becomes richer in light components as it passes up the column and a liquid phase that becomes richer in heavy components as it cascades downward. The overall separation achieved between the distillate and the bottoms depends primarily on the *relative volatilities* of the components, the number of contacting trays, and the ratio of the liquid-phase flow rate to the vapor-phase flow rate.

If the feed is introduced at one point along the column shell, the column is divided into an upper section, which is often called the *rectifying* section, and a lower section, which is often referred to as the *stripping* section. These terms become rather indefinite in *multiple-feed columns* and columns from which a product *sidestream* is withdrawn somewhere along the column length in addition to the two end-product streams.

Equilibrium-Stage Concept Energy and mass-transfer processes in an actual distillation column are much too complicated to be readily modeled in any direct way. This difficulty is circumvented by the *equilibrium-stage model*, in which vapor and liquid streams leaving an equilibrium stage are in complete equilibrium with each other and thermodynamic relations can be used to determine the temperature of and relate the concentrations in the equilibrium streams at a given pressure. A hypothetical column composed of equilibrium stages (instead of actual contact trays) is designed to accomplish the separation specified for the actual column. The number of hypothetical equilibrium stages required is then converted to a number of actual trays by means of *tray efficiencies*, which describe the extent to which the performance of an actual contact tray duplicates the performance of an equilibrium stage.

Use of the equilibrium-stage concept separates the design of a distillation column into three major steps: (i) Thermodynamic data and methods needed to predict equilibrium-phase compositions are assembled. (ii) The number of equilibrium stages required to accomplish a specified separation, or the separation that will be accomplished in a given number of equilibrium stages, is calculated. (iii) The number of equilibrium stages is converted to an equivalent number of actual contact trays or height of packing, and the column diameter is determined.

All separation operations require energy input in the form of heat or work. In the conventional distillation operation, energy required to separate the species is added in the form of heat to the reboiler at the bottom of the column, where the temperature is highest. Also, heat is removed from a condenser at the top of the column, where the temperature is lowest. This frequently results in a large energy-input requirement and low overall thermodynamic efficiency. With recent dramatic increases in energy costs, complex distillation operations that offer higher thermodynamic efficiency and lower energy-input requirements are being explored.

Related Separation Operations The simple and complex distillation operations just described all have two things in common: (i) both rectifying and stripping sections are provided so that a separation can be achieved between two components that are adjacent in volatility; and (ii) the separation is effected only by the addition and removal of energy and not by the addition of any mass separating agent (MSA) such as in liquid-liquid extraction. Sometimes, alternative single- or multiple-stage vapor-liquid separation operations, of the types shown in Fig. 3-2, may be more suitable than distillation for the specified task.

2. Batch Distillation

Batch distillation, which is the process of separating a specific quantity (the charge) of a liquid mixture into products, is used extensively in the laboratory and in small production units that may have to serve for many mixtures. When there are N components in the feed, one batch column will suffice where $N-1$ simple continuous-distillation columns would be required.

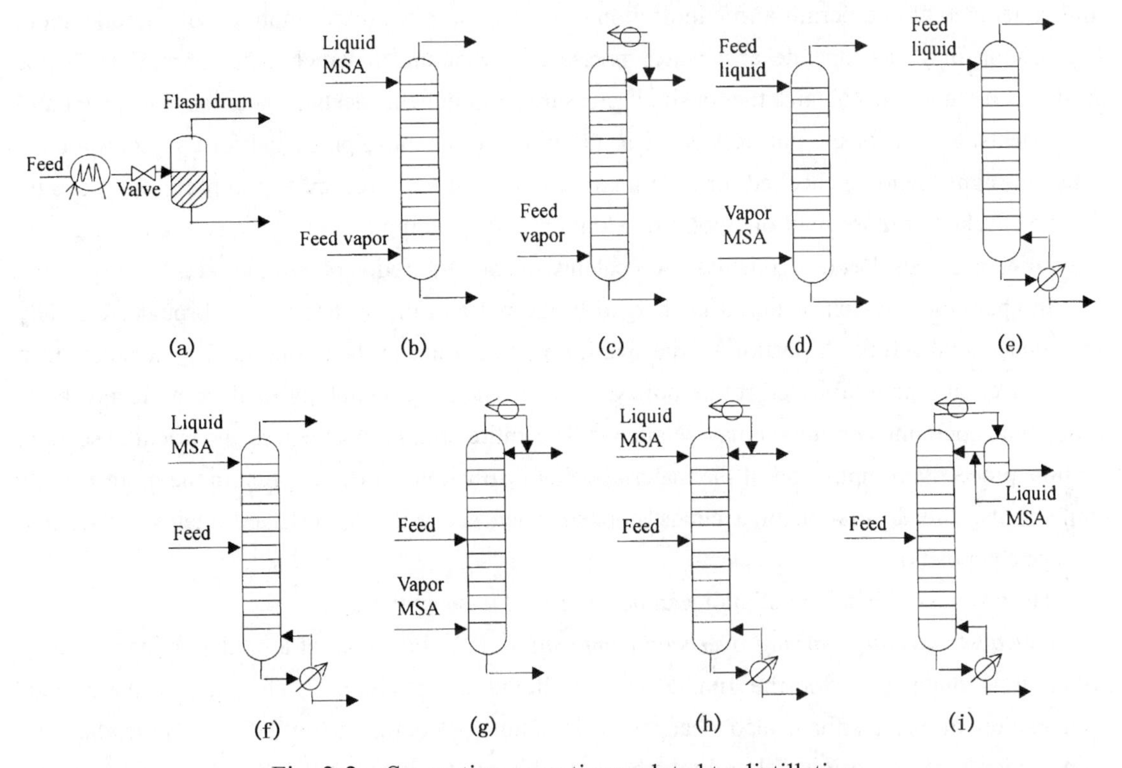

Fig. 3-2 Separation operations related to distillation

(a) Flash vaporization or partial condensation; (b) Absorption; (c) Rectifier; (d) Stripping; (e) Reboiled stripping; (f) Reboiled absorption; (g) Refluxed stripping; (h) Extractive distillation; (i) Azotropic distillation

Many larger installations also feature a batch still. Material to be separated may be high in solids content, or it might contain tars or resins that would plug or foul a continuous unit. Use of a batch unit can keep solids separated and permit convenient removal at the termination of the process.

Simple Batch Distillation The simplest form of batch still consists of a heated vessel (pot or boiler), a condenser, and one or more receiving tanks. No trays or packing are provided. Feed is charged into the vessel and brought to boiling. Vapors are condensed and collected in a receiver. No reflux is returned. The rate of vaporization is sometimes controlled to prevent "bumping" the charge and to avoid overloading the condenser, but other controls are minimal. This process is often referred to as Rayleigh distillation.

The simple batch still provides only one theoretical plate of separation. Its use is usually restricted to preliminary work in which products will be held for additional separation at a later time, when most of the volatile component must be removed from the batch before it is processed further, or for similar noncritical separations.

Batch Distillation with Rectification To obtain products with a narrow composition range, a rectifying batch still is used that consists of a pot (or reboiler), a rectifying column, a condenser, some means of splitting off a portion of the condensed vapor (distillate) as reflux, and one or more receivers. Temperature of the distillate is controlled in order to return the reflux at or near the column temperature to permit a true indication of reflux quantity and to improve column operation. The column may also operate at elevated pressure or vacuum, in which case appropriate device must be included to obtain the desired pressure. Equipment design methods for batch-still components, except for the pot, follow the same principles as those presented for continuous units, but the design should be checked for each mixture if several mixtures are to be processed. It should also be checked at more than one point of a mixture, since composition in the column changes as distillation proceeds. Pot design is based on batch size and required vaporization rate.

In operation, a batch of liquid is charged to the pot and the system is first brought to steady state under total reflux. A portion of the overhead condensate is then continuously withdrawn in accordance with the established reflux policy. Cuts are made by switching to alternate receivers, at which time operating conditions may be altered. The entire column operates as an enriching section. As time proceeds, composition of the material being distilled becomes less rich in the more volatile components, and distillation of a cut is stopped when accumulated distillate attains the desired average composition.

The progress of batch distillation can be controlled in several ways:

(i) *Constant reflux, varying overhead composition.* Reflux is set at a predetermined value at which it is maintained for the run. Since pot liquid composition is changing, instantaneous composition of the distillate also changes. Distillation is continued until the average distillate composition is at the desired value. In the case of a binary, the overhead is then diverted to another receiver, and an intermediate cut is withdrawn until the remaining pot liquor meets the required specification. The intermediate cut is usually added to the next batch. For a multicomponent mixture, two or more intermediate cuts may be taken between product cuts.

(ii) *Constant overhead composition, varying reflux.* If it is desired to maintain a constant overhead composition in the case of a binary, the amount of reflux returned to the columns must be constantly increased throughout the run. As time proceeds, the pot is gradually depleted of the lighter component. Finally, a point is reached at which the reflux ratio has attained a very high value. The receivers are then changed, the reflux is reduced, and an intermediate cut is taken as before. This technique can also be extended to a multicomponent mixture.

(iii) *Other control methods.* A cycling procedure can be used to set the pattern for column operation. The unit operates at total reflux until equilibrium is established. Distillate is then taken as total draw-off for a short period of time, after which the column is again returned to total-reflux operation. This cycle is repeated through the course of distillation. Another possibility is to optimize the reflux ratio in order to achieve the desired separation in a minimum of time. Complex operations may involve withdrawal of sidestreams, provision for intercondensers, addition of feeds to trays, and periodic charge addition to the pot.

Selected from "*Chemical Process Equipment*, Stanley M. Walas, Butterworth Publishers, 1988"

Words and Expressions

1. dumped packing　乱堆填料
2. ordered packing　整砌填料，规整填料
3. hold-down　n. 压具(板，块)，压紧（装置），固定
4. feed　[fi:d]　n. 进料，加料；加工原料
5. cascade　[kæs'keid]　v.;n. 梯流，阶流式布置；级联，串级
6. boil-up　蒸出（蒸汽）
7. bottom　['bɔtəm]　n. (pl.) 底部沉积物，残留物，残渣
8. relative volatility　相对挥发度（性）
9. rectify　['rektifai]　vt. 精馏，精炼，蒸馏
10. rectifying section　精馏段
11. stripping　['stripiŋ]　n. 洗提，汽提，解吸
12. stripping section　提馏段
13. multiple-feed　多口进料
14. sidestream　n. 侧线馏分，塔侧抽出物
15. circumvent　[sə:kəm'vent]　vt. 绕过，回避，胜过
16. hypothetical　[ˌhaipə'θetikəl]　a. 假定(设，说)的，有前提的
17. duplicate　['dju:plikeit]　vt. 重复，加倍，复制
18. mass separating agent　质量分离剂
19. flash drum　闪蒸槽
20. rectifier　['rektifaiə]　n. 精馏器(塔)；整流器
21. bump　[bʌmp]　v. 扰动，暴沸；冲击，造成凹凸
22. condensate　[kən'denseit]　n. 冷凝物，冷凝液　v. 冷凝，凝结
23. binary　['bainəri]　a.;n. 二，二元的
24. deplete　[di'pli:t]　vt. 放空，耗尽，使枯竭；贫化，减少

Exercises

1. *Completing the summary of the text. Choose **No More Than Three Words** from the text for each answer.*

The separation of liquid mixtures by distillation depends upon the [1]______________ of the components, the number of [2]______________, and the ratio of the liquid-phase flow rate to the vapor-phase flow rate.

The basic equipment required for continuous distillation consists of a still or [3]________, a column and [4] ___________________. Part of the condensate from the condenser is returned to the top of the column as [5]__________ and part of the liquid from the base of the column is vaporized in the reboiler and returned to provide the vapor flow. Vapor flows up the column and liquid counter-currently drown the column. The vapor and liquid are brought into contact on [6]_______, or [7]________. The section below the feed is often called the [8] ______________, while the section above the feed is known as the enriching or [9]________________. Distillation employs heat to generate vapors and cooling to effect partial or total condensation as needed, which usually results in a large [10]________________ and low [11]________________________.

With equilibrium-phase compositions, the number of equilibrium stage can be calculated and actual contact trays or height of packing can be converted by considering the [12]__________________.

[13]______________ should be considered when the quantity to be distilled is small; when it is produced at irregular intervals; or when a range of products has to be produced. In batch distillation the [14]______________ changes as distillation proceeded. To get products with a narrow composition range [15]__________________ still is used and the progress of batch distillation can be controlled in several ways.

2. *Completing the following table by referring to the passage of* ***"Selection of Plate Type"*** *in the reading material of* ***"Plate Columns and Packed Columns".***

	Sieve plate	*Bubble-cap plates*	*Valve plates*
Cost			
Capacity			
Operating range			
Efficiency	same	same	same
Pressure drop			

3. *Put the following into Chinese:*

dumped packing	ordered packing	sidestream	mass separating agent
flash	perforate	mild steel	manway
offset	bump	riser	foam

4. *Put the following into English:*

相对挥发度	精馏段	提馏段	空隙率
二元的	进料	级联	假设
降液管	溢流堰	筛板塔	极限负荷比
等板高度	传质单元高度	冷凝液	底部残留物

Reading Material 14:

Plate Columns and Packed Columns

1. Plate Columns

Cross-flow plates are the most common type of plate contactor used in distillation and absorption columns. In a cross-flow plate the liquid flows across the plate and the vapor up though the plate. The flowing liquid is transferred from plate to plate through vertical channels called "downcomers". A pool of liquid is retained on the plate by an outlet weir.

Other types of plate are used which have no downcomers (non-cross-flow plates), the liquid showering down the column through large openings in the plates (sometimes called shower plates). These, and, other proprietary non-cross-flow plates, are used for special purposes, particularly when a low-pressure drop is required.

Three principal types of cross-flow tray are used, classified according to the method used to contact the vapor and liquid.

(i) *Sieve plate* (*perforated plate*). This is the simplest type of cross-flow plate. The vapor passes up through perforations in the plate; and the liquid is retained on the plate by the vapor flow. There is no positive vapor liquid seal. And at low flow-rates liquid will "weep" through the holes, reducing the plate efficiency. The perforations are usually small holes, but larger holes and slots are used. These are much simpler in construction, with small holes in the tray. The liquid flows across the tray and down the segmental downcomer.

(ii) *The bubble-cap plates*. In which the vapor passes up through short pipes, called risers, covered by a cap with a serrated edge, or slots. The bubble-cap plate is the traditional, oldest, type of cross-flow plate, and many different designs have been developed. Standard cap designs would now be specified for most applications.

The most significant feature of the bubble-cap plate is that the use of risers ensures that a level of liquid is maintained on the tray at all vapor flow-rates.

(iii) *Valve plates* (*floating cap plates*). Valve plates are proprietary designs, they are essentially sieve plates with large-diameter holes covered by movable flaps, which lift as the vapor flow increases. As the area for vapor flow varies with the flow-rate, valve plates can operate efficiently at lower flow-rates than sieve plates: the valves closing at low vapor rates. Some very elaborate valve designs have been developed, but the simple type is satisfactory for most applications.

Selection of Plate Type

The principal factors to consider when comparing the performance of bubble-cap, sieve and valve plates are: cost, capacity, operating range, efficiency and pressure drop.

Cost. Bubble-cap plates are appreciably more expensive than sieve or valve plates. The relative cost will depend on the material of construction used; for mild steel the ratios, bubble-cap ∶ valve ∶ sieve, are approximately 3.0 ∶ 1.5 ∶ 1.0.

Capacity. There is little difference in the capacity rating of the three types (the diameter of the column required for a given flow-rate); the ranking is sieve, valve, bubble-cap.

Operating range. This is the most significant factor. By operating range is meant the range of vapor and liquid rates over which the plate will operate satisfactorily (the stable operating range). Some flexibility will always be required in an operating plant to allow for changes in introduction rate, and to cover start-up and shut-down conditions. The ratio of the highest to the lowest flow rates is often referred to as the "turn-down" ratio. Bubble-cap plates have a positive liquid seal and can therefore operate efficiently at very low vapor rates.

Sieve plates rely on the flow of vapor through the holes to hold the liquid on the plate, and cannot operate at very low vapor rates. But, with good design, sieve plates can be designed to give a satisfactory operating range; typically, from 50 per cent to 120 per cent of design capacity. Valve plates are intended to give greater flexibility than sieve plates at a lower cost than bubble-caps.

Efficiency. The Murphree efficiency of the three types of plate will be virtually the same when operating over their design flow range, and no real distinction can be made between them.

Pressure drop. The pressure drop over the plates can be an important design consideration, particularly for vacuum columns. The plate pressure drop will depend on the detailed design of the plate but, in general, sieve plates give the lowest pressure drop, followed by valves, with bubble-caps giving the highest.

Summary. Sieve plates are the cheapest and are satisfactory for most applications. Valve plates should be considered if the specified turn-down ratio cannot be met with sieve plates. Bubble-caps should only be used where very low vapor (gas) rates have to be handled and a positive liquid seal is essential at all flow-rates.

In considering the design of a column for a given separation, the number of stages required and the flowrates of the liquid and vapor streams must first be determined. In the mechanical design of the column, tower diameter, tray spacing, and the detailed layout of each tray will be investigated. In the first place, a diameter is established, based on the criterion of absence from liquid entrainment in the vapor stream, and then the weirs and the downcomers are designed to handle the required liquid flow. It is then possible to consider the tray geometry in more detail, and finally, to examine the general operating conditions for the tray and to establish its optimum range of operation.

2. Packed Columns

Distillation-type separation operations may be conducted in packed rather than tray-type columns. In prior years, except for small columns, plate columns were heavily favored over packed columns. However, development of more efficient packing materials and the need to increase capacity or reduce pressure drop in many applications has resulted in more extensive use of packed columns in larger sizes in recent years. Packed columns may employ dumped (random) packing, e.g., pall rings, or ordered (arranged or stacked) packing, e.g., wire web. Tray-type columns generally employ valve, sieve, or bubble-cap trays with downcomers. The choice between a packed column and a tray-type column is based mainly on economics when factors of contacting efficiency, loadability, and pressure drop must be considered.

Choice of Plates or Packing

The choice between a plate or packed column for a particular application can only be made with complete assurance by costing each design. However, this will not always be worthwhile, or necessary, and the choice can usually be made, on the basis of experience by considering main advantages and disadvantages of each type; which are listed below:

(i) Plate columns can be designed to handle a wider range of liquid and gas flow-rates than packed columns.

(ii) Packed columns are not suitable for very low liquid rates.

(iii) The efficiency of a plate can be predicted with more certainty than the equivalent term for packing (HETP or HTU).

(iv) Plate columns can be designed with more assurance than packed columns. There is always some doubt that good liquid distribution can be maintained throughout a packed column under all operating conditions, particularly in large columns.

(v) It is easier to make provision for cooling in a plate column; coils can be installed on the plates.

(vi) It is easier to make provision for the withdrawal of side-streams from plate columns.

(vii) If the liquid causes fouling, or contains solids, it is easier to make provision for cleaning in a plate column; manways can be installed on the plates. With small-diameter columns it may be cheaper to use packing and replace the packing when it becomes fouled.

(viii) For corrosive liquids a packed column will usually be cheaper than the equivalent plate column.

(ix) The liquid hold-up is appreciably lower in a packed column than a plate column. This can be important when the inventory of toxic or flammable liquids needs to be kept as small as possible for safety reasons.

(x) Packed columns are more suitable for handling foaming systems.

(xi) The pressure drop per equilibrium stage (HETP) can be lower for packing than plates; and packing should be considered for vacuum columns.

(xii) Packing should always be considered for small diameter columns, say less than 0.6 m, where plates would be difficult to install, and expensive.

Packed-Column Design Procedures

The design of a packed column will involve the following steps:

(i) Select the type and size of packing.

(ii) Determine the column height required for the specified separation.

(iii) Determine the column diameter (capacity), to handle the liquid and vapor flow rates.

(iv) Select and design the column internal features: packing support, liquid distributor, redistributors.

Types of Packing

Many diverse types and shapes of packing have been developed to satisfy these requirements. They can be divided into two broad classes:

(i) Packings with a regular geometry: such as stacked rings, grids and proprietary structured packings.

(ii) Random packings: rings, saddles and proprietary shapes, which are dumped into the column and take up a random arrangement.

Grids have an open structure and are used for high gas rates, where low pressure drop is essential; for example, in cooling towers. Random packings and structured packing elements are more commonly used in the process industries.

Random packing. Raschig rings are one of the oldest specially manufactured types of random packing, and are still in general use. Pall rings are essentially Raschig rings in which openings have been made by folding strips of the surface into the ring. This increases the free area and improves the liquid distribution characteristics. Berl saddles were developed to give improved liquid distribution compared to Raschig rings. Intalox saddles can be considered to be an improved type of Berl saddle; their shape makes them easier to manufacture than Berl saddles.

Ring and saddle packings are available in a variety of materials: ceramics, metals, plastics and carbon. Metal and plastics (polypropylene) rings are more efficient than ceramic rings, as it is possible to make the walls thinner.

Raschig rings are cheaper per unit volume than Pall rings or saddles but are less efficient, and the total cost of the column will usually be higher if Raschig rings are specified. For new columns, the choice will normally be between Pall rings and Berl or Intalox saddles.

The choice of material will depend on the nature of the fluids and the operating temperature. Ceramic packing will be the first choice for corrosive liquids; but ceramics are unsuitable for use with strong alkalies. Plastic packings are attacked by some organic solvents, and can only be used up to moderate temperatures; so are unsuitable for distillation columns. Where the column operation is likely to be unstable metal rings should be specified, as ceramic packing is easily broken.

Structured packing. The term structured packing refers to packing elements made up from wire mesh or perforated metal sheets. The material is folded and arranged with a regular geometry, to give a high surface area with a high void fraction.

Structured packings are produced by a number of manufacturers. The basic construction and performance of the various proprietary types available are similar. The advantage of structured packings over random packing is their low HETP (typically less than 0.5 m) and low pressure drop (around 100 Pa/m). They are being increasingly used in the following applications :

(i) For difficult separations, requiring many stages: such as the separation of isotopes.

(ii) High vacuum distillation.

(iii) For column revamps: to increase capacity and reduce reflux ratio requirements.

The cost of structured packings per cubic meter will be significantly higher than that of random packings, but this is offset by their higher efficiency.

Selected from "*Chemical Process Equipment*, Stanley M. Walas, Butterworth Publishers, 1988"

Words and Expressions

1. cross-flow 错流，交叉流动，横向流动
2. downcomer n. 降液管
3. weir [wiə] n. 堰，溢流堰
4. shower plate 喷淋塔（板）
5. sieve [siv] n. 筛，筛子；滤网
6. sieve plate 筛板（塔）
7. perforate ['pə:fəreit] v. 打孔，穿孔
8. slot [slɔt] n. 长（方形）孔，狭槽，缝隙
9. riser ['raizə] n. 立（式）管（道），升气管

10. serrate [se'reit] vt. 使成锯齿形
11. valve plate 浮阀塔（板）
12. flap [flæp] n. 活盖，活板，簧片，阀门
13. mild steel 低碳钢，软钢
14. turn-down ratio 极限负荷比，操作弹性
15. entrainment n. 挟带；雾沫
16. Pall ring 鲍尔环，带孔环形填料
17.wire web 金属丝网，网体填料
18. HETP ＝ height equivalent to a theoretical plate 等板高度，理论塔板的当量高度
19. HTU = height of a transfer unit 传质单元高度
20. manway n. 人孔
21. foam [foum] v. （使）起泡沫，变泡沫 n. 泡沫
22. grid [grid] n. 栅格
23. structured packing 结构填料
24. Raschig ring 拉西环
25. Berl saddle 弧鞍形填料，贝尔鞍形填料
26. Intalox saddle 矩鞍形填料，英特洛克斯鞍形填料
27. mesh [meʃ] n. 网，筛
28. void fraction 空隙率
29. revamp ['ri:'væmp] vt. 改进，整形
30. offset ['ɔfset] n. vt. 补偿，弥补，抵销

Unit 15 Solvent Extraction,Leaching and Adsorption

After completing this unit, you should be able to:

1.Identify the features and industrial applications of solvent extractors.

2.Outline the main steps in leaching process.

3.Describe briefly the adsorption and ion exchange processes.

4.Discuss the increasing importance of chromatographic and membrane separation processes.

1. Solvent Extraction (Liquid-Liquid Extraction)

The separation of the components of a liquid mixture by treatment with a solvent in which one or more of the desired components is preferentially soluble is known as liquid-liquid extraction. Alternative terms are liquid extraction or solvent extraction.

A very general classification of liquid-liquid extraction equipment, their main characteristics and industrial applications is in Table 3-1.

Table 3-1 Features and Industrial Applications of Liquid-Liquid Extractors

Types of Extractors	*General features*	*Fields of applications*
Unagitated columns	Low capital cost Low operating and maintenance cost Simplicity in construction Handles corrosive material	Petrochemical Chemical
Mixer-settlers	High-stage efficiency Handles wide solvent ratios High capacity Good flexibility Reliable scale-up Handles liquids with high viscosity	Petrochemical Nuclear Fertilizer Metallurgical
Pulsed columns	Low HETS No internal moving parts Many stages possible	Nuclear Petrochemical Metallurgical
Rotary-agitation columns	Reasonable capacity Reasonable HETS Many stages possible Reasonable construction cost Low operating and maintenance cost	Petrochemical Metallurgical Pharmaceutical Fertilizer

续表

Types of Extractors	*General features*	*Fields of applications*
Reciprocating plate columns	High throughput Low HETS Great versatility and flexibility Simplicity in construction Handles liquids containing suspended solids Handles mixtures with emulsifying tendencies	Pharmaceutical Petrochemical Metallurgical Chemical
Centrifugal extractors	Short contacting time for unstable material Limited space required Handles easily emulsified material Handles systems with little liquid density difference	Pharmaceutical Nuclear Petrochemical

In the operation, it is essential that the liquid-mixture feed and solvent are at least partially if not completely immiscible and, in essence, three stages are involved:

(i) Bringing the feed mixture and the solvent into intimate contact,

(ii) Separation of the resulting two phases, and

(iii) Removal and recovery of the solvent from each phase.

Important applications of this technique include the separation of aromatics from kerosene-based fuel oils to improve their burning qualities and the separation of aromatics from paraffin and naphthenic compounds to improve the temperature-viscosity characteristics of lubricating oils. It may also be used to obtain, for example, relatively pure compounds such as benzene, toluene, and xylene from catalytically produced reformates in the oil industry, in the production of anhydrous acetic acid, in the extraction of phenol from coal tar liquors, and in the purification of penicillin. The important feature is the selective nature of the solvent, in that the separation of compounds is based on differences in solubilities, rather than differences in volatilities as in distillation.

In the single-stage batch process, the solvent and solution are mixed together and then allowed to separate into the two phases: the *extract* containing the required solute in the added solvent and the *raffinate* the weaker solution with some associated solvent. With this simple arrangement mixing and separation occur in the same vessel. Equilibria in such cases are represented conveniently on triangular diagrams, either equilateral or right-angled. Equilibria between any number of substances are representable in terms of activity coefficient correlations such as the UNIQUAC or NRTL. In theory, these correlations involve only parameters that are derivable from measurements on binary mixtures, but in practice the resulting accuracy may be poor and some multicomponent equilibrium measurements also should be used to find the parameters. Finding the parameters of these equations is a complex enough operation to require the use of a computer.

It may be seen that successful extraction processes are not to be judged simply by the performance of the extraction unit alone, but by assessment of the recovery achieved by the whole plant. The sections of the plant for mixing and for separation must be considered together when assessing capital cost, in addition, the cost of the organic solvents used in the metallurgical processes may also be high.

Equipment for extraction and leaching must be capable of providing intimate contact between two phases so as to effect transfer of solute between them and also of ultimately effecting a complete separation of the phases. The highest degree of separation with a minimum of solvent is attained with a series of countercurrent stages. In the operation, feed enters the first stage and final extract leaves it, and fresh solvent enters the last stage and final raffinate leaves it.

2. Leaching

Leaching is concerned with the extraction of a soluble constituent from a solid by means of a solvent. The process may be used either for the production of a concentrated solution of a valuable material, or in order to remove an insoluble solid, such as a pigment, from a soluble material with which it is contaminated. The method used for the extraction is determined by the proportion of soluble constituent present, its distribution throughout the solid, the nature of the solid and the particle size.

If the solute is uniformly dispersed in the solid, the material near the surface will be dissolved first, leaving a porous structure in the solid residue. The solvent will then have to penetrate this outer layer before it can reach further solute, and the process will become progressively more difficult and the extraction rate will fall. If the solute forms a very high proportion of the solid, the porous structure may break down almost immediately to give a fine deposit of insoluble residue, and access of solvent to the solute will not be impeded. Generally, the process can be considered in three parts: first the change of phase of the solute as it dissolves in the solvent, secondly its diffusion through the solvent in the pores of the solid to the outside of the particle, and thirdly the transfer of the solute from the solution in contact with the particles to the main bulk of the solution. Anyone of these three processes may be responsible for limiting the extraction rate, though the first process usually occurs so rapidly that it has a negligible effect on the overall rate.

In some cases the soluble material is distributed in small isolated pockets in a material which is impermeable to the solvent such as gold dispersed in rock, for example. In such cases the material is crushed so that all the soluble material is exposed to the solvent. If the solid has a cellular structure, the extraction rate will generally be comparatively low because the cell walls provide an additional resistance. In the extraction of sugar from beet, the cell walls perform the important function of impeding the extraction of undesirable constituents of relatively high molecular weight, and the beet should therefore be prepared in long strips so that a relatively small proportion of the cells is ruptured. In the extraction of oil from seeds, the solute is itself liquid and may diffuse towards the solvent.

3. Adsorption

Though used as a physical-chemical process over a long period it is only over the last three decades that adsorption has developed to a stage where it is now a major industrial separation process. In adsorption, molecules distribute themselves between two phases, one of which is a solid whilst the other can be a fluid—liquid or gas.

Unlike absorption, in which solute molecules diffuse from the bulk of a gas phase to the bulk of a liquid phase, in *adsorption* molecules diffuse from the bulk of the fluid to the surface of the solid adsorbent, forming a distinct adsorbed phase.

Typically, gas adsorbers are used for removing trace components from gas mixtures. The commonest example is the drying of gases to prevent corrosion, condensation or some unwanted side reaction. For items as diverse as electronic instruments and biscuits, sachets of adsorbent may be included in the packing to keep the relative humidity low. In processes using volatile solvents it is necessary to guard against the incidental loss of solvent carried away with the ventilating air; recovery can be effected by passing the air through a packed bed of adsorbent.

Adsorption can be equally effective in removing trace components from the liquid phase and may be used either to recover the component or simply to rid an industrial effluent of a noxious substance.

Any potential application of adsorption has to be considered along with alternatives, notably distillation, absorption and liquid extraction. Each separation process exploits some difference between a property of the components to be separated. In distillation, it is volatility; in absorption, it is solubility; in extraction, it is distribution coefficient. Separation by adsorption depends on one component being more readily adsorbed than another. The selection of a suitable process may also depend on the ease with which the separated components can be recovered.

Separating *n*- and *iso*-paraffins by distillation requires a large number of stages because of the low relative volatility of the components. It may be economic, however, to use a selective adsorbent which separates on the basis of slight differences in mean molecular diameters. *n*- and *iso*-pentane have diameters of 0.489 and 0.558 nm respectively. When an adsorbent with pore size of 0.5 nm is exposed to a mixture of the gases, the smaller molecules diffuse to the adsorbent surface and are retained; the larger are excluded. In another stage of the process, the retained molecules are desorbed by reducing the total pressure or increasing the temperature.

All such processes suffer one drawback, that the capacity of the adsorbent for the adsorbate in question is limited. At intervals, the adsorbent has to be removed from the process and regenerated, that is, restored to its original condition. For this reason, in its early applications in industry, the adsorption unit was considered to be more difficult to integrate with a continuous process than, say, a distillation column. Furthermore, it was difficult to manufacture adsorbents which had identical adsorptive properties from batch to batch. The design of a commercial adsorber and its operation had to be sufficiently flexible to cope with such variations.

These factors, together with the rather slow thermal regeneration that was common in early applications, resulted in the adsorber not being a popular option with plant designers. Since a greater variety of adsorbents has become available, each tailor-made for a specific application, the situation has changed, particularly as faster alternatives to thermal regeneration are often possible.

Adsorption occurs when molecules diffusing in the fluid phase are held for a period of time by forces emanating from an adjacent surface. The surface represents a gross discontinuity in the structure of the solid, and atoms at the surface have a residue of molecular forces which are not satisfied by surrounding atoms like those in the body of the structure. These residual or van der Waals forces are common to all surfaces and the only reason the certain solids are designated "adsorbents" is that they can be manufactured in a highly porous form, giving rise to a large internal surface. In comparison the external surface will make only a modest contribution to the total, even when the solid is finely divided. An average figure for the total surface of commercial adsorbents would be 400,000 m^2/kg.

Selected from "*Chemical Engineering, Vol 6*, 2nd Edition, R.K. Sinnott, Pergamon Press, 1996"

Words and Expressions

1. mixer-settler 混合澄清器
2. pulsed column 脉冲塔
3. HETS = height equivalent to a theoretical stage 等板高度，理论塔板的当量高度
4. rotary-agitation column 回转搅拌塔
5. reciprocating plate column 往复振动板式萃取柱（塔）
6. centrifugal extractor 离心萃取器
7. reformate n. （汽油）重整产品
8. anhydrous [æn'haidrəs] a. 无水的
9. extract ['ekstrækt] n. 萃取相，萃取液
10. raffinate ['ræfineit] n. 萃余液
11. equilateral ['i:kwi'lætərəl] a. 等边的，两侧对称的
12. activity coefficient 活度系数
13. UNIQUAC = universal quasichemistry activity coefficient 准化学活度系数
14. NRTL = nonrandom two-liquid model 非随机两液体模型
15. impede [im'pi:d] vt. 阻碍，阻止，妨碍，障碍
16. impermeable [im'pə:mjəbl] a. 不能透过的，不可渗透的，不透水的
17. cellular ['seljulə] a. 多孔的，细胞质的
18. beet [bi:t] n. 甜菜
19. adsorbent [æd'sɔ:bənt] n. 吸附剂，吸附物质
20. adsorber [æd'sɔ:b] n. 吸附器
21. sachet ['sæʃei] n. （熏衣用的）香囊，小香袋
22. humidity [hju:'miditi] n. 湿度，湿气，水分含量
23. ventilate ['ventileit] vt. 通风，排气，开气孔，装以通风设备
24. petane ['pentein] n. （正）戊烷
25. emanate ['eməneit] v. 发出，放射，析出，发源 from

Exercises

1. *Filling in the spaces in the following paragraphs by referring to the text. Choose* ***No More Than Three Words*** *from the passage for each answer.*

(1) Extraction is a process whereby a mixture of several substances in the liquid phase is at least partially separated upon addition of [1]______________ in which the original substances have different [2]__________. When some of the original substances are solids, the process is called

[3]__________. In a sense, the role of solvent in extraction is analogous to the role of enthalpy in [4]________. The solvent-rich phase is called the [5]__________, and the solvent-poor phase is called the [6]_________. A high degree of separation may be achieved with several extraction stages in series, particularly in [7]_____________ flow.

(2) Adsorption separation of the components of [8]_________ can be effected by contacting them with a solid that has a preferential attraction for some of them, forming a distinct [9]____________. Such processes are quantitatively significant when the specific surfaces of the solids are measured in average of [10]_________ m^2/kg. Adsorbents are restored to essentially their [11]______________ for reuse by desorption by elevating the temperature, or reducing the [12]________________, or by passing the air through a packed bed of adsorbent.

2. *Complete the following paragraphs by referring to the reading material. Choose* ***No More Than Three Words*** *from the passage for each answer.*

(1) In ion exchange equipment, cations or anions from the fluid deposit in the solid and displace [13]___________________ of other ions from the solid. A typical exchange is that of [14]__________ ions from the solid for some undesirable ions in the solution. Eventually all of the ions in the solid are replaced by a suitable [15]__________. To design a new ion exchanger, we should take into considering some process parameters such as [16]___________, regenerant quantities and flow rates, rinsing operations, and even [17]_________________ with repeated cycles.

(2) Chromatography is a technique used for analyzing or separating mixtures of gases, liquids, or dissolved substances. Separations even between [18]____________ substances can be very sharp. In general, all types of chromatography involve two distinct phases—the [19]___________and the [20]__________________, eluent or carrier. The separation depends on the differing [21]__________________ of the components of the mixture between the two phases.

(3) In living organisms, all the necessary separations are achieved by [22]_______________. Nowadays, membranes, usually of [23]___________ materials, have been widely applied to a range of conventionally difficult separations. Their advantages are [24]_____________ operation, relatively low capital and running costs, and modular construction. Some well-established large-scale industrial processes are microfiltration (MF), [25]_______________ (UF) and [26]_________________.

3. *Put the following into Chinese:*

pulsed column　　reformate　　anhydrous　　impede
impermeable　　adsorbent　　deterioation　　impregnate
inherent　　category　　elution　　desalination

4. *Put the following into English:*

混合澄清槽　　萃取相　　萃余液　　活度系数
无水的　　湿度　　凝胶　　色谱
流动相　　固定相　　洗脱液　　载体
微孔过滤　　超滤　　反渗透　　电渗析

Reading Material 15:

Ion Exchange

Ion exchange stands as a unit operation in its own right, often sharing theory with adsorption or chromatography but having its own special areas of application. Its oldest and most enduring application is for water treatment, to soften or demineralize water before industrial use, to recover components from an aqueous effluent before it is discharged or recirculated. Ion exchange can be used to separate ionic species in various liquids. Ion exchangers can be manufactured which catalyze specific reactions or which are suitable to use for chromatographic separations.

In the present context, the *exchange* is that of equivalent numbers of similarly charged ions, between an immobile phase, which may be a crystal lattice or a gel, and a liquid surrounding the immobile phase. If the exchanging ions carry a positive charge, the ion exchanger is termed *cationic*, and, if a negative charge, *anionic*. The rate at which ions diffuse between exchanger and liquid is determined not only by the concentration differences in the two phases, but also by the necessity of maintaining electroneutrality in both phases.

Ion exchange processes function by replacing undesirable ions of a liquid with ions such as H^+ or OH^- from a solid material in which the ions are sufficiently mobile, usually some synthetic resin. Eventually the resin becomes exhausted and may be regenerated by contact with a small amount of solution with a high content of the desired ion. Resins can be tailored to have selective affinities for particular kinds of ions.

Commercial columns range up to 6 m dia and bed heights from 1 to 6 m, most commonly 1~3 m. Freebroad of 50%~100% is provided to accommodate bed expansion when regenerant flow is upward. The liquid must be distributed and withdrawn uniformly over the cross section. Perforated spiders are suitable. The usual support for the bed of resin is a bed of gravel or layers of ceramic balls of graded sizes, balls sometimes are placed on top of the bed to aid in distribution or to prevent disturbance of the top level. Since the specific volume of the material can change 50% or more as a result of water absorption and ion-ion exchange, the distributor must be located well above the initial charge level of fresh resin.

If the proposed process is similar to known commercial technology, a new design can be made with confidence. Otherwise laboratory work must be performed. Experts claim that tests on columns 2.5 cm dia and 1 m bed depth can be scaled up safely to commercial diameters. The laboratory work preferably is done with the same bed depth as in the commercial unit, but since the active exchange zone occupies only a small proportional to the bed height, and tests with columns 1 m high can be dependably scaled up. The laboratory work will establish process flow rates, regenerant quantities and flow rates, rinsing operations, and even deterioration of performance with repeated cycles.

Operating cycles for liquid contacting processes such as ion exchange consist of these steps:

(i) Process stream flow for a proper period.

(ii) A rinse for recovering possibly valuable occluded process solution.

(iii) A backwash to remove accumulated foreign solids from the top of the bed and possibly to reclassify the particle size distribution.

(iv) The flow of regenerant for a proper period.

(v) Rinse to remove occluded regenerant.

As complex a cyclic process as this may demand cycle times of more than a few hours. Very high ion concentrations or high volumetric rates may require batteries of vessels and automatic switching of the several streams, or continuously operating equipment. Several continuous ion exchange plants are being operated successfully.

1. Chromatographic Separations

Chromatographic methods of separation are distinguished by their high selectivity, that is their ability to achieve separation between components of closely similar physical and chemical properties. Many mixtures which are difficult to separate by other methods can be separated by chromatography. The range of materials which can be processed covers the entire spectrum of molecular weights, from hydrogen to proteins.

Chromatographic techniques have been used routinely for chemical analysis since the 1950s, and for automated analysis of process streams in process control (*process chromatography*) since 1961. They have also been extensively developed as rapid and accurate methods of measuring a great variety of thermodynamic, kinetic and other physico-chemical properties. We are concerned here with their use as a commercial separation process. This is often called *production* or *large-scale chromatography* (or sometimes, confusingly, process chromatography) to distinguish it from its smaller, laboratory-scale relative, *preparative chromatography* (Fig.3-3). Production chromatography is a relatively new entrant to the range of unit operations available to chemical engineers. Its use is increasing as the demand for high purity materials grows.

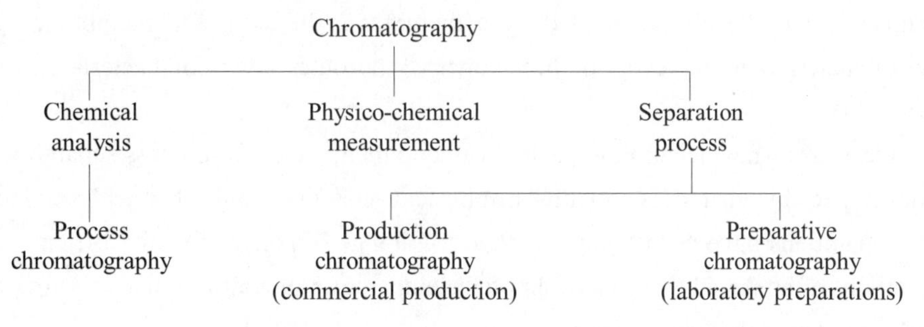

Fig. 3-3 Uses of chromatography

In production chromatography the components of a mixture are separated as they pass through a column. The column contains a *stationary phase* which may be a packed bed of solid particles or a liquid with which the packing is impregnated. The mixture is carried through the column dissolved in a gas or liquid stream known as the *mobile phase*, *eluent* or *carrier*. Separation occurs because the differing distribution coefficients of the components of the mixture between the stationary and mobile phases result in differing velocities of travel.

Chromatography methods are classified according to the nature of the mobile and stationary phases used. The terms *gas chromatography* (GC) and the *liquid chromatography* (LC) refer to the nature of the mobile phase.

Both GC and LC may be operated in one of several modes. The principal modes currently used for large-scale separations are elution, selective adsorption or desorption, and countercurrent chromatography. Elution is the most used and best developed form of the technique.

2. Membrane Separation Processes

Effective product separation is crucial to economic operation in the process industries. However, certain types of materials are inherently difficult and expensive to separate. Prominent examples include:

(i) Finely dispersed solids, especially those which are compressible, have a density close to that of the liquid phase, have high viscosity, or are gelatinous.

(ii) Low molecular weight, non-volatile organics or pharmaceuticals and dissolved salts.

(iii) Biological materials which are very sensitive to their physical and chemical environment.

The processing of these categories of materials has become of increased importance in recent years, especially with the growth of the newer biotechnological industries and with the increasingly sophisticated nature of processing in the food industries. When difficulties arise in the processing of materials of biological origin, there is one question which is well-worth asking—how does nature solve the problem? The solution which nature has developed is likely to be both highly effective and energy efficient, though it may be slow in process terms. Nature separates biologically active materials by means of membranes. A membrane may be defined as "an interphase separating two phases and selectively controlling the transport of materials between those phases". It is an interphase rather than an interface because it occupies a finite, though normally small, element of space. Human beings are all surrounded by a membrane, the skin, and membranes control the separation of materials at all levels of life, down to the outer layers of bacteria and subcellular components.

Since the 1960s a new technology using synthetic membranes for process separations has been rapidly developed by materials scientists, physical chemists and chemical engineers. Such membrane separations have been widely applied to a range of conventionally difficult separations. They potentially offer the advantages of ambient temperature operation, relatively low capital and running costs, and modular construction.

Industrial membrane processes may be classified according to the size range of materials which they are to separate and the driving force used in separation. There is always a degree of arbitrariness about such classification. The pressure driven processes are microfiltration (MF), ultrafiltration (UF) and reverse osmosis (RO). These are already well-established large-scale industrial processes. For example, reverse osmosis is used world-wide for the desalination of brackish water, with about 1,000 plants in operation. Plants capable of producing up to 10^5 m^3/day of drinking water are planned. As a further example, it is now standard practice to include an ultrafiltration unit in paint plants in the car industry. The resulting recovery of paint from wash waters can produce savings of 10~30 per cent in paint usage, and allows recycling of the wash waters. The use of reverse osmosis and ultrafiltration in the dairy industry has led to substantial changes in production techniques and the development of new types of cheeses and related products. Electrodialysis is a purely electrically driven separation process used extensively for the desalination or concentration of brackish water. There are about 300 such plants in operation. However, economics presently favor reverse osmosis rather than electrodialysis for such separations. It may have a future role in the desalination of protein solutions. The major use of dialysis is in hemodialysis of patients with renal failure, where it is most appropriate to use such a gentle technique. Hemodialysis poses many interesting problems of a chemical engineering nature, but dialysis is a relatively slow process not really suited to large-scale industrial separations.

Selected from "*Chemical Engineering, Vol. 2*, 4th Edition, R.K. Sinnott, Pergamon Press, 1992"

Words and Expressions

1. demineralize vt. 脱(去)矿质，软化，除盐
2. immobile [i'məubail] a. 固定的，稳定的，静置的
3. lattice ['lætis] n. 晶格，点阵，格（栅，子，状）
4. gel [dʒel] n. 凝胶（体），冻胶
5. cationic [kætai'ɔnik] a. 阳(正)离子的
6. anionic a. 阴(负)离子的
7. electroneutrality n. 电中性
8. spider ['spaidə] n. 支架，机架
9. gravel ['grævəl] n. 砾（石），砂砾（层），石子
10. graded sizes 分级(规格)尺寸
11. rinse [rins] vt.;n. 漂洗，淋洗，清洗
12. deterioration [ditiəriə'reiʃən] n. 退化，变质，降低（品质）
13. occlude [ək'lu:d] vt. 吸留，夹杂，包藏
14. process chromatography （工艺）流程色谱（法），工程管理色谱（法）
15. production chromatography 生产色谱（法）
16. large-scale chromatography 大型色谱(法)
17. preparative chromatography 制备色谱(法)
18. stationary phase 固定相
19. impregnate ['impregneit] v. 浸润，饱和
20. mobile phase 流动相
21. eluent n. 洗脱液，洗脱剂
22. carrier ['kæriə] n. 载体
23. elution [i'lju:ʃən] n. 洗提，洗出
24. elution chromatography 洗脱色谱（法）
25. countercurrent chromatography 逆流色谱（法）

26. inherent [in'hiərənt] a. 固有的，生来的，内在的
27. gelatinous [dʒi'lætinəs] a. 胶状的，凝胶状的
28. category ['kætigəri] n. 种类，类型，范畴
29. subcellular a. 亚细胞的，子细胞的，亚晶胞的
30. microfiltration n. 微孔过滤
31. ultrafiltration n. 超滤(作用)
32. osmosis [ɔz'məusis] n. 渗透(性，作用)
33. reverse osmosis 反渗透
34. desalination n. 淡化，脱盐
35. brackish ['brækiʃ] a. 有盐味的，稍(半，微)咸的
36. electrodialysis n. 电渗析
37. dialysis [dai'ælisis] n. 渗析，渗透
38. hemodialysis n. 血液渗透(作用)
39. renal ['ri:nl] a. 肾脏的，肾的

Unit 16 Evaporation, Crystallization and Drying

Before reading this unit, try to answer the following questions:

1.What is the major consideration in the design and operation of evaporators?

2.Do you know the typical applications of the main types of crystallizer?

3.Can you show the features of some basic types of dryer?

4.Can you summarize various separation processes by listing their names, describing the processes and showing their applications?

1. Evaporation

Evaporators employ heat to concentrate solutions or to recover dissolved solids by precipitating them from saturated solutions. They are reboilers with special provisions for separating liquid and vapor phases and for removal of solids when they are precipitated or crystallized out. Simple kettle-type reboilers may be adequate in some applications, especially if enough freeboard is provided. The tubes may be horizontal or vertical, long or short; the liquid may be outside or inside the tubes, circulation may be natural or forced with pumps or propellers.

Natural circulation evaporators are the most popular. The forced circulation type of evaporator is most versatile for viscous and fouling services especially, but also the most expensive to buy and maintain. In the long tube vertical design, because of vaporization the liquid is in annular or film flow for a substantial portion of the tube length, and accordingly is called a rising film evaporator. In falling film evaporators, liquids distributed to the tops of the individual and flows down as a flow. The hydrostatic head is eliminated, the pressure drop is little more than the friction of the vapor flow, and heat transfer is excellent. Since contact time is short and separation of liquid and vapor is virtually complete, falling film evaporation is suitable for the materials of heat sensitivity.

Long tube evaporators, with either natural or forced circulation are the most widely used. Tubes range from 19 to 63 mm diameter, and 12~30ft in length. The calandria has tubes 3~5 ft long, and the central downtake has an area about equal to the cross section of the tubes. Sometimes circulation in calandrias is forced with built in propellers. In some type of evaporators, the solids are recirculated until they reach a desired size.

Thermal economy is a major consideration in the design and operation of evaporators. A single-effect evaporator is wasteful of energy since the latent heat of the vapor leaving is not used but is discarded. However, much of this latent heat can be recovered and reused by employing multiple-effect evaporators.

A great variety of evaporator designs have been developed for specialized applications in particular industries. The designs can be grouped into the following basic types.

Direct heated evaporators This type includes solar pans and submerged combustion units. Submerged combustion evaporators can be used for applications where contamination of the solution by the products of combustion is acceptable.

Long-tube evaporators In this type the liquid flows as a thin film on the walls of a long, vertical, heated tube. Both falling film and rising film types are used. They are high capacity units; suitable for low viscosity solutions.

Forced circulation evaporators In forced circulation evaporators the liquid is pumped through the tubes. They are suitable for use with materials which tend to foul the heat transfer surfaces, and where crystallization can occur in the evaporator.

Agitated thin-film evaporators In this design a thin layer of solution is spread on the heating surface by mechanical means. Wiped-film evaporators are used for very viscous materials and for producing solid products.

Short-tube evaporators, also called callandria evaporators, are used in the sugar industry.

Evaporator selection

The selection of the most suitable evaporator type for a particular application will depend on the following factors:

(1) The throughput required.

(2) The viscosity of the feed and the increase in viscosity during evaporation.

(3) The nature of the product required; solid, slurry, or concentrated solution.

(4) The heat sensitivity of the product.

(5) Whether the materials are fouling or non-fouling.

(6) Whether the solution is likely to foam.

(7) Whether direct heating can be used.

Auxiliary equipment Condensers and vacuum pumps will be needed for evaporators operated under vacuum. For aqueous solutions, steam ejectors and jet condensers are normally used. Jet condensers are direct-contact condensers, where the vapor is condensed by contact with jets of cooling water.

2. Crystallization

Crystallization is used for the production, purification and recovery of solids. Crystalline products have an attractive appearance, are free flowing, and easily handled and packaged. The process is used in a wide range of industries: from the small-scale production of specialized chemicals, such as pharmaceutical products, to the tonnage production of products such as sugar, common salt and fertilizers.

Crystallization equipment can be classified by the method used to obtain supersaturation of the liquor, and also by the method used to suspend the growing crystals. Supersaturation is obtained by cooling or evaporation. There are four basic types of crystallizer: *tank crystallizers, scraped-surface crystallizers, circulating magma crystallizers* (Fig. 3-4) and *circulating liquor crystallizers.*

Typical applications of the main types of crystallizer are summarized in Table 3-2.

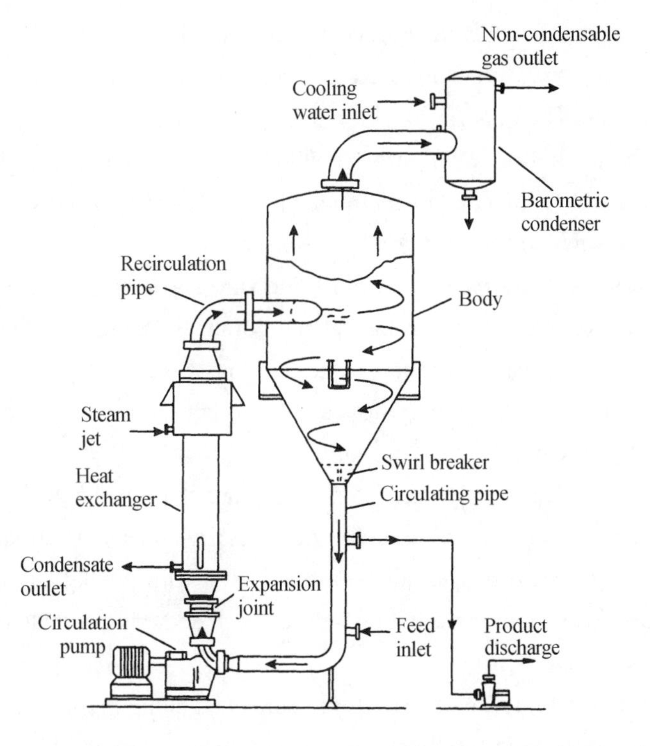

Fig. 3-4 Circulating magma crystalliser(evaporative type)

Table 3-2 Selection of crystallizers

Crystallizer type	Applications	Typical uses
Tank	Batch operation, small-scale production	Fatty acids, vegetable oils, sugars
Scraped surface	Organic compounds, where fouling is a problem, viscous materials	Chlorobenzenes, organic acids, paraffin waxes, naphthalene, urea
Circulating magma	Production of large-sized crystals. High throughputs	Ammonium and other inorganic salts, sodium and potassium chlorides
Circulating liquor	Production of uniform crystals (smaller size than circulating magma). High throughputs.	Gypsum, inorganic salts, sodium and potassium nitrates, silver nitrates

3. Drying

Drying is the removal of water, or other volatile liquids, by evaporation. Most solid materials require drying at some stage in their production. The overriding consideration in the selection of drying equipment is the nature and concentration of the feed. Drying is an energy-intensive process, and the removal of liquid by thermal drying will be more costly than by mechanical separation techniques.

Except for a few specialized applications, hot air is used as the heating and mass transfer medium in industrial dryers. The air may be directly heated by the products of combustion of the fuel used (oil, gas or coal) or indirectly heated, usually by banks of steam-heated finned tubes.

The basic types used in the chemical process industries are:

Tray dryers Batch tray dryers are used for drying small quantities of solids, and are used for a wide range of materials. The material to be dried is placed in solid bottomed trays over which hot air is blown; or perforated bottom trays through which the air passes. Batch dryers have high labor requirements, but close control can be maintained over the drying conditions and the product inventory, and they are suitable for drying valuable products.

Conveyor dryers (continuous circulation band dryers) In this type, the solids are fed on to an endless, perforated, conveyor belt, through which hot air is forced. The belt is housed in a long rectangular cabinet, which is divided up into zones, so that the flow pattern and temperature of the drying air can be controlled. The relative movement through the dryer of the solids and drying air can be parallel or, more usually, counter-current.

This type of dryer is clearly only suitable for materials that form a bed with an open structure. High drying rates can be achieved, with good product-quality control. Thermal efficiencies are high and, with steam heating, steam usage can be as low as 1.5 kg per kg of water evaporated. The disadvantages of this type of dryer are high initial cost and, due to the mechanical belt, high maintenance costs.

Rotary dryer In rotary dryers the solids are conveyed along the inside of a rotating, inclined, cylinder and are heated and dried by direct contact with hot air gases flowing through the cylinder. In some, the cylinders are indirectly heated.

Rotating dryers are suitable for drying free-flowing granular materials. They are suitable for continuous operation at high throughputs; have a high thermal efficiency and relatively low capital cost and labor costs. Some disadvantages of this type are: a non-uniform residence time, dust generation and high noise levels.

Fluidized bed dryers In this type of dryer, the drying gas is passed through the bed of solids at a velocity sufficient to keep the bed in a fluidized state; which promotes high heat transfer and drying rates. Fluidized bed dryers are suitable for granular and crystalline materials within the particle size range 1 to 3 mm. They are designed for continuous and batch operation. The main advantages of fluidized dryers are: rapid and uniform heat transfer, short drying times, with good control of the drying conditions; and low floor area requirements. The power requirements are high compared with other types.

Pneumatic dryers, also called flash dryers, are similar in their operating principle to spray dryers. The product to be dried is dispersed into an upward-flowing stream of hot gas by a suitable feeder. The equipment acts as a pneumatic conveyor and dryer. Contact times are short, and this limits the size of particle-that can be dried. Pneumatic dryers are suitable for materials that are too fine to be dried in a fluidized bed dryer but which are heat sensitive and must be dried rapidly. The thermal efficiency of this type is generally low.

Spray dryers Spray dryers are normally used for liquid and dilute slurry feeds, but can be designed to handle any material that can be pumped. The material to be dried is atomized in a nozzle, or by a disc-type atomizer, positioned at the top of a vertical cylindrical vessel. Hot air flows up the vessel (in some designs downward) and conveys and dries the droplets. The liquid vaporizes rapidly from the droplet surface and open, porous particles are formed. The dried particles are removed in a cyclone separator or bag filter.

The main advantages of spray drying are the short contact time, making it suitable for drying heat-sensitive materials, and good control of the product particle size, bulk density, and form. Because the solids concentration in the feed is low the heating requirements will be high.

Rotary drum dryers Drum dryers are used for liquid and dilute slurry feeds. They are an alternative choice to spray dryers when the material to be dried will form a film on a heated surface, and is not heat sensitive.

Selected from "*Chemical Engineering, Vol. 6*, 2nd Edition, R.K. Sinnott, Pergamon Press, 1996"

Words and Expressions

1. kettle-type reboiler 釜式再沸器，釜式重沸器
2. propeller [prɔ'pelə] n. 螺旋桨，推进器
3. natural circulation evaporator 自然循环蒸发器
4. forced circulation evaporator 强制循环蒸发器
5. rising film evaporator 升膜式蒸发器
6. falling film evaporator 降膜式蒸发器
7. hydrostatic head 静水压头
8. long tube evaporator 长管蒸发器
9. calandria [kə'lændriə] n. 排管式，加热管群
10. central downtake 中央降液管
11. single effect evaporator 单效蒸发器
12. multiple effect evaporator 多效蒸发器
13. direct heated evaporator 直接加热蒸发器
14. solar pan 盐池，盐田
15. submerged combustion 浸没燃烧
16. agitated thin-film evaporator 搅拌式薄膜蒸发器
17. wiped-film evaporator 刮膜式蒸发器
18. short tube evaporator 短管蒸发器
19. steam ejector 蒸汽喷射器
20. jet condenser 喷射式冷凝器
21. free flowing 自由流动的，流动性能良好的
22. supersaturation ['sju:pə'sætə'reiʃən] n. 过饱和(现象)
23. tank crystallizer 槽式结晶器
24. scraped-surface crystallizer 刮膜式结晶器
25. magma ['mægmə] n. 稀糊状混合物，岩浆，稠液
26. circulating magma crystallizer 晶浆循环结晶器
27. circulating liquor crystallizer 母液循环结晶器
28. non-condensable gas 不凝性气体

29. barometric condenser 气压冷凝器
30. swirl breaker 消旋板
31. expansion joint 膨胀节
32. gypsum ['dʒipsʌm] n. 石膏，灰泥板，
33. bank n. 一排，排，列，群，组
34. finned tube 翅片管
35. tray dryer 盘架干燥器
36. conveyor dryer 带式干燥器
37. continuous circulation band dryer 连续循环带式干燥器
38. cabinet ['kæbinit] n. 箱，室，壳体
39. fluidized bed dryer 流化床干燥器
40. pneumatic dryer 气流干燥器
41. flash dryer 气流干燥器
42. spray dryer 喷雾干燥器
43. pneumatic [nju: 'mætik] a. 气力的，气动的
44. bulk density 堆积密度
45. rotary drum dryer 转鼓式干燥器

Exercises

1. *Complete the following paragraph by referring to* ***"Evaporation"****. Choose* ***No More Than Three Words*** *from the passage for each answer.*

   In evaporation, heat is added to a solution to vaporize the solvent, which is usually water. It is normally used to [1]_____________, from which sometimes [2]________ can be precipitated or crystallized out. The type of equipment used depends primarily on the configuration of the heat-transfer surface and on the means employed to provide [3]__________. The selection of the most suitable evaporator type for a particular application will depend on the following factors: the throughput required, the [4]______________ of the feed, the nature of the product required, the [5]_____________of the product, and the tendency to foul the [6]_____________ . Among all evaporators, [7]___________ ones, with either natural or forced circulation, are the most widely used. Thermal economy is improved by operating several vessels, i.e., [8]________________. If the evaporators operate under [9]_______________, some auxiliary equipment, such as [10]___________ and vacuum pumps will be needed.

2. *Referring to* ***"Crystallization"****, especially Fig. 3-4, fill in the blanks in the following paragraph.*

   In this circulating-magma crystallizer in Fig.3-4, the liquor and growing crystals are circulated through the zone in which [11]___________ occurs. Feed comes into the circulating pipe and the magma is driven by a [12]_______________ to pass through the [13]______________, where its temperature is raised 2 to 6 K. The heated liquor then mixes with body slurry and boiling occurs at the liquid surface. This causes supersaturation in the swirling liquid near the surface, which causes deposits on the swirling suspended crystals until they leave again via the [14]_____________ and then [15]______________. [16]_____________ is discharged through the circulating pipe by a screw pump. The off vapors may be cooled and [17]____________ leaves off the top of [18]__________________. Operation under vacuum often is practiced.

3. *Summarize the information on dryers by completing the table below.*

Dryer type	*General features*	*Application*
Tray dryers		
Conveyor dryers		
Rotary dryer		
Fluidized bed dryers		
Pneumatic dryers		
Spray dryers		
Rotary drum dryers		

4. *Put the following into Chinese:*

calandria	barometric condenser	expansion joint	finned tube
orth-	meta-	para-	ferrous
retardation time	micron	sterilization	stack gas

5. *Put the following into English:*

过饱和现象	多效蒸发器	降膜式蒸发器	强制循环
晶浆循环结晶器	气力的	气流干燥器	喷雾干燥器
升华	冷冻干燥	堆积密度	不凝性气体

Reading Material 16:

Separation Processes

It will be recalled that before and after most reaction stages, separation steps are necessary. Also certain processes have no reaction stages and are just a series of physical unit operations, for example, milk processing or natural gas treatment. Prior to storage and subsequent sale, separation of desired products from by-products (if any) and from waste streams is obviously necessary.

It is important that the process engineer has the ability to select and then size the appropriate separation process. The production rate of plant is as high as the production rate of the weakest link within the overall process. Thus it is important that all pieces of equipment from pumps to reactors to pipe lines to separating vessels are sized correctly.

Tables 3-3 to 3-6 reveal the wide range of available processes for the purification of reactants or products. In order to achieve a separation it is necessary that the component parts of a process stream possess different properties that can be exploited by a particular operation. The thermal processes (for example, distillation, evaporation and crystallization) depend on differences in vapor pressure or solubility. In some cases the separating agent is not heat but another fluid or solid (for example, a non-condensable gas for stripping out volatile liquid component from less volatile liquid components, a solvent for extraction or a solid adsorbent). A further class of separations is based on either size differences, density differences or a combination of both.

Table 3-3 Separation Processes for Liquid Mixtures

Name	Type of process	Practical examples/comment
Stripping	An insoluble gas is bubbled through a liquid and the volatile liquids are removed in the gas stream	Removal of light hydrocarbons from crude oil fractions
Solvent extraction	An immiscible solvent is contacted with the liquids that need separating. One or more but not all, are soluble in the second solvent	Separation of aromatics from paraffins and naphthenes (cyclic nonaromatics)
Adsorption	The liquids are passed through a granular bed of solid. One of the liquids is retained upon the solid and removed later. Process depends upon differences in adsorption potential	Removal of trace amounts of water from hydrocarbon streams. Important if subsequent stage requires very low water levels. Separation of aqueous ethanol, close to the azeotropic composition, into pure water and pure ethanol
Gravity settling	For immiscible liquids the density difference may yield sufficient separation	Oil-water separation
Chromatography	Consists of a mobile phase and a stationary phase. Components of the mobile phase attach themselves to the stationary phase, but to different extents. As the retardation times differ, a separation of the components occurs	Principally used for analysis; but protein separations and other biotechnological separations need separators of this type within the manufacturing process itself

Table 3-4 Separation Processes for Liquid-Solid Mixtures

Name	Type of process	Practical examples/comment
Evaporation	Concentration of solutions by boiling off solvent. The vapors above the solution are pure solvent. Contrast with drying	Concentration of milk. Concentration of fruit juices. Concentration of sodium hydroxide solutions (chlorine-alkali plant). Evaporation of sea-water to produce potable water
Drying	Removal of a volatile solvent from a solid in the presence of a non-condensable gas, normally air	Wide range from drying of crystals to drying of biscuits
Crystallization	Solubility limit of desired solid is exceeded either by evaporating some of the solvent or simply by cooling	Production of raw sugar from the clarified juices. Separation of *p*-xylene from *o*- and *m*-xylene.

续表

Name	Type of process	Practical examples/comment
Precipitation	Addition of chemical reactant to give insoluble precipitate	Waste-water treatment
Sedimentation	Depends on density difference. Moderate sized particles will separate out in a reasonable time	Removal of silt from oil at well-head
Filtration	Depends on size of solid being greater than pore-size of filter	Widely used to protect equipment such as pumps and nozzles (for example, burner nozzles) and to recover solid product from liquid (for example, cells from fermentation liquor or waxes during processing of crude oil
Centrifugation	Imposition of larger gravitational forces aids separation of particles from liquid. Important if density difference small and/or particles small	Widely used, particularly in pharmaceutical industry. Crystals often concentrated in centrifuges, for example, *p*-xylene and sugar
Microfiltration	An extension of normal filtration to the micron level	
Ultrafiltration	An extension of normal filtration to the sub-micron level. Sieving on a molecular scale	The concept of pores within the filter is now inappropriate.
Dialysis	selective membrane: separation occurs because of different diffusion rates which depend on molecular weights	Artificial kidneys. Recovery of sodium hydroxide in rayon manufacture
Electrostatic precipitation	Very fine droplets can be charged and then attracted to collecting plates	Has been used to remove sulfuric acid mist from gaseous effluent.

Table 3-5 Gas-Liquid and Gas-Gas Separation Processes

Name	Type of process	Practical examples/comment
Gas-liquid		
stripping	Removal of a dissolved gas from a solution by bubbling an inert gas through the liquid	Removal of carbon dioxide from liquid by bubbling air through the solution
Gravity separators	Separation of gas from liquid by allowing sufficient time for (i) droplets of liquid to fall out of gas, and (ii) bubbles of gas to rise through liquid	Gas-oil separators. 'knock-out' vessels in front of compressors; the flue gas for gas turbines must be free of liquid droplets and these drop out in 'knock-out' vessels which are described later
cyclones	Depends on density differences. Liquid droplets thrown to wall	Removal of acid spray from gaseous effluent leaving the absorbers on a sulphuric acid plant
Gas-gas		
absorption	Preferential absorption of one component into a liquid	Removal of SO_3 from other gases. Removal of CO_2 from synthesis gas

续表

Name	Type of process	Practical examples/comment
Adsorption	Preferential adsorption of one component on to a solid surface	Removal of water vapor by silica gel or molecular sieves. Odor removal
Membranes	Small molecules diffuse through the membrane	Separation of hydrogen from other gases (for example, purge gas)
Diffusion	Different diffusion rates through porous barrier	Concentration of radioactive $^{235}UF_6$ from natural UF_6
Thermal diffusion	Different diffusion rates along a temperature gradient	Isotope separation

Table 3-6 Gas-Solid and Solid-Solid Separation Processes

Name	Type of process	Practical examples/comment
Gas-solid		
Cyclones	Depends on density differences. Solid particles thrown to wall	Recovery of fine solids from gas streams
Electrostatic precipitation	Fine solids are charged and then attracted on to collecting plates	Dust removal from stack gases. Often used at cement works
Filtration	Size of solid greater than pore-size of filter	Removal of dust
Microfiltration	Removal of harmful bacteria	Sterilization of air
Solid-solid		
Freeze drying	A thermal process in which ice is sublimated to water vapor to leave a water-free solid	Sterilization of air
Solvent extraction (leaching)	Preferential dissolution of one solid	Purification of penicillin. Recovery of sugar from crushed cane or beat
Supercritical gas extraction	Depends upon solubility of a component in a gas; variable solubility with pressure permits recovery of component and re-use of gas	De-caffeination of coffee using CO_2
Flotation	Surfactants and air bubbles required. One solid preferentially adheres to surfactant which is carried to surface by bubbles	Ore flotation, for example, recovery of ZnS
Magnetic separation	Attraction of materials in a magnetic field	Concentration of ferrous ores

Selected from "*Chemical Engineering: Introductory Aspects,* Robert W. Field, Macmillan Education, 1988"

Words and Expressions

1. size [saiz] vt. 依一定尺寸制造，定尺寸，估计大小

2. retardation time 保留时间
3. orth-，*o*- [词头]邻位，正，原
4. meta-，*m*- [词头]间位，偏
5. para-，*p*- [词头]对位，仲，副
6. silt [silt] n. 淤泥，泥沙，泥浆
7. well-head （油）井口
8. micron ['maikrɔn] n. 微米，10^{-6}米；百万分之一
9. submicron n. 亚微米，亚微型，亚微细粒
10. kidney ['kidni] n. 肾
11. knock-out vessel 分离器
12. purge gas 吹扫气体
13. stack gas 烟道气
14. sterilization [sterilai'zeiʃən] n. 消毒，灭菌
15. freeze drying 冷冻干燥
16. sublimate ['sʌblimeit] v. 升华
17. supercritical gas extraction 超临界气体萃取
18. de-caffeination n. 脱咖啡因，除去咖啡因
19. ferrous ['ferəs] a. (亚，二价，含)铁的，铁类的

Unit 17 Chemical Reaction Engineering

Before reading this unit, try to answer the following questions:

1.What are the basic questions in the reactor design?

2.What kinds of information, knowledge and experience may be used in reactor design?

3.In what way would you classify chemical reactions?

4.Can you outline some basic reactors and their main applications?

Every industrial chemical process is designed to produce economically a desired product from a variety of starting materials through a succession of treatment steps. Fig. 3-5 shows a typical situation. The raw materials undergo a number of physical treatment steps to put them in the form in which they can be reacted chemically. They then pass through the reactor. The products of the reaction must then undergo further physical treatment—separations, purifications, etc.—for the final desired product to be obtained.

Design of equipment for the physical treatment steps is studied in the unit operations. Here we are concerned with the chemical treatment step of a process. Economically this may be an inconsequential unit, say a simple mixing tank. More often than not, however, the chemical treatment step is the heart of the process, the thing that makes or breaks the process economically.

Design of the reactor is no routine matter, and many alternatives can be proposed for a process. In searching for the optimum it is not just the cost of reactor that must be minimized. One design may have low reactor cost, but the materials leaving the unit may be such that their treatment requires much higher cost than alternative designs. Hence, the economics of the over-all process must be considered.

Reactor design uses information, knowledge, and experience from a variety of areas—thermodynamics, chemical kinetics, fluid mechanics, heat transfer, mass transfer, and economics. Chemical reaction engineering is the synthesis of all these factors with the aim of properly designing a chemical reactor.

The design of chemical reactors is probably the one activity which is unique to chemical engineering, and it is probably this function more than anything else which justifies the existence of chemical engineering as a distinct branch of engineering.

In chemical reactor design there are two questions which must be answered:

(i) What change can we expect to occur?

(ii) How fast will they take place?

The first question concerns thermodynamics, the second the various rate processes—chemical kinetics, heat transfer, etc. Putting these all together and trying to determine how these processes are interrelated can be an extremely difficult problem; hence we start with the simplest of situations and build up our analysis by considering additional factors until we are able to handle the more difficult problems.

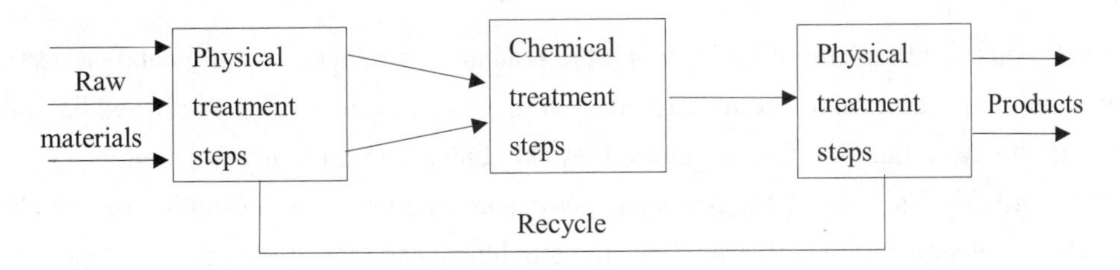

Fig. 3-5 Typical chemical process

1. Thermodynamics

Thermodynamics gives two important pieces of information needed in design, the heat liberated or absorbed during reaction and the maximum possible extent of reaction.

Chemical reactions are invariably accompanied by the liberation or absorption of heat, the magnitude of which must be known for proper design. Consider the reaction

$$aA \longrightarrow rR + sS, \Delta H_r \begin{cases} \text{positive, endothermic} \\ \text{negative, exothermic} \end{cases} \tag{2}$$

The heat of reaction at temperature T is the heat transferred from surroundings to the reacting system when a moles of A disappear to form r moles of R and s moles of S, with the system measured at the same temperature and pressure before and after reaction. With heats of reaction known or estimable from thermochemical data, the magnitude of the heat effects during reaction can be calculated.

Thermodynamics also allows calculation of the equilibrium constant K from the standard free energies of the reacting materials. With the equilibrium constant known, the expected maximum attainable yield of the products of reaction can be estimated.

2. Chemical Kinetics

Under appropriate conditions feed materials may be transformed into new and different materials which constitute different chemical species. If this occurs only by rearrangement or redistribution of the constituent atoms to form new molecules, we say that a chemical reaction has occurred. Chemistry is concerned with the study of such reactions. It studies the mode and mechanism of reactions, the physical and energy changes involved and the rate of formation of produces.

It is the last-mentioned area of interest, chemical kinetics, which is of primary concern to us. Chemical kinetics searches for the factors that influence the rate of reaction. It measures this rate and proposes explanations for the values found. For the chemical engineer the kinetics of a reaction must be known if he is to satisfactorily design equipment to effect these reactions on a technical scale. Of course, if the reaction is rapid enough so that the system is essentially at equilibrium, design is very much simplified. Kinetic information is not needed, and thermodynamic information alone is sufficient.

3. Homogeneous and Heterogeneous Reactions

Homogeneous reactions are those in which the reactants, products, and any catalyst used form one continuous phase: gaseous or liquid. Homogeneous gas phase reactors will always be operated continuously; whereas liquid phase reactors may be batch or continuous. Tubular (pipe-line) reactors are normally used for homogeneous gas-phase reactions; for example, in the thermal cracking of petroleum crude oil fractions to ethylene, and the thermal decomposition of dichloroethane to vinyl chloride. Both tubular and stirred tank reactors are used for homogeneous liquid-phase reactions.

In a heterogeneous reaction two or more phases exist, and the overriding problem in the reactor design is to promote mass transfer between the phases. The possible combination of phases are:

(i) Liquid-liquid: immiscible liquid phases; reactions such as the nitration of toluene or benzene with mixed acids, and emulsion polymerizations.

(ii) Liquid-solid: with one, or more, liquid phases in contact with a solid. The solid may be a reactant or catalyst.

(iii) Liquid-solid-gas: where the solid is normally a catalyst; such as in the hydrogenation of amines, using a slurry of platinum on activated carbon as a catalyst.

(iv) Gas-solid: where the solid may take part in the reaction or act as a catalyst. The reduction of iron ores in blast furnaces and the combustion of solid fuels are examples where the solid is a reactant.

(v) Gas-liquid: where the liquid may take part in the reaction or act as a catalyst.

4. Reactor geometry (type)

The reactors used for established processes are usually complex designs which have been developed (have evolved) over a period of years to suit the requirements of the process, and are unique designs. However, it is convenient to classify reactor designs into the following broad categories.

Stirred tank reactors Stirred tank (agitated) reactors consist of a tank fitted with a mechanical agitator and a cooling jacket or coils. They are operated as batch reactors or continuously. Several reactors may be used in series.

The stirred tank reactor can be considered the basic chemical reactor, modeling on a large scale the conventional laboratory flask. Tank sizes range from a few liters to several thousand liters. They are used for homogeneous and heterogeneous liquid-liquid and liquid-gas reactions; and for reactions that involve finely suspended solids, which are held by the agitation. As the degree of agitation is under the designer's control, stirred tank reactors are particularly suitable for reactions where good mass transfer or heat transfer is required.

When operated as a continuous process the composition in the reactor is constant and the same as the product stream, and, except for very rapid reactions, this will limit the conversion that can be obtained in one stage.

The power requirements for agitation will depend on the degree of agitation required and will range from about 0.2 kW/ms for moderate mixing to 2 kW/ms for intense mixing.

Tubular reactor Tubular reactors are generally used for gaseous reactions, but are also suitable for some liquid-phase reactions.

If high heat-transfer rates are required, small-diameter tubes are used to increase the surface area to volume ratio. Several tubes may be arranged in parallel, connected to a manifold or fitted into a tube sheet in a similar arrangement to a shell and tube heat exchanger. For high-temperature reactions the tubes may be arranged in a furnace.

Packed bed reactors There are two basic types of packed-bed reactor: those in which the solid is a reactant, and those in which the solid is a catalyst. Many examples of the first type can be found in the extractive metallurgical industries.

In the chemical process industries the designer will normally be concerned with the second type: catalytic reactors. Industrial packed-bed catalytic reactors range in size from small tubes, a few centimeters diameter to large diameter packed beds. Packed-bed reactors are used for gas and gas-liquid reactions. Heat-transfer rates in large diameter packed beds are poor and where high heat-transfer rates are required fluidized beds should be considered.

Fluidized bed reactors The essential features of a fluidized bed reactor is that the solids are held in suspension by the upward flow of the reacting fluid; this promotes high mass and heat-transfer rates and good mixing. The solids may be a catalyst; a reactant in fluidized combustion processes; or an inert powder, added to promote heat transfer. Though the principal advantage of a fluidized bed over a fixed bed is the higher heat-transfer rate, fluidized beds are also useful where it is necessary to transport large quantities of solids as part of the reaction processes, such as where catalysts are transferred to another vessel for regeneration.

Fluidization can only be used with relatively small sized particles, $< 300\mu m$ with gases.

A great deal of research and development work has been done on fluidized bed reactors in recent years, but the design and scale up of large diameter reactors is still an uncertain process and design methods are largely empirical.

Batch or continuous processing

In a batch process all the reagents are added at the commencement; the reaction proceeds the compositions changing with time, and the reaction is stopped and the product withdrawn when the required conversion has been reached. Batch processes are suitable for small-scale production and for processes where a range of different products, or grades is to be produced in the same equipment; for instance, pigments, dyestuffs and polymers

In continuous processes the reactants are fed to the reactor and the products withdrawn continuously; the reactor operates under steady-state conditions. Continuous production will normally give lower production costs than batch production, but lacks the flexibility of batch production. Continuous reactors will usually be selected for large-scale production. Processes that do not fit the definition of batch or continuous are often referred to as semi-continuous or semi-batch. In a semi-batch reactor some of the reactants may be added, or some of the products withdrawn, as the reaction proceeds. A semi-continuous process can be one which is interrupted periodically for some purpose; for instance, for the regeneration of catalyst.

Selected from "*Chemical Reaction Engineering*, 2nd edition, O.Levenspiel, John Wiley & Sons, Inc. , 1992"

Words and Expressions

1. endothermic [endəu'θəmik] a. 吸热的
2. thermochemical ['θə:məu'kemikəl] a. 热化学的
3. tubular reactor 管式反应器
4. stirred tank reactor 搅拌釜式反应器
5. amine [ə'mi:n] n. 胺
6. activated carbon 活性炭
7. blast furnace 高炉，鼓风炉
8. manifold ['mænifəuld] n. 总管，集气管，导管
9. tube sheet 管板
10. shell and tube heat exchanger 管壳式换热器，列管式换热器
11. extractive metallurgical 湿法冶金的
12. commencement n. 开始，开端，开工

Exercises

1. *Fill in the gaps in the passage with* ***appropriate*** *words* ***(No More Than Three Words)****.*

Chemical Reaction Engineering and Unit Operations

Chemical reaction engineering (CRE) is concerned with thc [1]_________, operation, [2]_______________, and [3]_________ of processing equipment called chemical reactors. CER is the counterpart to [4]_________________, which is concerned with processing equipment in which no chemical reactions take place. Both chemical reaction engineering and unit operations integrate [5]_________________ to attain practical engineering goals. They differ from the engineering science subjects of [6]___________, [7]_____________, [8]____________, and transport phenomena that seek to isolate and analyze an individual aspect of a complex piece of machinery or to understand and describe quantitatively the material behavior at [9]______________ or molecular scales.

The main difference between chemical reaction engineering and unit operations lies in the presence or absence of [10]_____________. Except for purely separational process, the heart of any chemical process is one or more chemical reaction that transform less valuable feed material to [11]_____________. In the case of combustion, the main products are heat and energy rather than material products. In the case of pollution control equipment, the conversion of a harmful feed to [12]____________ is the main objective. Chemical reactors lie in the heart of any chemical plant, and the unit operations equipment [13]____________ or compensates for the inadequacies of the chemical reactors. The design of a chemical plant must start with [14] __________________, which usually run 10%~20% of the total plant cost. When you look over the [15] ___________ of a process, you will find the chemical reactor as a small unit in a very large network; yet, the design of all other equipment revolves around the chemical reactors. The optimum design of a chemical reactor does not [16] __________ lead to the optimum design of a chemical plant. The peripheral equipment of unit operations (the tail) usually wages the chemical reactors (the dog). A good design engineer chooses the dog that has the smallest [17] _______.

In a comparison of the salient features, the following may be noted.

	Chemical Reactors	*Unit Operations*
Function	Chemical reactions	Physical operations needed to service the reactors
Design	Individually tailored for [18] ________________	Modular; often can be ordered from catalogs
Cost	10%~20% of total plant	80%~90% of total plant
Performance	Highly nonlinear due to kinetic dependence on [19] ______________ ______________________	Nearly [20] _________
Intellectual Collaborators	Chemists and chemical engineers	Mechanical engineers

2. *Put the following into Chinese:*

thermal tubular reactor　　trickle bed reactor
ebullating bed reactor　　slurry reactor
chemical vapor deposition　　hydrodesulfrization
pursuit　　ozonation　　chelation　　carbonylation
epitaxy　　water gas　　zeolite　　maleic anhydride

3. *Put the following into English:*

吸热的　　放热的　　绝热的　　等温的
连续的　　间歇的　　停留时间　　返混
均相的　　非均相的　　管式反应器　　连续搅拌釜式反应器
列管式换热器　　湿法冶金的　　流体动力学　　多相反应器

Reading Material 17:

Reactor Technology

Reactor technology comprises the underlying principles of chemical reaction engineering (CRE) and the practices used in their application. Reactor designs evolve from the pursuit of new products and uses, higher conversion, more favorable reaction selectivity, reduced fixed and operating costs, intrinsically safe operation and environmentally acceptable processing. All the factors are interdependent and must be considered together, requirements for contacting reactants and removing products are a central focus in applying reactor technology; other factors usually are set by the original selection of the reacting system, intended levels of reactant conversion and product selectivity, and economic and environmental considerations. These issues should be taken into account when determining reaction kinetics from laboratory and bench-scale data, designing and operating pilot units, scaling up to large units, and ultimately in designing, operating, and improving industrial plant performance.

Most reactors have evolved from concentrated efforts focused on one type of reactor. Some processes have emerged from parallel developments using markedly different reactor types. In most cases, the reactor selected for laboratory study has become the reactor type used industrially because further development usually favors extending this technology. Following are illustrative examples of reactor usage, classified according to reactor type.

Batch Reactors. The batch reactor is frequently encountered in petrochemical, pharmaceutical, food, and mining processes, e.g., alkylation, emulsion polymerization, hydrocarbon fermentation, glycerolysis of fats, ozonation, and metal chelation. The processes often require achieving uniform dispersions of micrometer-sized drops and providing adequate exothermic heat removal especially where product quality is adversely affected by temperature.

Batch reactors are used in manufacturing plastic resins, eg, polyesters, phenolics, alkyds, urea-formaldehydes, acrylics, and furans. Such reactors generally are 6~40 m^3 baffled tanks, in which there are blades or impellers connected from above by long shafts, and heat is transferred either through jacketed walls or by internal coils.

Semibatch Reactors. Semibatch reactors are the most versatile of reactor types. Thermoplastic injection molds are semibatch reactors in which shaped plastic articles are produced from melts.

Reaction injection molding (RIM) circumvents the problems with injection molds and provides the technology for fabricating large articles, such as polyurethane automobile fenders and bumpers.

Continuous -Flow Stirred-Tank Reactors. The synthesis of *p*-tolualdehyde from toluene and carbon monoxide has been carried out using CSTR equipment. *p*-Tolualdehyde (PTAL) is an intermediate in the manufacture of terephthalic acid. Hydrogen fluoride-boron trifluoride catalyzes the carbonylation of toluene to PTAL. In the industrial process, separate stirred tanks are used for each process step. Toluene and recycle HF and BF_3 come in contact in a CSTR to form a toluene-catalyst complex; the toluene complex reacts with CO to form the PTAL-catalyst complex in another CSTR. Once the complex decomposes to the product and the catalyst is regenerated, hydrated HF-BF_3 is processed in a separate vessel, because by-product water deactivates the catalyst and promotes corrosion.

Thermal Tubular Reactors. Tubular reactors have been widely used for low temperature, liquid-phase noncatalytic oxidation, eg, butane to acetic acid and methyl ethyl ketone (MEK), *p*-xylene to terephthalic acid, cyclohexane to cyclohexanone and cyclohexanol, and *n*-alkanes to secondary alcohols, and high temperature pyrolysis, e.g., thermal cracking of petroleum feeds to olefins-particularly ethylene. Generally, conversion and selectivity to any given product are low for these oxidations. Because runaway branch-chain reactions are possible, heat dissipation must be assured and oxygen concentrations controlled. These considerations often favor the use of a series of tubular reactors in plug flow with some back-mixing in each reactor to maintain sufficient radical concentrations to propagate the reactions.

The epitaxy reactor is a specialized variant of the tubular reactor in which gas-phase precursors are produced and transported to a heated surface where thin crystalline films and gaseous by-products are produced by further reaction on the surface. Similar to this chemical vapor deposition (CVD) are physical vapor depositions (PVD) and molecular beam generated deposits. Reactor details are critical to assuring uniform, impurity-free deposits and numerous designs have evolved.

Bubble Columns. Bubble columns are finding increasing industrial application such as in ethylene dimerization, polymer manufacture, and liquid-phase oxidation. Bubble column processing offers the advantages of simplicity, favorable operating costs, and potentially superior product quality. Ethylene dimerization using homogeneous catalysts to produce 1-butene is favored compared to 1-butene produced by steam cracking, where butadiene must be separated and hydrogenated. Butadiene separation is complicated by the need to chemically remove the closely boiling isobutene, an impurity that later produces sticky polymers in some ethylene polymerizations.

Bubble columns in series have been used to establish the same effective mix of plug-flow and back-mixing behavior required for liquid-phase oxidation of cyclohexane, as obtained with staged reactors in series. Well-mixed behavior has been established with both liquid and air recycle.

Airlift Reactors. Airlift reactors are hydrodynamic variants of the bubble column in which the liquid or slurry circulates between two physically separated zones as a result of sparged gas in one zone inducing a density difference between the zones. The reactors have well-established uses in producing industrial and pharmaceutical chemicals, and in treating industrial and municipal wastes. Further applications stem from opportunities for waste minimization, eg, converting ethylene and chlorine to dichloroethane. Important features in an airlift reactor design are the means used for ensuring liquid circulation, establishing high gas-liquid interfacial areas, and efficiently separating gas and liquid. Numerous configurations are in use including physically separated internal loops and draft tubes, and external loops. Also employed are vertical vessels with circulation induced by the downward injection of a bubbly liquid at velocities sufficient to force circulation.

Loop reactors are particularly suitable as bioreactors to produce, for example, single-cell protein. In this process, intense mixing and broth uniformity are essential, and must be accomplished without foaming, segregation of either bouyant or heavy components, or recourse to either chemical additives or mechanical agitation.

Spray Columns. Spray columns have diverse specialized uses in biotechnology processing, catalyst manufacture, and minimization of waste products. Spray columns are used in the production of milk powder, cheese, and other fermentation products for direct heat-induced conversion of proteins, microorganism and enzymes, thus affecting color, flavor, nutritive value, and biological safety. Incineration, pyrolysis, and partial oxidation are carried out in spray columns for the disposal of plastic wastes.

Tubular Fixed-Bed Reactors. Bundles of downflow reactor tubes filled with catalyst and surrounded by heat-transfer media are tubular fixed-bed reactors. Such reactors are used most notably in steam reforming and phthalic anhydride manufacture. Steam reforming is the reaction of light hydrocarbons, preferably natural gas or naphthas, with steam over a nickel-supported catalyst to form synthesis gas, which is primarily H_2 and CO with some CO_2 and CH_4.

Additional conversion to the primary products can be obtained by iron oxide-catalyzed water gas shift reactions, but these are carried out in large-diameter, fixed-bed reactors rather than in small-diameter tubes.

Fixed-Bed Reactors. *Single-Phase Flow* Fixed-bed reactors supplied with single-phase reactants are used extensively in the petrochemical industry, for ammonia synthesis, catalytic reforming, other hydroprocesses, eg, hydrocracking and hydrodesulfurization, and oxidative dehydrogenation. The feeds in these processes are gases or vapors. The reactors generally are of large diameter, operate adiabatically, and often house multiple beds in individual pressure vessels. Bed geometries usually are determined by catalyst reactivity, so that the beds can be either tall and thin or short and squat. Variations of designs result from issues associated with the specific properties of the reactants or catalysts and differences in operating conditions. Either interbed cooling (or heating) or liquid quench additions are used to remove or supply reaction heat from the effluent of each bed. Multicomponent heterogeneous catalysts that require special activation treatments or unique handling requirements are used in most cases. Provisions must be made for restoring catalyst activity, either by replacement with fresh catalyst or by regeneration. Although reactants generally flow downward, air may be injected for catalyst regeneration at the bottom of the reactor.

Fixed-Bed Reactors. *Multiphase Flow* Flow regimes and contacting mechanisms in fixed-bed reactors that operate with mixtures of liquids and gases are totally different from those with single-phase feeds. Nevertheless, mixed-phase, downflow fixed-bed reactor designs are extensions of single-phase, fixed bed hydroprocessing technology and outwardly resemble such reactors. The most generally used mixed-phase reactor is the trickle bed. Special distributors are used to uniformly feed the two-phase mixtures. Hydrodesulfurization, hydrocracking, hydrogenation, and oxidative dehydrogenation are carried out with high boiling feeds in such reactors. Pressures generally are higher than in their single-phase flow counterparts. Though some of these reactors may operate in the pulsed-flow regime, these reactors retain their trickle bed name because the same configurations are used. Furthermore, reactor instrumentation may not be suited for recording the pulsation, thus the flow regime would not be noted. Where required, the temperature rise in trickle-bed reactors is controlled as with single-phase reactors. Generally, liquid quench systems are preferred.

Increased global urbanization provides the impetus to exploit improvements in feed distribution and catalyst utilization to achieve very low (<500 ppm) sulfur levels in existing hydrodesulfurization reactors for a wide range of feeds. High boiling feeds that have been successfully processed include virgin and cracked heavy gas oils and residue. Such feeds contain metals, which are hydrodemetallized and removed by deposition within the catalyst porous structures. Catalysts that are low in cost relative to noble metal supported catalysts slowly deactivate and are replaced after one to three years of use, depending on the severity of service. Vapor-liquid equilibria play an important role in catalyst deactivation. Moving trickle beds are also used in these applications. Catalysts can be fed as an oil slurry to the top and then flow downward through a series of beds. The conical bottom of each bed is designed to assure plug flow of catalyst.

Fluid-Bed Reactors. The range of fluid-bed applications is large and diverse. One of the earliest and most well-known applications is fluid catalytic cracking (FCC). In FCC, gas oils are cracked at ca 500~525 ℃ to produce gasoline and other light hydrocarbons, fine silica-alumina-based catalysts averaging ca 50~60 μm dia are used. The reactors are dense-phase fluid beds, dilute-phase transfer lines, or combinations of the two fluidization regimes. In the various configurations developed for this process, deactivated catalyst, which flows downward through a steam-stripping zone to remove residual products, is air lifted into a regenerator, where air at 600~700 ℃ is used to burn the coke. Regenerated catalyst is recalculated to the reactor.

The advent of high activity catalysts containing zeolites widened the range of design configurations, feed properties, and operating conditions. These units are large and can process 6000 t/d of feed.

Numerous other processes have followed the catalytic cracking lead, including fluid-bed coking of residue alone and combined with coke gasification, catalytic reforming and catalytic oxidation of aromatics, eg, benzene, toluene, and naphthalene, to maleic and phthalic anhydrides, ammoxidation to acrylonitrile; and hydrogen chloride oxidation to chlorine. Process developments outside the petrochemical industry include iron ore reduction and spent nuclear fuel reprocessing. Thermal and catalytic coal gasification, oil-shale retorting, flue-gas desulfurization, and ethanol dehydration to produce ethylene represent new and renewed initiatives for fluidization technology.

Gas-Liquid-Solid Fluidization Reactors. The logical extensions of gas-fluidization technology are the ebullating bed gas-liquid-solid and slurry reactors, where both liquid and gas fluidize the solids. Such reactors can be used for catalytically hydrodesulfurizing and hydrodemetalizing residual fuels, upgrading heavy gas oils and residue for further processing, and converting non-pumpable heavy crudes and bitumens into transportable lighter crudes suitable for conventional processing. Liquid recycle increases the total flow rate to that desired for good fluidization. Catalyst activity is maintained by periodic addition and removal through lock hoppers.

Indirect coal liquefaction is carried out in an ebullating bed reactor, in which synthesis gas together with inert hydrocarbon liquids fluidize the copper-zinc catalyst particles. Similarly, Fischer-Tropsch hydrocarbon synthesis is carried out in gas-liquid-solid reactors. The synthesis gas is generated from natural gas with both thermal partial oxidation and catalytic steam reforming carried out in a single fluid-bed reactor. The highly integrated combination produces clean products and exhibits high thermal efficiency, efficient heat removal, and economy of scale, features of increasing focus in the development and evolution of reactor technology.

Selected from "*Encyclopedia of Chemical Technology*, Vol. 20, R. E. Kirk and D.F. Othmer, Interscience, 3rd edition 1996"

Words and Expressions

1. pursuit [pə'sju:t] n. 追求，从事，研究
2. glycerolysis of fats 脂肪甘油水解
3. ozonation n. 臭氧化作用
4. chelation [ki'leiʃən] n. 螯合作用
5. phenolics n. 酚醛塑料(树脂)
6. furan n. 呋喃
7. fender ['fendə] n. 挡泥板，防护板
8. bumper ['bʌmpə] n. 保险杠
9. *p*-tolualdehyde n. 对甲苯甲醛
10. CSTR =continuously stirred tank reactor 连续搅拌釜反应器
11. carbonylation n. 羰化作用
12. deactivate [di:'æktiveit] vt. 减活，去活化，钝化
13. thermal tubular reactor 热管反应器
14. ketone ['ki:təun] n. （甲）酮
15. cyclohexanone n. 环己酮
16. cyclohexanol n. 环己醇
17. secondary ['sekəndəri] 仲 (指 $CH_3\cdots CH(CH_3)$-型支链烃，或指二元胺及 R_2CHOH 型的醇)
18. back-mixing 返混
19. epitaxy [epi'tæksi] n. 晶体取向生长
20. chemical vapor deposition 化学气相淀积
21. physical vapor deposition 物理气相淀积
22. molecular beam 分子束
23. molecular beam generated deposit 分子束淀积
24. bubble column 鼓泡塔
25. dimerization [daimərai'zeiʃən] n. 二聚（作用）
26. isobutene n. 异丁烯
27. airlift reaction 升气式反应器
28. hydrodynamic ['haidrəudai'næmiks] n. 流体动力学
29. municipal [mju:'nisipəl] a. 市政的，城市的
30. loop reactor 环路反应器
31. segregation n. 分离，分凝，分开
32. incineration [insinə'reiʃən] n. 焚化，灰化，煅烧
33. tubular fixed-bed reaction 管式固定床反应器
34. phthalic anhydride 邻苯二甲酸酐

35. water gas　水煤气
36. hydroprocess　n. 加氢过程
37. hydrodesulfurization　n. 加氢脱硫过程
38. mixed-phase reactor　多相反应器
39. counterpart　['kauntəpɑ:t]　n. 对应物，配对物，对方；一对东西中之一，副本
40. trickle bed reactor　滴流床反应器
41. impetus　['impitəs]　n. （推）动力，促进；动量，冲量
42. sulfur=sulphur
43. virgin oil　直馏油
44. hydrodementallize　v. 加氢脱金属
45. moving trickle bed reactor　移动滴流床反应器
46. dense-phase　密相
47. dilute-phase　稀相
48. zeolite　['zi:əlait]　n. 沸石
49. maleic anhydride　顺丁烯二酸酐, 马来酐
50. ammoxidation　n. 氨氧化反应,氨解氧化
51. oil-shale　油页岩
52. oil-shale retorting　油页岩干馏
53. ebullating bed　沸腾床，流化床
54. slurry reactor　淤浆反应器
55. hopper　['hɔpə]　n. 漏斗，装料斗，接收器(阀)

PART 4 FRONTIERS OF CHEMICAL ENGINEERING

Unit 18 Chemical Engineering Modeling

Before reading this unit, try to answer the following questions:

1. What are the main features of the modeling and empirical approaches in chemical engineering?
2. Can you list some advantages of a combined modeling and simulation approach?
3. Can you show the major stages in the modeling procedure?
4. How many basic concepts do you know in process control?

Compared to purely empirical methods of describing chemical process phenomena, the modeling approach attempts to describe performance, by the use of well-established theory, which when described in mathematical terms, represents a working model for the process. In carrying out a modeling exercise, the modeler is forced to consider the nature of all the important parameters of the process, their effect on the process and how each parameter can be defined in quantitative terms, i.e., the modeler must identify the important variables and their separate effects, which in practice may have a very highly interactive effect on the overall process. Thus the very act of modeling is one that forces a better understanding of the process, since all the relevant theory must be critically assessed. In addition, the task of formulating theory into terms of mathematical equations is also a very positive factor that forces a clear formulation of basic concepts.

Once formulated, the model can be solved and the behavior predicted by the model compared with experimental data. Any differences in performance may then be used to further redefine or refine the model until good agreement is obtained. Once the model is established it can then be used, with reasonable confidence, to predict performance under differing process conditions, and used for process design, optimization and control. Input of plant or experimental data is, of course required in order to establish or validate the model, but the quantity of data required, as compared to the empirical approach is considerably reduced.

A comparison of the modeling and empirical approaches are given below.

Empirical Approach. Measure productivity for all combinations of plant operating conditions, and make correlations.

Advantage: Little thought is necessary.

Disadvantage: Many experiments are required.

Modeling Approach. Establish a model and design experiments to determine the model parameters. Compare the model behavior with the experimental measurements. Use the model for rational design, control and optimization.

Advantages: Fewer experiments are required and greater understanding is obtained .
Disadvantage: Time is required for developing models.

1. General Aspects of the Modeling Approach

An essential stage in the development of any model, is the formulation of the appropriate mass and energy balance equations. To these must be added appropriate kinetic equations for rates of chemical reaction, rates of heat and mass transfer and equations representing system property changes, phase equilibrium, and applied control. The combination of these relationships provides a basis for the quantitative description of the process and comprises the basic mathematical model. The resulting model can range from a simple case of relatively few equations to models of great complexity. The greater the complexity of the model, however the greater is then the difficulty in identifying the increased number of parameter values. One of the skills of modeling is thus to derive the simplest possible model, capable of a realistic representation of the process.

A basic use of a process model is to analyse experimental data and to use this to characterize the process, by assigning numerical values to the important process variables. The model can then also be solved with appropriate numerical data values and the model predictions compared with actual practical results. This procedure is known as simulation and may be used to confirm that the model and the appropriate parameter values are "correct". Simulations, however, can also be used in a predictive manner to test probable behavior under varying conditions, leading to process optimization and advanced control strategies.

The application of a combined modeling and simulation approach leads to the following advantages.

(1) **Modeling improves understanding.** In formulating a mathematical model, the modeler is forced to consider the complex cause-and-effect sequences of the process in detail, together with all the complex inter-relationships that may be involved in the process. The comparison of a model prediction with actual behavior usually leads to an increased understanding of the process, simply by having to consider the ways in which the model might be in error.

(2) **Models help in experimental design.** It is important that experiments be designed in such a way that the model can be properly tested. Often the model itself will suggest the need for certain parameters, which might otherwise be neglected. Conversely, sensitivity tests on the model may indicate that certain parameters may be negligible and hence can be neglected in the model.

(3) **Models may be used predictively for design and control.** Once the model has been established, it should be capable of predicting performance under differing process conditions that may be difficult to achieve experimentally. Models can also be used for the design of relatively sophisticated control systems and can often form an integral part of the control algorithm. Both mathematical and knowledge based models can be used in designing and optimizing new processes.

(4) **Models may be used in training and education.** Many important aspects of reactor operation can be simulated by the use of simple models. These include process start-up and shut down, feeding strategies, measurement dynamics, heat effects and control. Such effects are easily demonstrated by computer, but are often difficult and expensive to demonstrate in practice.

(5) **Models may be used for process optimization.** Optimization usually involves the influence of two or more variables, with one often directly related to profits and the other related to costs.

2. General Modeling Procedure

One of the more important features of modeling is the frequent need to reassess both the basic theory (physical model), and the mathematical equations, representing the physical model, (mathematical model), in order to achieve agreement, between the model prediction and actual plant performance (experimental data).

As shown in Fig. 4-l, the following stages in the modeling procedure can be identified:

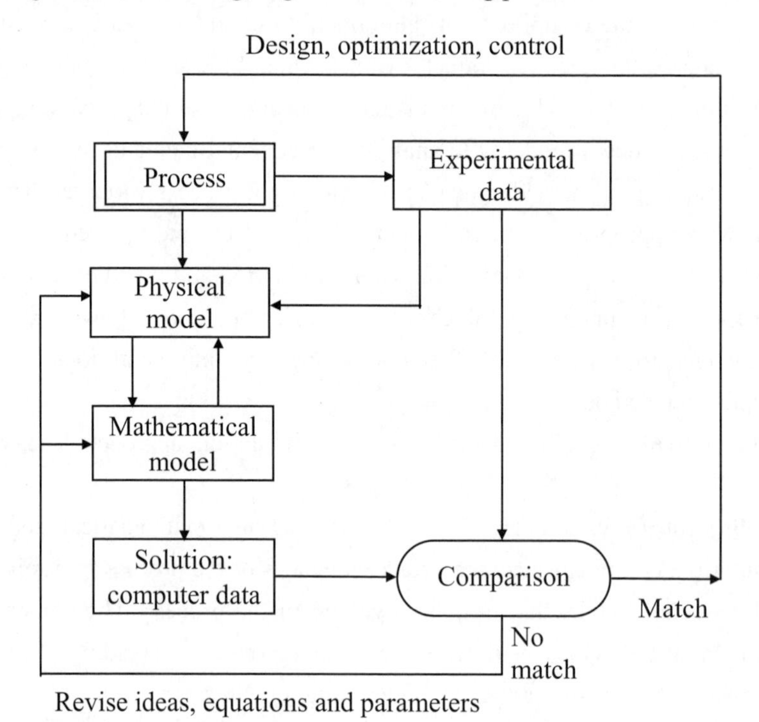

Fig. 4-1 Information flow in model building and its verification.

(i) The first involves the proper definition of the problem and hence the goals and objectives of the study. All the relevant theory must be assessed in combination with any practical experience, and perhaps alternative physical models need to be developed and examined.

(ii) The available theory must then be formulated in mathematical terms. Most reactor operations involve many different variables (reactant and product concentrations, temperature, rates of reactant consumption, product formation and heat production) and many vary as a function of time (batch, semi-batch operation). For these reasons the mathematical model will often consist of many differential equations.

(iii) Having developed a model, the equations must then be solved. Mathematical models of chemical engineering systems, are usually quite complex and highly non-linear and are such that an analytical means of solution is not possible. Numerical methods of solution must therefore be employed.

Digital simulation languages are designed specially for the solution of sets of simultaneous differential equations, based on the use of numerical integration.

Many fast and efficient numerical integration routines are now available, such that many digital simulation languages are able to offer a choice of integration routine. Sorting algorithms within the structure of the language enable very simple programs to be written, having an almost one-to-one correspondence with the way in which the basic model equations are originally formulated. The resulting simulation programs are therefore very easy to understand and also to write. A further major advantage is a convenient output of results, in both tabulated and graphical form, obtained via very simple program commands.

(iv) The validity of the computer prediction must be checked and steps (i) to (iii) will often need to be revised at frequent intervals. The validity of the solution depends on the correct choice of theory (physical and mathematical model), the ability to identify model parameters correctly and accuracy in the numerical solution method.

In many cases, the system will not be fully understood, thus leaving large areas of uncertainty. The relevant theory may also be very difficult to apply. In such cases, it is then often necessary to make simplifying assumptions, which may subsequently be eliminated or improved as a better understanding is obtained. Care and judgement must be taken such that the model does not become over complex and that it is not defined in terms of immeasurable parameters. Often a lack of agreement can be caused by an incorrect choice of parameter values, which can even lead to quite contrary trends being observed during the course of the simulation. It is evident that these parameters to which the model response is very sensitive have to be chosen or determined with greatest care.

It should be noted that often the model does not have to give an exact fit to data as sometimes it may be sufficient to simply have a qualitative agreement with the process.

Selected from "*Chemical Engineering Dynamics*, J. Ingham, VCH Publishers, Inc., 1994"

Words and Expressions

1. sensitivity [sensi'tiviti] n. 灵敏性，灵敏度
2. algorithm ['ælgəriðəm] n. 算术，算法
3. reassess ['ri:'ses] vt. 对…再估(评)价，再鉴定
4. revise [ri'vaiz] vt. 修正，修改，校正
5. verification [verifi'keiʃən] n. 检验，验证，核实；证明，证实

Exercises

1. *Complete the summary of the text, by choosing* ***No More Than Three Words*** *from the passage for each answer.*

   Process modeling and computer simulation have been powerful engineering tools for the design, [1]______________ and control of process industries. Developing process simulation requires that modelers develop the following skills: a better understanding of the process and formulating theory into terms of [2]_____________. Although developing models requires [3]__________, fewer [4]_____________ are needed and [5]________________ is obtained for rational design, control and optimization.

Since simulation relies upon a scientific rather than [6]_____________ to engineering, it has served to stimulate the understanding of the process and help in [7]_____________. It is usually a lot easier to predict performance under [8]_____________ and evaluate via a mathematical model than by experiment methods. It is very useful in the design of relatively sophisticated [9]_____________. Modeling is a convenient way to investigate the process start-up and shut down, [10]________________, and the effects of system parameters and process disturbances upon operation, so it is beneficial in [11]________________. There are some definite limitations of process simulation of which the engineer must be aware. These include the following: a lack of fully understanding of process mechanisms, difficulty to apply the relevant theory and an incorrect choice of parameters. However, it is sometimes good enough to simply have a qualitative agreement with the process.

The general strategy for the simulation of complex processes follows a path. The first step is the [12] _____________, and physical models may be formed. Then the engineer is ready to write the appropriate [13]________________. The next step is to solve the formulated model by employing some [14]__________. A convenient output of results may be in [15]____________ form. Finally, the behavior predicted by the model compared with [16]________________. Note that [17]________________travels in both directions, indicating the adaptive nature of the development of any successful simulation.

2. *By referring to the paragraph of* ***"Process Simulation"*** *in the reading material* ***"Computer-Aided Engineering"****, complete the following notes.*

Computer simulation in the chemical industry

where	*To study*
Research and development	Assess [1]__________ of the process and the effects of [2]________________ Scale-up process Interpreting [3]________________ Study of many [4]__________________
Design	Study [5]_________ between new plant and modernization of existing plant Investigation [6]__________ operation Analyze flexibility of plant to handle a range of [7]____________ [8]___________ plant and process design Reduce capital and operating costs of new plant
Existing plant	Improve [9]____________ Reduction of raw materials and [10]_________ requirements Removing [11]____________ of the process Improving [12]________________ [13]____________ of plant to incorporate technological advances (e.g., [14]______________ , solvent or process unit)

3. *Put the following into Chinese:*

algorithm	discrete	by and large	update
rate	revise	deploy	constraint
dynamic	static	correlation	generalization

4. *Put the following into English:*

算法	灵敏度	动态模型	预测
参数	系数	关系式	变量
模拟	最优化	权衡	验证

Reading Material 18:

Computer-Aided Engineering (CAE)

Engineering may be defined as a creative activity whereby a person uses the laws of nature and the knowledge of science for the benefit of humanity, while taking economic considerations into account. The laws of science, especially those of physics and chemistry, are generally stated as mathematical equations. Thus, engineering consists of applying those mathematically stated laws to the design and analysis of systems for useful purposes. Specifically, an engineer builds a mathematical model of an engineering system, such as a reactor or a chemical processing plant, in terms of the laws of physics and chemistry; then determines the parameters for the model, and finally, manipulates the mathematical model to arrive at conclusions about that system, such as its performance or its design.

A significant part of this work involves making engineering calculations, in other words, finding numerical solutions to a set of mathematical equations. The equations used may be linear or nonlinear and may or may not involve the derivatives and integrals of variables. The variables themselves may be discrete or continuous. From the time when computers were first available, engineers have used them to perform such numerical computations. Some unique problems arise because computers represent numbers electronically in binary form as they perform mathematical operations on the numbers stored in their memory. The discipline of numerical analysis has arisen to deal with such issues. It is often necessary to perform numerical analysis when developing computer programs; sometimes it must even be applied when using them to solve complex engineering problems.

Whenever a computer is used for engineering computations, several layers of programming are involved. Fig. 4-2 represents those layers and their relationships with each other. Computer hardware cannot function for any practical purpose without an operating system that manages the various components of the hardware. By and large, modeling systems are written in higher level languages, which are then compiled (or translated) into a computer's machine language before the operating system presents them to the machine. *FORTRAN* is the most popular language for writing engineering programs because of its ability to represent mathematical expressions easily. *BASIC*, *C* and C^{++} are other languages that engineers employ increasingly.

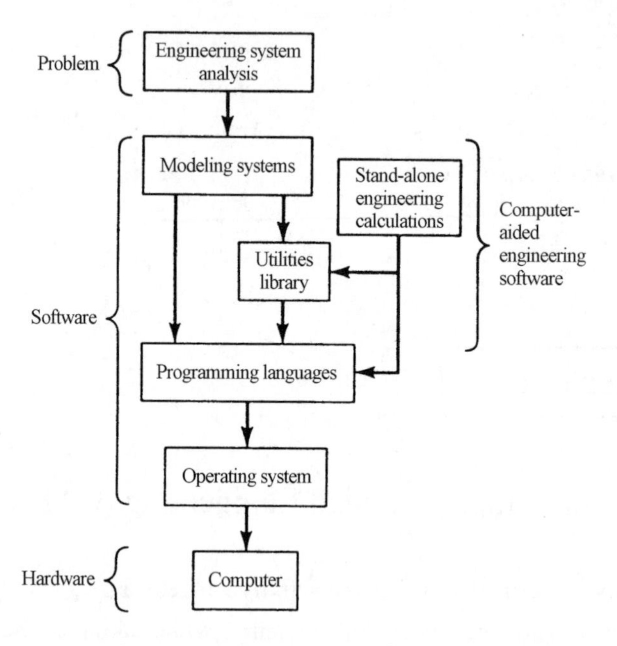

Fig. 4-2 Layers of programming with engineering computation software

1. Process Simulation

At the simplest level, process simulation involves making material and energy balances for a process flow sheet. Generally, it involves much more detailed modeling of any type of process unit to the next. Simulators have been used to model processes in chemical and petrochemical industries, petroleum refining, oil and gas processing, synthetic fuels, power generation, metals and minerals, pulp and paper, food, pharmaceuticals, and biotechnology.

Flow-sheet models are used at all stages in the life cycle of a process plant during process development, for process design and retrofits, and for plant operations. During process development, a model can be developed as soon as a conceptual flow sheet has been formulated. This model can be updated as more information about the process is obtained. Even at an early stage in the project, the model can be used to assess the preliminary economics of the process and the effect of technological changes on these economics. The model can aid in interpreting pilot-plant data and allows the study of many process alternatives.

During process design, once the decision has been made to build a new plant or to modernize an existing plant, simulation models can be used to study trade-offs, to investigate off-design operation, and to analyze the flexibility to handle a range of feedstocks. Simulation studies during process design can avoid costly mistakes before committing to plant hardware. Process engineers can use a simulation model to optimize the design of the process by making a series of cases studies to ensure that the plant will work properly under a wide range of operating conditions.

For an existing plant, a model can serve as a powerful tool for plant engineers to improve plant operations, to enhance yield and throughput, and to reduce energy use. The model can guide plant operations to reduce cost and improve productivity. Finally, the model can be used to study possible plant modifications for removing bottlenecks or for revamping the plant to incorporate technology advances such as an improved catalyst, a new solvent, or a new process unit.

Using simulation offers several advantages. Simulation makes it possible to investigate and experiment with the complex internal interactions of the system being studied whether a single process, an overall plant, or a complete company. It allows investigation of the sensitivity of a system to small changes in internal parameters or environmental conditions and this helps determine the accuracy to which these factors must be known. Simulation also allows the testing of the model system in regimes of operation that would be too costly, too dangerous, too time-consuming, or beyond the operating ranges of any one particular physical system, i.e., system's sizes, construction materials, etc.

2. Process Equipment Design and Rating

There is a wide array of computer programs that have been developed for the sizing and detailed mechanical design of processing equipment such as distillation and other separation columns, heat exchangers, compressors, etc. Process simulation programs define the material and energy flows through such pieces of equipment for a particular process. The next step in the design of any process is the sizing of the equipment.

Some computer programs can both design and rate equipment, whereas some can only design or rate the performance of the equipment. For the design of equipment, the process conditions are given as input to the program, which then produces all the size parameters of the equipment as the output. In rating, on the other hand, the physical dimensions or the size of existing equipment are input into the program, which then predicts the performance of the equipment and the outlet conditions of the process streams from the equipment. Rating programs are useful for studying alternative uses of existing equipment for purposes other than what it might have originally been designed for, and for monitoring the internal condition of equipment in service, such as the fouling of a heat exchanger or proper operation of trays or packing in separation columns. They can also be used to identify material and energy losses arising from internal breakdowns of equipment such as tube ruptures.

3. Optimization

Finding the best solution when a large number of variables are involved is a fundamental engineering activity. The optimal solution is with respect to some critical resources, most often the cost (or profit). For some problems, the optimum may be defined as, e.g., minimum solvent recovery. The calculated variable that is maximized or minimized is called the objective or the objective function.

In the design of a distillation column for a given separation, increasing the reflux ratio would reduce column height and increase its diameter and the operating cost for the column. An optimum reflux ratio can be found for the minimum total cost. In designing or developing a process with a reactor, separator, and recycle of unreacted materials, the engineer can optimize the design and size of the reactor and determine the size of the separator and the recycle constraints.

Many process simulators come with optimizers that vary any arbitrary set of stream variables and operating conditions and optimize an objective function.

4. Dynamic Models and Process Control

Mathematically speaking, a process simulation model consists of a set of variables (stream flows, stream conditions and compositions, conditions of process equipment, etc.) that can be equalities and inequalities. Simulation of steady-state processes assume that the values of all the variables are independent of time; a mathematical model results in a set of algebraic equations. If, on the other hand, many of the variables were to be time dependent (in the case of simulation of batch processes, shutdowns and startups of plants, dynamic response to disturbances in a plant, etc), then the mathematical model would consist of a set of differential equations or a mixed set of differential and algebraic equations.

There are special numerical analysis techniques for solving such differential equations. New issues related to the stability and convergence of a set of differential equations must be addressed. The differential equation models of unsteady-state process dynamics and a number of computer programs model such unsteady-state operations. They are of paramount importance in the design and analysis of process control systems.

5. Process Synthesis

Process synthesis is the step in design when the chemical engineer selects component parts and the interconnection between them to create the flow sheet. This formal approach to design includes developing a representation of the synthesis problem using a means to evaluate alternatives, and following a strategy to search the almost infinitely large space of possible alternatives. Effective solutions depend heavily on the nature of the synthesis problem being addressed.

Typically, process synthesis involves the synthesis of the following: heat-exchanger networks, separation systems, chemical reaction paths, complete flow sheets, and control systems. Significant progress has been made in developing insights to aid in the design of heat-exchanger networks. Although synthesis of heat-exchanger networks can be used for grass-roots design of new chemical plants, it also provides a systematic technique for optimal retrofit of existing heat-exchanger networks.

6. Artificial Intelligence① and Expert Systems②

Computers that started out as machines to carry out programmed calculations were soon used as information-processing machines. The next progression was to use them for processing nonnumerical, nonquantitative information and program them so that they would simulate the way a human mind processes such nonquantitative information.

Expert systems require a depository of relevant facts (known by experts) for the field or discipline the system is set up for. Most of the facts are in the form of IF-THEN conditional statements, known as rules. The software deploys and stays within the confines of all rules of logic. The system must deal with vast volumes of information and complex linguistic representations of such information and inquires for practically useful applications.

In addition to the knowledge based on the experience of human experts, the expert system might contain information about fundamental laws of physics, chemistry, or other sciences. This could be in the form of a mathematical mode of a process. To deal with deep knowledge, large computer memory and much computer time are required. Currently, there are no mature or industrially significant systems in existence that operate at that level.

The process of design, including the design of chemical is a complex nonquantitative process requiring a vast amount of information, deep knowledge of the field, and expert experience. Artificial intelligence will most likely be applied in developing process designs in the future. This is a promise and a possibility that is a target of current research.

Selected from "*Encyclopedia of Chemical Technology*, Vol. 7, R. E. Kirk and D.F. Othmer, Interscience, 3rd edition 1996"

Words and Expressions

1. discrete [dis'kri:t] a. 离散的，不连续的，独立的，个别的
2. by and large 一般来说，总的讲，大体上，基本上
3. retrofit ['retrəfit] v.; n. 改型，式样翻新
4. update [ʌp'deit] v. 适时修正，不断改进，使…适合新的要求
5. trade-off n. (对不能同时兼顾的因素的)权衡，比较评定，放弃
6. incorporate [in'kɔ:pəreit] v. 引入；体现；使结合，使合并
7. rate [reit] v. (对…)评价，估计，估价，计算
8. array [ə'rei] n. 序，列，组；族，系，类
9. constraint [kən'streint] n. 限制，制约，约束
10. dynamic model 动态模型
11. equality [i:'kwɔliti] n. 等式，相等
12. dynamic response 动态响应
13. grass-roots ['grɑ:sru:ts] n. 基础，根本；草根
14. deploy [di'plɔi] v.;n. 展开，使用，利用
15. linguistic [liŋ'gwistik] a. 语言（学，研究）的

Notes

① artificial intelligence：人工智能 (1) 一种概念认为，计算机可由程序设计来取得模拟人类智能的能力，例如，学习、推理、适应和自我校正。(2) 计算机科学的一个广泛的分支，包括模式识别、知识系统、计算机视觉、机械人、景物分析、自然语言处理和机械理论的证明，现已涉及更多的新领域。缩略语 AI。

② expert system：专家系统 指设计的能起到专家咨询作用的软件。一般有两部分组成，即一个组织好的易于扩充的专家知识库和一组用以找到结论的规则。

Unit 19 Introduction to Process Design

Before reading this unit, try to answer the following questions:

1.What does the sustainable industrial activity mean?

2.How does a chemical process design start?

3.What kinds of process documents should be included in a process design?

4.Can you explain the concept of successful scaleup?

The purpose of chemical processes is not to make chemicals: The purpose is to make money. However, the profit must be made as part of a sustainable industrial activity which retains the capacity of ecosystems to support industrial activity and life. This means that process waste must be taken to its practical and economic minimum. Relying on methods of waste treatment is usually not adequate, since waste treatment processes tend not so much to solve the waste problem but simply to move it from one place to another. Sustainable industrial activity also means that energy consumption must be taken to its practical and economic minimum. Chemical processes also must not present significant short-term or long-term hazards, either to the operating personnel or to the community.

When developing a chemical process design, it helps if it is recognized that there is a hierarchy which is intrinsic to chemical processes. Design starts at the reactor. The reactor design dictates the separation and recycle problem. The reactor design and separation problem together dictate the heating and cooling duties for the heat exchanger network. Those duties which cannot be satisfied by heat recovery dictate the need for external utilities. This hierarchy is represented by the layers in the onion diagram (see Fig. 4-3).

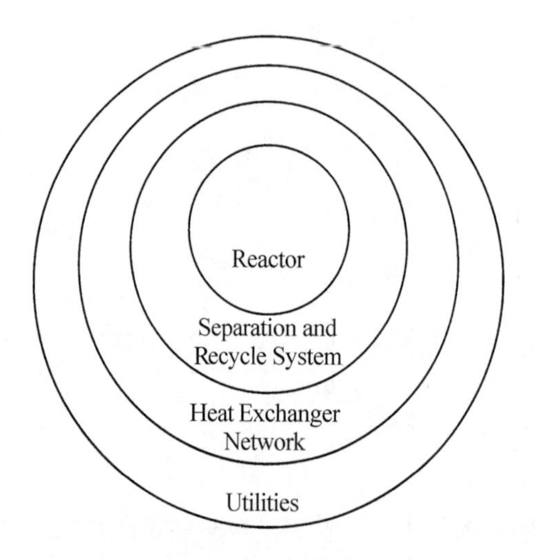

Fig.4-3 The " onion model " of process design.A reactor design is needed before the separation and recycle system can be designed,and so on.

Following this hierarchy, all too often safety, health and environmental considerations are left to the final stages of design. This approach leaves much to be desired, since early decisions made purely for process reasons often can lead to problems of safety, health and environment that require complex solutions. It is better to consider them as the design progresses. Designs which avoid the need for hazardous materials, or use less of them, or use them at lower temperatures and pressures, or dilute them with inert materials will be inherently safe and not require elaborate safety systems. Designs which minimize waste will not require elaborate treatment systems. These considerations need to be addressed as the design progresses, as each layer of the design is added.

1. The Hierarchy

(1) *Choice of reactor.* The first and usually most important decisions to be made are those for the reactor type and its operating conditions. In choosing the reactor, the overriding consideration is usually raw materials efficiency (bearing in mind materials of construction, safety, etc.). Raw materials costs are usually the most important costs in the whole process. Also, any inefficiency in raw materials use is likely to create waste streams that become an environmental problem.

The design of the reactor usually interacts strongly with the rest of the flowsheet. Hence a return must be made to the reactor when the process design has progressed further.

(2) *Choice of separator.* For a heterogeneous mixture, separation usually can be achieved by phase separation. Such phase separation normally should be carried out before any homogeneous separation. Phase separation tends to be easier and usually should be done first.

Distillation is by far the most commonly used method for the separation of homogeneous fluid mixtures. No attempt should be made to optimize pressure, reflux ratio, or feed condition of distillation in the early stages of design. The optimal values will almost certainly change later once heat integration with the overall process is considered.

The most common alternative to distillation for the separation of low-molecular-weight materials is absorption. Liquid flow rate, temperature, and pressure are important variables to be set, but no attempt should be made to carry out any optimization at this stage.

(3) *The synthesis of reaction-separation systems.* The recycling of material is an essential feature of most chemical processes. The use of excess reactants, diluent, or heat carriers in the reactor design has a significant effect on the flowsheet recycle structure. Sometimes the recycling of unwanted byproduct to the reactor can inhibit its formation at the source.

(4) *Distillation sequencing.* Unless there are constraints severely restricting heat integration, sequencing of simple distillation columns can be carried out in two steps: (i) identify the best few nonintegrated sequences, and (ii) study the heat integration. In most cases there is no need to solve the problems simultaneously. Complex column arrangements offer large potential savings in energy compared with sequences of simple columns.

(5) *Heat exchanger network and utilities targets.* Having established a design for the two inner layers of the onion (reaction and separation and recycle), the material and energy balance is known. This allows the hot and cold streams for the heat recovery problem to be defined.

Energy targets can then be calculated directly from the material and energy balance. It is not necessary to design a heat exchanger network in order to establish the energy costs. Alternative utility scenarios and combined heat and power schemes can be screened quickly and conveniently using the grand composite curve.

Targets also can be set for total heat exchange area, number of units, and number of shells for shell-and-tube heat exchangers. These can be combined to establish a target for capital costs, taking into account mixed materials of construction, pressure rating, and equipment type. Furthermore, the targets for energy and capital cost can be optimized to produce an optimal setting for the capital/energy tradeoff before any network design is carried out.

Once a design is known for the first two layers of the onion (i.e., reactors and separators only), the overall total cost of this design for all four layers of the onion (i.e., reactors, separators, heat exchanger network, and utilities) is simply the total cost of all reactors and separators (evaluated explicitly) plus the total cost target for heat exchanger network and utilities.

(6) *Economic tradeoffs.* Interactions between the reactor and the rest of the process are extremely important. Reactor conversion is the most significant optimization variable because it tends to influence most operations through the process. Also, when inerts are present in the recycle, the concentration of inerts is another important optimization variable, again influencing operations throughout the process.

In carrying out these optimizations, targets should be used for the energy and capital cost of the heat exchanger networks. This is the only practical way to carry out these optimizations, since changes in reactor conversion and recycle inert concentration change the material and energy balance of the process, which in turn, changes the heat recovery problem. Each change in the material and energy balance, in principle, calls for a different heat exchanger network design. Furnishing a new heat exchanger network design for each setting of reactor conversion and recycle inert concentration is just not practical. On the other hand, targets for energy and capital cost of the heat exchanger network are by comparison easily generated.

(7) *Effluent treatment.* It has been emphasized that waste minimization (along with safety and health considerations) should be considered as the design progresses. Inevitably, however, there will be some waste, and its treatment and disposal should be considered before the design is finalized. If treatment of the waste is particularly problematic, this might require fundamental design changes to reduce or change the nature of the waste.

(8) *Process changes for improved heat integration.* Having minimized process waste, energy costs and utility waste can be reduced further by directing process changes to allow the energy targets to be reduced.

The sequence of distillation columns should be addressed again at this stage and the possibility of introducing complex configurations considered. Prefractionator arrangements (both with and without thermal coupling) can be used to replace direct or indirect distillation pairings. Alternatively, direct pairings can be replaced by side-rectifiers and indirect pairings replaced by side-strippers.

(9) *Heat exchanger network design.* Having explored the major degrees of freedom, the material and energy balance is fixed, and the hot and cold streams which contribute to the heat exchanger network are firmly defined. The remaining task is to design the heat exchanger network.

The pinch design method is a step-by-step approach which allows the designer to interact as the design progresses. For more complex network designs, especially those involving many constraints, mixed equipment specifications, etc., design methods based on the optimization of a reducible structure can be used.

2. The Final Design and Project Documentation

Although the sequence of the design follows the onion diagram in Fig. 1, the design rarely can be taken to a successful conclusion by a single pass. More often there is a flow in both directions. This follows from the fact that decisions are made for the inner layers on the basis of incomplete information. As more detail is added to the design in the outer layers with a more complete picture emerging, the decisions might need to be readdressed, moving back to the inner layers, and so on.

As the flowsheet becomes more firmly defined, the detailed process (Pipe and Instrumentation diagrams) and mechanical design of the equipment can progress. The control scheme must be added and detailed hazard and operability studies carried out.

The design and engineering of a chemical process requires the co-operation of many specialist groups. Effective co-operation depends on effective communications, and all design organizations have formal procedures for handling project information and documentation. The project documentation will include:

(1) General correspondence within the design group and with: government departments, equipment vendors, site personnel and the client;

(2) Calculation sheets: design calculations, costing and computer print-out;

(3) Drawings: flow-sheets, piping and instrumentation diagrams, layout diagrams, plot/site plans, equipment details, piping diagrams, architectural drawings and design sketches;

(4) Specification sheets for equipment, such as heat exchangers and pumps;

(5) Purchase orders: quotations and invoices.

All documents should be assigned a code number for easy cross referencing, filing and retrieval.

3. Process Manuals

Process manuals are often prepared by the process design group to describe the process and the basis of the design. Together with the flow-sheets, they provide a complete technical description of the process.

Operating manuals give the detailed, step by step, instructions for operation of the process and equipment. They would normally be prepared by the operating company personnel, but may also be issued by a contractor as part of the contract package for a less experienced client. The operating manuals would be used for operator instruction and training, and for the preparation of the formal plant operating instructions.

Selected from "*Chemical Process Design,* Robin Smith, McGraw-Hill, 1995"

Words and Expressions

1. sustainable a. 可持续的，能支撑住的
2. ecosystem [i:kə'sistəm] n. 生态系（统）
3. hierarchy ['haiərɑ:ki] n. 体系，系统；层次

4. dictate [dik'teit] v. 支配，命令；口述
5. scenario [si'nɑ:riəu] n. (pl) 剧情概要，情况[意大利语]
6. explicitly ad. 明确地，清楚地；显然
7. problematic [prɔbli'mætik] a. 成问题的，有疑问的；疑难的，未定的
8. prefractionator n. 初步分馏塔
9. side-rectifier 侧线（馏分）精馏塔
10. side-stripper 侧线（馏分）汽提塔
11. degree of freedom 自由度
12. operability [ɔpərə'biliti] n. （可）操作性(度)
13. client ['klaiənt] n. 顾客，买主，当事人
14. invoice ['invɔis] n. 发票，发货单，装货清单
15. retrieval [ri'tri:vəl] n. （数据，信息）检索

Exercises

1.*Complete the summary of the text, by choosing* ***No More Than Three Words*** *from the passage for each answer.*

Chemical process design starts with the selection of a series of processing steps and their interconnection into [1]__________ to transform raw materials into desired products. Then the detailed process (P&ID) and mechanical design of the equipment can progress. The [2]___________ must be added and detailed hazard and operability studies carried out. The project documentation will include all process documents as well as [3]____________ and operating manuals.

Economic considerations are obviously a major constraint on any engineering design: plants must make a [4]__________. Chemical processes will in the future need to be designed as part of a [5]__________ which retains the capacity of ecosystems to support industrial activity and life. Emphases should be put on [6]__________ minimization and energy efficiency as well as good economic performance. The process also must meet required [7] _________ and [8]__ criteria.

Our attempt to develop a methodology will be helped if we have a clearer picture of the structure of the problem. If the process requires [9]____________, this is where the design starts. High raw material efficiency will lead to an economic process and minimize waste. Design of the separation and recycle system follows reactor design. Some economic separation unit operations are considered in this stage, but no attempt should be made to carry out any optimization at this stage in the design. The synthesis of reactor-separation systems and recycle system designs together define the process heating and cooling duties. Thus heat exchanger network design comes third. Those heating and cooling duties which cannot be satisfied by heat recovery dictate the need for external utilities. Thus utility selection and design come fourth. Once the basic performance of the design has been evaluated, some economic [10]____________ are still needed and changes can be made to improve the performance; in other words, [11]___________ are carried out. The "onion diagram" emphasizes the sequence, or [12]_____________, in the process design.

2. *Unexpected problems are often encountered in scaleup. Completing the following notes by referring to the reading material of **"Major issues in Scaleup"**.*

Problem	*Unexpected results*	*Possible cause*
Water as impurity		
Determination of explosive limits		
Storage of unstable materials		

3. *Put the following into Chinese:*

side-stripper	retrieval	ramification	degree of freedom
soak up	intrinsic	diagram	hierarchy
dictate	tradeoff	catastrophic	interplay

4. *Put the following into English*

可持续的	可操作性	侧线精馏塔	爆炸极限
生态系统	冷模	设想	假说

Reading Material 19:

Major Issues in Scaleup

When a new chemical process or a change in some part of a process moves from the laboratory to a commercial manufacturing operation, unexpected problems are often encountered. The problems may be of a physical nature, a chemical nature, or involve some aspects of both. Some examples of the difficulties that may be encountered in scaleup of a chemical process will illustrate the nature of the problems that can arise. Three examples will be considered: water as an impurity, determination of explosive limits[①], and the storage of unstable materials.

One of the most serious and frustrating problems that can be encountered in a commercial operation is the presence of impurities that were not considered or studied in the smaller scale laboratory or pilot plant studies. Some impurities can completely change the character of a catalytic process by deactivating the catalyst or by increasing the quantity of the by-products that are formed. Moreover, once a commercial installation has been built without giving adequate consideration to the removal of impurities from process streams, modifications can be made only with great difficulty and at significant expense.

Water is a common impurity in commercial hydrocarbon streams. In a large manufacturing unit there are many opportunities for water to "leak" into a process unit. While in principle water can be eliminated from process streams by rather straightforward manufacturing procedures and mechanical features, these can be costly and the mechanical features must be provided during the construction of a commercial plant. Otherwise, a small steam leak in a heat exchanger will result in sufficient water entering a process stream to hydrolyze chlorinated hydrocarbons, "kill" a catalyst, or seriously modify its performance. The critical features of water and similar impurities as well as their potential ramifications, if any, must be understood before the design of a commercial unit is undertaken.

Similarly, the explosive limits for hydrocarbon/oxygen/nitrogen mixtures as measured in small-size laboratory equipment are narrower (and, therefore, apparently safer and easier to handle) than when the same measurements are made in commercial size equipment. The apparent narrower explosive limits are the result of the higher heat transfer rates, especially through conduction and radiation, which are made to the walls and surfaces of laboratory equipment. Higher heat transfer rates slow down the catastrophic temperature-time buildup that leads to explosions. Moreover, small-scale equipment provides a larger heat sink relative to the combustion energy evolved. Soaking up energy also helps hold down the temperature rise.

Often, temperature-unstable materials can be stored and safely handled on a small scale with minimum difficulty by following well-established procedures. In a commercial unit the storage of such materials must be examined from a critical mass point of view to be certain that the heat removal capability of the equipment to be used is substantially greater than the potential spontaneous exothermic rate of heat release. Failure to recognize the limitations of small-scale data for unstable materials has led to a number of serious and expensive explosions and fires in plants utilizing air oxidation processes and those storing ammonium nitrate, wood chips, and powdered coal.

Implicit in all of these examples is the concept of *scaleup*. In this book scaleup is defined as: The successful startup and operation of a commercial size unit whose design and operating procedures are *in part* based upon experimentation and demonstration at a smaller scale of operation.

The concept of *successful* must include production of the product at planned rates, at the projected manufacturing cost, and to the desired quality standards. Implicit in the term cost are not only the obvious factors such as the purchase prices for raw materials, the product yield, and the return on capital, but also the overall safety of the contemplated operation to plant personnel, the public, and the environment. The timing of project completion is also in most instances a critical factor. An experience in scaleup that results in the startup being completed later than planned is not a very successful experience.

To be successful at the scaleup of chemical processes requires the utilization of a broad spectrum of technical skills and a mature understanding of the total problem under study. Scaleup procedures do not involve only technical decisions and compromises. The selected compromise always has an economic aspect since it is never possible to establish exactly what an industrial process should be. There are always restrictions of time and money availability for the total development program of which scaleup is only a part. Therefore, *calculated risks*[②] will have to be taken in the design, construction, and startup of a "first commercial unit." The scope of the risks (and, the resulting financial uncertainties) will have to be considered against the additional expenses required to improve still further one's knowledge of the process.

The required interplay of chemical engineering and the underlying sciences can be clearly seen in the decision process required to establish reactor geometry and mode of operation for economic performance. The specific combination of chemical kinetics and reactor type used to arrive at a level of reactor performance (an optimum one) can be determined entirely from either simple engineering methods or through a sophisticated analysis of the interacting physical and chemical rate phenomena. This interplay of scientific and engineering disciplines changes at each stage of the selection and development of a reactor, as shown in Fig. 4-4. The preferred path of development is rarely the simple direct one based on either theory or empiricism but rather some hybrid.

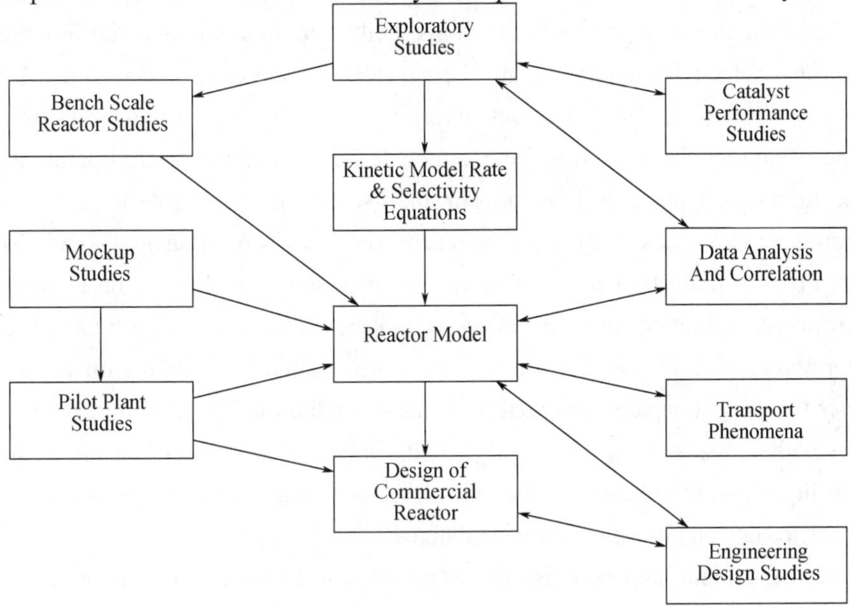

Fig. 4-4 Structure of reactor design.

Indeed, to follow a *direct path* from laboratory data to a commercial design requires either a fund of information that is often (or almost always) unavailable or scientific and engineering judgments beyond those normally considered possible or desirable. However, if only minor changes are contemplated in processes where there is considerable practical experience at several scales of operation, the direct path may be both feasible and desirable.

The first step in the development or modification of a reactor design must be the derivation of some rate and selectivity expressions from an analysis of laboratory data. Where the laboratory studies have only been exploratory in nature and directed primarily at determining the feasibility of reaction scheme, it is unlikely that even a simplified usable model can be extracted from the available data. At a minimum, reaction studies at the bench scale will be required to obtain even a marginally useful kinetic model.

However, proceeding from a kinetic model to a reactor design implies that the physical processes occurring in the reactor such as diffusion and velocity distribution are sufficiently well understood that their impact on conversion and selectivity can be allowed for. This is frequently *not* the case. When the reaction involves several phases, for example, not all of the phenomena of interest are influenced in the same manner by the dimensions of the physical equipment.

Not surprisingly, a laboratory reactor with a large surface/volume ratio can understate or even conceal a potential heat transfer problem. Pilot plant studies, therefore, are often necessary to ensure that the reactor model developed from laboratory studies can be related (and extrapolated) to the design and performance of a commercial reactor.

While small-scale experiments often permit the development and verification of fundamental hypotheses that will be used in developing a model, a note of caution is in order. As one proceeds with scaleup studies, it is critical to verify that the hypotheses developed from those early experiments are still valid. For example, for a tubular continuous reactor the hypothesis of plug flow must be verified both on small- and full-scale units. Failure to do this may result in laboratory data on conversion and selectivity apparently not being valid for the commercial unit. Model studies utilizing mockups (that is, flow without chemical reaction)[③] are often used to study the hydrodynamic behavior of a system to help establish the commercial scale operating conditions required to ensure that a hypothesis derived from small-scale experiments is still valid.

Considerable research has been done in recent years on two-phase gas/liquid flow through catalyst beds. From an industrial point of view, however, much remains to be learned about this regime. Even pressure drop in many instances cannot be calculated with a reasonable degree of accuracy. Variations of ±100 percent are not unknown. Laboratory studies on pressure drop in small-diameter tubes must be supplemented by mockup studies on the distribution of the liquid and gas phases over the cross section of a catalyst bed. Only in this manner can one ensure that the distribution of liquid and gas phases will be reasonably uniform, a minimum requirement to achieve good catalyst efficiency and minimum reactor volume.

Mockup studies should help establish the variables that determine the flow conditions of each phase in a reactor. In a pilot reactor with a small inside diameter (often less than 5 cm), uniform gas/liquid distributions are obtained even where the linear velocities of both fluids are considerably lower than those in a commercial unit. Low linear velocities can have a marked impact on gas-liquid mass and heat transfer, particularly in processes such as hydrocracking where large quantities of hydrogen are consumed. An industrial unit may appear to have higher catalyst activity and stability as compared to pilot unit runs if the pilot unit runs have not been made at conditions where the fluid linear velocities are close to those in commercial units.

Selected from "*Scaleup of Chemical Processes*, Attilio Bisio, John Wiley & Sons, Inc., 1985"

Words and Expressions

1. explosive limit　爆炸极限
2. frustrate　[frʌs'treit]　v. 挫败，破坏，使无效
3. catastrophic　[kætə'strɔfic]　a. 灾难性的，大变动的
4. soak up　吸收
5. contemplate　['kɔntempleit]　v. 设想，打算，预期；注视，仔细考虑
6. interplay　['intə'plei]　n.;vi. 相互作用(影响)，相互关系
7. mockup　['mɔkʌp]　n. 冷模，(1∶1)的模型，同实物等大的研究用模型
8. hypothesis　[hai'pɔθisis]　n. (pl. hypotheses)　假定，假说，前提

Notes

① explosive limit: 爆炸极限。指可燃气体、可燃蒸气或粉尘与空气组成的混合物在一定浓度范围内，当遇到明火或其它火源时，就会发生爆炸。此浓度范围，就是某物质的爆炸极限。可燃气体、可燃蒸气或粉尘在空气中形成爆炸混合物的最低浓度称作爆炸下限，最高浓度称作爆炸上限。

② calculated risk: 预计无可避免的危险；成败（或利害）参半的风险。

③ mockup: 冷模（试验）。化学反应的规律不因设备尺寸而异，可以在小型装置中进行研究。而流体流动和传热、传质规律一般随设备尺寸而变。在大型装置中，在没有化学反应的条件下，利用水、空气、砂子、瓷环等廉价的物料进行试验，以探明反应器传递过程的规律，这一过程称为冷态模型试验，简称冷模试验，以区别于热模试验，即真正的反应过程试验。

Unit 20 Material Science and Chemical Engineering

Before you reading this unit, try to answer the following questions:

1.Can you describe the background of chemical engineers and show how it can be used in materials areas?

2.Can you outline some challenging areas in materials science?

3.What are the fields which bioengineering encompasses?

4.What is genetic engineering?

A few years ago, who would have dreamed that an aircraft could circumnavigate the earth without landing or refueling? Yet in 1986 the novel aircraft *Voyager* did just that. The secret of *Voyager's* long flight lies in advanced materials that did not exist a few years ago. Much of the airframe was constructed from strong, lightweight polymer-fiber composite sections assembled with durable, high-strength adhesives; the engine was lubricated with a synthetic multicomponent liquid designed to maintain lubricity for a long time under continuous operation. These special materials typify the advances being made by scientists and engineers to meet the demands of modern society.

The future of industries such as transportation, communications, electronics, and energy conversion hinges on new and improved materials and the processing technologies required to produce them. Recent years have seen rapid advances in our understanding of how to combine substances into materials with special, high-performance properties and how to best use these materials in sophisticated designs.

The revolution in materials science and engineering presents both opportunities and challenges to chemical engineers. With their basic background in chemistry, physics, and mathematics and their understanding of transport phenomena, thermodynamics, reaction engineering, and process design, chemical engineers can bring innovative solutions to the problems of modern materials technologies. But it is imperative that they depart from the traditional "think big" philosophy of the profession; to participate effectively in modern materials science and engineering they must learn to "think small." The crucial phenomena in making modern advanced materials occur at the molecular and microscale levels, and chemical engineers must understand and learn to control such phenomena if they are to engineer the new products and processes for making them. This crucial challenge is illustrated in the selected materials areas described in the following sections.

1. Polymers

The modern era of polymer science belongs to the chemical engineer. Over the years, polymer chemists have invented a wealth of novel macromolecules and polymers. Yet understanding how these molecules can be synthesized and processed to exhibit their maximum theoretical properties is still a frontier for research. Only recently has modern instrumentation been developed to help us understand the fundamental interactions of macromolecules with themselves, with particulate solids, with organic and inorganic fibers, and with other surfaces. Chemical engineers are using these tools to probe the microscale dynamics of macromolecules. Using the insight gained from these techniques, they are manipulating macromolecular interactions both to develop improved processes and to create new materials.

The power of chemical processing for controlling materials structure on the microscale is illustrated by the current generation of high-strength polymer fibers, some of which have strength-to-weight ratios an order of magnitude greater than steel. This spontaneous orientation is the result of both the processing conditions chosen and the highly rigid linear molecular structure of the aramid polymer. During spinning①, the oriented regions in the liquid phase align with the fiber axis to give the resulting fiber high strength and rigidity. The concept of spinning fibers from anisotropic phases has been extended to both solutions and melts of newer polymers, such as polybenzothiazole, as well as traditional polymers such as polyethylene. Ultrahigh-strength fibers of polyethylene have been prepared by gel spinning②. The same concept, controlling the molecular orientation of polymers to produce high strength, is also being achieved through other processes, such as fiber-stretching③ carried out under precise conditions.

In addition to processes that result in materials with specific high-performance properties, chemical engineers continue to design new processes for the low-cost manufacture of polymers.

2. Polymer Composites

Polymer composites consist of high-strength or high-modulus fibers embedded in and bonded to a continuous polymer matrix. These fibers may be short, long, or continuous. They may be randomly oriented so that they impart greater strength or stiffness in all directions to the composite (isotropic composites), or they may be oriented in a specific direction so that the high-performance characteristics of the composite are exhibited preferentially along one axis of the material (anisotropic composites). These latter fiber composites are based on the principle of one-dimensional microstructural reinforcement by disconnected, tension-bearing "cables" or "rods."

To achieve a material with improved properties (e.g., strength, stiffness, or toughness) in more than one dimension, composite laminates④ can be formed by bonding individual sheets of anisotropic composite in alternating orientations. Alternatively, two-dimensional reinforcement can be achieved in a single sheet by using fabrics of high-performance fibers that have been woven with enough bonding in the crossovers that the reinforcing structure acts as a connected net or trusswork. One can imagine that an interdisciplinary collaboration between chemical engineers and textile engineers might lead to ways of selecting the warp, woof, and weave in fabrics of high-strength fibers to end up with trussworks for composites with highly tailored dimensional distributions of properties.

First-generation polymer composites (e.g., fiberglass) used thermosetting epoxy polymers reinforced with randomly oriented short glass fibers. The filled epoxy resin could be cured into a permanent shape in a mold to give lightweight, moderately strong shapes.

The current generation of composites is being made by hand laying woven glass fabric onto a mold or preform, impregnating it with resin, and curing to shape. Use of these composites was pioneered for certain types of military aircraft because the lighter airframes provided greater cruising range. Today, major components for aircraft and spacecraft are manufactured in this manner as are an increasing number of automobile components. The current generation of composites are being used in automotive and truck parts such as body panels, hoods, trunk lids, ducts, drive shafts, and fuel tanks. In such applications, they exhibit a better strength-to-weight ratio than metals, as well as improved corrosion resistance. For example, a polymer composite automobile hood is slightly lighter than one of aluminum and more than twice as light as one of steel. The level of energy required to manufacture this hood is slightly lower than that required for steel and about 20 percent of that for aluminum; molding and tooling costs are lower and permit more rapid model changeover to accommodate new designs.

The mechanical strength exhibited by these composites is essentially that of the reinforcing glass fibers, although this is often compromised by structural defects. Engineering studies are yielding important information about how the properties of these structures are influenced by the nature of the glass-resin interface and by structural voids and similar defects and how microdefects can propagate into structural failure. These composites and the information gained from studying them have set the stage for the next generation of polymer composites, based on high-strength fibers such as the aramids.

3. Advanced Ceramics

For most people, the word “ceramics” conjures up the notion of things like china, pottery, tiles, and bricks. Advanced ceramics differ from these conventional ceramics by their composition, processing, and microstructure. For example:

- Conventional ceramics are made from natural raw materials such as clay or silica; advanced ceramics require extremely pure man-made starting materials such as silicon carbide, silicon nitride, zirconium oxide, or aluminum oxide and may also incorporate sophisticated additives to produce specific microstructures.
- Conventional ceramics initially take shape on a potter’s wheel or by slip casting and are fired (sintered) in kilns; advanced ceramics are formed and sintered in more complex processes such as hot isostatic pressing.
- The microstructure of conventional ceramics contains flaws readily visible under optical microscopes; the microstructure of advanced ceramics is far more uniform and typically is examined for defects under electron microscopes capable of magnifications of 50,000 times or more.

Advanced ceramics have a wide range of application. In many cases, they do not constitute a final product in themselves, but are assembled into components critical to the successful performance of some other complex system. Commercial applications of advanced ceramics can be seen in cutting tools, engine nozzles, components of turbines and turbochargers, tiles for space vehicles, cylinders to store atomic and chemical waste, gas and oil drilling valves, motor plates and shields, and electrodes for corrosive liquids.

4. Ceramic Composites

Like polymer composites, ceramic composites consist of high-strength or high-modulus fibers embedded in a continuous matrix. Fibers may be in the form of "whiskers"[5] of substances such as silicon carbide or aluminum oxide that are grown as single crystals and that therefore have fewer defects than the same substances in a bulk ceramic. Fibers in a ceramic composite serve to block crack propagation; a growing crack may be deflected to a fiber or might pull the fiber from the matrix. Both processes absorb energy, slowing the propagation of the crack. The strength, stiffness, and toughness of a ceramic composite is principally a function of the reinforcing fibers, but the matrix makes its own contribution to these properties. The ability of the composite material to conduct heat and current is strongly influenced by the conductivity of the matrix. The interaction between the fiber and the matrix is also important to the mechanical properties of the composite material and is mediated by the chemical compatibility between fiber and matrix at the fiber surface. A prerequisite for adhesion between these two materials is that the matrix, in its fluid form, be capable of wetting the fibers. Chemical bonding between the two components can then take place.

As with advanced ceramics, chemical reactions play a crucial role in the fabrication of ceramic composites. Both defect-free ceramic fibers and optimal chemical bonds between fiber and matrix are required for these composites to exhibit the desired mechanical properties in use. Engineering these chemical reactions in reliable manufacturing processes requires the expertise of chemical engineers.

5. Composite Liquids

A final important class of composite materials is the composite liquids. Composite liquids are highly structured fluids based either on particles or droplets in suspension, surfactants, liquid crystalline phases, or other macromolecules. A number of composite liquids are essential to the needs of modern industry and society because they exhibit properties important to special end uses. Examples include lubricants, hydraulic traction fluids, cutting fluids, and oil-drilling muds. Paints, coatings, and adhesives may also be composite liquids. Indeed, composite liquids are valuable in any case where a well-designed liquid state is absolutely essential for proper delivery and action.

Chemical engineers have long been involved with materials science and engineering. This involvement will increase as new materials are developed whose properties depend strongly on their microstructure and processing history. Chemical engineers will probe the nature of microstructure—how it is formed in materials and what factors are involved in controlling it. They will provide a new fusion between the traditionally separate areas of materials synthesis and materials processing. And they will bring new approaches to the problems of fabricating and repairing complex materials systems.

Selected from "*Frontiers in Chemical Engineering: Research Needs and Opportunities*, National Academy Press, 1988"

Words and Expressions

1. airframe ['ɛəfreim] n. （飞行器，飞机）机架，构架
2. hinge [hindʒ] v. 依...为转移，依赖
3. imperative [im'perətiv] a. 不可避免的，绝对必要的
4. probe [prəub] v. 试探，探测；（用探针，探测器）探查
5. spinning n. 纺，纺丝，拉丝，旋压成型
6. align [ə'lain] v. 与...合作，一致，匹配
7. anisotropic [ænaisəu'trɔpic] a. 非均质的，各相异性的
8. polybenzothiazole n. 聚苯并噻唑
9. gel spinning 冻胶纺丝法
10. fiber-stretching 纤维拉伸
11. matrix ['meitriks] n. 母体，基体，本体，[数]矩阵
12. isotropic [aisəu'trɔpik] a. 各向同性的，均质的
13. laminate ['læminit] n. 层压塑料，层压制件
14. crossover ['krɔsəuvə] n. 截面，交叉，跨接结构
15. weave [wi:v] n. 织法; v. (wove, woven) 织，编（织）
16. trusswork n. 桁架
17. collaboration [kəlæbə'reiʃən] n. 合作，共同研究
18. warp [wɔ:p] n. 经线
19. woof [wu:f] n. 纬线
20. fiberglass n. 玻璃纤维
21. cure [kjuə] v. 塑化，固化，硫化，硬化；处理
22. cruise [kru:z] n.;v. 巡航，航行；巡逻
23. hood [hud] n. （车）棚，外壳，帽，盖，罩
24. duct [dʌkt] n. （导，输送）管，（管，渠，地，风，烟）道，槽
25. conjure ['kʌndʒə] v. 想象，用幻想作出
26. conjure up 凭幻想(想象)作出
27. pottery ['pɔtəri] n. 陶器
28. tile [tail] n. 瓦（片），（瓷，面）砖
29. silicon ['silikən] n. 硅 Si
30. zirconium [zə:'kəunjəm] n. 锆 Zr
31. potter ['pɔtə] n. 陶工
32. slip casting 粉浆浇铸
33. sinter ['sintə] vt.; n. 烧结，粉末冶金
34. isostatic [aisəu'stætik] a. 等压的，(地壳)均衡的
35. isostatic pressing （特种陶瓷的）等静压成型法
36. flaw [flɔ:] n. 裂缝，裂纹
37. magnification [mægnifi'keiʃən] n. 放大（倍数），倍率
38. turbocharger 涡轮（透平）增压器

39. whisker ['hwiskə] n. 晶须
40. deflect [di'flekt] v. （使）偏（移，斜，离，向）
41. mediate ['mi:dieit] v. 调停，处于中间
42. compatibility [kəmpætə'biliti] n. 兼容性，相容性，适应性
43. prerequisite ['pri: 'rekwizit] n. 先决条件，必要条件，前提（to , for）
44. traction ['trækʃən] n. 牵引（力）；拖拉；吸引力

Notes

① spinning: 纺丝。成纤聚合物在溶剂中溶解成溶液，或将成纤聚合物切片在螺杆挤出机中加热熔融成熔体，经纺前准备工序后入纺丝机，用纺丝泵将纺丝溶液或熔体定量、连续、均匀地从喷丝头的细孔压出，这种细流在水、凝固液或空气中固化，生成初生纤维。

② gel spinning: 冻胶纺丝。将浓聚合物溶液或塑化的冻胶从喷丝头细孔挤出到某气体介质中，细流冷却，伴随溶剂挥发，聚合物固化成纤维，又称半熔体纺丝。

③ fiber-stretching: 纤维拉伸。纺丝后得到的卷绕丝在拉伸机上进行拉伸，使大分子沿纤维轴向取向排列，同时发生结晶，以进一步提高初生纤维的结晶度，或改变晶型结构，形成一定的超分子结构，从而显著提高纤维强度。

④ laminate: 层压制品。借加热、加压把多层相同或不同的材料结合为整体的成型加工方法，称为层压，其产品称为层压制品。如将浸有合成树脂的纸张、织物、玻璃布、特种纤维等层叠起来，加热、加压即可得各种层压制品。

⑤ whisker: 晶须。通过晶体生长而得到的细而结实的晶丝或纤维，如碳化硅、蓝宝石等的丝。

Exercises

1. *Summarize the information about research activities in the some material areas, by completing following table.*

Materials areas	*Research activities*
Polymer	
Polymer Composites	
Advanced Ceramics	
Ceramic Composites	
Composite Liquids	

2. *Referring to Fig. 4-5 in the reading material 20, filling in the gaps in the following basic steps of a microbiological synthesis process.*

(1) A highly productive culture of a microorganism [1]____________________ is prepared.

(2) A suitable [2]____________________, called the substrate, is prepared to sustain the producing species.

(3) The producing species is grown.

(4) The producing species is cultivated under specified conditions so that the desired microbial reactions take place. This is the [3]______________________.

(5) The [4] ________________ is thickened and separated or the desired end product is extracted and purified. This [5] ________________ step is effected in separators, flotators, filters, and evaporators.

(6) The thickened biomass is dried by some [6] ________________.

(7) The finished [7] ________________ is obtained.

(8) Some of the broth drawn off at the biomass thickening step is recycled to the fermenter, while the remainder such as [8] ____________ is subjected to [9] ____________ and withdrawn from the process.

3. *Put the following into Chinese:*

imperative	probe	gel spinning	matrix
crossover	cure	duct	sinter
flaw	tissue culturing	hybridization	substrate
uptake	hydrolysate	DNA	corollary

4. *Put the following into English:*

各向同性的	各向异性的	放大倍数	氧化还原电势
锰 Mn	硅	锆	兼容性
必要条件	葡萄糖	好氧的	层压塑料

Reading Material 20:

An Outline of Bioengineering

Bioengineering, or biotechnology, is an up-coming and rapidly expanding division of the high-technology field. As it stands today, bioengineering encompasses microbiological synthesis, genetic engineering, fermentation technology, tissue culturing①, cell hybridization, and some other fields.

1. Microbiological Synthesis

Microbiological synthesis is based on microbial activity which brings about complex biochemical conversion to yield a desired biomass or the products of its life processes.

The reactions involved here take place in and outside the cell of microorganisms—bacteria and yeasts—under the influence of the enzymes secreted by these microorganisms. Commercial processes use microorganisms capable of reproduction at a very high rate (to date, bacteria and yeasts have been isolated that can build up their biomass 500 times faster than do the most high-yield crops) and also of oversynthesis (that is, the formation of metabolites, such as amino acids, vitamins, nucleotides, etc., in excess of what is needed to sustain the microbial cell).

Such microorganisms can be isolated from natural sources or grown artificially, using the techniques of genetic engineering or other methods. Fig. 4-5 shows a typical microbiological synthesis process.

The growth and development of the microorganisms selected for synthesis purposes are governed by a large number of factors related to the environment. The most important among them are the substrate, oxygen uptake, temperature, pressure, pH value, and redox potential.

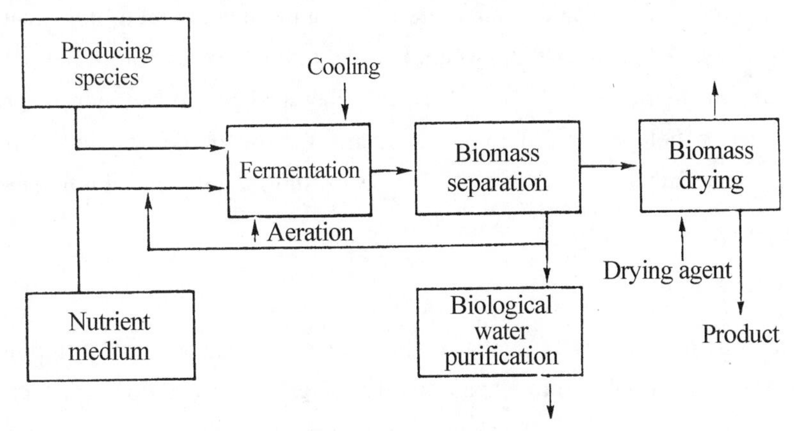

Fig. 4-5 Production of biomass

The substrate consists of organic and inorganic compounds. The carbon required for the growth of the microorganisms can be obtained from various hydrocarbons, such as n-paraffins, methane, and gas oil. The best sources of carbon are carbohydrates. The current industrial practice gives preference to the derivation of proteins from purified liquid paraffins. In the future it is planned to use methanol on a large scale for the purpose. Protein biosynthesis from methanol is relatively easy to effect and does not call for heavy energy expenditures.

The essential inorganic components of the substance are nitrogen, phosphorus, magnesium, potassium, iron, zinc, and manganese. The substrate also includes the trace amounts of the elements molybdenum, copper, cobalt, calcium, nickel, sulphur, chlorine, sodium, and some others. The deficiency in any of these inorganic elements might cause heavy damage to the development and composition of the cell.

The required concentration of inorganic elements in the substrate can be found from the balances on the nutrients in the process and their uptake by the microorganisms.

The productivity of microbiological synthesis is markedly affected by oxygen. Oxygen takes part in the respiration of aerobic microorganisms as the electron acceptor on the respiratory circuit of the cell. It is also a part of the substrate that makes up the cell mass.

For analysis and design purposes, it is assumed that the products of biosynthesis are only biomass, water, and carbon dioxide.

The principal step of microbiological synthesis is the biochemical conversion effected in a biochemical reactor called the fermenter or fermentator. Fermenters may be continuous or cyclic, sterile (hermetically sealed) or non-sterile. The mechanical design of a fermenter depends on the substrated to be used, which may be liquids (such as paraffins, distillates, and hydrolysates) or gases (such as methane or carbon dioxide), and also on the quantity of oxygen required to sustain the process, and the thermal effect of the biosynthesis reaction. Among the key requirements to be met by a fermenter are provision for high-rate mass and heat transfer, high level of homogenization, and turbulence in the reactor.

Micro biological technology mainly produces crop-stimulating agents, animal-feed supplements, including feed-grade yeasts and the essential amino acids (notably lysine), premixes, vitamins, enzymes, feed-grade and veterinary antibiotics, microbiological pesticides and disinfectants, bacterial fertilizers, etc. There is a continuous expansion in the production of agents for the textile, food processing, pharmaceutical, chemical and other industries and for research. Special promise is held by microbiological agents for the processing hides, pelts and furs, the manufacture of perfumes and cosmetics, flax processing, detergent manufacture, and some other fields.

2. Genetic Engineering

Genetic engineering is essentially the art and science of "cutting and stitching" deoxyribonucleic acid (DNA) into what is known as reformant *DNA* or *rDNA,* carrying the desired genetic information. It is one of the most promising divisions of bioengineering as it offers a means of introducing into a bacterial host cell the genetic code, or genes, from practically any organism, including the human being, thus converting it into a highly efficient protein factory for medicine, agriculture, and industry. When suitable foreign genes are 'stitched' into the cells of bacteria, these cells will then manufacture human protein, such as interferon, insulin, growth hormones and other valuable drugs and diagnostic reagents. It also offers a means for the improvement and/or development of highly efficient bacterial strains for the manufacture of antibiotics, amino acids, vitamins, and new microbial cultures that can in turn be utilized in the chemical process and food industries and as energy sources.

Genetic engineering has proved a success in plant breeding. By introducing new genes into plant cells, it is possible to endow plants with qualities that will enhance their resistance to environmental factors and step up photosynthesis rate, and with the ability to fix molecular nitrogen from the air into usable forms by themselves or to establish symbiotic relating high-rate photosynthesis and nitrogen-fixing abilities, wheat, rice and other cereal crops can be converted into varieties of an extremely high protein content without having to put in more fertilizers. As a corollary, this will also save energy, notably gas and petroleum which are used as feed stocks in the manufacture of nitrogen fertilizers.

3. Tissue Culture

It comprises isolating and growing isolated cells. These cells could be from plants, animals including human beings. The isolated cells are put in a media which could nourish them, where they multiply. Techniques have also been developed to allow them to grow rapidly. Plant cells grow relatively more easily, while human tissue is most difficult to grow.

4. Cloning

When a single cell or tissue is placed in a medium and where they multiply, they reproduce identical cells, i.e. cells possessing similar characteristics. These are clones[②]. This method is useful for replicating some characteristics in a large number of cells. The technique is useful for reproducing a large number of cells to meet a specific purpose, as for example in the production of a particular substance, a chemical, through cell metabolism. It is also useful in producing a plant which is resistant to a particular disease.

5. Fermentation Technology

Fermentation technology, or the use of enzymes as biocatalysts in the industrial production of a wide gamut of substances, is a highly promising division of bioengineering. Enzymes increase the rate of reaction millions of times. As they do so, they also allow a substantial reduction in the temperature and pressure used in chemical processes, thus making them less energy-intensive and independent of expensive inorganic catalysts. Importantly, fermentation synthesis of polymers does not pollute the atmosphere in which respect it compares favorably with the chemical synthesis of these materials.

In some cases, enzymes are immobilized, or trapped, in a suitable substrate –this makes them more convenient to handle and to use repeatedly.

Among other things, fermentation technology is to be used for the preparation of prostaglandins, biologically active substances of high value to medicine, livestock breeding, and veterinary science. Work is under way on a fermentation process for the production of glucose from the cellulose of cotton lint. When commercialized, the process will help to expand the production of this valuable product many times and to obtain a high economic benefit.

6. Commercialization of biotechnology

Commercialization of biotechnology is not opportunity-limited. Successful and rapid commercialization may depend as much on developments in bioprocess engineering as on innovations in genetics. This need for research and development on bioprocess systems presents a unique challenge to the chemical engineering profession. It is entirely possible that as much as a quarter of the profession will be involved in biotechnology or related activities within the next decade. The supply of adequately trained biochemical engineers familiar with the basic principles of the new biology is woefully lacking. Likewise, there presently exists a shortage of experienced faculty members in this field.

There is a critical need to expand the chemical engineering knowledge base to include:

(i) The design and scale-up of bioreactors.

(ii) Adaptation of existing separation and purification techniques to include bioproducts as well as the creation of novel separations techniques particularly suited for bioproducts.

(iii) The creation of biosensors, control algorithms, and process models enabling optimal control of bioprocesses.

The commercialization of developments in biotechnology will require a new breed of chemical engineer, one with a solid foundation in the life sciences as well as in process engineering principles. This engineer will be able to bring innovative and economic solutions to problems in health care delivery and in the large-scale implementation of advances in molecular biology.

The biologically oriented chemical engineer will focus on areas ranging from molecular and cellular biological systems (biochemical engineering) to organ and whole-body systems and processes (biomedical engineering). Biochemical engineers will focus on the engineering problems of adapting the "new", biology to the commercial production of therapeutic, diagnostic, and food products. Biomedical engineers will apply the tools of chemical engineering modeling and analysis to study the function and response of organs and body systems, to elucidate the transport of substances in the body; and to design artificial organs, artificial tissues, and prostheses.

Selected from "*Science, Technology and Development*, A. Rahman, Bloomsbury Publishing Plc., 1995"

Words and Expressions

1. microbiological [maikrəubaiə'lɔdʒikəl] a. 微生物的
2. tissue ['tisju:] n. (细胞)组织，体素；薄纸，织物
3. culture ['kʌltʃə] n.;vt. (人工，细菌)培养(繁殖)，栽培；文化(明)
4. tissue culturing (细胞)组织培养
5. hybridization [haibridai'zeiʃən] n. 杂交，杂化，混成
6. metabolite [me'tæbəlait] n. 代谢物
7. nucleotide ['nju:kliətaid] n. 核苷酸
8. nutrient ['nju:triənt] a. 营养的 n. 营养基，营养素，养分
9. substrate ['sʌbstreit] n. 培养基，被酶作用物，基质
10. uptake ['ʌpteik] n. 吸收；领会，理解
11. redox = reduction-oxidation n. 氧化还原（作用）
12. redox petential 氧化还原电势
13. manganese [mæŋg'ni:z] n. 锰 Mn
14. deficiency [di'fiʃənsi] n. 缺少，不足
15. respiration [respə'reiʃən] n. 呼吸（作用）
16. aerobic [ɛə'rəubik] a. 好氧的，需氧的，有氧的
17. respiratory [ris'paiərətəri] a. 呼吸（作用）的
18. hermetically [hə:'metikəli] ad. 密封着，气密，不透气地
19. hydrolysate 水解产物
20. lysine ['laisin] n. 赖氨酸
21. premix [pri:'miks] n. 预混合料
22. hide [haid] n. 兽皮，大（原料）皮，皮革
23. pelt [pelt] n. 毛皮
24. perfume ['pə:fju:m] n. 香水，香料；香味，芬芳
25. cosmetic [kɔz'metik] n. 化妆品 a. 化妆用的，整容的
26. flax [flæks] n. 亚麻；亚麻纤维，亚麻织物
27. stitch [stitʃ] v. 缝合，接合
28. deoxyribonucleic acid 脱氧核糖核酸
29. reformant 重组
30. hormone ['hɔ:məun] n. 激素，荷尔蒙，内分泌

31. endow [in'dau] vt. 赋予（with），资助，捐赠
32. photosynthesis [fəutəu'sinθəsis] n. 光合作用
33. symbiotic [simbai'ɔtik] a. 共生的，共栖的
34. corollary [kə'rɔləri] n. 推论，（必然的）结果
35. nourish ['nɔriʃ] vt. 给以营养，养育
36. multiply ['mʌltiplai] v. （使）增殖
37. clone n. 克隆，无性繁殖系
38. replicate ['replikeit] vt. 复制
39. metabolism [me'tæbəlizəm] n. （新陈）代谢（作用）
40. gamut ['gæmət] n. 全范围，全部；音阶
41. prostaglandin [prɔstə'glændin] n. 前列腺素
42. glucose ['glu:kəus] n. 葡萄糖；右旋糖
43. lint [lint] n. 皮棉，棉花纤维，棉花绒
44. therapeutic [θerə'pju:tik] a. 治疗的，关于治病的
45. elucidate [i'lu:sideit] v. 阐明，解释，说明
46. prosthesis ['prɔsθisis] n. (pl. prostheses) [医] 修复术；假体

Notes

① culture: 培养。微生物，组织或器官在培养基或其它支撑物中或上生长。

② clone: 克隆，无性繁殖系。通过无性繁殖，从单一亲代派生的生物体、细胞或微生物，它们有近乎一致的基因型。

Unit 21 Chemical Industry and Environment

Before reading this unit, try to answer the following questions:
1.Which chemical compound is responsible to stratospheric ozone depletion?
2.What is an "environmentally benign" process?
3.What should be done to make environmental friendly products?
4.Can you outline some frontiers in processing of energy and natural resources?

How can we reduce the amount of waste that is produced? And how can we close the loop by redirecting spent materials and products into programs of recycling? All of these questions must be answered through careful research in the coming years as we strive to keep civilization in balance with nature.

1. Atmospheric Chemistry

Coal-burning power plants, as well as some natural processes, deliver sulfur compounds to the stratosphere①, where oxidation produces sulfuric acid particles that reflect away some of the incoming visible solar radiation. In the troposphere②, nitrogen oxides produced by the combustion of fossil fuels combine with many organic molecules under the influence of sunlight to produce urban smog. The volatile hydrocarbon isoprene, well known as a building block of synthetic rubber, is also produced naturally in forests. And the chlorofluorocarbons, better known as CFCs, are inert in automobile air conditioners and home refrigerators but come apart under ultraviolet bombardment in the mid-stratosphere with devastating effect on the earth's stratospheric ozone layer. The globally averaged atmospheric concentration of stratospheric ozone itself is only 3 parts in 10 million, but it has played a crucial protective role in the development of all biological life through its absorption of potentially harmful short-wavelength solar ultraviolet radiation.

During the past 20 years, public attention has been focused on ways that mankind has caused changes in the atmosphere: acid rain, stratospheric ozone depletion, greenhouse warming, and the increased oxidizing capacity of the atmosphere. We have known for generations that human activity has affected the nearby surroundings, but only gradually have we noticed such effects as acid rain on a regional then on an intercontinental scale. With the problem of ozone depletion and concerns about global warming, we have now truly entered an era of global change, but the underlying scientific facts have not yet been fully established.

2. Life Cycle Analysis

Every stage of a product's life cycle has an environmental impact, starting with extraction of raw materials, continuing through processing, manufacturing, and transportation, and concluding with consumption and disposal or recovery. Technology and chemical science are challenged at every stage. Redesigning products and processes to minimize environmental impact requires a new philosophy of production and a different level of understanding of chemical transformations. Environmentally friendly products require novel materials that are reusable, recyclable, or biodegradable[3]; properties of the materials are determined by the chemical composition and structure. To minimize waste and polluting by-products, new kinds of chemical process schemes will have to be developed. Improved chemical separation techniques are needed to enhance efficiency and to remove residual pollutants, which in turn will require new chemical treatment methods in order to render them harmless. Pollutants such as radioactive elements and toxic heavy metals that cannot be readily converted into harmless materials will need to be immobilized in inert materials so that they can be safely stored. Finally, the leftover pollution of an earlier, less environmentally aware era demands improved chemical and biological remediation techniques.

Knowledge of chemical transformations can also help in the discovery of previously unknown environmental problems. The threat to the ozone layer posed by CFCs was correctly anticipated through fundamental studies of atmospheric chemistry, eventually leading to international agreements for phasing out the production of these otherwise useful chemicals in favor of equally functional but environmentally more compatible alternatives. On the other hand, the appearance of the ozone hole over the Antarctic came as a surprise to scientists and only subsequently was traced to previously unknown chlorine reactions occurring at the surface of nitric acid crystals in the frigid Antarctic stratosphere. Thus it is critically important to improve our understanding of the chemical processes in nature, whether they occur in fresh water, saltwater, soil, subterranean environments, or the atmosphere.

3. Manufacturing with Minimal Environmental Impact

Discharge of waste chemicals to the air, water, or ground not only has a direct environmental impact, but also constitutes a potential waste of natural resources. Early efforts to lessen the environmental impact of chemical processes tended to focus on the removal of harmful materials from a plant’s waste stream before it was discharged into the environment. But this approach addresses only half of the problem; for an ideal chemical process, no harmful by-products would be formed in the first place. Any discharges would be at least as clean as the air and water that were originally taken into the plant, and such a process would be “environmentally benign.”

Increasing concern over adverse health effects has put a high priority on eliminating or reducing the amounts of potentially hazardous chemicals used in industrial processes. The best course of action is to find replacement chemicals that work as well but are less hazardous. If a substitute cannot be found for a hazardous chemical, then a promising alternative strategy is to develop a process for generating it on-site and only in the amount needed at the time.

Innovative new chemistry has begun delivering environmentally sound processes that use energy and raw materials more efficiently. Recent advances in catalysis, for example, permit chemical reactions to be run at lower temperatures and pressures. This change, in turn, reduces the energy demands of the processes and simplifies the selection of construction materials for the processing facility. Novel catalysts are also being used to avoid the production of unwanted by-products.

4. Control of Power Plant Emissions

Coal-, oil-, and natural-gas-fired power generation facilities contribute to the emissions of carbon monoxide, hydrocarbons, nitrogen oxides, and a variety of other undesired by-products such as dust and traces of mercury. A rapidly increasing array of technologies are now available to reduce the emissions of unwanted species to meet national or local standards. Chemists and chemical engineers have made major contributions to the state of the art, and catalytic science is playing a critical role in defining the leading edge.

The simultaneous control of more than one pollutant is the aim of some recently developed catalyst or sorbent technologies. For example, catalytic methods allow carbon monoxide to be oxidized at the same time that nitrogen oxides are being chemically reduced in gas turbine exhaust. Other research efforts are aimed at pilot-plant evaluation of the simultaneous removal of sulfur and nitrogen oxides from flue gas by the action of a single sorbent and without the generation of massive volumes of waste products.

5. Environmentally Friendly Products

Increased understanding of the fate of products in the environment has led scientists to design "greener" products. A significant early example comes from the detergent industry in the 1940s and 1950s, new products were introduced that were based on synthetic surfactants called branched alkylbenzene sulfonates. These detergents had higher cleaning efficiency, but it was subsequently discovered that their presence in waste water caused foaming in streams and rivers. The problem was traced to the branched alkylbenzene sulfonates; unlike the soaps used previously, these were not sufficiently biodegraded by the microbes in conventional sewage treatment plants. An extensive research effort to understand the appropriate biochemical processes permitted chemists to design and synthesize another new class of surfactants, linear alkylbenzene sulfonates. The similarity in molecular structure between these new compounds and the natural fatty acids of traditional soaps allowed the microorganisms to degrade the new formulations, and the similarity to the branched alkylbenzene sulfonates afforded outstanding detergent performance.

Novel biochemistry is also helping farmers reduce the use of insecticides. Cotton plants, for example, are being genetically modified to make them resistant to the cotton bollworm. A single gene from a naturally occurring bacterium, when transferred into cotton plants, prompts the plant to produce a protein that is ordinarily produced by the bacterium. When the bollworm begins to eat the plant, the protein kills the insect by interrupting its digestive processes.

6. Recycling

Increasing problems associated with waste disposal have combined with the recognition that some raw materials exist in limited supply to dramatically increase interest in recycling. Recycling of metals and most paper is technically straightforward, and these materials are now commonly recycled in many areas around the world. Recycling of plastics presents greater technical challenges. Even after they are separated from other types of waste, different plastic materials must be separated from each other. Even then, the different chemical properties of the various types of plastic will require the development of a variety of recycling processes.

Some plastics can be recycled by simply melting and molding them or by dissolving them in an appropriate solvent and then reformulating them into a new plastic material. Other materials require more complex treatment, such as breaking down large polymer molecules into smaller subunits that can subsequently be used as building blocks for new polymers. Indeed, a major program to recycle plastic soft drink bottles by this route is now in use.

A great deal of research by chemists and chemical engineers will be needed to successfully develop the needed recycling technologies. In some cases, it will be necessary to develop entirely new polymers with molecular structures that are more amenable to the recycling process.

7. Separation and Conversion for Waste Reduction

New processes are needed to separate waste components requiring special disposal from those that can be recycled or disposed of by normal means. Development of these processes will require extensive research to obtain a fundamental understanding of the chemical phenomena involved.

Metal-bearing spent acid waste. Several industrial processes produce acidic waste solutions in large quantities. Could this waste be separated into clean water, reusable acid, and a sludge from which the metals could be recovered? Such processes would preserve the environment, and their costs could be competitive with disposal costs and penalties.

Industrial waste treatment. The hazardous organic components in industrial wastewater could be destroyed with thermocatalytic or photocatalytic processes. A promising line of research employs "supercritical" water at high temperatures and pressures. Under these conditions, water exhibits very different chemical and physical properties. It dissolves and allows reactions of many materials that are nearly inert under normal conditions.

High-level nuclear waste. Substantial savings would be achieved if the volume and complexity of nuclear waste requiring storage could be significantly reduced; this reduction would require economic separation of the radioactive components from the large volumes of other materials that accompany the nuclear waste. The hazardous chemical waste might then be disposed of separately. The disposal of nuclear waste will require major research and development efforts over many years.

Membrane technology. Separations involving semipermeable membranes offer considerable promise. These membranes, usually sheets of polymers, are impervious to some kinds of chemicals but not to others. Such membranes are used to purify water, leaving behind dissolved salts and providing clean drinking water. Membrane separation techniques also permit purification of wastewater from manufacturing. Membrane separations are also applicable to gases and are being used for the recovery of minor components in natural gas, to enhance the heating value of natural gas by removal of carbon dioxide, and for the recovery of nitrogen from air. Research challenges include the development of membranes that are chemically and physically more resilient, that are less expensive to manufacture, and that provide better separation efficiencies to reduce processing costs.

Biotechnology. Scientists have turned to nature for help in destroying toxic substances. Some microorganisms in soil, water, and sediments can adapt their diets to a wide variety of organic chemicals; they have been used for decades in conventional waste treatment systems. Researchers are now attempting to coax even higher levels of performance from these gifted microbes by carefully determining the optimal physical, chemical, and nutritional conditions for their existence. Their efforts may lead to the design and operation of a new generation of biological waste treatment facilities. A major advance in recent years is the immobilization of such microorganisms in bioreactors, anchoring them in a reactor while they degrade waste materials. Immobilization permits high flow rates that would flush out conventional reactors, and the use of new, highly porous support materials allows a significant increase in the number of microorganisms for each reactor.

Selected from "*Critical Technologies: the Role of Chemistry and Chemical Engineering,* National Research Council, National Academy of Sciences, 1992"

Words and Expressions

1. strive [straiv] vi. 努力，奋斗，力求；斗争，反抗
2. stratosphere ['strætəusfiə] n. 同温层，平流层
3. troposphere ['trɔpəsfiə] n. 对流层
4. isoprene ['aisəupri:n] n. 异戊二烯
5. building block 结构单元；预制件；积木
6. chlorofluorocarbon n. 含氯氟烃(CFC)
7. ultraviolet ['ʌltrə'vaiəlit] a. 紫外的，紫外线的
8. bombardment [bɔm'bɑ:dmənt] n. 照射，辐照；轰击，打击
9. devastate ['devəsteit] vt. 破坏，毁坏，使荒芜
10. ozone ['əuzəun] n. 臭氧
11. greenhouse ['gri:nhaus] n. 温室，暖房
12. intercontinental [intəkɔnti'nentl] a. 洲际的
13. biodegradable a. 可生物降解的
14. leftover a.;n. 剩余的（物）
15. remediation n. 补救，修补；治疗
16. pose [pəuz] v. 造成，形成，提出
17. compatible [kəm'pætəbl] a. 兼容的，可共存的；一致的，相似的，协调的
18. Antarctic [ænt'ɑ:ktik] n.;a. 南极地带（的）
19. frigid ['fridʒid] a. 寒冷的，严寒的
20. subterranean [sʌbtə'reinjən] a. 地下的，隐藏的，秘密的
21. benign [bi'nain] a. 有益于健康的，良好的，[医]良性的
22. on-site a. （在）现场的，就地的
23. sorbent ['sɔ:bənt] n. 吸附剂，吸收剂

24. alkylbenzene sulfonate 烷基苯磺酸盐
25. microbe ['maikrəub] n. 微生物，细菌
26. insecticide [in'sektisaid] n. 杀虫剂，农药
27. bollworm n. 螟蛉
28. insect ['insekt] n. 昆虫
29. digestive [di'dʒestiv] a. 消化的，助消化的
30. subunit ['sʌbˌju:nit] n. 副族，子单元，亚组，子群
31. sludge [slʌdʒ] n. 淤泥，泥状沉积物；淤渣
32. penalty ['penlti] n. 罚款；损失
33. impervious [im'pə:vjəs] a. 不能透过的，不可渗透的
34. resilient [ri'ziliənt] a. 有弹性的，能恢复原状的
35. sediment ['sedimənt] n. 沉积物；沉积，沉淀
36. diet ['daiət] n. 食物，饮食
37. coax [kəuks] vt. 耐心地处理，慢慢地把…弄好；诱，哄
38. immobilization [i'məubilai'zeiʃən] n. 固定，定位，降低流动性

Notes

① stratosphere: 平流层。对流层顶（tropopause）以上到离地约 50km 的大气层，因大气多平流运动，故名。其层内温度一般随高度增加而升高。

② troposphere: 对流层。大气的低层，对流运动显著的气层。其厚度由地球表面向上至不同的高度，极地约 9km，赤道约 17km。层内的温度随高度颇有规则地降低。

③ biodegradation: 生物降解。物质被细菌分解。

Exercises

1. *Complete the summary of the text, by choosing* ***No More Than Three Words*** *from the passage for each answer.*

The growing public concern about environmental protection gives the impetus to environment research. [1]___________ and other science help us to understand the nature of environmental degradation problems, such as the effects of CFCs on [2]____________ and the effects of [3]____________ on a regional then on a global scale. Understanding of the environmental fate of various products, scientists are searching for ways to make them “greener”, i.e., to design[4]_____________. For example, a new class of surfactants, linear alkylbenzene sulfonates, which are [5]_____________, has replaced some earlier synthetic surfactants.

Although removing harmful materials from a plant’s waste stream before it was discharged into the environment, an ideal chemical process should have no [6]________ formed in the first place and no damage on the air and water. Considerations should be put on every stage of a product’s life, including using energy and raw materials more [7]___________.

Chemistry and chemical engineering face important research challenges associated with the control of [8]_____________, and catalytic science is playing a critical role. Recycling is necessary for natural resources are in limited supply. Unlike recycling of metals and most paper,

[9]_____________ should be separated from each other and then a variety of recycling processes is required.

Some new processes are using to separate waste components, which can then be [10]____________ of by normal means. The special challenge is treating [11]_____________ in large quantities. "Supercritical" water may be used to treat hazardous [12]_____________ in industrial wastewater. Another challenge is the disposal of nuclear waste. Recent development of [13]_____________offers many applications. However, this technology still calls for modifications. Recent developments in [14]______________ offer many new concepts for destroying toxic substances. Bioreactors immobilized useful [15]________________ have been put into use.

2. *Important intellectual challenges await chemical engineers in the frontiers listed in the reading material of "**Processing of Energy and Natural Resources**". Identify the research activities in each area by completing following table.*

Frontier	*Research activities or problem faced*
In-site processing	
Process solids	
Separation process	
Materials	
Design and scale-up	

3. *Put the following into Chinese*:

stratosphere	troposphere	CFC	bombardment
devastate	remediation	on-site	microbe
insecticide	coax	domain	retrenchment
ubiquitous	pervasive	serviceability	prevail

4. *Put the following into English*:

紫外的	臭氧	可生物降解的	烷基苯磺酸盐
污水	温室效应	污染	膜分离
气力输送	粉煤灰	辛烷值	氢脆

Reading Material 21:

Processing of Energy and Natural Resources

Energy processing and natural resources processing share numerous fundamental technical problems, many of which fall squarely in the domain of the chemical engineer. The current retrenchment in research in both fields does not imply that the problems have largely been solved. Indeed, the problems are as challenging as ever, and they are not going to be solved overnight, now is the time to conduct the fundamental research needed for their solution.

In the early part of this century, technologies were developed for exploiting apparently limitless reservoirs of gaseous and liquid fossil fuels. Because these fuels are easier to handle and cleaner than coal, they made great inroads on the use of coal as a primary energy source. However, in recent years, it has become apparent that easily accessible, high-quality reservoirs of gaseous and liquid fossil fuels are not inexhaustible. Moreover, the demand for energy continues to increase as the population increases and labor-sparing machines are developed.

It is a basic premise that this challenge can best be met by developing technologies for more efficient use of existing resources and for utilizing previously untapped sources of energy.

1. Intellectual Frontiers

The demands for energy and materials continue to increase, and the accessibility of natural resources to meet them continues to fall as the most easily recovered fossil fuel and mineral deposits are depleted. The gap between rising demand and falling availability must be bridged by technology that improves the efficiency of materials. The development of such technology takes long lead times, and there is a paramount long-term need to maintain momentum in research on the frontiers of chemical and process engineering.

In-Situ Processing

Available resources of fuels and materials in the accessible parts of the earth's crust are becoming increasingly scarce. The alternative to moving greater and greater amounts of crust, whether it is mixed with the valued substance or simply overlies it, is in-situ processing. Although this technology is well established in petroleum recovery, the long-term incentive to increase its efficiency is great. The incentives for other in-situ technologies vary but are bound to intensify in the future. The development of in-situ processes involves long lead times in research and development. Field tests are large-scale, prolonged projects that may last many months. The potential environmental problems are considerable. By the time the need for an in-situ process becomes acute, it is too late to commence research. The prize goes to those who are prepared.

Problems with in-situ processing share certain elements. Fluid phases move through a vast, complex network of passages in a porous medium. The process is inherently nonsteady state. The physical transformations or chemical reactions proceed in zones or fronts that migrate through the porous structure. The fluids interact physically with the solid walls that define the passages. The passages are irregular, and their dimensions and structure change with distance. This structural inhomogeneity imposes uncertainties that make processing in situ riskier than processing in designed and constructed plants. Further, the potential adverse environmental impacts of in-situ processing have proved to be important barriers to the widespread commercialization of in-situ processes for oil shale and coal.

Processing Solids

Solids handling is ubiquitous in the processing of energy and natural resources. To liberate the desired components, crystalline solids (e.g., rocks) must be broken into grains; these may have to be comminuted to yet finer particles. Current crushing and grinding processes are highly energy inefficient; typically 5 percent or less of the total energy expended is used to accomplish solids fracture. These processes also produce a broad distribution of particle sizes, including fines that are difficult to process further. Solids comminution could be greatly improved by a process that fractured crystalline solids selectively along grain boundaries.

The handling of coal, oil shale, and ores would be improved by research on the mechanics of pneumatic and slurry transport of particulate solids, particularly on the mechanisms of failure through plugging, attrition, and erosion. Improved processes for coal liquefaction and gasification could come from research on particulate transport in fluidized beds, including high-pressure gas-fluidized beds of large particles, ebulated beds, and liquid slurry reactors. We must also understand chemical reaction processes in systems of moving particles, especially at high temperatures and pressures. There are the related critical issues of particles being consumed or created by chemical reaction, particle agglomeration and sintering, and transport and separation of hot sticky particles.

Equipment design and scale-up present particularly great challenges whenever solids are to be processed on a large scale. Consequently, advances in the basic understanding of solids processing will be for naught if they are not translated into practical, reliable designs. This will require close cooperation among the fields of mechanical, mineral, and chemical engineering and physical sciences.

Separation Processes

Separations play a vital role in the processing of energy and natural resources. Improved separations can lead to improved efficiency of existing processes or to economical means for exploiting alternative resources. For example, the petroleum refining industry is based on separations of natural and synthetic hydrocarbons. Improved separations could lead to better concentrations of aromatic hydrocarbons in gasoline to enhance the octane rating① and paraffinic hydrocarbons in jet fuel to improve burning characteristics. The winning of critical metals such as copper, uranium, and vanadium from low-grade domestic ores requires chemical extraction followed by recovery from the dilute extractant solution. More selective extractants are needed, as are better separations to remove fly ash, sulfur oxides, and nitrogen oxides from power plant and other gaseous emissions to protect air and water quality.

Every separation process divides one or more feeds into at least two products of different composition. Separation processes that operate on heterogeneous feeds usually involve screening or settling. Those that involve physically homogeneous mixtures must use more subtle means to create products of different composition. These latter processes are pervasive in industry; they consume large amounts of energy and require sophisticated research and design.

Separation processes are based on some difference in the properties of the substances to be separated and may operate kinetically, as in settling and centrifugation, or by establishing an equilibrium, as in absorption and extraction. Better separations follow from higher selectivity or higher rates of transport or transformation. The economics of separation hinges on the required purity of the separated substance or on the extent to which an unwanted impurity.

Most methods of separating molecules solution use direct contact of immiscible fluids or a solid and a fluid. These methods are helped by dispersion of one phase in the other fluid phase, but they are hindered by the necessity for separating the dispersed phase. Fixed-bed adsorption processes overcome the hindrance by immobilizing the solid adsorbent, but at the cost of cyclic batch operation. Membrane processes trade direct contact for permanent separation of the two phases and offer possibilities for high selectivity.

There is already intensive research on membrane separations for energy and natural resource processing. Applications have so far centered on organic polymeric membranes for mild service conditions, but research could lead to both organic and inorganic membranes that can operate under harsher conditions. Zeolites and other shape-selective porous solids appear to offer a fertile field of research for separation applications. Chemically selective separation agents that distinguish between absorptive, cheating, or other molecular properties are also attracting study.

Research should continue on traditional separation methods. For example, there is a continuing need for more selective extraction agents for liquid-liquid and ion-exchange extractions. High-temperature processes that use liquid metals or molten salts as extraction agents should have potential in nuclear fuel reprocessing and metals recovery; basic thermodynamic data on such high-temperature systems are lacking.

Researchers in separation science and technology draw on and contribute to a variety of related fields, including

- phase-equilibrium thermodynamics ,
- mass transfer and transport phenomena;
- interfacial phenomena, including surface and colloid chemistry,
- mechanisms of chemical reactions, especially complexation reactions,
- analytical chemistry, and
- computer-assisted process and control engineering

Future progress in separation science and technology will require continued cooperative research between scientists and engineers in these fields.

Materials

Research on materials can lead to more economical processing under extreme conditions and to reduced capital and operating costs. There are strong incentives to find construction materials for process units that are derived from domestic resources, that are less contaminating of process and environment, and that have the following properties:

- greater strength and more resistance to abrasion and corrosion;
- longer life and less subject to degradation by cycling conditions;
- serviceability under more severe conditions of temperature, pressure, or neutron flux , and greater resistance to hydrogen embrittlement②.

There are comparable incentives to develop new process-related materials that are more selective as catalysts, extractant, or separation membranes and more effective in controlling flow in porous media. In addition, the development of materials that are less energy intensive in terms of production and use is a goal equivalent to other means of energy conservation.

Materials science is an intrinsically interdisciplinary field. Materials scientists include physicists, chemists, metallurgists, mechanical engineers, and chemical engineers. It is the latter who have the best opportunity to establish specifications for needed materials and to join in research on ways to meet those specifications.

Advanced Methods for Design and Scale-up

Many of the shortcomings of energy and natural resource processing arise from lack of sufficiently powerful design and scale-up procedures for the practicing chemical engineer. A goal of research is to design large units from first principles and small-scale experiments. This has been done in the past; scale-up factors of 50,000 are common in petroleum refining technology. However, in much of energy and natural resource production, there is such complexity and lack of basic data, especially for large-scale solids processing, that empiricism will continue to prevail until pilot plants and demonstration projects are successfully modeled. Scale-up factors in solids processing typically range from two to five.

For example, research on moving hot solids will require individual pieces of equipment, then whole systems, from which reliable data for scale-up can be obtained. Costs of such research would be out of reach for all but the largest industrial and government laboratories. The application of research results to improved commercial oil shale retorting would require large pilot plants costing tens of millions of dollars, followed by demonstration plants or single commercial modules costing hundreds of millions. Such research will require interdisciplinary teams and sustained activity over periods of years.

2. Implication of Research Frontiers

Each of the generic research areas discussed here has a strong multidisciplinary character. While the underlying fundamentals of some are amenable to investigation by individual chemical engineers, in many cases collaboration will be required between chemical engineers and other scientists and engineers skilled in geology, geophysics, hydrology, mechanical engineering, physics, mineralogy, materials science, metallurgy, surface and colloid science, and all branches of chemistry. They should seek ways to involve government and industrial scientists in interdisciplinary activities. There must be free flow of information between industry, university and government, professional disciplines, and academic departments.

The educational background of chemical engineers makes them particularly well suited to solve problems in the areas discussed herein. Chemical engineers are used to working with concepts from all the related fields, and their training has evolved to cover most of the skills needed to solve technical problems. Interdisciplinary research in the relevant areas can only strengthen the chemical engineering cadre in the energy and natural resource processing industry.

Selected from "*Frontiers in Chemical Engineering: Research Needs and Opportunities,* National Academy Press, 1988"

Words and Expressions

1. domain [də'mein] n. 领域，范围，范畴
2. retrenchment n. 紧缩，节约，减少
3. inroad ['inrəud] n. （突然）侵害，(pl.)损害，侵蚀

4. overlie [əuvə'lai] v. 覆盖（在…上面）
5. acute [ə'kju:t] a. 尖锐的，剧烈的，严重的，急剧的
6. commence [kə'mens] v. 开始，开始（做）
7. migrate [mai'greit] v. 迁移，移动，流动
8. inhomogeneity ['inhɔmoudʒe'ni:iti] n. 不均匀性，多相性，不同类
9. ubiquitous [ju:'bikwitəs] a. （同时）普遍存在的，处处存在的
10. comminute ['kɔminju:t] vt. 粉碎，磨碎，分割
11. fracture ['fræktʃə] v.;n. （使）破碎，断裂
12. attrition [ə'triʃən] n. 磨损，研磨
13. erosion [i'rəuʒən] n. 磨蚀，风化，腐蚀，侵蚀
14. naught [nɔ:t] n. 无（价值），零
15. octane ['ɔktein] n. （正）辛烷，辛烷值
16. octane rating 辛烷值
17. fly ash 粉煤灰，烟灰
18. pervasive [pə'veisiv] a. 遍布的，弥漫的
19. hinder ['hində] v. 妨碍，阻止，阻碍
20. hindrance ['hindrəns] n. 阻碍，干扰
21. abrasion [ə'breiʒən] n. 磨损，磨蚀，剥蚀
22. serviceability n. 使用中的可靠性，耐用性
23. neutron ['nju:trɔn] n. 中子
24. embrittlement n. 脆裂，脆性
25. hydrogen embrittlement （钢的）氢脆
26. prevail [pri'veil] vi. 占优势，盛行，普遍；成功，奏效
27. geology [dʒi'ɔlədʒi] n. 地质学
28. geophysics [dʒi:əu'fiziks] n. 地球物理学
29. hydrology [hai'drɔlədʒi] n. 水文学
30. mineralogy [minə'rælədʒi] n. 矿物学
31. cadre ['kɑ:dr] n. 核心，骨干，骨架

Notes

① octane rating: 辛烷值。汽油蒸气和空气的混合物在发动机汽缸内压缩点火燃烧时抗爆性能的量度单位。测定辛烷值的标准物质是异辛烷和庚烷，其辛烷值分别规定为 100 和 0。汽油样品在单缸发动机内，在规定的测试条件下，其抗爆性能如相当于某一组成的异辛烷-庚烷混合物（标准燃料），则样品的辛烷值等于标准燃料中异辛烷的体积百分数，抗爆性能好的汽油辛烷值高。苯及其同系物的辛烷值高于支链烷烃，支链烷烃又高于直链烷烃。汽油中加入四乙基铅可改善抗爆性能。因其带来环境问题，正逐步被淘汰。

② hydrogen embrittliment: 氢脆或氢蚀。在高温、高压下，氢与钢材中的碳原子能化合生成甲烷，使钢材变脆，称为氢蚀或氢脆。

APPENDIXES

Appendix 1

Reading and Searching a Patent

Patent is an official license from the government giving one person or business the exclusive right to make, use, and sell an invention for a limited period. Ideas are not eligible, neither is anything not new. The earliest known patent for an invention in England is dated 1449.

Reviewing patent documents requires the skill of understanding the significance of what is being disclosed. Legal counsel should always assist in interpreting the legal effect of any patent on commercial activity. However, a patent attorney or agent often must seek the assistance of technical personnel to gain a full understanding of the technology disclosed and claimed in a given patent. Further, an understanding of the form, content, and function of the various sections of a U.S. patent assists the nonlawyer in understanding the commercial importance of any issued patent.

The cover or front page of an U.S. patent must follow the form requirements placed on issued patents by the U.S. PTO. Specifically, the front cover discloses the inventor in two locations. The first named inventor is generally used as a head note for the patent. A given patent may often be referred to in an informal sense by this inventor's name.

Once the patent is issued, the inventor is referred to as the *patentee*. The first named inventor, if there is more than one, is printed prominently in the upper left-hand corner of the front page of the patent. All of the inventors or patentees are listed beneath the *invention title* along with the inventors' full names, addresses, and citizenship if other than the United States.

The title of the invention is generally written so as to use the shortest possible accurate description of the invention described fully in the patent and found in the claims. The *patent application number* and *filing date* are printed beneath the title. The application number and filing date are important because the patent application filing date may be used to eliminate other publications of third parties that might be used to limit the legal scope of the applicant's rights.

Also printed on the front page of the patent is *a coded classification listing*. This coding is complex and largely unnecessary to a lay person's understanding of a patent. This classification stems from the specific technology area to which the patent application was assigned during processing in the U.S. PTO. The classification also results from the search or review of prior patents completed by the Patent Examiner.

Apart from the technical classification information, the front page of the patent also contains a listing of publications or references cited during examination, including "United States Patent

Documents," "Foreign Patent Documents," and "Other Publications" such as trade literature, journal articles, and product descriptions.

The front cover of the patent generally also identifies the U.S. Patent Examiner who reviewed and allowed the patent application, as well as the patent attorney, agent, or firm who worked with the Patent Examiner on the application.

Also provided is an *abstract*, which describes the invention, specifically highlighting its most valuable properties and distinguishing features. By doing so, the abstract assists those searching for prior patents which disclose developments relevant to an invention or patent application presently under examination. Another aid to patent searchers is the listing of claims and drawing sheets. *A representative drawing* may also often be found on the front page of the patent, if figures are provided by the inventor. Figures or drawings are not required to receive a patent. However, where figures are essential to a full and complete understanding of the invention, they must be included. Further, the figures should show those elements of the invention which are found in the claims.

Within the body of the issued patent, the title is generally repeated to maintain clarity. A field of invention is then provided. The field of invention should direct the reader to the general area of technology to which the invention relates, and to specific improvements in the identified areas of application.

A description or explanation of the background of the invention may also be provided by the inventor. This background section discusses previous developments of inventors working in the same area of technology and may also list publications or patents that have discussed these developments and predate the filing date of the patent application. The background section may also point to deficiencies in the prior developments that the inventor intends to overcome.

To complement the discussion of problems and prior publication in the background of the invention, the inventor may generally provide a summary of the invention disclosed in instant patent. The summary of the invention should provide an explanation of the invention in the broadest and simplest terms and should also discuss how the invention disclosed in the patent solves problems remaining in prior work in this area of technology.

The patent should also provide a brief description of any drawings or figures. This brief description is often given in the technical terms used by engineering draftsmen to explain the various views illustrated in the figures.

The next section of the patent is titled "The Detailed Description of the Preferred Embodiment", often a multipage work serving several functions. First, the detailed description should provide an illustration of the invention in both its broadest or simplest sense and in its most preferred sense. Any elements of the invention that the inventor believes are crucial to the success or performance of the invention must also be included within this description. Further, this description should provide an explanation of the invention that is definite and illustrative, so as to allow persons having nothing but the patent before them to practice or use the invention in the manner intended. This description should be understood by those who work in the area that covers the subject matter of the patent.

Elements often include a detailed explanation of the various elements of the invention comprising the function of those elements, a written description of those elements, and an analysis of the elements that relies on any figures present in the patent application. The Detailed Description of the Preferred Embodiment may also include one or more working examples, especially if the invention is related to chemical technology. That is, in cases relating to chemistry, biochemistry, and chemical engineering, working examples are more often included than not. These working examples may serve any number of functions, including illustrating the formulation, applicability, and performance of the invention. Working examples may also be used to illustrate how the invention is distinguishable from those inventions previously developed and patented. As such, these working examples may include data such as adhesion and cohesion performance for adhesives, disinfecting and sanitizing efficacy for cleaners, or data on chemical and physical properties for polymer systems.

The final section of an issued patent is the claims. A United States patent is required by law to have at least one claim. The claims represent the legal definition and boundaries of the rights resulting from the patent grant. Patent claims are analogous to the legal description which one might find on a title to real estate.

When evaluating an issued patent for purposes of determining the patentability of a new invention, the entire patent must be considered. As a result, the figures and The Detailed Description of the Preferred Embodiment are every bit as important to an issued patent as the claims. At certain times any one of these elements may become more relevant than another. For example, claims tend to be more relevant to determinations of patent infringement or violation. However, in determinations concerning the patentability of new inventions, the figures and The Detailed Description of the Preferred Embodiment may be the most relevant aspects of any previous patent.

Patent Searches. Because valid patent claims can only be issued on an invention that is novel and innovative in light of prior art, it is necessary to search the prior art for previous references either to the composition of matter, press, or machine defined in the claims of a patent application, or to any similar composition, process, or apparatus that would render the claimed invention obvious to a person skilled in the field of the invention. Inventions that have been described in a publication or embodied in a product are said to have been anticipated in the prior art and are not patentable. Patentability searches are performed by examiners employed by the national and regional patent offices and are an important step in the examination of patent applications. Patentability searches should also be performed by the representatives of inventors prior to the filing of a patent application so that the claims will not overlap with any publication in the prior art. These searches may encompass the full scope of the published literature, including patents, technical journals, gray literature, and even catalogs. Individuals or organizations who are making plans to introduce a new product or process must conduct infringement searches to ensure that they will not infringe patents that belong to others. Infringement searches need only consider patents in force and pending applications that may result in patents in countries where manufacturing or marketing are contemplated. After a patent application has been published and/or a patent has been granted, organizations that wish to practice the invention may also conduct validity searches to be used as ammunition for opposition proceedings or invalidity lawsuits. Validity searches, like patentability searches, should include all forms of published literature, but are limited to publications with effective dates earlier than the filing date of the patent application being challenged.

Searches of scientific and technical literature are performed using any of the information retrieval tools suitable for searches done for other purposes. Patent offices have devised special classification systems to facilitate searches among the individual patent documents in their collections. These patent classification systems were designed to subdivide patents into groups covering similar inventions were claimed in later applications. All of the existing fields of science and technology were defined and provided with a class code and subdivisions of the fields were given narrower classification designations. Patents belonging to each subclass were stacked together in drawers or on shelves similar to the stacks of boxes in a shoestore, and examiners or members of the public could extract a stack of patents and search for information in the subfield of interest by flipping through paper copies of the patent documents. As new fields of science and technology have developed, each patent classification system has been revised so chat the emerging technologies can be searched. Patents are assigned classification codes by the examining office and the relevant primary classification and any cross-reference classifications are printed on the first page of the patent. Although patent classifications originated as tools for manual searches, they can be searched through printed or electronic indexes as well.

Patent systems were conceived encouraging the dissemination of information on technological developments. Information dissemination is therefore essential for the patenting process. Patent offices have traditionally announced the issuance of new patents in bulletins and gazettes. Other organizations, notably scientific and technical societies and for profit publishers, have produced value-added patent information services. These secondary sources of patent information serve multiple purposes, among which are current awareness alerting, document delivery, and retrospective searching. Traditionally, such products have appeared as printed publications, but increasingly they have found second use in electronic form in on-line databases, and in the 1990s there has been rapid growth of optical storage of information, especially as Compact Disk-Read Only Memory (CD-ROM) products. Patent documentation is a field in considerable ferment, with rapid introduction of new products and capabilities.

Printed Patent Office Gazettes. The issuance of patents is announced by patent offices in publications typically known as gazettes and bulletins, which are published most commonly at the time of the patent's publication, but there are exceptions. Advance information is published in a patent gazette by some countries prior to the publication of patent documents, typically as a notification of filing details. However, some patent gazettes do not appear until well after the effective publication date of the patents they announce. The amount of information included in patent gazettes varies. Typically, they include bibliographic details on published patent applications and granted patents, including patent number, title, inventor, patentee, patent classification, application number and date, and priority application details if relevant. Some gazettes also provide the front page abstract of the patent and a representative drawing. In addition to announcement of new patents and applications, the various gazettes typically include listings of patents that have been rejected, challenged, or disclaimed, patents that have been allowed to lapse, and in some instances even listings of new applications that have been made but that will not be published for some time, if ever. Gazettes often include indexes to the information they contain; the amount of indexing available varies from country to country.

Information from Other Sources. Some of the abstracting and indexing services produced by scientific and technical societies have traditionally included patent information, especially in the field of chemistry. For instance, *Chemical Abstracts* (CA), produced by the American Chemical Society since 1907, has always covered patents. On the other hand, some notable information services have not included patent coverage. One example, despite the fact that many patents are based on some aspects of engineering, is the *Engineering Index*. *Science Abstracts*, covering physics, electricity, and electronics, is another example, which has not covered patents since 1976. However, even where patents are covered, the focus may not be ideal for those concerned with the legal aspects of patents. Thus, CA in its patent coverage documents the new chemistry involved, but shies away from the legal aspect of patents. For these and other reasons, others have stepped in to develop a variety of patent information services, e.g., Derwent information Ltd. of London.

Selected from "*Encyclopedia of Chemical Technology*, Vol. 19, R. E. Kirk and D.F. Othmer, Interscience, 3rd edition 1996"

Words and Expressions

1. attorney [ə'tə:ni] n. 代理人，律师
2. U.S.PTO = United States Patent Office 美国专利局
3. patentee [pætən'ti:] n. 专利权所有人
4. lay [lei] a. 外行的，局外的
5. draftsman = draughtsman ['drɑ:ftsmən] n. 制图员，绘图员，起草者
6. embodiment [im'bɔdimənt] n. 具体化，具体体现
7. infringement n. 侵害，违反
8. gazette [gə'zet] n. 公报，报纸
9. lapse [læps] n.;v. 失效，终止

Appendix 2

Design Information and Data

Information on manufacturing processes, equipment parameters, materials of construction, costs and the physical properties of process materials are needed at all stages of design; from the initial screening of possible processes, to the plant start-up and production.

When a project is largely a repeat of a previous project, the data and information required for the design will be available in the Company's process files, if proper detailed records are kept. For a new project or process, the design data will have to be obtained from the literature, or by experiment (research laboratory and pilot plant), or purchased from other companies. The information on manufacturing processes available in the general literature can be of use in the initial stages of process design, for screening potential process; but is usually mainly descriptive, and too superficial to be of much use for detailed design and evaluation.

The literature on the physical properties of elements and compounds is extensive, and reliable values for common materials can usually be found. Where values cannot be found, the data required will have to be measured experimentally or estimated. Methods of estimating (predicting) the more important physical properties required for design are given in this chapter.

Readers who are unfamiliar with the sources of information, and the techniques used for searching the literature, should consult one of the many guides to the technical literature that have been published.

1. Sources of Information on Manufacturing Processes

In this section the sources of information available in the open literature on commercial processes for the production of chemicals and related products are reviewed. The chemical process industries are competitive, and the information that is published on commercial processes is restricted. The articles on particular processes published in the technical literature and in textbooks invariably give only a superficial account of the chemistry and unit operations used. They lack the detailed information needed on reaction kinetics, process conditions, equipment parameters, and physical properties needed for process design. The information that can be found in the general literature is, however, useful in the early stages of a project, when searching for possible process routes. It is often sufficient for a flow-sheet of the process to be drawn up and a rough estimate of the capital and production costs made.

The most comprehensive collection of information on manufacturing processes is probably the *Encyclopedia of Chemical Technology* edited by Kirk and Othmer (1978, 1991ff), which covers the whole range of chemical and associated products. Another encyclopedia covering manufacturing processes is that edited by McKetta (1977). Several books have also been published which give brief summaries of the production processes used for the commercial chemicals and chemical products. The most well known of these is probably Shreve's book on the chemical process industries, now updated by Austin, Austin (1984).

The extensive German reference work on industrial processes, *Ullman's Encyclopedia of Industrial Technology*, is now available in an English translation, Ullman (1984).

Specialized texts have been published on some of the more important bulk industrial chemicals, such as that by Miller (1969) on ethylene and its derivatives; these are too numerous to list but should be available in the larger reference libraries and can be found by reference to the library catalogue.

Books quickly become outdated, and many of the processes described are obsolete, or at best obsolescent. More up-to-date descriptions of the processes in current use can be found in the technical journals. The journal *Hydrocarbon Processing* publishes an annual review of petrochemical processes, which was entitled *Petrochemical Developments* and is now called

Petrochemicals Notebook; this gives flow-diagrams and brief process descriptions of new process developments. Patents are a useful source of information; but it should be remembered that the patentee will try to write the patent in a way that protects his invention, whilst disclosing the least amount of useful information to his competitors. The examples given in a patent to support the claims often give an indication of the process conditions used; though they are frequently examples of laboratory preparations, rather than of the full-scale manufacturing processes. Several short guides have been written to help engineers understand the use of patents for the protection of inventions, and as sources of information.

2. General Sources of Physical Properties

International Critical Tables (1933) is still probably the most comprehensive compilation of physical properties, and is available in most reference libraries. Though it was first published in 1933, physical properties do not change, except in as much as experimental techniques improve, and ICT is still a useful source of engineering data.

Tables and graphs of physical properties are given in many handbooks and textbooks on Chemical Engineering and related subjects. Many of the data given are duplicated from book to book, but the various handbooks do provide quick, easy access to data on the more commonly used substances.

An extensive compilation of thermophysical data has been published by Plenum Press, Touloukian (1970~1977). This multiple-volume work covers conductivity, specific heat, thermal expansion, viscosity and radiative properties.

The Engineering Sciences Data Unit (ESDU) was set up to provide authenticated data for engineering design. Its publications include some physical property data, and other design data and methods of interest to chemical engineering designers. They also cover data and methods of use in the mechanical design of equipment.

Caution should be exercised when taking data from the literature, as typographical errors often occur. If a value looks doubtful it should be cross-checked in an independent reference, or by estimation.

The values of some properties will be dependent on the method of measurement; for example, surface tension and flash point, and the method used should be checked, by reference to the original paper if necessary, if an accurate value is required.

The results of research work on physical properties are reported in the general engineering and scientific literature. The *Journal of Chemical Engineering Data* specializes in publishing physical property data for use in chemical engineering design. A quick search of the literature for data can be made by using the abstracting journals; such as *Chemical Abstracts* (American Chemical Society) and *Engineering Index* (Engineering Index inc., New York).

Computerized physical property data banks have been set up by various organizations to provide a service to the design engineer. They can be incorporated into computer-aided design programs and are increasingly being used to provide reliable, authenticated, design data.

3. Sources of Information on Chemical Engineering

Journals

(1) Chemical Engineering Science (England)

(2) International Journal of heat and Mass Transfer (England)

(3) The Chemical Engineering Journal (England)

(4) I and EC—Process Design and Development (America)

(5) I and EC—Product Research and Development (America)

(6) I and EC—Fundamentals (America)

(7) Chemical Engineering Progress (America)

(8) Journal of the American Institute of Chemical Engineers (AIChE Journal)

(9) Chemical Engineering (America)

(10) ChemTech (America)

(11) Environmental and Technology (America)

(12) Journal of Chemical and Engineering Data (America)

(13) Hydrocarbon (America)

(14) Oil and Gas and Petroleum Equipment (America)

(15) Journal of Petroleum Technology (America)

(16) Advances in Heat Transfer (America)

(17) Journal of Applied Polymer Science (America)

(18) The Canadian Journal of Chemical Engineering

Abstract

(1) Engineering Index

(2) Chemical Abstracts (America)

(3) Theoretical Chemical Engineering Abstracts

Handbooks and Encyclopaedia

(1) Chemical Engineers' Handbook

R. H. Prrry and C. H. Chilton, 6th edn., McGraw-Hill,1984

(2) Handbook of Heat Transfer

W. H. Rohaenow and J. P. Hartnett, McGraw-Hill,1973

(3) Chemical Engineering Practice

H. W. Gremer and T. Davies, Butterworths, 1956~1960

(4) Encyclopaedia of Chemical Technology

Kirk-Othmer, 2th edn, Wiley,1963-

(5) The Materials Handbook

George S. Brady, 10th edn, McGraw-Hill, 1971

References:

(1) *An Introduction to Industrial Chemistry,* 2nd Edition, C.A. Heaton, Blackie & Son Ltd., 1997

(2) *Chemical Engineering, Vol 6*, 2nd Edition, R.K. Sinnott, Pergamon Press, 1996

Words and Expressions

1. International Critical Tables　国际标准数据表
2. Engineering Sciences Data Unit　工程科学数据组织（英）
3. flash point　闪点

Appendix 3

化学化工常用构词

1. aci-	酸式
2. aero-	空气
3. -al	醛
4. ald-	醛
5. -aldehyde	醛
6. -amide	酰胺
7. -amine	胺
8. amino-	氨基
9. -ane	烷
10. anhydro-	脱水
11. anti-	反，抗，对，解，阻
12. aryl-	芳（香）基
13. -ase	酶
14. –ate	[词尾] 用于由词尾为-ic的酸所成的盐类或酯类的名称
15. auto-	自，自动
16. benz-	苯基
17. bi-	二，两个，双
18. bio-	生物的
19. bis-	两个，双
20. -carboxylic acid	羧酸
21. chemico-	化学的
22. chemo-	化学
23. chlor-	氯
24. chloro-	氯代，氯（基） Cl—
25. chromato-	色谱
26. chromo-	色
27. cis-	顺式
28. co-	共，同，相互
29. counter-	反，逆
30. cyan-	氰基 CN—
31. cycl(o)-	环（合，化），（循）环
32. de-	脱，去，除，解，减，消，反，止
33. deca-	十，癸
34. dehydro-	脱氢
35. dextro-	右旋的
36. di-	二，双（指基的数目）；联（二）指两个基以一价相联；双（指两个单体相接合）
37. dodeca-	十二
38. electro-	电
39. -en	[词尾]指烃或环型化合物
40. endo-	内，桥（环内桥接）
41. -ene	烯
42. epoxy-	环氧
43. -ether	醚
44. ferri-	铁
45. ferro-	亚铁
46. fluo-	氟，荧
47. fluoro-	氟代，氟（基）
48. haem-	血的
49. halo-	卤
50. hepta-	七，庚
51. hetero-	杂，不同
52. hexa-	六，己
53. homo-	同（型），高
54. hydro-	氢化的，氢的，水
55. -ic anhydride	酸酐
56. -ide	一化物
57. infra-	在下，较低
58. inter-	（在）中（间），互相，　合，一起
59. intra-	内
60. iso-	异；同，等
61. -ketone	酮

62. -lactone 内酯
63. laevo- 左旋
64. lipo- 酯的
65. *m*- (=meta) 间
66. meso- 内消旋；中（间）
67. meta- 间（位）（有机系统名用）；偏（无机酸用）
68. mono- 一，单
69. multi- 多
70. nitro- 硝基
71. non- 不，非，无
72. nona- 九，壬
73. *o*- (= ortho) 邻（位）一
74. octa- 八，辛
75. -oic acid 酸
76. -ol 醇；酚
77. -one 酮
78. ortho- 正，原，邻（位）
79. -ose 糖
80. -oside 糖苷
81. over- 过（度），超，在外 oxo- 氧化，氧代，含氧的
82. para- （位次）对；仲
83. penta- 五，戊
84. per- 高，过，全
85. phono- 声，音
86. photo- 光，感光的
87. poly- 多，聚
88. pre- 预，前，先，在上
89. pyro- 火，热，高温，焦
90. radio- 放射，辐射
91. re- 再，重；回，向后；相互；相反
92. retro- 向后
93. rheo- 流
94. stereo- 立体，固（体）
95. sub- 下，亚，次；副
96. sulf- [词头] 表示有硫存在
97. sulfo- 硫代，磺基
98. -sulfonic acid 磺酸
99. super- 过，超，高于
100. syn- 同，共，与；顺式
101. tauto- 互变（异构）
102. tetra- 四，丁
103. thio- 硫代
104. trans- 反（式）；超，跨，过，（以）外，后
105. tri- 三，丙
106. ultra- 超，过，（以）外；极端，异常，过度
107. under- 在下，底下，不足，从属
108. uni- 单，一
109. -yl （某）基
110. -ylene （某）烯
111. -yne （某）炔

常见有机基团

1. acetenyl = ethynyl 乙炔基
2. acetoxy 乙酸基，乙酰氧基
3. acetyl 乙酰基
4. aldo （表示有醛基存在）醛（元），氧代
5. alkoxy 烷氧基
6. amino 氨基
7. amyl = pentyl 戊基
8. anilino 苯胺基
9. anthraquinonyl 蒽醌基
10. anthryl 蒽基
11. axo 偶氮基
12. azido 叠氮基
13. benzoxy = benzoyloxy 苯甲酸基
14. butyl 丁基
15. carbonyl 羰基
16. carboxy(l) 羧基
17. decyl 癸基
18. diazo 重氮基
19. ethyl 乙基
20. formyl 甲酰
21. heptyl 庚基
22. hexyl 己基
23. hydroxy(l) 羟基
24. methene = methylene 亚甲基
25. methenyl = methylidyne 次甲基
26. methyl 甲基
27. naphthyl 萘基

28. nitro 硝基
29. nitroso 亚硝基
30. nonyl 壬基
31. octyl 辛基
32. pentyl 戊基
33. phenyl 苯基
34. propenyl 丙烯基
35. propyl 丙基
36. sulfo 磺基
37. thio 硫代
38. vinyl 乙烯基

Appendix 4

Nomenclature of Organic Compounds

Common or trivial name	***Systematic (or IUPAC) name***	***Structure***
Paraffin	Alkane	—
Cycloparaffins or	Cycloalkanes	—
Naphthenes		—
Olefins	Alkenes	—
Acetylenes	Alkynes	
Methacrylates	2-Methylpropenoates	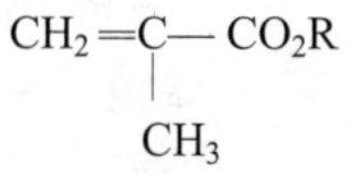 $CH_2=C(CH_3)-CO_2R$
Ethylene	Ethene	$CH_2=CH_2$
Propylene	Propene	$CH_3CH=CH_2$
Styrene	Phenylethene	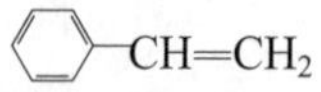 $C_6H_5-CH=CH_2$
Acetylene	Ethyne	$HC\equiv CH$
Isoprene	2-Methylbuta-l, 3-diene	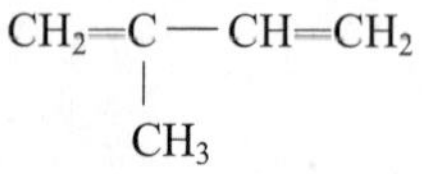 $CH_2=C(CH_3)-CH=CH_2$
Ethylene oxide	Oxirane	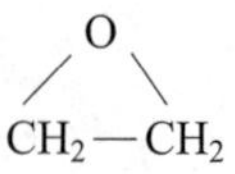 CH_2-CH_2 (bridged by O)
Propylene oxide	1- Methyloxirane	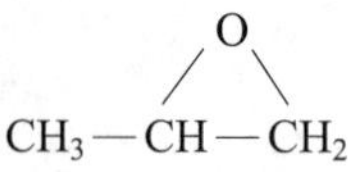 $CH_3-CH-CH_2$ (CH and CH_2 bridged by O)
Methyl iodide	Iodomethane	CH_3I
Methyl chloride	Chloromethane	CH_3Cl
Methylene dichloride	Dichloromethane	CH_2Cl_2
Chloroform	Trichloromethane	$CHCl_3$
Carbon tetrachloride	Tetrachloromethane	CCl_4
Vinyl chloride	Chloroethene	$CH_2=CH-Cl$
Ethylene dichloride	1, 2-Dichloroethane	$ClCH_2CH_2Cl$

Common or trivial name	***Systematic (or IUPAC) name***	***Structure***
Allyl chloride	3-Chloroprope	$CH_2{=}CH-CH_2-Cl$
Chloroprene	2-Chlorobuta-l,3-diene	$CH_2{=}C(Cl)-CH{=}CH_2$
Epichlorohydrin	1-Chloromethyloxirane	$ClCH_2CH-CH_2$ (epoxide, O bridging CH and CH_2)
Ethylene glycol	Ethane- l,2-diol	$HOCH_2CH_2OH$
Propargyl alcohol	Prop-2- yn -1-ol	$H-C{\equiv}C-CH_2OH$
Allyl alcohol	Prop-2- en -1-ol	$CH{=}CH-CH_2OH$
Iso-Propanol	2-Propanol	$CH_3CH(OH)CH_3$
Glycerol	Propane-1,2,3-triol	$HOCH_2-CH(OH)-CH_2OH$
Sec-Butanol	2-Butanol	$CH_3CH(OH)CH_2CH_3$
Pentaerythritol	2,2-Di (hydroxymethyl) Propane-1,3- diol	$HOCH_2-C(CH_2OH)_2-CH_2OH$
Lauryl alcohol	Dodecanol	$CH_3(CH_2)_{10}CH_2OH$
Acetone	Propanone	CH_3COCH_3
Methylisobutyl ketone	4-Methylpentan-2-one	$CH_3COCH_2CH(CH_3)CH_3$
Formaldehyde	Methanal	$HCOH$
Acetaldehyde	Ethanal	CH_3CHO
Chloral	2,2,2-Trichloroethanal	Cl_3CCHO
Propionaldehyde	Propanal	CH_3CH_2CHO
Acrolein	Propenal	$CH_2{=}CHCHO$
Butyraldehyde	Butanal	$CH_3CH_2CH_2CHO$
Formic acid	Methanoic acid	HCO_2H
Methyl formate	Methyl methanoate	HCO_2CH_3
Acetic acid	Ethanoic acid	CH_3CO_2H
Acetic anhydride	Ethanoic anhydride	$(CH_3CO)_2O$
Peracetic acid	Perathanoic acid	CH_3CO_3H
Vinyl acetate	Ethenyl Ethanoate	$CH_2{=}CHO_2CCH_3$
Acrylic acid	Propenoic acid	$CH_2{=}CH-CO_2H$
Dimethyl oxalate	Dimethyl ethanedioate	$CO_2CH_3-CO_2CH_3$

Common or trivial name	***Systematic (or IUPAC) name***	***Structure***
Propionic acid	Propaonic acid	$CH_3CH_2CO_2H$
Methyl methacrylate	Methyl 2- Methylpropenoate	$CH_2{=}C(CH_3){-}CO_2CH_3$
Maleic acid	Cis-Butenedoic acid	H H; C=C; H_2OC CO_2H
Maleic anhydride	Cis-Butenedioic anhydride	O; O=C C=O; C=C; H H
Citric acid	2-Hydroxypropane-1,2,2-tricarboxylic acid	CH_2CO_2H; $HO{-}C{-}CO_2H$; CH_2CO_2H
Methyl laurate	Methyl dodecanoate	$CH_3(CH_2)_{10}CO_2CH_3$
Stearic acid	Octadecanoic acid	$CH_3(CH_2)_{!6}CO_2H$
Acrylonnitrile	Propenonitrile	$CH_2{=}CH{-}CN$
Adiponitrile	Hexane-1,6-dinitrile	$NC{-}(CH_2)_6{-}CN$
Urea	Carbamide	H_2NCONH_2
Ketene	Ethenone	$CH_2{=}C{=}O$
Toluene	Methyl benzene	CH_3
Aniline	Phenylamine	NH_2
Cumene	iso-Propylbenzene	CH_3 CH_3; CH
Benzyl alcohol	Phenylmethanol	CH_2OH
o-Xylene	1,2- Dimethylbenzene	CH_3; CH_3

Common or trivial name	*Systematic (or IUPAC) name*	*Structure*
m-Xylene	1,3- Dimethylbenzene	CH_3 CH_3
p-Xylene	1,4- Dimethylbenzene	CH_3 CH_3
Phthalic acid	Benzene-1,2- dicarbxylic Acid	CO_2H CO_2H
Isophthalic acid	Benzene-1,3- dicarbxylic Acid	CO_2H CO_2H
Terephthalic acid	Benzene-1,4- dicarbxylic Acid	CO_2H CO_2H
0-Toluic acid	2- Methylbenzoic acid	CO_2H CH_3
p-Toluic acid	4- Methylbenzoic acid	CO_2H CH_3
p-Tolualdehyde	4- Methylbenzaldehyde	CHO CH_3
Benzidine	4,4'-Biphenyldiamine	H_2N— —NH_2
Furfural	2-Formylfuran	O CHO
HFA 134a	1,1,1,2-Tetrafluoroethane	CF_3CH_2F
LTBE	Ethyl t-butyl ether	$CH_3CH_2OC(CH_3)_3$
MTBE	Methyl t-butyl ether	$CH_3OC(CH_3)_3$
TAME	t-Amyl methyl ether	$H_3C—C—OCH_3$ / \ H_3C CH_2CH_3

Appendix 5

总 词 汇 表

abrasion n. 磨损，磨蚀，剥蚀
absorption n. 吸收（作用）
accessory n. (pl.) 辅助设备(装置)，附件 a. 附属的，辅助的
accountant n. 会计（员），出纳（员）
acenaphthene n. 苊
acetal n. 乙缩醛，乙醛缩二乙醇
acetate n. 醋酸盐(脂)，乙酸盐(酯，根)；醋酸纤维素
acetic a. 醋（酸）的，酸的
acetic acid 醋酸
acetone n. 丙酮
acetylene n. 乙炔
acrylic a. 聚丙烯的，丙烯酸（衍生物）的
acrylonitrile n. 丙烯腈
activated carbon 活性炭
activity coefficient 活度系数
acute a. 尖锐的，剧烈的，严重的，急剧的
additive n. 添加剂，加成剂 a. 附加的，加成的
adhere v. 粘附（于），附着（于）； 坚持；追随
adhesive n. 胶粘剂，粘结剂
adiabatically ad. 绝热地
adsorbent n. 吸附剂，吸附物质
adsorber n. 吸附器
adsorption n. 吸附（作用）
advent n. 到来，出现，来临
aerate vt. 充气,鼓气,通风,鼓风
aerobic a. 好氧的，需氧的，有氧的
affinity n. 亲和力，亲和势，化合力
agglomeration n. 附聚，凝聚，
agitated thin-film evaporator 搅拌式薄膜蒸发器
agitator n. 搅拌器，搅拌装置
agreed-upon a. 约定的，（各方）同意的
agrochemical n. 农用化学品；农业化肥；农产品中提炼出的化学品
airframe n.（飞行器，飞机）机架，构架
airlift reaction 升气式反应器
albeit conj. 虽然，即使
alcohol n. （乙）醇，酒精
alert vt. 使警觉，使留心
algebraic a. 代数（学）的
algorithm n. 算术，算法
align v. 与…合作，一致，匹配
aliphatic a. 脂肪族的，无环的
alkali n. 碱（性，质)，强碱
alkaline n. 碱性 a. 强碱的
alkane n. 烷(属)烃，(链)烷
alkene n. 烃烯
alkyd n. 醇酸（树脂）
alkyd resin 醇酸树脂，聚酯树脂
alkyl n. 烷基，烃基
alkylation n. 烷基化，烷基取代
alkylbenzene sulfonate 烷基苯磺酸盐
alkyne n. 炔（属烃）
ally n. 同盟国(者)；伙伴，助手 v. 结盟
alumina n. 矾土，氧化铝
aluminum=aluminium n. 铝 Al
amalgamation n. 合并，混合；汞合，汞齐作用
ambient a. 周围的，包围着的
amenable a. 服从的，适合于…的（to）
amine n. 胺
amino a. 氨基的
ammonia n. 氨(水)
ammoniacal a. (含)氨的，氨性的
ammoniated a. 充氨的，含氨的
ammonium n. 铵(基)
ammonium carbamate 氨基甲酸铵
ammoxidation n. 氨氧化反应,氨解氧化
amorphous a. 无定形的，非晶体的
analogy n. 类似，相似（性），类推
anatomy n. 解剖，分解；构造，组织
angular a. 角的，角度的，有角的
anhydrous a. 无水的
aniline n. 苯胺
anionic a. 阴(负)离子的

anisotropic a. 各相异性的，非均质的
anode n. 阳极，正极
Antarctic n.;a. 南极地带（的）
anthracene n. 蒽，并三苯
antibiotic n. 抗生[菌]素，抗生素学 a. 抗菌的
antiknock a. 抗爆的，防爆的，抗震的
antimalarial a. 抗疟疾的
antioxidant n. 抗氧化剂，防老化剂
apex n. 顶点，最高点，脊
appendix n. 附录，附言；附属（物），附加（物）
aptly ad. 适当地，合适地
aqueous a.（含，多，似）水的，水成[化，样，多]的
aquifer n. 蓄水层，含水层
aramid n. 芳香族聚酰胺
aromatic a. 芳香（族）的，芳（香）烃的
aromatization n. 芳构化
array n. 序，列，组；族，系，类
arsenical a. (含)砷的 n. 含砷制剂
artificial intelligence 人工智能
aryl n. 芳基
asphalt n. （地）沥青，柏油
asphalt base crude 沥青基石油
asset n. 宝贵的人（或物）；财产
atactic a. 无规立构的
athletic a. 体育的，运动的；运动员的
atomize vt. 使雾化，喷雾
atrophy n. 退化，衰退，萎缩
attrition n. 磨损，研磨
authenticity n. 可靠性,真实性
autoclave n. 压煮器, 高压釜
aviation n. 航空，飞行
awe n.;v. （使）敬畏（畏惧）
azeotrope n. 恒沸物，共沸混合物
backbone n. 构架, 骨干, 主要成分
back-mixing 返混
bacteria n. (bacterium 的复数)细菌
bacterial a. 细菌的
baffle n. 挡板；折流板；缓冲板
bag filter 袋滤器
bakelite n. 胶木, 酚醛树脂, 电木
bale n. 大包，大捆
ban vt. 禁止，取缔
bank n. 一排，排，列，群，组
barometric condenser 气压冷凝器
base n. 碱
batch a. 间歇的，分批的
bauxite n. 铝土矿，矾土
be akin to 类似（于），近似
beet n. 甜菜
belt filter 带式过滤机
bench n. 实验台，装置
benign a. 有益于健康的，良好的，[医]良性的
benzene n. 苯
benzenesulphonic acid 苯磺酸
benzenoid a. 苯（环）型的
benzole n. (粗)苯，安息油
benzothiophene n. 苯并噻吩
Berl saddle 弧鞍形填料，贝尔鞍形填料
beset vt. 包围，缠绕，为…所苦
bestow vt. 使用，花费把…赠(给)与
beverage n. 饮料
bicarbonate n. 碳酸氢盐，酸式碳酸盐
bid v.; n. 出[报，喊]价，投标
bifunctional a. 双官能团的
binary a.;n. 二，二元的
binder n. 粘合剂;铺路沥青
biochemical a. 生物化学的
biodegradable a. 可生物降解的
biomass n. 植物茎杆或动物废弃物；生物量
biomedicine n. 生物医学
biopolymer n. 生物聚合物
biotechnology n. 生物工艺学
bisphenol A n. 双酚 A
bitumen n. 地沥青
blast furnace 高炉，鼓风炉
bleaching n. 漂白 a. 漂白的
blockade n.;vt. 封锁，禁运
blow-moulding 吹模法
blue sky a. 纯理论的；（股票等）价值极微的
blue-chip a. （在行业中）最赚钱, 第一流的；（股票等）热门的，靠得住的，
blur v. （使）变模糊；弄污
bog down （使）陷入泥沼[困境]，（使）停顿，阻碍
boiler n. 锅炉
boiling point 沸点
bollworm n. 螟蛉
bombardment n. 照射，辐照；轰击，打击
bond n.;v. （化学）键，键合
boom n.（商业等的）景气，繁荣；激增，暴涨
borate n. 硼酸盐(酯)

borax n. 硼砂
boric acid 硼酸
bottom n. (pl.) 底部沉积物，残留物，残渣
boundary layer 边界层
brackish a. 有盐味的，稍(半，微)咸的
brine n. 盐水，卤水，海水
brittle a. 脆的, 易碎的
broth n.肉汤（指细菌培养液），液体培养基
Brownian motion 布朗运动
Btu = British thermal unit 英热量单位 (＝252 卡)
bubble column 鼓泡塔
bubble-cap towe 泡罩塔
buck n.（美俚）元
builder n. 组分，增加洗涤剂清洁作用的物质
building block 结构单元；预制件；积木
bulk a. 散装的；大块的
bulk carrier 散装大船
bulk density 堆积密度
bulk polymerization 本体聚合
bump v. 扰动，暴沸；冲击，造成凹凸
bumper n. 保险杠
buoyancy n. 浮力，浮性
buoyant a. 有浮力的，能浮的，易浮的
bust n. 商业上的大不利；失败
butadiene n. 丁二烯
butane n. 丁烷
butene n. 丁烯
butyl- n. 丁基
by and large 一般来说，总的讲，大体上，基本上
ca = circa [拉丁语] prep.;ad. 大约
cabinet n. 箱，室，壳体
cadre n. 核心，骨干，骨架
calandria n. 排管式，加热管群
calcine v.; n. 煅烧,烧成（灰）
calcium n. 钙 Ca
calorific value 热值，发热量
capital-intensive a. 资本密集的，资本集约的
capsule n. （密封）（座）舱；胶囊
carbamate n. 氨基甲酸酯
carbamide n. 尿素，碳酰二胺
carbide n. 碳化物，硬质合金；碳化钙
carbohydrate n. 碳水化合物，糖
carbolic acid = phenol 苯酚，石炭酸
carbon black 炭黑
carbonaceous a. 碳的，碳质的，含碳的
carbonate n. 碳酸盐，碳酸脂 vt. 碳化，使化合成碳酸盐（脂）；充碳酸气于
carbonium n. 阳碳, 正碳
carbonization n. 碳化处理，渗炭，焦化
carbonylation n. 羧化作用
carrier n. 载体
carton n. 纸板箱（或盒）
cascade v.; n. 梯流，阶流式布置；级联，串级
casing-head gas 油井气，油田气
catalysis n. 催化（作用，反应）
catalyst n. 催化剂
catalytic a. 催化的
catastrophic a. 灾难性的，大变动的
category n. 种类，类型，范畴
catenation n. 耦合，连接
cathedral n.（一个教区内的）总教堂，大教堂
a.（象）大教堂的，权威的
cathode n. 阴极，负极
cationic a. 阳（正）离子的
caustic a. 苛性的 n. 苛性物，氢氧化物
cellular a. 多孔的，细胞的，由细胞组成的
celluloid n. 赛璐珞, 硝酸纤维素
cellulose n. 纤维素，细胞膜质 a. 细胞的
centralize v. 集中，形成中心，由中心统一管理
centrifugal a. 离心力的，利用离心力的
centrifuge n.;v. 离心；离心机，离心器
cephalosporin n. 头孢菌素
ceramic a. 陶器的，陶瓷的，制陶的
cereal n.;a. 谷类(的)，谷子，谷物(的)
certitude n. 确实，必然性
CFC = chlorofluorocarbon n. 含氯氟烃
char n. 炭，木炭
chelation n. 螯合作用
chemical vapor deposition 化学气相淀积
chlor(o)- [词头] 氯（化）
chloralkali n. 氯碱
chlorate n. 氯酸盐
chloride n. 氯化物，漂白剂
chlorinate vt. 使氯化，使与氯化合，用氯气处理
chlorine n. 氯（气） Cl
cholesterol n. 胆固醇
chromate n. 铬酸盐
chromatography n. 色谱(法,学)，色层法
cinchona n. 金鸡纳树属，金鸡纳皮，奎宁
circumvent vt. 绕过，回避，胜过
clear-cut a. 明确的，鲜明的； 轮廓清楚的
client n. 顾客，买主，当事人

clink v.; n. 响裂（钢锭缺陷），（铸件）裂纹，（发出）碰撞声
clone n. 克隆，无性繁殖系
cloning n. 克隆，无性繁殖
coagulation n. 凝结（聚, 固）;胶凝, 絮凝
coal carbonization 煤干馏
coal-tar 煤焦油
coarse a. 粗的，大的
coax vt. 耐心地处理，慢慢地把…弄好；诱哄
cobalt n. 钴 Co
coefficient n. 系数
coke n. 焦炭，焦 vt. 炼焦，焦化
collaboration n. 合作，共同研究
colloid n. 胶体，胶粒 a. 胶状的，胶体的
combustion n. 燃烧
commence v. 开始，开始（做）
commencement n. 开始，开端，开工
comminute vt. 粉碎，磨碎，分割
commission v. 交工试运转，投产
commodity n. 日用品，商品
compactness n. 致密（性)，密集（性)，紧凑
compatibility n. 兼容性，相容性，适应性
compatible a. 兼容的，可共存的；一致的，相似的，协调的
complement n. 补充，互补，补充物；配套
comply vi. 同意，遵照，履行，根据（with）
composite n. 复合材料, 合成 （复合, 组合）物
composition n. 组成，成分，结构
conceive v. 设想，想象；想到（出）（of）
concomitant a. 相伴的，伴随的
concrete n. 混凝土 a. 混凝土的
condensate n. 冷凝物，冷凝液 v. 冷凝，凝结
condenser n. 冷凝器
conduction n. 传导(性，率，系数)，导热（电）(性，率，系数)
conductivity n. 传导率，导热系数
conduit n. 导管，输送管， (大)管道
configuration n. 构造，结构；外形，轮廓
confluence n. 合流(点)，汇合(处)；集合，聚集
conical a. （圆）锥形的
conjure up 凭幻想(想象)作出
conjure v. 想象，用幻想作出；祈求
conserve vt. 节省；保存；守恒
console n. 控制台，操纵台；托架，支柱
consolidation n. 巩固，加强；合并，联合
constituent n. 组成，组分，成分
constraint n. 限制，制约，约束
consultant n. 顾问，咨询
contaminate vt. 污染，弄脏，毒害
contemplate v. 设想，打算，预期；注视，仔细考虑
continuum n. 连续介质；连续（统一体)；连续光谱
controversy n. 争论，论战
convection n. (热，电)对流，迁移
converge v. 会聚，汇合，[数]收敛
conveyor dryer 带式干燥器
coordinate n. 坐标；一致；配位 a. 坐标的，协调的，配位的 v. 使协调，配合，配位
coordination n. 配位, 配合
copolymer n. 共聚物
corollary n. 推论，（必然的）结果
correlation n. 相关（性），（相互，对比）关系
corrosion n. 腐蚀，锈蚀
cosmetic n. 化妆品 a. 化妆用的，整容的
counter current 逆流
cocounterpart n. 对应物，配对物，对方；一对东西中之一，副本
covalent a. 共价的
cracking n. 裂化，裂解
crease n. (衣服、纸等的)折缝，皱痕
creosote n. 木馏油，木材防腐油
cresol n. 甲酚，甲氧甲酚，甲氧基
criterion n. (pl.) criteria 判据，准则，判断标准
critical velocity 临界速度
cross section （横）截面，剖面，断面
cross-current n. 错流，正交流
cross-flow 错流，交叉流动，横向流动
cross-link v. (聚合物)交联,横向耦合
crossover n. 截面，交叉，跨接结构
cruise n.;v. 巡航，航行；巡逻
crystalline a. 结晶的，结晶状的；水晶的
crystallization n. 结晶（作用，过程）
CSTR =continuously stirred tank reactor 连续搅拌釜反应器
culmination n. 顶点，极点，最高潮
culture n.;vt. (人工，细菌) 培养（繁殖)，栽培；文化[明]
cumene n. 枯烯，异丙基苯
cure v. 塑化，固化，硫化，硬化；处理
curricula n. curriculum 的复数
curriculum n. （一门，全部）课程

cyanamide n. 氰胺，氨基氰
cyanide n. 氰化物
cybernetics n. 控制论
cycloalkane n. 环烷烃
cyclohexane n. 环己烷
cyclohexanol n. 环己醇
cyclohexanone n. 环己酮
cyclone n. 旋风分离器，旋流器
dashboard n. （车辆的）挡泥板，仪表板
deactivate vt. 减活，去活化，钝化
debit vt.;n. （记入）借方
de-caffeination n. 脱咖啡因，除去咖啡因
decantation n. 倾析（法)，倾滤，滗析
decline v.;n. 下降，减少，倾斜，衰落
decomposition n. 分解,离解
decouple v. 消除...间的影响，分隔；去耦
dedicate vt. 把(时间、力量等)用在…(to)；奉献
deficiency n. 缺少，不足
definiteness n. 明确，确定，肯定
deflect v. （使）偏（移，斜，离，向）
degradation n. 降解；退化；(能量的)衰变；降级
dehydrate v.; n. 脱水，干燥
dehydration v.; n. 去(脱，除)水(物)，(使)干燥
dehydrogenation n. 脱氢（作用）
deliberately ad. 故意地，蓄意地；审慎地，深思熟虑地
delineation n. 描述，叙述
demethylation n. 脱甲烷（作用）
demineralize vt. 脱[去]矿质，软化，除盐
dense-phase 密相
deoxyribonucleic acid 脱氧核糖核酸
deplete vt. 放空，耗尽，使枯竭；贫化，减少
deploy v.;n. 展开，使用，利用
derivative n. 衍生物；导数
desalination n. 淡化，脱盐
desalt vt. 脱盐
desulphurisation n. 脱硫,除硫
detergent n. 洗涤剂，去污剂
deterioration n. 退化，变质，降低（品质）
devastate vt. 破坏，毁坏，使荒芜
devolatilization n. 脱(去)挥发份(作用)
di- [词头]二，重，双
diagnose v. 判断，诊断；确定，分析，识别，断定（…的原因）
diagnostic a. 诊断的，（有）特征的 n. 诊断，症状，特征
dialysis n. 渗析，渗透
diammonium hydrogen phosphate 磷酸氢二铵
diamond n. 金刚石，钻石
diaphragm n. 隔膜，隔板
dichloroethane n. 二氯乙烷
dichotomy n. 两分法
dictate v. 支配，命令；口述
diesel n. 内燃机，柴油机
diesel oil 柴油
diet n. 食物，饮食
differential a.; n. 微分（的），差分（的）；（有）差别（的）
differentiate v. 区分，区别；求微分，求导数
diffuse v. 扩散，散布
digestive a. 消化的，助消化的
dilemma n. 困境，进退两难；二难推论
dilute a. 稀（薄，释）的， 淡的 v. 稀释，冲淡
dilute-phase 稀相
dimensionless a. 无因次的，无量纲的
dimentional a. …维的；因次的；维数的；尺寸的
dimerization n. 二聚（作用）
dimethyl benzene 二甲苯
diminish v. 减少，递减，削弱，由大变小
dinitrogen n. 分子氮，二氮
dioxide n. 二氧化物
dipole n. 偶极(子)
disastrous a. 灾难性的，造成惨重损失的
disc filter 盘滤机
discrete a. 离散的，不连续的，独立的，个别的
disinfectant n. 杀菌剂，消毒剂
dispatch vt. （迅速地）发送，派遣；迅速办理，了结
dispersion n. 分散（体系，作用）；扩散（现象）
dissipate v. 使耗散，消除，消耗
dissipation n. 耗散，损耗，消散
dissolution n. 溶解，溶化
dissolve v.; n. 使溶解，溶化
distil(l) vt. 蒸馏，用蒸馏法提取；提取…的精华
distillate n. 馏出物，馏出液；精华
distillation n. 蒸馏（作用)，馏份
divert vt. 使转向，使变换方向，转移
dodecanol n. 十二（烷）醇
domain n. 领域，范围，范畴
down time 停车时间，故障期
downcomer n. 降液管
drag n. 阻力，曳力

drip-dry vi. 易快速晾干，晾干自挺
droplet n. 液滴，微滴，小滴
duct n. （导，输送）管，（管，渠，地，风，烟）道，槽
dumped packing 乱堆填料
duplicate vt. 重复，加倍，复制
dyestuff n. 染料，颜料，着色剂
dynamic model 动态模型
dynamic response 动态响应
dynamics n. （动）力学，动态（特性）
dynamite n. 黄色炸药，硝化甘油炸药
earth vt. 接地，通地
ebullating bed 沸腾床
ecosystem n. 生态系（统）
eddy n. (水，风，气等的)涡，旋涡
effluent a.; n 流出（的，物），废水及废气
elastomer n. 合成橡胶，人造橡胶；弹性体，高弹体
electrochemical a. 电化学的
electrode n. 电极
electrodialysis n. 电渗析
electrolyse vt. 电解（= electrolyze）
electrolysis n. 电解（法，作用），电分析
electrolytic a. 电解的，电解质的
electroneutrality n. 电中性
electrostatic a. 静电的
elegant a. 优雅的，精美的
elucidate v. 阐明，解释，说明
elude vt. 使困惑，难倒
eluent n. 洗脱液，洗脱剂
elution n. 洗提，洗出
elution cromatography 洗脱色谱（法）
emanate v. 发出，放射，析出，发源
embed vt. 把…嵌入；栽种
embrittlement n. 脆裂，脆性
emission-free a. 无排放的，零排放的
emulsion n. 乳胶，乳(化，状，浊)液，乳剂
emulsion polymerization 乳液聚合
enamore vt. 使倾心，使迷恋
encapsulate v. 压缩，节略；封装，用胶囊包起来
encompass vt. 包含，包括；完成；围绕
encyclopedia n. 百科全书；某科全书
endeavor n. 努力，尽力
endothermic a. 吸热的
endow vt. 赋予（with），资助，捐赠
end-product 最后产物，最终结果
engross vt. （使）全神贯注，吸引（注意）
enhance vt. 提高，增强
enthalpy n. 焓，热函，（单位质量的）热含量
entity n. 存在，实体，统一体
entrained bed 气流床
entrainment n. 挟带；雾沫
entropy n. 熵
envisage vt. 设想，预计，重视
enzymic a. 酶的，酵素的
epitaxy n. 晶体取向生长
epoxy n. 环氧树脂
equality n. 等式，相等
equilateral a. 等边的，两侧对称的
equilibrium n. 平衡
equilibrium stage 平衡级
erosion n. 磨蚀，风化，腐蚀，侵蚀
erratically ad. 不规律的，不稳定的
erroneous a. 错误的，不正确的
ester n. 酯
ethane n. 乙烷
ethanol n. 乙醇，酒精
ethanolamine n. 乙醇胺
ethene n. 乙烯
ether n. 醚，乙醚；以太
ethics n. 职业规矩，道德标准，伦理观
ethyl n. 乙基，乙烷基
ethylbenzene n. 乙（基）苯
ethylene n. 乙烯
evaporation n. 蒸发，挥发，汽化
evoke vt. 引起,召唤，制定出
exothermic a. 放热的
expansion joint 膨胀节
expenditure n. （时间、金钱等的）支出，花费，使用
expert system 专家系统
explicitly ad. 明确地，清楚地；显然
explosive limit 爆炸极限
exponent n. 指数，幂(数)，阶
externalize vt. 使客观化，使具体化，给…以外形
extract n. 萃取相，萃取液 vt. 萃取，提炼
extraction n. 萃取，提炼；抽出物，提取的
extractive metallurgical 湿法冶金的
extruder n. 挤压机, (螺旋)压出机
fabricate vt. 制造，生产，制备；装配，安装，组合
facet n. （多面体的）面，（题目、思想等的）面 vt. 在…上刻画

falling film evaporator　降膜式蒸发器
famine　n. 饥荒；严重的缺乏
fascinate　v. 使着迷，强烈吸引住
fascination　n. 感染力，吸引力
fatty acid　脂肪酸
feed　n. 进料，加料；加工原料
fender　n. 挡泥板，防护板
fermentation　n. 发酵
fermenter　n. 发酵罐
ferrous　a. (亚，二价，含)铁的，铁类的
fertilizer　n. 肥料（尤指化学肥料）
fiberglass　n. 玻璃纤维
fiber-stretching　纤维拉伸
filament　n. （细）丝，（细）线；灯丝，游丝
filler　n. 填充物，填料
filter aid　助滤剂
filter　n. （过）滤器[机，层，纸]　v. 过滤
filtrate　v. 过滤，滤除　n. 滤液，滤过的水
filtration　n. 过滤
fine chemical　精细化学药品
finishing　n. 精加工，最终加工
finite　a. 有限的，受限制的
finned tube　翅片管
fixed bed　固定床
fizzle　vi. （在开始时大有成功希望的计划等）终于失败
flammability　n. 易燃性，可燃性，燃烧性
flap　n. 活盖，活板，簧片，阀门
flare　v. 端部张开，（向外）扩张（成喇叭形）
flare line　火舌管，（石油）废气燃烧管路
flash drum　闪蒸槽
flash dryer　气流干燥器
flask　n. 烧瓶，长颈瓶
flaw　n. 裂缝，裂纹
flax　n. 亚麻；亚麻纤维，亚麻织物
fledged　a. 羽毛已长成的
flooding　液泛，溢流
flow sheet　工艺流程图，程序方框图
fluctuation　n. 脉动，波动，起伏，增减
flue　n. 烟道，风道
fluffy　a. 蓬松的,松软的
fluidized bed dryer　流化床干燥器
fluidized bed　流化床
fluoride　n. 氟化物
fluorinated　a. 氟化的
fluorine　n. 氟　F
fluorite　n. 萤石，氟石
flux　n. 通量
fly ash　粉煤灰，烟灰
foam　v. （使）起泡沫，变泡沫　n. 泡沫
forced circulation evaporator　强制循环蒸发器
fore　ad. 在前面　n. 前部
foreseeable　a. 可预见到的
foresight　n. 先见，预见，预见的能力
forge ahead　向前迈进，迎头赶上
formaldehyde　n. 甲醛
formica　n. 胶木
formulate　vt. 配方（制），按配方制造
formulation　n. 配方，组成；公式化，列方程式
fossil fuel　化石燃料，石油
foster　vt. 培养，促进，鼓励；养育
foul　n. 污物（垢）　v. 结垢，弄脏
foundry　n. 铸造, 翻砂
fraction　n. 馏份，分馏物；分数，部分
fractional distillation　分馏（作用）
fractionate　vt. 使分馏，把…分成几部分
fracture　v.; n. （使）破碎，断裂
Frash process　地下熔融法
free flowing　自由流动的，流动性能良好的
free radical mechanism　自由基机理
freeze drying　冷冻干燥
friction　n. 摩擦，摩擦力
frigid　a. 寒冷的，严寒的
froth flotation　泡沫浮选
frustrate　v. 挫败，破坏，使无效
functional group　官能团
fungi　n. (fungus 的复数) 真菌
funnel　n. 漏斗　a. 漏斗状的
furan　n. 呋喃
fuse　v. 熔融，熔化
gallon　n. 加仑
gamut　n. 全范围，全部；音阶
garment　n. （一件）衣服；［pl.］服装
gas oil　粗柴油, 瓦斯油, 汽油
gas retort　干馏甑，干馏炉
gasification　n. 气化（法，作用）
gasifier　n. 气化炉
gauze　（金属丝，纱，线）网
gel　n. 凝胶（体），冻胶
gel spinning　凝胶纺丝法
gelatinous　a. 胶状的，凝胶状的
gem　n. 宝石，玉，珍宝

gene n. 基因
generalization n. 归纳，概述，通则；普遍化，法则化
generic a. （同，定）属的，类（属性）的；一般的，普通的
geological a. 地质(学，上)的
geology n. 地质学
geophysics n. 地球物理学
glamorous a. 吸引人的，动人的
glaze n. 釉面，上釉 vt. 上釉于，给陶（瓷）器上釉
glucose n. 葡萄糖；右旋糖
glyceride n. 甘油脂
glycerol n. 甘油，丙三醇
glycol n. 乙二醇
(be) good for 对…适用，有效，有利，有好处
graded sizes 分级规格尺寸
gradient n. 梯度，变化率，坡度
grandeur n. 宏伟，壮观；伟大，崇高；富丽堂皇，豪华
granulate vt. 使成颗粒，使成粒状
grass-roots n. 基础，根本；草根
gravel n. 砾（石），砂砾（层），石子
gravity settling 重力沉降
grease n. 脂肪；润滑脂（俗称牛油，黄油）
greenhouse n. 温室，暖房
grid n. 栅格
gutter n. 排水沟，水槽
gypsum n. 石膏，灰泥板，
hallmark n. 标志，品质证明
hard coal 硬煤，无烟煤
hardware n. 硬件，硬设备，计算机
haunt vt.（鬼魂等）常出没于，作祟；常去，缠住
H-bond n. 氢键
heat exchanger 热交换器
heavy distillate 重馏分
heavy flotation oil 重质浮选油
heavy mineral oil 重质矿物油
hemodialysis n. 血液渗透(作用)
heretofore ad. 至今，到现在为止；在此以前
hermetically ad. 密封着，气密地，不透气地
heteroatom n. 杂原子, 异质原子
heterocyclic a. 杂环的
heterogeneous a. 多相的, 非均匀的
HETP = height equivalent to a theoretical plate 等板高度，理论塔板的当量高度
HETS = height equivalent to a theoretical stage 等板高度，理论塔板的当量高度
hierarchy n. 体系，系统；层次
highlight vt. 使突出，使显著；以强烈光线照射
hinder v. 妨碍，阻止，阻碍
hindrance n. 阻碍，干扰
hinge v. 依…为转移，依赖
hold-down n. 压具[板，块]，压紧（装置），固定
holdup n. 滞留量，滞液量
homogeneous a. 均相的，均匀的，同质的
hone vt. 把…放在磨石上磨，磨石
hood n. （车）棚，外壳，帽，盖，罩
hopper n. 漏斗，装料斗，接收器[阀]
horizontal pan filter 卧式盘滤机
hormone n. 激素，荷尔蒙，内分泌
HTU = height of a transfer unit 传质单元高度
hue n. 色彩，色调，色泽
humanity n. 人性，人类；the humanities 人文学科
humidification n. 增湿作用，湿润
humidity n. 湿度，湿气，水分含量
hunidifier n. 增湿器，湿润器
hybridization n. 杂交，杂化，混成
hide n. 兽皮，大（原料）皮，皮革
hydrate v. （使）水合，（使）成水合物
hydraulics n. 水力学；液压系统
hydrocarbon n. 烃，碳氢化合物
hydrochloric acid 盐酸
hydrocracking n. 加氢裂化, 氢化裂解
hydrocyclone n. 水力旋流器
hydrodesulfurization n. 加氢脱硫过程
hydrodynamic n. 流体动力学
hydroelectricity n. 水电
hydrofluoric a. 氟化氢的，氢氟酸的
hydrogen embrittlement （钢的）氢脆
hydrogenate vt. 使与氢化合，使氢化
hydrogenation n. 加氢（作用）
hydrogenolysis n. 氢解（作用），用氢还原
hydrology n. 水文学
hydrolysate 水解产物
hydrolysis n. 水解（作用），加水分解
hydrometallize v. 加氢脱金属
hydroprocess n. 加氢过程
hydrostatic head 静水压头
hydroxide n. 氢氧化物
hygiene n. 卫生（学），保健学

hypochlorite n. 次氯酸盐
hypochlorous acid 次氯酸
hypothesis n. (pl. hypotheses) 假定，假说，前提
hypothetical a. 假定（设，说）的，有前提的
iimmobilization n. 固定，定位，降低流动性
immerse vt. 浸（入，没），沉入；专心，埋头于，投入
immiscible a. 不混溶的，不互溶的
immobile a. 固定的，稳定的，静置的
immune a. 免除的，可避免的；不受影响的
impart vt. 给予，把…分给；告诉
impede vt. 阻碍，阻止，妨碍，障碍
imperative a. 不可避免的，绝对必要的
impermeable a. 不能透过的，不可渗透的，不透水的
impervious a. 不能透过的，不可渗透的
impetus n. （推）动力，促进；动量，冲量
impingement n. （气体等的）撞击；水捶
implement vt. 实现，完成，履行
implicitly ad. 含蓄地；无疑地，无保留地，绝对地
impregnate v. 浸润，饱和
impurity n. 杂质，夹杂物；不纯，污染
in one's turn 值班，替代，依次
in situ 就地，原地，在现场
inasmuch as 因为，由于
incentive a. 刺激的，鼓励的 n. 刺激，诱因
incineration n. 焚化，灰化，煅烧
inconceivable a. 不可想象的，不可思议的，难以置信的
incorporate v. 引入；体现；使结合，使合并
incredible a. 难以置信的，不可思议的，惊人的
inductive a. 引入的，导论的，诱导的
ineluctable a. 不可避免的，必然发生的
inert a. 惰性的，不活泼的；惯性的
infancy n. 初期，摇篮时代；婴儿期，幼年期
infinitesimal a. 无穷小的；细微末节的
infrared a. 红外线的，红外区的
ingredient n. （混合物的）成分，组分，配料
inherent a.固有的，生来的，内在的
inhibit vi. 有禁止力,起抑制作用 vt. 禁止;抑制,约束
inhomogeneity n. 不均匀性，多相性，不同类
injection-moulding 塑料注塑成型, 注模
innovation n. 创新，改革；新方法，新事物
inorganic a. 无机的，无机物的
inroad n. （突然）侵害， (pl.)损害，侵蚀
insect n. 昆虫
insecticide n. 杀虫剂，农药
insight n. 见识，洞察(力)，理解，领会
institute vt. 设立，创立
instrumental a. 有帮助的，起作用的；仪器的
insulation n. 绝缘，绝热；孤立，隔离
insulin n. 胰岛素
Intalox saddle 矩鞍形填料，英特洛克斯鞍形填料
integrate vt. 使一体化，使结合；[数]求…的积分
integrity n. 完整，完全，完善
intercontinental a. 洲际的
interfacial a. 界面的，面际的，层间的；
interferon n. 干扰素
interficial polymerization 界面聚合
intermediate distillate 中间馏分
intermittently ad. 间歇地；断断续续地；周期性地
interplay n.;vi. 相互作用 （影响），相互关系
intrinsic a. 内在的，固有的；本质的
intrusion n. 侵入
inventory n. 库存量；（商品、物资等）清单
invoice n. 发票，发货单，装货清单
ion n. 离子
ionize v. 使电离，离子化，游离（化）
ironically ad. 令人啼笑皆非地，讽刺地
irrotational a. 无旋的，不旋转的
iso- [词头]（相）等，（相）同的，（同分）异构
isobutene n. 异丁烯
isocyanate 异氰酸盐（酯）
isomerism n. 同分异构(现象)
isomerization n. 异构化(作用)
isoprene n. 异戊二烯
isostatic a. 等压的，(地壳)均衡的
isostatic pressing （特种陶瓷的）等静压成型法
isotactic a. 全同立构的, 等规立构的
isothermal a.;n. 等温（的），等温线（的）
isotope n. 同位素
isotropic a. 各向同性的，均质的
jet condenser 喷射式冷凝器
jet fuel 喷气式发动机燃料
jungle n. 丛林， 密林
jurisdiction n. 权限，管辖权
kernel n.（果实的）核，仁；原子核，核心
kerosene n. 煤油，火油
ketone n. （甲）酮
kettle-type reboiler 釜式再沸器，釜式重沸器

kidney n. 肾
kiln n. 窑,炉 v. 窑烧
kilowatt n. 千瓦（特）
kinetics n. 动力学
knock-out vessel 分离器
laminar a. 层流的，层状的
laminate n. 层压塑料，层压制件
latent heat 潜热
lateral a. 横向的，水平的
latex n. 橡胶, 乳状液, (天然橡胶, 人造橡胶)乳液
lattice n. 晶格，点阵，格（栅，子，状）
lauryl n. 月桂基，十二烷基
leaching n. 浸取，浸提
lead chamber process 铅室法
leaf filter 叶滤机
leeway n. 余地，可允许的误差；落后
leftover a.;n. 剩余的（物）
legislation n. 法规，立法
leguminous a. 豆科的，似豆科植物的
liability n.责任，义务
liaison n.; v. 联络，联系（人），协作
light distillate 轻馏分
light heating oil 轻质燃料油
lignite n. 褐煤
linear a. （直）线的，直线型的；线性的，线性化的
linguistic a. 语言（学，研究）的
lint n. 皮棉，棉花纤维，棉花绒
lipid = lipiod n. 类脂（化合物），类脂体
liquefaction(=liquification) n.液化（作用）
literally ad. [口]不加夸张地，确实地
livestock n. (总称)家畜，牲畜
lixiviate vt. 浸提[析，出]，溶滤
logistics n. 后勤（学），后勤保障
loop reactor 环路反应器
lot n. （商品的）一批；批量；份额
LPG = liquefied petroleum gas 液化石油气
lubricate vt. 使润滑
lubricating oil 润滑油
lutidine= dimethyl pyridine n. 二甲基吡啶，卢剔啶
lysine n. 赖氨酸
macro- [词头]宏（观），大（量），常量
macromer n. 高聚物
macromolecule n. 大分子
macroscale n. 宏观尺度（刻度，标度）
macroscopic a. 宏观的；肉眼可见的
magma n. 稀糊状混合物，岩浆，稠液
magnesite n. 镁矿
magnesium n. 镁 Mg
magnification n. 放大（倍数），倍率
magnitude n. （数）量级；大小
mainstream n. 干流，主流；主要倾向
maleic anhydride 顺丁烯二酸酐,马来酐
manganese n. 锰 Mn
manifold n. 总管，集气管，导管
manipulate v. 操作，控制，运算
manway n. 人孔
margarine n. 人造黄油，代黄油
mass separating agent 质量分离剂
matrix n. 母体，基体，本体， [数]矩阵
maturity n. 成熟；老化，陈化
mauve n. 苯胺紫（染料） a. 紫红色的，淡紫色的
maximize v. 使达到最大，使极大，极限化
mechanics n. 力学，机械学
mechanism n. 机理；机制；历程；机械
mediate v. 调停，处于中间
medicinal a. 药的，药用的 n. 药物，药品
melamine n. 密胺，三聚氰(酰)胺
membrane n. 膜,膜片,隔板
mentor n. 顾问，指导者，教练，师傅
mercaptan n. 硫醇
mercury n. 汞, 水银 Hg
merger n. （企业等的）合并，吞并；合并者
mesh n. 网，筛
meso- [词头]中（间，等，央），中等的；内消旋；介，新
mesoscale n. 中间尺度（刻度，标度）
messiness n. 混乱，弄脏，肮脏；困境
meta-，*m*- [词头]间位，偏
metabolism n. （新陈）代谢（作用）
metabolite n. 代谢物
metallurgical a. 冶金（学、术）的
metallurgy n. 冶金学，冶金术
metaphor n. 隐喻，比喻
metathesis n. 复分解(作用), 置换(作用)
methanation n. 甲烷化作用
methane n. 甲烷，沼气
methanol n. 甲醇
methycyclopentane n. 甲基环戊烷
methyl n. 甲基
methylchloroform n. 三氯乙烷,甲基氯仿

methylnaphthalene 甲基萘
methylphenol 甲酚
methyl-pyridine 甲基吡啶
micro- n. [词头]微（量，型，观）；显微；百万分之一
microbe n. 微生物，细菌
microbial a. 微生物的, (因)细菌(而引起)的
microbiological a. 微生物的
microelectronics n. 微电子学，微电子技术
microfiltration n. 微孔过滤
micron n. 微米，10^{-6}米；百万分之一
micro-organism n. 微生物
microprocessor n. 微信息处理机
microscale n. 微（观）尺度（刻度，标度）
microscopic a. 微观的，微小的；显微镜的
migrate v. 迁移，移动，流动
mild steel 低碳钢，软钢
millennium n. 一千年
mineral acid 无机酸
mineralogy n. 矿物学
miscellanneous a. 杂的, 各种的, 多方面的
mixed base crude 混合基石油
mixed-phase reactor 多相反应器
mixer-setller 混合澄清器
mobile phase 流动相
mockup n. 冷模，(1∶1)的模型，同实物等大的研究用模型
modulus n. 模数, 系数, 指数
molecular beam 分子束
molybdenum n. 钼 Mo
momentum n. 动量，冲量
mono- [词头]单一，单一的
monomer n. 单体，单聚物
monoxide n. 一氧化物
motivation n. 动机的形成，促进因素，动力
mould n. 霉菌；（模）型，模（具）
moving trickle bed reactor 移动滴流床反应器
multiple effect evaporator 多效蒸发器
multiple-feed 多口进料
multiply v. （使）增殖
multitude n. 大批，大群，大量，众多
municipal a. 市政的，城市的
myriad n. （一）万，无数
naphtha n. 石脑油，粗汽油， (粗)挥发油
naphthalene n. 萘
naphthene base crude 环烷基石油
naphthene n. 环烷烃
nasty a. 难处理的，极脏的，(气味)令人作呕的
natural circulation evaporator 自然循环蒸发器
naught n. 无（价值），零
negligible a. 可忽略的，不计的，很小的
neutron n. 中子
nickel n. 镍 Ni
nitrate n. 硝酸盐(根，酯)
nitration n. 硝化(作用)，渗氮(法)
nitric a. (含)氮的，硝酸根的
nitrile n. 腈
nitro- [词头] 硝基
nitrocellulose n. 硝化纤维（素），棉纤维火药，硝化棉
nitrogenous a. 含氮的
nitroglycerine n. 硝化甘油(炸药)，硝酸甘油
nomenclature n. 术语，命名(法)，名称，(某一学科的）术语表
non-condensable gas 不凝性气体
nourish vt. 给以营养，养育
noxious a. 有毒的，有害的，不卫生的
nozzle n. 喷嘴(管，头)，接管嘴
NRTL ＝nonrandom two-liquid model 非随机两液体模型
nucleic acid 核酸
nucleotide n. 核苷酸
numerical a. 数（量，字，值）的，用数字表示的
nut n. 螺帯(帽)；(美俚)傻瓜，（行为或信仰方面的）怪人，狂热者
nutrient a. 营养的 n. 营养基，营养素，养分
Nutsche 真空吸滤机
nylon n. 酰胺纤维，尼龙，耐纶
obliterate vt. 除去，删去，消除
obsolete a. 已废弃的，过时的
occlude vt. 吸留，夹杂，包藏
octadecanoic acid 十八（碳）（烷）酸
octane n. （正）辛烷，辛烷值
octane rating 辛烷值
offgas n. 废气，气态废物
offset n. vt. 补偿，弥补，抵销
off-the-shelf a. 成品的，现成的
oil-shale 油页岩
oil-shale retorting 油页岩干馏
olefin n.（链）烯（烃)，烯族烃
oleum n. 发烟硫酸
oligomer n. 齐(分子量)聚(合)物

olive n. 橄榄 a. 橄榄（色）的
on a par with 和…同等，等于…
on one's toes 准备行动的
one-pass 单程，非循环过程
on-line 联机，在线，机内
onset n. （有力的）开始，发动，
on-site a. （在）现场的，就地的
opaque a. 不透明的；不传导的；无光泽的
open-cast a.;ad. 露天开采的（地）
operability n. （可）操作性 （度）
opt vi. 选择，挑选 (for, between)
optimize v. （使）最优（佳）化，优选
optimum a.;n. 最佳（的，点，值），最优（的，值）
ordered packing 整砌填料，规整填料
organofluorine compound 有机氟化合物
orient v. 定向，取向，定位；（使）适应
orifice n. 孔板；锐孔
orifice scrubber 孔板涤气器
orphan n. 孤儿
orth-，*o*- [词头]邻位，正，原
osmium n. 锇 Os
osmosis n. 渗透(性，作用)
overflow v. 溢出，溢流
overhead n. 企业一般管理费；[化]塔顶馏出物
overlap n. 重迭（部分）
overlie v. 覆盖（在…上面）
overriding a. 基本的，最主要的，占优势的
oxidation n. 氧化（反应，作用）
oxidize vt. 使氧化
ozonation n. 臭氧化作用
ozone n. 臭氧
packed tower 填充塔，填料塔
pale v. 用栅栏围住 n. 界限，范围；栅栏
Pall ring 鲍尔环，带孔环形填料
palladium n. 钯 Pd
palm n. 棕榈（树，叶，枝）
panoramic a. 全景的，全貌的
para-，*p*- [词头]对位，仲，副
paradoxically ad. 似非而可能是，自相矛盾地，荒谬地
paraffin n. 链烷（属）烃，石蜡
parameter n. 参数，系数
paramount a. 最高的，高过，优于（to）
Parr bomb 派氏氧弹
particulate a. 颗粒的，微粒的 n. 颗粒，微粒，粒子
patent n. 专利，专利权 vt. 取得…的专利权
peculiar a. 特有的，独特的，特殊的；奇怪的
pedagogical a. 教学法的，教师的
pedestrian a. 普通的，平凡的 n. 非专业人员
PEEK ＝ polyetheretherketone 聚醚醚酮
pelletize v. 造粒, 做成丸（球, 片）状
pelt n. 毛皮
penalty n. 罚款；损失
penicillin n. 青霉素，盘尼西林
penicillium chrysogenum 黄青霉
penicillium notatum 青霉菌
pentane n. （正）戊烷
pentoxide n. 五氧化物
perceive vt. 觉察，发觉；看见，看出；领悟，理解
perforate v. 打孔，穿孔
perfume n. 香水，香料；香味，芬芳
peripheral a. 周边的，周围的，边缘的
peroxide n. 过氧化物
perseverance a. 能坚持的
pervasive a. 遍布的，弥漫的
pest n. 害虫，灾害
pesticide n. 农药，杀虫剂
petrochemical a. 石油化学的 n. 石油化学制品
petrolatum 石蜡油, 软石蜡, 矿酯
pharmaceutical n. 药物（品, 剂） a. 医药的，制药的，药物的，
phenanthrene n. 菲
phenol n. (苯)酚，石碳酸
phenol-formaldehyde resin 酚醛树脂
phenolics n. 酚醛塑料（树脂）
phenylamine n. 苯胺
phosphate n. 磷酸盐（酯），磷肥
phosphoric a. 磷的，含磷的，含五价磷的
phosphorus n. 磷 P，磷光体; 启明星, 金星
photosynthesis n. 光合作用
phthalic anhydride 邻苯二甲酸酐
physical vapor deposition 物理气相淀积
picoline n. 皮考啉，甲基吡啶
pigment n. 颜料，色料；色素
pilot-plant n. 中间（试验性）工厂，试验生产装置
plasticizer n. 增塑剂
plate and frame press 板框式压滤机
plate tower 板式塔

platinum n. 铂 Pt, 白金
plug flow 活塞流, 平推流
plump vi. 投票赞成，坚决拥护（for）
plywood n. 胶合板
pneumatic a. 气力的，气动的
pneumatic dryer 气流干燥器
poly (styrene-butadiene) rubber 丁苯橡胶
poly vinyl chloride 聚氯乙烯
poly- [词头] 多，聚，重，复
poly n. 多，聚
polyamide n. 聚酰胺，尼龙
polybenzothiazole n. 聚苯并噻唑
polybutylene terephthalate 聚丁烯对苯二酸酯
polycarbonate n. 聚碳酸酯
polyester n. 聚酯
polyethylene n. 聚乙烯
polymer n. 聚合物（体），高（多）聚物
polymerization n. 聚合(反应，作用)
polyoxymethylene n. 聚甲醛, 聚氧化亚甲基
polyphenylene oxide 聚苯氧
polypropylene n. 聚丙烯
polysaccharide n. 多糖
polystyrene 聚苯乙烯
polytetrafluoroethylene n. 聚四氟乙烯
polythene n.聚乙烯（=polyethylene）
polyurethane n. 聚氨基甲酸(乙)酯，聚氨酯
polyurethane 聚氨酯，聚氨基甲酸乙酯
pore n. 细[毛，微，气]孔，孔隙
porous a. 多孔的，疏松的；能渗透的
pose v. 造成，形成，提出
potash n. 钾碱
potassium n. 钾 K
potential n. 势（能），位（能），电势（位，压）
potential flow 势流
potter n. 陶工
pottery n. 陶器
precarious a. 靠不住的，不安全的；不稳定的，不确定的
precipitate n. 沉淀物 v. 沉淀，析出
preclude vt. 预防，排除
precursor n. 产物母体, 前身, 先驱
predominate vi. 占优势，居支配地位
prefractionator n. 初步分馏塔
premium n. 额外费用；奖励，奖金
premix n. 预混合料
preoccupation n. 急务，使人全神贯注的事物
prerequisite n. 先决条件，必要条件，前提（to , for）
prestigious a. 有威信的，受尊敬的
prevail vi. 占优势，盛行，普遍；成功，奏效
priority n. （在）先，（在）前；优先（权，次序），重点
probe v. 试探，探测；（用探针，探测器）探查
problematic a. 成问题的，有疑问的；疑难的，未定的
proficiency n. 熟练，精通
prohibitively ad. （价格）过高地
prolong vt. 延伸，引伸；延长，拖延
propagation n. 增长, 繁殖, 传播, 波及
propane n. 丙烷
propanol n. 丙醇
propeller 螺旋桨，推进器
propene n. 丙烯
proprietary a. 专利的，专有的，有专利权的 n. 所有权，业主
propylene n. 丙烯
prostaglandine n. 前列腺素
prosthesis n. (pl. prostheses)[医] 修复术；假体
protein n. 蛋白质，朊
Protland cement 硅酸盐水泥，波特兰水泥，普通水泥
protocol n. (条约等的)草案，会谈备忘录， (外交)协定书
proton n. 质子
protonate v. 使质子化
p-tolualdehyde n. 对甲苯甲醛
pulp n. 浆状物，纸浆；矿浆
pulsed column 脉冲塔
pulverize vt. 使成粉末，研磨，粉碎
purge gas 吹扫气体
purification n. 净化，提纯
purity n. 纯度，品位；纯净，洁净；纯化
pursuit n. 追求，从事，研究
PVC = poly vinyl chloride n. 聚氯乙烯
pyridine n. 吡啶，氮（杂）苯
pyrite n. 黄铁矿
pyritic a. 黄铁矿的
pyrolysis n. 热解(作用)，高温分解
pyrolyze vt. 热(分)解
qualitative a. 定性的；质的，质量的；性质上的
qualitatively ad. 定性地
quantitative a. 定量的；数量的
quantitatively ad. 定量地

quantum n. 量子
quarry v. 挖掘，（露天）开采
quartz n. 石英，水晶
quench v.; n. 急冷，淬冷
quicklime n. 生石灰，氧化钙
quinine n. 奎宁，金鸡纳碱（霜）
quinoline n .喹啉，氮(杂)茂
racquet = racket n.（网球、羽毛球等的）球拍；乒乓球拍
radial a. 径向的，（沿）半径的
radiator n. 辐射体，散热器，暖气装置
radical n. 基，原子团；根部；根式
raffinate n. 萃余液
ramification n. 细节，门类；结果；衍生物
random a. 随机的，无规则的，偶然的
rapeseed n. 油菜籽
Raschig ring 拉西环
rate v. (对…)评价，估计，估价，计算
rayon n. 人造丝，人造纤维
reactant n. 反应物
reaction injection moulding 反应注射成型
reactive a. 反应性的，活性的；反应的
reactive processing of molten polymers 熔融聚合物的反应加工
reactivity n. 反应性，反应活性；反应
reactor n. 反应器，反应堆
reagent n. 试剂，反应物
reassess vt. 对…再估（评） 价，再鉴定
reboiler n. 再沸器
recession n.（工商业的)衰退；（价格的）暴跌；后退
reciprocating plate column 往复振动板式萃取柱（塔）
recruit vt. 征募，吸收（新成员）
rectangular a. 矩形的，长方形的
rectifier n. 精馏器（塔）；整流器
rectify vt. 精馏，精炼，蒸馏
rectifying section 精馏段
redox = reduction-oxidation n. 氧化还原（作用）
redox potential 氧化还原电势
reduce v.（使）还原；减少
refinery n. 炼油厂，提炼厂
reflux n. 回流，倒流
reformant 重组
reformate n. （汽油）重整产品
reforming n. 重整，转化
refractory a. 难熔的，耐火的 n. 耐火材料
refrigerant n. 致冷剂，冷冻剂
regeneration n. 再生，更新，新生
relative volatility 相对挥发度（性）
relevance n. 关联，关系；适当，贴切，中肯
relish vt. 乐于，爱好，欣赏，玩味
remediation n. 补救，修补；治疗
renal a. 肾脏的，肾的
render v. 使得，使变为；提炼，提取
repel v. 排斥，推开，击退，弹回
replicate vt. 复制
reproducibility n. 再生性, 还原性
residence time 停留时间
residue n. 残余物，残渣，剩余物
resilient a. 有弹性的，能恢复原状的
resin n. 树脂 vt. 用树脂处理
respiration n. 呼吸（作用）
respiratory a. 呼吸（作用）的
retardation time 保留时间
reticence n. 缄默，保留
retort n. 蒸馏釜, 甑
retrenchment n. 紧缩，节约，减少
retrieval n. （数据，信息）检索
retrofit v.; n. 改型，式样翻新
revamp vt. 改进，整形
reverse osmosis 反渗透
reverse-flow cyclone 回流型旋风分离器
reversible a. 可逆的，双向的
revise vt. 修正，修改，校正
revolve v. （使）绕（旋）转；循环；思索，反复思考
revolve around … 围绕着…盘算，绕…旋转
rhetoric n. 言语，修辞学
rhodium n. 铑 Rh
rigorous a. 严格的，严密的，精确的；严厉的，苛刻的
rinse vt.;n. 漂洗，淋洗，清洗
riser n. 立（式）管（道），升气管
rising film evaporator 升膜式蒸发器
road oil 铺路沥青
rotary drum dryer 转鼓式干燥器
rotary dryer 旋转干燥器
rotary-agitation column 回转搅拌塔
rotating bed 转动床
rotating-drum filter 转鼓式过滤机
round-the-clock 连续一整天（或一昼夜）

run-off　n. 流出，流泻，径流；流量
rupture　n.;v. 破裂，断裂，破损
rupture disk　安全（隔）膜
saccharide　n. 糖类，糖化物
sachet　n. （熏衣用的）香囊，小香袋
salable　a. 畅销地，销路好的
salutary　a. 有益的，有益于健康的
sanction　n.;v. 批准，许可，承认
saponification　n. 皂化（作用）
saturate　v. 使饱和；浸透　a. 饱和的
scalar　n. 标量，纯量
scale-up　n. （按比例）放大，增加，升高
scavenger　n. 清除剂, 净化剂
scenario　[意大利语]　n. (pl)剧情概要，情况
schematically　ad. 用示意图，用图解法，示意地，大略地
scraped-surface crystallizer　刮膜式结晶器
screen　v. 筛分，筛选；屏蔽，隐藏
scrub　v. 气体洗涤，涤气，洗涤，清洗
seam　n.　(煤，矿)层
secondary　仲（指 $CH_3\cdots CH(CH_3)$-型支链烃，或指二元胺及 R_2CHOH 型的醇）
secondary reformer　二段（次）转化炉（器）
sediment　n. 沉积物；沉积，沉淀
sedimentation　n. 沉积，沉淀，沉降，淀积
segment　n. 部分；切片
segregation　n. 分离，分凝，分开
selectivity　n. 选择性，选择
self-evident　a. 不言而喻的，自明的，不需证明的
seminar　n. 研究班，（专家）研讨班，讨论会
semipermeable　a. 半渗透性的
semi-technical　n. 半工业化的
sensing device　传感装置（器），遥感装置
sensitivity　n. 灵敏性，灵敏度
sensor　n. 传感器，探测器
septicemia　n. 败血症
serrate　vt. 使成锯齿形
serviceability　n. 使用中的可靠性，耐用性
settling　n. 沉降，沉淀
sewage　n. 污水，下水道（系统）
shaft　n. （传动，旋转）轴
shear stress　剪应力
shed light on　阐明，把…弄明白
shell and tube heat exchanger　管壳式换热器，列管式换热器
shift　n. (换，轮）班，工作班
shift reaction　变换反应，转移反应
shortcut　n. 近路，捷径　v. 简化
shower plate　喷淋塔（板）
shutdown　n. 停工，停车，停止运转
side-rectifier　侧线（馏分）精馏塔
sidestream　n. 侧线馏分，塔侧抽出物
side-stripper　侧线（馏分）汽提塔
sieve　n. 筛，筛子；滤网　vt. 筛分，过筛，过滤
sieve plate　筛板
silica　n. 二氧化硅，硅石
silica-gel　(氧化)硅胶
silicate　n. 硅酸盐（酯）
silicon　n. 硅　Si
silt　n. 淤泥，泥沙，泥浆
similarity　n. 相似性，类似，相象
simulate　vt. 模拟，仿真，模型化，模型试验
simultaneously　ad. 同时地；同时发生地
single effect evaporator　单效蒸发器
sinter　vt.; n. 烧结，粉末冶金
size　vt. 依一定尺寸制造，定尺寸，估计大小
sketch　n. 示意图，简图，设计图
slag　n. (炉,熔,矿）渣
slakedlime　n. 熟石灰,消石灰
slip casting　粉浆浇铸
slot　n. 长（方形）孔，狭槽，缝隙
sludge　n. 淤泥，泥状沉积物；淤渣
slurry　n. 稀浆，淤浆；悬浮液[体]
slurry polymerization　淤浆聚合
slurry reactor　淤浆反应器
snag　n. 暗礁，隐患，意外困难
soak up　吸收
soda　n. 苏打，纯碱，碳酸钠；碳酸氢钠，小苏打
soda-ash　n. 纯碱，无水碳酸钠，苏打灰
sodium　n. 钠，Na
sodium dichromate　n. 重铬酸钾
software　n. 软件，程序，程序计算方法；设计计算方法
solar pan　盐池，盐田
solubility　n. 溶解度，溶解性
solubility product　溶度积
solubilization　n. 溶液化，增溶（化）
solute　n. 溶质，溶解物
solution polymerization　溶液聚合
solvent　n. 溶剂，溶媒
solvent naphtha　溶剂石脑油
sorbent　n. 吸附剂，吸收剂

soya n. 或 soybean 大豆，黄豆
spaghetti n. 通心粉
spare part n. 备件
spec = specification n. 说明书；（pl.）（尺寸）规格，技术要求；明细表
speciality n. 特制品，特殊产品；专门化，专业（化）
spectre n. 鬼怪，幽灵
spectroscopy n. 光谱学
spectrum n.（光，波，能，质）谱，频谱；范围，领域
sperm n. 巨头（抹香）鲸，鲸油
spider n. 支架，机架
spin off n. 有用的副产品
spinning n. 纺，纺丝，拉丝，旋压成型
spiral a. 螺旋（形）的，螺线的
splitting n. 分解，分裂，蜕变
spontaneous a. 自发的，自然的
spray dryer 喷雾干燥器
spray tower 喷淋塔
stack gas 烟道气
stainless a. 不锈的；纯洁的
stand … in good stead 对…很有用（很有帮助）
standby a. 备用的，后备的 n. 备用设备
starch n. 淀粉，浆（糊）
startup n. 开动，运转
stationary phase 固定相
stationary a. 静止的，固定的，不变的
steam ejector 蒸汽喷射器
stearic a. 硬脂的
stearic acid 硬脂酸，十八（碳）（烷）酸
stereochemical a. 立体化学的
stereoregular a. 有规立构的，立体定向的
sterile a. 无菌的，消过毒的
sterilization n. 消毒，灭菌
stiffness n. 刚性(度)，韧性
still n. 蒸馏釜，蒸馏
stimulus n. 刺激，促进因素
stirred tank reactor 搅拌釜式反应器
stitch v. 缝合，接合
stoichiometry n. 化学计算,化学计量,理想配比法
straight run gasoline 直馏汽油
straightforward a. 直接了当的，简单明了的，易懂的
strain n. 菌株（种），品系，种
stratosphere n. 同温层，平流层
streptomycin n. 链霉素
stripper n. 汽提塔，解吸塔
stripping n. 洗提，汽提，解吸
stripping section 提馏段
strive vi. 努力，奋斗，力求；斗争，反抗
structured packing 结构填料
styrene n. 苯乙烯
subbituminous coal (黑色，褐色)次烟煤
subcellular a. 亚细胞的，子细胞的，亚晶胞的
subject-matter 主题，题材，要点，内容
sublerranean a. 地下的，隐藏的，秘密的
sublimate v. 升华
submerged combustion 浸没燃烧
submicron n. 亚微米，亚微型，亚微细粒
subordinate a. 下级的，次要的，从属的
subsidy n. 补助费，津贴
substrate n. 培养基，被酶作用物，基质
subtle a. 微细的，巧妙的；稀薄的
subunit n. 副族，子单元，亚组，子群
sucrose n. 蔗糖，砂糖
suffice vi. 足够，有能力 vt. 满足（…的需要）
sugar-cane n. 甘蔗
sulfide n. 硫化物
sulfur = sulphur
sulphate n. 硫酸盐(酯)
sulphite n. 亚硫酸盐（酯）
sulphonate n. 磺酸盐，磺化 vt. 使磺化
sulphur n. 硫 S, 硫磺
sulphuric a. (正，含)硫的，(含)硫磺的
supercritical gas extraction 超临界气体萃取
superiority n. 优越（性），优势
supersaturation n. 过饱和现象
supersede vt. 代替，取代，废弃
superstructure n. 上层（上部）结构，上层建筑
supervision n. 监督，管理
surface-active agent 表面活性剂
surfactant n. 表面活性剂
suspension polymerization 悬浮聚合
sustainable a. 可持续的，能支撑住的
swap vt. 用…作交易，交换
symbiotic a. 共生的，共栖的
syngas 合成气
tailor-made a. 特制的，专用的，定做的；合适的，恰到好处的
tangentially ad. 成切线
tank crystallizer 槽式结晶器
tap vt. 开发，发掘

tar acid　焦油酸
teamwork　n. 协力，协作，配合，协同作战
teflon　n. （商品名）特氟隆，聚四氟乙烯
tension　n. 张力，弹力
terephthalic acid　对苯二甲酸
terminology　n. 术语，专门用语
terylene　n. 涤纶，聚（对苯二甲酸乙二醇）酯纤维，的确良
tetra-alkyl lead　四烷基铅
tetraethyl lead　四乙基铅
the lion's share　较大部分，最大部分
the Solvay process　索尔维法
therapeutic　a. 治疗的，关于治病的
thermal　a. 热（量，力）的，温的
thermal tubular reactor　热管反应器
thermochemical　a. 热化学的
thermodynamics　n. 热力学
thermoplastic　n. 热塑性塑料　a. 热塑性的
thermoset　n. 热固性　a. 热固性的
thiophene　n. 噻吩，硫（杂）茂
thoroughness　n. 彻底性，充分性，完全性
throughput　n. 生产量，生产率，生产能力
tile　n. 瓦（片），（瓷，面）砖
timber　n. 木材，树木
tissue　n. (细胞)组织，体素；薄纸，织物
tissue culturing　(细胞)组织培养
titanium　n. 钛 Ti
TM ＝ trademark　n. 商标
to the fore　在前面，在显著的位置；在近处
toluene　n. 甲苯
toxic　a. （有）毒的，毒性的　n. 毒药[物，剂]
toxicity　n. 毒性，毒力
traction　n. 牵引（力）；拖拉；吸引力
trade-off　n. (对不能同时兼顾的因素的)权衡，比较评定，放弃
transition　n. 过渡(段)，转变，变化
transparent　a. 透明的，半透明的，某种辐射线可以透过的
tray dryer　盘架干燥器
tri-　[词头] 三（重，倍，回）
trialkyl　三烷（烃）基
trichloroethene　n. 三氯乙烯
trickle bed reactor　滴流床反应器
tricky　a. （工作等）复杂的，棘手的；靠不住的
tricresyl phosphate　磷酸三甲苯酯
trihydric　a. 三价的，三元的，含有三个 OH 基的，三价酸式的
trinitrotoluene　n. 三硝基甲苯，TNT 炸药
–triol　[词尾]三醇
triphenyl　n. 三苯基
tripolyphosphate　n. 三聚磷酸盐(酯)
trivial　a. 普通的，不重要的，无价值的
troposphere　n. 对流层
trusswork　n. 桁架
tube sheet　管板
tubular　a. 管的，管式的，由管构成的
tubular fixed-bed reaction　管式固定床反应器
tubular reactor　管式反应器
turbine　n. 透平（机），叶轮机，汽轮机，涡轮（机）
turbo　n. 涡轮（透平）（机）
turbocharger　涡轮（透平）增压器
turbulent　a. 湍流的，紊流的；扰动的
turn-down ratio　极限负荷比，操作弹性
turpentine　n. 松节油，松香水
ubiquitous　a. （同时）普遍存在的，处处存在的
U-boat　n. 潜水艇
ultrafiltration　n. 超滤(作用)
ultraviolet　a. 紫外的，紫外线的
unbound electron　自由电子
underbrush　n. 下木，下层林木（长在树林下的矮树丛）
underlie　v. 构成(作为) …的基础；位于…的下面
unfold　v. 展开，显露，呈现；发展，伸展
unify　vt. 统一，使一致，使成一体
unimpressive　a. 给人印象不深的，平淡的，不令人信服的
UNIQUAC ＝ universal quasichemistry activity coefficient　准化学活度系数
unlagged　a. 未保温的，未隔热的；未绝缘的，
unsaturated　a. 不饱和的
untapped　a. 未利用的，未开发的
unto　prep. 到，对；直到，到…为止
update　v. 适时修正，不断改进，使…适合新的要求
uptake　n. 吸收；领会，理解
uranium　n. 铀　U
urea　n. 尿素，脲
urea-formaldehyde resin　脲(甲)醛树脂
validity　n. 有效，合法性；正确，确实
valve　n. 阀，活门
valve plate　浮阀塔（板）

vanadium n. 钒 V
vaporize vt. （使）汽化，（使）蒸发
vector n. 矢量，向量
vendor n. 卖主，小贩，自动售货机
ventilate vt. 通风，排气，开气孔，装以通风设备
venturi n. 文氏管
venturi scrubber 文丘里涤气器
verification n. 检验，验证，核实；证明，证实
veterinary n. 兽医 a. 兽医的
via prep. ［拉丁语］经（过），（经）由，通过；借助于
viable a. 可行的
vinyl n. 乙烯基，乙烯树脂
virgin oil 直馏油
viscosity n. 粘度
viscous a. 粘（性，滞，稠）的，
viz = videlicet ［拉丁语］即，就是
void n. 空隙，空隙率；空间，空位
void fraction 空隙率
volatile a. 易挥发的，挥发性的
vortex n. 旋涡；涡流（面），旋涡（体）
vulcanization n. 硫化，硬化
ward vt. 挡住，避开，防止（off）
warfare n. 战争（状态），竞争，斗争
warp n. 经线
water gas 水煤气
weave n. 织法 v. (wove, woven) 织，编（织）
weir n. 堰，溢流堰
well-head （油）井口
wet scrubber 湿洗器
whale n. 鲸（鱼）
whisker n. 晶须
wiped-film evaporator 刮膜式蒸发器
wire web 金属丝网，网体填料
with the advent of 随着…的到来（出现）
woof n. 纬线
workaholic n. 为免遭辞退而工作过分卖力的人
xylene n. 二甲苯
yeast n. 酵母，发酵粉
zeolite n. 沸石
zinc n. 锌 Zn
zirconium n. 锆 Zr